A DAVID L. WOLPER PRODUCTION

"THE MAN WHO SAW TOMORROW"

with

ORSON WELLES

Executive Producer

DAVID L. WOLPER

Produced by

**ROBERT GUENETTE,
LEE KRAMER
PAUL DRANE**

Screenplay by

ROBERT GUENETTE
and
ALAN HOPGOOD

Directed by

ROBERT GUENETTE

THE PROPHECIES OF NOSTRADAMUS

TRANSLATED, EDITED AND INTRODUCED BY ERIKA CHEETHAM

BERKLEY BOOKS, NEW YORK

THE PROPHECIES OF NOSTRADAMUS

A Berkley Book / published by arrangement with
G. P. Putnam's Sons

PRINTING HISTORY
First published in Great Britain by Neville Spearman Ltd.
First American Edition 1974
Capricorn edition published 1975
Berkley edition / March 1981
Fifth printing / April 1982

ISBN: 0-425-05772-0

A BERKLEY BOOK ® TM 757.375
Berkley Books are published by Berkley Publishing Corporation,
200 Madison Avenue. New York. New York 10016.
The name ''BERKLEY'' and the stylized ''B'' with design
are trademarks belonging to Berkley Publishing Corporation.
PRINTED IN THE UNITED STATES OF AMERICA

To Alexander and Jamie

THE PROPHECIES OF NOSTRADAMUS

INTRODUCTION

In the autumn of 1939, soon after Germany had declared war on Europe, Frau Dr. Goebbels was lying in bed reading an obscure book on occult literature. It contained some predictions made by a certain Nostradamus, printed in 1568. Her husband was asleep, but Frau Dr. Goebbels was so excited by what she had read that she woke him and made him read the relevant passages. He was sufficiently impressed to arrange that his Propaganda Ministry hired the services of an astologer named Krafft who was soon to be found reproducing material based on Nostradamus' Prophecies, using them to some effect psychologically in occupied Europe. How could an obscure medieval French doctor cause such consternation in both Goebbels and Himmler's Departments? How could he also cause the British Secret Service to spend a reputed sum of £80,000 on retaliatory propaganda?

He was Michel de Nostredame, more commonly known by the Latinized form of his name, Nostradamus, born at noon on 14th December 1503 by the old calendar, in St. Rémy de Provence. His family were not the illustrious line of Jewish-Italian doctors working at the Courts of King René of Anjou and of his son, as has commonly been claimed, but people of simple lineage from around Avignon. His grandfather was Peyrot or Pierre de Nostredame, an established grain-dealer, who married a Gentile girl named Blanche. Their son Jaume or Jacques, Nostradamus' father, moved to St. Rémy in 1495 and gave up the family trade. Here he married Reyniere de St. Rémy who was the granddaughter of an ex-doctor, turned tax-collector. The family were converted from Judaism to the Catholic faith by the time Nostradamus was nine years old, as his parents are listed in 1512 as being part of the new Christian community. It is important to remember the Jewish element of Nostradamus' childhood when trying to decipher the Prophecies, as he was greatly influenced by occult Jewish literature. Nostradamus was the oldest son, and had four brothers; of the first three we know little; the youngest, Jean, wrote a great many ribald Provençal songs and commentaries, and eventually became Procureur of the Parliament of Provence.

Nostradamus' great intellect became apparent while he was still very young, and his education was put into the hands of his grandfather, Jean, who taught him the rudiments of Latin, Greek, Hebrew, Mathematics and what Nostradamus calls celestial science, Astrology. When this grandparent died the boy returned to his parents' house in the rue de Barri and his other grandfather endeavoured to continue his education. Soon, however, Nostradamus was sent to Avignon to study, and probably stayed with some of the many cousins he had in the town.

He already showed a great interest in astrology and it became common talk among his fellow students. He upheld the Copernican theory that the world was round and circled around the sun more than 100 years before Galileo was prosecuted for the same belief. His parents were quite rightly worried by this attitude because theirs was the age of the Inquisition, and as ex-Jews they were more vulnerable than most. So they sent him off to study medicine at Montpellier in 1522. Nostradamus was now nineteen years old and had the advantage of some of the most progressive medical minds in Europe to stimulate him. He obtained his bachelor's degree (baccalauréat) after three years, with apparent ease, and once he had his licence to practise medicine he decided to leave the University and go out into the countryside and help the many victims of the plague.

Plague was endemic in Southern France during the 16th Century, in particular a very virulent form known locally as '*le charbon*' because of the great black pustules that appeared on the body of the victim. Nostradamus had many detractors throughout his lifetime but not one has ever denied his courage in facing disease, his humanity, his kindness towards the sick, and his generosity towards the poor. It was at this early stage, 1525, that his reputation as a healer became known. Nostradamus went from town to stricken town dispensing his own cures, the prescriptions for some of which are found later in a book he published in 1552. He was very unsettled and went from Narbonne to Carcassonne where incidentally he prescribed an elixir of life for the local bishop, which if it did all the author claimed for it would be the salvation of every jaded man! Next we hear of him at Toulouse in the rue de la Triperie, again at Bordeaux where the plague was severe and then back to Avignon where he remained studying for some months. His interest in magic and the occult may spring

6

from this period of his life, for the library at Avignon held many occult books. At the same time he managed to concoct a delicious recipe for quince jelly for the Papal Legate and the Grand Master of the Knights of Malta who were then in the town. It is a good recipe but with rather too much sugar for modern tastes.

After nearly four years of sporadic travelling he returned to Montpellier to complete his doctorate and re-enrolled on 23rd October 1529. Nostradamus had some trouble in explaining his unorthodox remedies and treatments, for his success and renown had made him enemies among the faculty. Nevertheless his learning and ability could not be denied and he obtained his doctorate. He remained teaching at Montpellier for a year but by this time his new theories, for instance his refusal to bleed patients, were causing trouble and he set off upon another spate of wandering, moving from place to place as his work and fancy took him. Throughout his life he was to suffer from this wanderlust. Dressed in his dark scholar's cap and gown he must have looked the epitome of the Wandering Jew.

While practising in Toulouse he received a letter from Julius-César Scaliger, the philosopher considered second only to Erasmus throughout Europe. Apparently Nostradamus' reply so pleased Scaliger that he invited him to stay at his home in Agen. This life suited Nostradamus admirably, and *circa* 1534 he married a young girl 'of high estate, very beautiful and admirable', whose name unfortunately has not come down to us. He had a son and a daughter by her and his life seemed complete. His practice was famous and profitable and he had the brilliant mind of Scaliger to help sharpen his wits. Then a series of tragedies struck. The plague came to Agen and, despite all his efforts, killed Nostradamus' wife and two children. The fact that he was unable to save his own family had a disastrous effect on his practice. Then he quarrelled with Scaliger and lost his friendship—a not unlikely happening, as Scaliger quarrelled with all his friends sooner or later. His late wife's family tried to sue him for the return of her dowry and as the final straw, in 1538, he was accused of heresy because of a chance remark made some years before, which had been reported to the authorities. To a workman casting a bronze statue of the Virgin, Nostradamus had commented that he was making devils. His plea that he was only describing the lack of aesthetic appeal inherent in the statue was ignored and the Inquisitors sent for him to go to Toulouse. Nostradamus, naturally having no wish to stand trial nor to suffer the rack or the stake, immediately set out on his wanderings again, keeping well clear of the Church authorities for the next six years.

We know very little about this period of his life. From references in his later books we know that he travelled in the Lorraine and went to Venice and Sicily, making a point of meeting the apothecaries of each place and noting down those who were efficient or bad for his book, the Traité des Fardmens.

It was probably around this period that he started to translate the Horapollo of Philippus from the Greek into French. It is nothing but a collection of treatises on ethics and philosophy and is of no great literary merit. Legends about Nostradamus' prophetic powers also start to appear at this time. Apparently when in Italy he saw a young monk who had been a swineherd pass by him in the street, and immediately knelt down and called him 'Your Holiness'. Felice Peretti became Sextus V in 1585, long after Nostradamus' death.

There is another amusing tale concerning a certain Seigneur de Florinville, who was discoursing with Nostradamus about prophecy and asked him to put his gift to the test by telling him the fates of the two suckling pigs in his yard. Nostradmus replied that the Seigneur would eat the black pig and a wolf the white one. Immediately de Florinville went to his cook and ordered the white pig to be killed for that night's dinner, which it duly was. Unfortunately a tame wolf-cub, belonging to the lord's men, stole the meat. The terrified cook killed the black pig and served it for dinner. Seigneur de Florinville then told Nostradamus that they were now eating the white pig. When Nostradamus insisted that it was the black one, the cook was sent for and confessed to the whole incident.

By 1554 Nostradamus had settled in Marseilles. In November of that year, Provence experienced one of the worst floods of its history. The plague redoubled in virulence, spread by the waters and the polluted corpses. Nostradamus worked ceaselessly. Most doctors had fled with those people who were still well enough to move, thus carrying the infection farther. According to contemporary memoirs, the plague was particularly bad at Aix, the capital of Provence, and the city sent for his help on 1st May. Nostradamus was alone throughout the epidemic, working among the sick, curing many, and insisting on fresh air and unpolluted water. The sense of hopelessness was so great when he first arrived in the city that he saw one sick woman sewing herself into her own shroud because she knew there would be no one to do it for her when she was dead.

8

Once the city had recovered, Nostradamus moved on to Salon, which he found so pleasant a town that he determined to settle there for the rest of his life. But almost immediately the city of Lyons sent for him to cure a pestilence which may, in fact, have been an epidemic of whooping cough. Whatever it was, once over, Nostradamus returned home laden with yet more gifts from the grateful citizens. Characteristically, he gave many away to the poor of the town before leaving. It is difficult to separate truth from legend in these reports of his great generosity but they almost certainly have some foundation in fact.

Back home in Salon in November, he married Anne Ponsart Gemelle, a rich widow. The house in which he spent the remainder of his days can still be seen off the Place de la Poissonnerie. Now Nostradamus seems to have led a quieter existence. His interest in the occult was strong and presumably he was still experiencing odd flashes of prophetic insight. He does not seem to have practised much medicine at this period, and appears to have concentrated more upon his writings. After 1550 he produced a yearly Almanac —and after 1554 The Prognostications—which seem to have been successful, and encouraged him to undertake the much more onerous task of the Prophecies.

Nostradamus converted the top room of his house at Salon into a study and as he tells us in the Prophecies, worked there at night with his occult books. He also mentions later that he burnt a lot of them once he had finished with them, but it is difficult to believe that a true scholar could possibly do this. It was more probably an attempt to mislead the Church authorities. The main source of his magical inspirations was a book called *De Mysteriis Egyptorum*, a copy of which was published at Lyons in 1547, and which Nostradamus almost certainly possessed, as he quotes from it line for line in his prophecies.

It was also about this time, 1554, that Jean Aymes de Chavigny, a former mayor of Beaune, gave up his position in that city and came to Nostradamus as a pupil to study judicial astrology and astronomy. He wrote several books about Nostradamus after the prophet's death and certainly helped to edit the first complete edition of the Prophecies, but, like Nostradamus' son César, he seems to have exaggerated his own importance with regard to the prophet. The evidence for this lies in Nostradamus' will, a long and detailed document referring not only to to his money but detailing all his possessions. There is no reference to Chavigny concerning Nostradamus' papers which he states specifically are to be left to whichever of his sons on reaching maturity 'has drunk the smoke of the lamp' i.e. is a true scholar. Chavigny did, however, edit a great many of Nostradamus' papers, probably with the consent of his widow.

By 1555 Nostradamus had completed the first part of his book of prophecies that were to contain predictions from his time to the end of the world. The word Century has nothing to do with one hundred years; it was so called because there were a hundred verses, or quatrains, in each book, of which Nostradamus intended to write ten, making one thousand quatrains in all. For some unknown reason, the Seventh Century was never completed, and there are indications among his papers that Nostradamus was considering adding an Eleventh and Twelfth Century, which were prevented by his death.

The verses are written in a crabbed, obscure style, with a polyglot of vocabulary of French, Provençal, Italian, Greek and Latin. In order to avoid being prosecuted as a magician, Nostradamus writes that he deliberately confused the time sequence of the Prophecies so that their secrets would not be revealed to the non-initiate.

It is extraordinary how quickly the fame of Nostradamus spread across France and Europe on the strength of the Prophecies, published in their incomplete form of 1555. The book contained only the first three Centuries and part of the fourth. At this time books were an expensive luxury and were usually owned and read only by the rich, for most of the population were illiterate. The Prophecies became all the rage at Court, and one or two seemed to invoke a certain uneasiness among the courtiers, particularly the one which appeared to predict the king's death (I. 35). Be that as it may, the Queen, Catherine de' Medici, sent for Nostradamus to come to Court, and he set out for Paris on 14th July 1556. The journey took only one month because the Queen had horses posted for him, instead of the more usual eight weeks. On 15th August, Nostradamus booked a room at the Inn of St. Michel, near Notre Dame. The Queen must have been very anxious to see him because she sent for him the next day and the Chief Constable took him to the Court of St. Germain en Laye.

One could only wish that there had been a witness to record their meeting. Nostradamus and the Queen spoke together for two hours. She is reputed to have asked him about the quatrain concerning the king's death and to have been satisfied with Nostradamus' answer. Certainly she continued to believe in Nostradamus' predictions until her death. The king, Henri II, granted Nostradamus only a brief audience and was obviously not greatly interested, although he sent Nostradamus one hundred golden crowns, and Catherine sent another thirty. This seemed poor recompense to Nostradamus, who had expended one hundred crowns on his journey alone. However, his lodgings were exchanged for the grandeur of the palace of the Archbishop of Sens, where he remained for some two weeks seeing people who came for advice, drawing up horoscopes, and offering prophetic guidance. The Queen then sent for him a second time and now Nostradamus was faced with the delicate and difficult task of drawing up the horoscopes of the seven Valois children, whose tragic fates he had already revealed in the Centuries. All he would tell Catherine was that all of her sons would be kings, which is slightly inaccurate since one of them, François, died before he could inherit. If on the other hand what he actually said was that he saw four kings to come, then the prediction was accurate because Henri III was king of Poland before returning to be king of France.

Soon afterwards Nostradamus was warned that the Justices of Paris were enquiring about his magic practices, and he returned quickly to Salon. He was welcomed home as a person of importance. From this time on, suffering from gout and arthritis, he seems to have done little except draw up horoscopes for his many distinguished visitors and complete the writing of the Prophecies. Apparently he allowed a few manuscript copies to circulate before publication, because many of the predictions were understood and quoted before the completed book came off the printing press in 1568, two years after his death.

The reason for this reticence was probably the king's death in 1559. Nostradamus had predicted it in I. 35 and may have felt that it was too explicit for comfort and that it would be advisable to wait a few more years until things had quietened down. But the following year, 1560, King Francis II, married to Mary Queen of Scots, died, and this time the courtiers openly quoted quatrain 39 of Century X.

'The eldest son; a widow of an unfortunate marriage with no children; two islands in discord; before eighteen still a minor; for the other one the betrothal will take place when even younger.' Francis II was Henri II's eldest son. He died six weeks before reaching the age of eighteen leaving a widow, Mary Queen of Socts, whose return to her country was to put two realms at discord. Francis' younger brother, Charles, had been betrothed at the early age of eleven to Elizabeth of Austria.

In 1564 Catherine, now Queen Regent, decided to make a Royal Progress through France with her second son Charles IX and the rest of her family. The progress was to take two years and the court entourage was reduced to a minimum of eight hundred people. While travelling through Provence Catherine naturally came to Salon to see Nostradamus. He dined with the King and Queen and she also visited him at his house and admired his children. This time Catherine gave Nostradamus three hundred gold crowns and the title Physician in Ordinary, which carried with it a salary and other fringe benefits, which doubtless pleased him.

Another interesting incident occurred during this visit to Salon when Nostradamus asked to see the moles on the body of a young boy in the entourage. This was a common form of prediction, but the child was shy and ran away. Nostradamus went to see him the next day while asleep and declared that he would one day be king of France, although Catherine still had two sons living. The boy was Henri of Navarre, who later became Henri IV.

By now the gout from which he suffered was turning to dropsy and Nostradamus, the doctor, realized that his end was near. He made his will on 17th June 1566 and left the large sum, for those days, of 3,444 crowns over and above his other possessions. On 1st July he sent for the local priest to give him the last rites, and when Chavigny took leave of him that night, told him that he would not see him alive again. His body was found the next morning, as he himself had predicted, 'trouvé tout mort pres du lit & du banc'. He was buried upright in one of the walls of the Church of the Cordeliers at Salon, and his wife Anne erected a splendid marble plaque to his memory. Nostradamus' grave was opened by superstitious soldiers during the Revolution but his remains were reburied in the other church at Salon, the Church of St. Laurent, where his grave and portrait can still be seen.

HISTORY OF THE CENTURIES SINCE PUBLICATION

In evaluating the works of anyone who claims to have prophetic powers it is essential to know which of those writings attributed to him are really his own, and which publication dates are genuine. Nostradamus in particular has been the victim of many forgeries over the centuries which may help to account for his undeservedly bad reputation.

There is great confusion about all the early editions of Nostradamus' works, including the Prophecies, because they were first printed in two parts, in 1555 and 1568. Several of the oldest editions are undated and there are several counterfeit 'first' editions which have altered texts and were printed more than one hundred years later than the date on their frontispiece.

There are so many editions of the Prophecies that it is impossible to list them here, but Nostradamus is probably the only author who could claim that his work has never been out of print for over four hundred years, apart from the Bible. The interest he generates is extraordinary. On an average about thirty books, either editions of the Prophecies, or critical appreciations of them, have been published each century since his death. Of course, times of crisis, such as the French Revolution, and the First and Second World Wars, produce a spate of such books. Some are frankly bad, and make no attempt at impartiality of judgment and often change the text to suit themselves. Others are sceptical and critical, but none manage wholly to dismiss out of hand the small hard core of Nostradamus' accurate predictions.

Nostradamus was used as a propaganda machine as early as 1649 and as late as 1943. In 1649 the opponents of Cardinal Mazarin, who felt he had too great an influence in the French Court, published an edition of the Prophecies, dating it 1568, in which they planted two obvious quatrains against the Cardinal. When the Bastille was stormed on 14th July 1789, the Revolutionaries recognized themselves in the Preface to the Prophecies, for apparently a copy was laid open on a table in the prison, and for ten days the people filed past, to read confirmation of their achievements. Napoleon's attention was drawn to the Prophecies by the Empress Josephine, but he was also the victim of an unscrupulous forgery which was declared to have been written by Nostradamus, called the Prophecies of Olivarius. It was a fake and its true date is *circa* 1820. A later similar forgery appeared in 1839 called the Prophecy of Orval. Neither of these works have anything to do with Nostradamus.

His fame was not confined to France. Editions of the Prophecies appeared all over Europe within twenty-five years of their first publication. Again it is impossible to list them all here, but if one mentions that twenty-six known editions and four forged ones were published in Europe between 1555 and 1643, at a time when books were valuable, one is given some idea of the strength of Nostradamus' popularity, which has continued to the present day.

From 1860 onwards a provincial French curé, called the Abbé Torné to which he added the surname Chavigny after Nostradamus' pupil, produced a series of interpretations of Nostradamus' quatrains which shook France and affected many political decisions of the time. He was convinced that the Bourbon line would be restored to the French throne. Equally he was certain that in the next war France would be invaded by means of Switzerland, and it was because of this information that the then French Chief of Staff ordered the drawing up of the disastrous Maginot line on the strength of Quatrain 80 in Century IV. Incredible but true.

Hitler's interest in Nostradamus was first aroused by the notorious Hister quatrains discovered by Frau Dr. Goebbels who, as I have mentioned, drew her husband's attention to them in 1939. By May 1940 onwards, the Germans were dropping from aircraft crude forgeries of various quatrains from the Prophecies which predicted that Hitler would be victorious and that the war would not affect South-eastern France. By this means the Germans hoped to clear the roads to Paris and the Channel ports. In retaliation, British Intelligence, 'inspired' by Louis de Wohl, who was probably as great a charlatan as any, spent an enormous sum on anti-German propaganda, carefully composing and imitating selected German Nostradamus quatrains which Allied pilots dropped over France and Belgium. This occurred as late as 1943. Books have continued to be written about Nostradamus ever since.

The final problem remaining with regard to Nostradamus is as to whether the man was a prophet or fraud. He believed himself to possess certain powers, although there is reason to believe he could not draw on these to order. They certainly sometimes let him down in the Prophecies. The reader must decide whether it is possible to believe in prediction, whether a man who wrote over four hundred years ago could possibly glimpse incidents in the future, or whether it is just inspired guesswork. It is essential for thinking man to believe in free will, to believe that his future can be changed by thought and action. Prophecy denies this and declares that all futures are immutable and fixed, that nothing man strives towards is relevant, as is already preordained by whatever governs his future, be it God or Destiny. I believe that mankind must have free will; but also I must admit the disturbing fact that although I can dismiss ninety-five per cent of Nostradamus' predictions as historical coincidence, there remain a few quatrains which are hard to reconcile with this. What about the one describing Louis XVI's flight to Varennes, the ones mentioning Napoleon and Hitler? What about the verses giving the actual month and year of an occurrence, such as that which describes the obscure treaty between the Persians and the Turks in October

1727, or another which gives the day and month of the assassination of a Prince? (III. 96) I find this type of quatrain difficult to explain away completely. They appear to me to be more than coincidence.

The modern disciples of Einstein recognize nothing but an eternal present which was also what the ancient mystics believed. If the future exists already then precognition is a fact. The whole trend of advanced knowledge is to place the laws of physics in a four dimensional continuum, that is, the eternal present. If this is so then past, present and future exist simultaneously. Perhaps it is only our consciousness that moves? One day we may know and then precognition would become an accepted fact.

But, on the other hand, the answer may lie in Dunne's concept of alternative variable futures which run parallel to each other. Each man receives the future dependent upon his earlier actions. Nostradamus could have glimpsed these parallels of time which may or may not have occurred, depending upon the earlier freely determined actions of other men. No man can be in any sense an island; all our actions affect someone else. Thus if Louis XVI had done the sensible thing and stayed in Paris instead of fleeing in a panic to Varennes, there would have been another incomprehensible quatrain in this book. Equally, however appalling it may appear, if Hitler's attention had not been drawn to the Prophecies and the connection between Poland and Britain, would he have gone to war at that time?

The reader can try to reconcile the concept of free will with the mathematical probability of chance. By means of E.S.P. or some similar faculty, possibly the future may be vaguely seen and grasped at—a future conditioned by the education of the man who receives it. Humanity does seem to repeat its mistakes, or as Dr. Inge says, resemble itself to a remarkable degree. This is proven by the fact that some of the quatrains—the ones I call split quatrains—will quite accurately predict events separated by over a century in time. But it seems that if we wish to avoid the gloomy future that Nostradamus foresees for mankind, we must break away from our present behaviour pattern, conditioned over the last few hundred years, and grow outwards towards a new concept of worldwide peace and brotherhood, and away from Nostradamus' medieval concepts of famine, war and tragedy.

THE TEXT, TRANSLATION AND COMMENTARY

Throughout this edition I have used the text of the first edition, published by Benoit Rigaud in 1568. The concessions I have made to the reader are mainly in the realm of spelling. I have changed *u* to *v* when required, *y* to *i*, *f* to *s*, and added *n* or *m* when only indicated by an accent, e.g. *côplaire = complaire*. I have copied the same punctuation, accents and capital letters as the original.

Opposite each quatrain I have given a very literal translation, which may seem nonsensical at first sight because I have kept as closely as possible to the Latin style of the original. I explain proper names and obscure words in footnotes. Below the translation is a prose commentary with a heading summarizing the subject matter when possible, for those who wish to skip quickly through the book. In the list of subjects at the beginning of each quatrain I have marked the interesting ones with an asterisk and those that possibly apply to our future, or which are especially intriguing, with an F? or an *. Those quatrains which I cannot decipher I leave to the ingenuity and patience of the reader.

I have omitted the Preface to the first edition and the Epistle to Caesar, which is placed before the Seventh Century because of length and obscurity. I will deal with them in detail in the companion book to this one on Nostradamus' life and beliefs.

January 1972

CENTURY I

17

KEY: * Of interest. F? Possibly referring to the future.

Estant assis de nuict secret estude
Seul reposé sur la selle d'aerain;
Flambe exiguë sortant de soli-
tude
Fait prosperer qui n'est à croire
vain.

Sitting alone at night in secret study; it is placed on the brass tripod. A slight flame comes out of the emptiness and makes successful that which should not be believed in vain.

DIVINATION

Both this and the following quatrain describe Nostradamus' method of divination, they are not predictions. Nostradamus used the methods of the 4th Century neo-Platonist Iamblichus, a reprint of whose book *De Mysteriis Egyptorum* was published at Lyons in 1547 and almost certainly read by Nostradamus. It may well have been the source of his experiments with prophecy, for soon afterwards his almanacs started to appear.

All the ingredients for magical practices are in this quatrain. It is night. Nostradamus is alone in his study reading the secret forbidden books which inspire his prophecies; the brass tripod is a method used by Iamblichus—on it was placed a bowl of water into which the seer gazed until the water became cloudy and pictures of the future were revealed. *Flambe exiguë* is the light of inspiration which seizes Nostradamus as he begins to prophesy.

2

La verge en main mise au milieu
des BRANCHES[1]
De l'onde il moulle[2] *& le limbe*[3]
& le pied:
Un peur & voix fremissant par les
manches:
Splendeur divine. Le divin pres
s'assied.

The wand in the hand is placed in the middle of the tripod's legs. With water he sprinkles both the hem of his garment and his foot. A voice, fear; he trembles in his robes. Divine splendour; the god sits nearby.

DIVINATION

Nostradamus continues to explain his method. He touches the middle of the tripod with his wand, and then moistens his robe and his feet with the water placed on it. This is the same method as was used to obtain inspiration by the Apollonian prophetess at the

---

[1] *Branches*—Capitals in original = (*a*) The three limbs or branches of the tripod. (*b*) Indirect reference to the prophetess of Branchus.

[2] *moulle*—Modern french *mouille* = to moisten.

[3] *limbe*—Latin, *limbus* hem of a garment.

oracles of Branchus in Classical times. Nostradamus is afraid of the power he evokes when it comes to him; he hears it, as well as sees it; it appears to speak to him and he writes down the prophecies. He is unafraid once the gift has possessed him. This dual aspect of his vision is most important when interpreting the centuries.

3

Quand la licture du tourbillon versee,
Et seront faces de leurs manteaux convers:
La republique par gens nouveaux vexée,
Lors blancs & rouges jugeront à l'envers.

When the litters are overturned by the whirlwind and faces are covered by cloaks, the new republic will be troubled by its people. At this time the reds and the whites will rule wrongly.

FRENCH REVOLUTION

The French Revolution of 1789, which Nostradamus calls the Common Advent, the coming of the ordinary men in the Preface, is here described. The aristocracy were always carried in litters, and this, their symbol, is overturned by the violent whirlwind of revolution. Could the line mentioning the heads covered by cloaks refer to the many exiles who fled from France, or possibly to the heads which fell from the guillotine and were hidden from sight? It is interesting that Nostradamus should here refer to France as a republic, and to one that was greatly troubled by its new rulers. The era of Danton, Murat and Robespierre during the terror springs vividly to mind. White was the colour of the Bourbon kings and red, of course, that of the revolutionaries. The last line 'à l'envers' may also imply that the law givers, i.e. the church and aristocracy, were judged by the populace who were unsuited for this work.

4

Par l'univers sera faict un monarque,
Qu'en paix & vie ne sera longuement,
Lors se perdra la piscature¹ barque,
Sera regie en plus grand detriment.

In the world there will be made a king who will have little peace and a short life. At this time the ship of the Papacy will be lost, governed to its greatest detriment.

¹ piscature—Latin, piscature = fishing, but a common synonym for the Papacy.

NAPOLEON AND PIUS VII

Napoleon crowned himself king and Emperor of France on 18th May 1804 and abdicated in April 1814, ruling for the short time of ten years. Peace was certainly not a characteristic of his era. Pius VII (1800–23) first came to France to crown Napoleon as Emperor, but on his second visit he came as a prisoner. The French army, under General Miollis, captured Rome in 1809 and the Papal States were joined to the French Empire in 1810; the Pope was held prisoner by Napoleon and only released by the abdication at Fontainbleau on 23rd January 1814. The last line refers to the general religious anarchy that existed in France from the time of the dissolution of the Clergy in 1792.

5

Chassés seront pour faire long combat,
Par le pays seront plus fort grevés:
Bourg & Cité auront plus grand debat,
Carcas[1] Narbonne auront coeur esprouvéz.

They will be driven away for a long drawn out fight. The countryside will be most grievously troubled. Town and country will have the greater struggle. Carcassonne and Narbonne will have their hearts tried.

HUGUENOT STRUGGLES IN PROVENCE, 1562–98

The whole of southern France was greatly afflicted by the religious wars which broke out between Huguenots and Catholics before the accession of Henri IV. Carcassonne declared itself for the Catholic League but the Huguenots seized part of the town, and Narbonne also suffered a great deal of fighting. A general quatrain covering a wide period of over thirty years. Nostradamus was always greatly interested in the fate of France and those towns he knew and had lived in during his wanderings.

6

L'oeil de Ravenne sera destitué,
Quand à ses pieds les ailles failliront:
Les deux de Bresse auront constitué,
Turin, Derseil[2] que Gaulois fouleront.

The eye of Ravenna will be forsaken, when his wings will fail at his feet. The two of Bresse will have made a constitution for Turin and Vercelli, which the French will trample underfoot.

[1] Apocope of Carcassonne.
[2] Read *Versail* = Vercelli, Piedmont, Italy.

FRENCH OCCUPATION OF BRESSE, 1601,
TURIN, 1640 etc. VERCELLI 1904 etc. CAPTURED
FROM THE PAPAL STATES

Ravenna has been part of the Papal States since 1509, and the
most likely interpretation of this quatrain concerns the fates of the
states mentioned above, Bresse, Turin and Vercelli, which were all
occupied by the French at some period. Bresse was ceded to
France in 1601, Turin was taken by the French in 1640 and 1798–
1814. Vercelli was also captured in 1704 and 1798–1814. All that is
certain is that each of these places, except for Ravenna, suffered
French occupation after the Centuries were written.

7

Tard arrivé l'execution faicte,[1]	Arrived too late, the act has
Le vent contraire lettres aux	been done. The wind was
chemin prinses:	against them, letters inter-
Les conjurez xiiii d'une secte:	cepted on their way. The
Par le Rousseau semez[2] *les entre-*	conspirators were fourteen of
prinses.	a party. By Rousseau shall
	these enterprises be under-
	taken.

DREYFUS CASE, 1894–1906.
M. WALDECK ROUSSEAU, 1899

Alfred Dreyfus, a Jewish French soldier was condemned for
treason, selling military secrets to the Germans in 1894, and pub-
licly degraded and transported to a penal colony, l'Ile du Diable in
1895. In 1899 he was brought back to France for a public retrial but
due to strong anti-semitic influences was again found guilty, but
with extenuating circumstances. President Loubet pardoned him
ten days later and the courts ordered further investigation of the
case. The letters which convicted him were declared forgeries and
Dreyfus innocent. The case troubled French society for some years
to come. Nostradramus describes the proof of Dreyfus' innocence
as arriving too late, for his sentence has already been passed and he
is in the penal colony. *Vent contraire* is interpreted as political, i.e.
anti-semitic, feeling running high against Dreyfus. The minister
who was called upon to revise the Dreyfus case in 1899 was M.
Waldeck Rousseau, whose name is given in the last line. He was vio-
lently anti-Dreyfus, finding him guilty a second time until the

[1] *faicte*—Normal spelling of the period for fait.
[2] Two alternatives. Either *semez*, to spread, which I accept, or
senez = wise.

public pardon. The number of conspirators may well have been fourteen, but it is impossible to prove at this date.

8

Combien de fois prinse cité solaire	How often will you be captured, O city of the sun? Changing laws that are barbaric and vain. Bad times approach you. No longer will you be enslaved. Great Hadrie will revive your veins.
Seras changeant les loix barbares &	
vaines:	
Ton mal s'approche. Plus sera	
tributaire,	
La grand Hadrie¹ recourira des	
veines.	

HENRI IV. SIEGE OF PARIS, 1590

After his accession to the French throne Henri IV de Navarre had to besiege Paris for six months before he could enter the city in September 1590. It is called Solaire, city of the sun, a suitable epithet if one thinks of Louis XVI, the Sun King. The barbarous laws refer to the innovations of the Seize which was the first truly revolutionary faction to govern Paris. '*Ton mal s'approche*'; the siege occurred less than thirty years after Nostradamus' death and he seems to feel the accession of a Huguenot king deeply. The last line is interesting in that throughout the siege from April to September Henri IV allowed food to be passed through the lines to the starving people of Paris. Perhaps this line is to be taken in its most literal form, or more metaphorically in that the new line of the Navarre family will revive the greatness of France and the French kings?

9

De l'Orient viendra la coeur	From the Orient will come the African heart to trouble Hadrie and the heirs of Romulus. Accompanied by the Libyan fleet the temples of Malta and nearby islands shall be deserted.
Punique	
Facher Hadrie & les hoirs²	
Romulides	
Accompagné de la classe³ Libyque	
Temples Mellites⁴ & proches isles	
vuides.	

¹ *Hadrie*—Henry by anagram, one letter being altered according to Nostradamus' rules.
² *hoirs* = heirs. The heirs of Romulus are of course the Italians.
³ *classe*—Latin, *classis* = fleet.
⁴ *Mellites* = adjective, Maltese.

1. HENRI IV AND THE DUC DE PARME.
2. THE SIEGE OF MALTA

This quatrain should be divided into two parts. Lines 1–2 continue from the last verse and refer again to Henri IV. The man who troubles him from the East is the Duke of Parma who compelled Henri to raise his siege of Paris in 1590 in order to meet the Spanish army advancing from Flanders. This annoyed the Pope (the heir of Romulus) who favoured the Navarre claim and was hostile to Spanish policy at this point.

Lines 3–4 most probably refer to the siege of Malta in 1565 and the Libyan fleet is then the Turkish navy which roamed the Mediterranean. These are not quite contemporary events.

10

Serpens[1] *transmis dans la caige de fer,*	A coffin is put into the vault of iron, where the seven children of the king are held. The ancestors and forebears will come forth from the depths of hell, lamenting to see thus dead the fruit of their line.
Ou les enfans septaines[2] *du Roy sont pris:*	
Les vieux & peres ·sortiront bas de l'enfer,	
Ains mourir voir de fruict mort & cris.	

FATES OF VALOIS CHILDREN AND HENRI III's DEATH, 1610

This complicated quatrain refers to the fall of the House of Valois and in particular to the removal of the remains of the last Valois king, Henri III, in 1610 to the family sepulchre at Saint Denis. The theme of the seven Valois children of Catherine de' Medici, Queen of France, wife of Henri II, recurs several times in the quatrains. Nostradamus seems clearly aware that the line will die out although it is only fair to admit that Henri III was not the last to die, as Marguerite de Navarre lived until 1615. Line three is a poetic reference to the family ghosts who return to mourn the end of the Valois line.

[1] *Serpens*—From *serpos*, Gk. = Shroud.
[2] *enfans septaines* = (a) François II, 1549–60. (b) Elisabeth 1545–68. (c) Claude 1547–75. (d) Charles IX 1550–74. (e) Henri III 1551–89. (f) Marguerite 1552–1615. (g) François duc d'Alençon 1554–84.

Le mouvement de sens, coeur, pieds
　　& mains,
Seront d'accord Naples, Lyon,[1]
　　Sicille:
Glaves, feux, eaux puis aux
　　nobles Romains,
Plongez tuez mors par cerveau
　　debile.

The motion of senses, heart, feet and hands will be in agreement between Naples, Lyon and Sicily. Swords, fire, floods, then the noble Romans drowned, killed or dead because of a weak brain.

All the places mentioned, if one accepts the reading Leon for Lyon, were part of the Spanish Hapsburg Empire. The weak mind may imply that some Pope would cause trouble between the Vatican and the Empire?

Dans peu dira faulce brute fragile,
De bas en haut eslue prompte-
　　ment:
Puis un instant desloyale & labile,
Qui de Veronne aura gouverne-
　　ment.

There will soon be talk of a treacherous man, who rules a short time, quickly raised from low to high estate. He will suddenly turn disloyal and volatile. This man will govern Verona.

From 1405–1562 Verona was governed by podestas, the office of a captain which was meant to change yearly. After that date it was ruled by a council of proveditors. The last podesta was Jacapo Sansebastiani 1539/62, but he was not a traitor.

Les exilez par ire, haine intestine,
Feront au Roy grand conjuration:
Secret mettront ennemis par la
　　mine,
Et ses vieux siens contre aux
　　sedition.

Through anger and internal hatreds, the exiles will hatch a great plot against the king. Secretly they will place enemies as a threat, and his own old (adherents) will find sedition against them.

CONSPIRACY OF AMBOISE, 1560 (?)

This is a generally worded quatrain concerning the Conspiracy of Amboise 1560. The coming to power of the Guise family in France, caused other parties, in particular the Montmorencys and the Bourbons, to conspire to kill the Duc de Guise and kidnap the

[1] *Lyon*—Alternative reading = Leon.

King, Francis II. However the plot leaked out in advance and was suppressed.

14

De gent esclave[1] *chansons, chants* *& requestes,* *Captifs par Princes & Seigneur*[2] *aux prisons:* *A l'avenir par idiots sans testes,*[3] *Seront reçus par divines oraisons.*	From the enslaved populace, songs, chants and demands, while Princes and Lords are held captive in prisons. These will in the future be received by headless idiots as divine prayers.

FRENCH REVOLUTION, 1789

Most commentators accept this quatrain as referring to the songs and demands of the populace while Louis XVI was imprisoned with his family in the Temple. The idiots who lose their heads are the early ringleaders of the terror who in their turn will follow the aristocracy to the guillotine, but who are regarded at first as inspired leaders of the Revolution.

15

Mars nous menace par la force *bellique,*[4] *Septante fois fera le sang espandre:* *Auge*[5] *& ruine de l'Ecclesiastique,* *Et plus ceux qui d'eux rien* *voudront entendre.*	Mars threatens us with the force of war and will cause blood to be spilt seventy times. The clergy will be both exalted and reviled moreover, by those who wish to learn nothing of them.

DIFFICULTIES FACING THE CHURCH

Commentators of the early 19th Century, such as Nicollaud, take lines 1–2 as referring to Napoleon (Mars) and the many wars of the Empire. The church was both humbled and exalted during this period. In 1792 the clergy were disbanded and religion almost vanished from France during the early days of the Directoire. However by 1804 Napoleon had recognized the Pope and the position of the clergy in order to legitimize his coronation. The troubles facing the Catholic Church in the future is a common theme through the Prophecies. Religious practice is certainly declining in most western countries at the present time.

[1] *esclave* = (*a*) enslaved, (*b*) Slav or Russian?
[2] Singular use of *Seigneur* may indicate King Louis XVI.
[3] *testes*—O.F. for *têtes* = heads.
[4] *bellique*—Latin, *bellicus* = warlike.
[5] *Auge*—Latin, *augere* = to increase.

Faulx[1] *à l'estang*[2] *joint vers le Sagitaire,*[3]
En son hault AUGE[4] *de l'exaltation,*
Peste, famine, mort de main militaire,
La siecle approche de renouvation.

A scythe joined with a pond in Sagittarius at its highest ascendant. Plague, famine, death from military hands; the century approaches its renewal.

POSSIBLE WAR TOWARDS THE END OF THE CENTURY?

When Saturn and Aquarius are in conjunction with Sagittarius in the ascendant, towards the end of a century, we should expect a great war, together with disease and famine. This description is so general that it could fit our century as well as any other. Nostradamus does refer later in Centuries to the possibility of a third war towards the end of this Century. See I. 91, II. 41, 46, 62, VI. 97, VIII. 59, 77, X. 49, 72, 74, 75.

17

Par quarante ans l'Iris n'apparoistra,
Par quarante ans tous les jours sera veu:
La terre aride en siccité croistra,
Et grans deluges quand sera aperceu.

For forty years the rainbow will not be seen. For forty years it will be seen every day. The dry earth will grow more parched, and there will be great floods when it is seen.

FLOODS AND DROUGHT

This must be left to the reader. There is no record of a forty-year drought followed by forty years of flooding. One of the general quatrains of gloom and doom.

18

Par la discorde negligence Gauloise,
Sera passaige à Mahommet ouvert:
De sang trempé la terre & mer Senoise,
Le port phocen[5] *de voiles & nefs convert.*

Because of French discord and negligence an opening shall be given to the Mohammedans. The land and sea of Siena will be soaked in blood, and the port of Marseilles covered with ships and sails.

[1] *Faulx* = a scythe, the sign of Saturn.
[2] *l'estang* = a pond, or water sign, i.e. Saturn in Aquarius.
[3] *Sagitaire* = (Nov.–Dec.) sign of the Zodiac.
[4] *Auge*—Latin, *augere* = increase.
[5] *phocen* = Marseilles, founded by the people of Phocaea, the mother city in W. Asia Minor.

FRANCE AND NORTH AFRICA.
SECOND WORLD WAR

This refers to the chaos in France during 1940 which allowed the Italian armies to march into North Africa without hindrance. The Italian blood spilt would refer to the battles in the desert; the harbour at Marseilles was constantly operative, although in German hands.

19

Lors que serpens viendront cir-
cuir[1] l'are,[2]
Le sang Troyen vexé par les
Espaignes:
Par eux grand nombre en sera
faicte tare.
Chef fruict,[3] caché aux mares[4]
dans les saignes.[5]

When the snakes surround the altar, and the Trojan blood is troubled by the Spanish. Because of them, a great number will be lessened. The leader flees, hidden in the swampy marshes.

CATHERINE DE' MEDICI

Catherine de' Medici, Queen mother of France, changed her emblem after her husband's death to a serpent biting its tail curled round a star, not an altar. Trojan blood is the usual Nostradamus description of Royal blood derived from the medieval legend that the French Royal family were descended from Francus, a mythical son of Priam. The French trouble with Spain did not really occur until the interregnum 1589–94, and the later war of the Spanish succession. Another suggestion is that the snakes refer to the Huguenots pressing hard around the Catholic altar, but the reference to Trojan blood links it to Catherine de' Medici and the French royal line. The last line is unclear.

20

Tours, Orleans, Blois, Angiers,
Reims, & Nantes,
Cités vexées par subit changement:
Par langues estranges seront ten-
dues tentes,[6]
Fleuves, dards Rones, terre & mer
tremblement.

The cities of Tours, Orleans, Blois, Angers, Reims and Nantes are troubled by sudden change. Tents will be pitched by (people) of foreign tongues; rivers, darts at Rennes, shaking of land and sea.

[1] circuir—Latin, circuire = to encircle.
[2] are—Latin, ara = altar.
[3] fruict—fuit = flee.
[4] mares—O.F. = swamp marsh.
[5] seigne—O.F. = swamp, marsh.
[6] tentes = (a) Tents pitched by invaders. (b) Latin, tentare, to attack. These cities will be attacked by invaders. The meaning is substantially the same.

All the cities, except for Reims, are situated on the Loire and have suffered several foreign invasions, mainly the Prussian and Russian armies in 1815, the Prussians again in 1871 and 1940, and also the Americans in 1917–19 and 1944–5. There is no record of an earthquake at Rennes since publication.

21

Profonde argille blanche nourrit rochier, *Qui d'un abisme istra[1] lactineuse:[2]* *En vain troublez ne l'oseront toucher,* *Ignorans estre au fond terre argilleuse.*	The rock holds in its depths white clay which will come out milk-white from a cleft. Needlessly troubled people will not dare touch it, unaware that the foundation of the earth is of clay.

No connection with local historical events can be found to explain this odd verse. I wonder whether the language has alchemistic undertones?

22

Ce que vivra & n'ayant ancien sens, *Viendra leser à mort son artifice:* *Austun, Chalan, Langres & les deux Sens,* *La gresle & glace fera grand malefice.*	A thing existing without any senses will cause its own end to happen through artifice. At Autun, Chalan, Langres and the two Sens there will be great damage from hail and ice.

MEDICAL? c. 1613

A very interesting solution to this quatrain occurs in Garancières. He states that in 1613 a petrified embryo was removed by operation (artifice) from the womb of a woman called Colomba Chantry who lived at Sens. This quite a rare event; examples can be found in medical textbooks, and a woman living in Italy two years ago was found to have been carrying a petrified embryo well into her sixties; an interesting medical sideline from Nostradamus the doctor. All the towns mentioned belong to the Duchy of Burgundy. The reference to the weather seems very general, the quatrain implying that it occurred around the same period, 1613. The second town of Sens is near Louhans.

[1] *istra*—O.F. = *aller* to go (ira).
[2] *lactineuse*—Latin, *lac* = milk. *lacticineum* = milk food.

30

Au mois troisiesme se levant le soleil
Sanglier, Liepard au champ Mars pour combattre:
Liepard laissé, au ciel extend son oeil,
Un aigle autour du Soleil voit s'esbattre.

In the third month, at sunrise, the Boar and the Leopard meet on the battlefield. The fatigued Leopard looks up to heaven and sees an eagle playing around the sun.

BATTLE OF WATERLOO. 18th JUNE 1815.
NAPOLEON'S 100 DAYS

This is one of Nostradamus' most fascinating quatrains. The background to the battle of Waterloo was that Blücher, the Prussian Boar, had been beaten back at Ligny and the joining up of the British and Prussian forces had therefore not been able to take place when Wellington decided to make his stand at Waterloo. This was in June, just over three months after Napoleon's return from Elba in February 1815 (*au mois troisiesme*). It may also contain a reference to Napoleon's reign of 100 days which this battle brought to an end. Equally, dating from the March solstice, which Nostradamus would have done, we are given the month of June for the date of the battle. This is a typical example of Nostradamus' convoluted style where meaning after meaning appears to be contained in one phrase. The French troops battered the English Leopard all day from sunrise to evening while Wellington waited for his ally Blücher to turn the French flank. Wellington's position was facing south so he would have seen Napoleon's Imperial eagles flying against the sun. As the day drew to a close, the British were exhausted. A cloud of dust was seen. Napoleon thought it was Grouchy, but it was Blücher. The end had come. This is a vivid and poetic quatrain of a much higher standard than most. The Imperial Eagle is often used in the Centuries as a synonym for Napoleon himself. On this occasion it refers both to the standards and to the man. Napoleon used to call the English heraldic lion the Leopard of England.

A cité neufue pensif pour condemner,
L'oisel de proye au ciel se vient
offrir:
Apres victoire à captifs pardonner,
Cremone & Mantoue grands maux
aura souffert.

At the New City he is thoughtful to condemn; the bird of
prey offers himself to the gods.
After victory he pardons his
captives. At Cremona and
Mantua great hardships will
be suffered.

NAPOLEON AT VILLA NOVA, AND THE
SIEGE OF MANTUA, 1796–97

During Napoleon's Italian campaigns 1795–7, he arrived at Villa
Nova uncertain how to proceed, having received no orders from
the Directoire in France. In June 1796 Napoleon besieged
Mantua which, despite terrific bombardments, held out until
February 1797. Napoleon is reputed to have treated the prisoners
generously on their defeat. Cremona is situated near Mantua
and must have suffered from the French invasion. Mantua's
peace, however, lasted a very short time. In 1799 it was again
taken by the Austrians and, although restored to the French
in 1801 (Lunéville) it became Austrian again from 1814 to 1866.
Cremona and Mantua both suffered severe political persecution as
did the whole of Lombardy between 1849–59 after the peace of
Villafranca. Note again the use of the metaphor of the bird of prey,
the eagle, for Napoleon.

Perdu trouvé, caché de si long siecle,
Sera Pasteur demi Dieu honoré:
Ains que la lune acheve son grand
siecle,
Par autres vents sera deshonoré.

The lost thing is discovered,
hidden for many centuries.
Pasteur will be celebrated
almost as a god-like figure.
This is when the moon com-
pletes her great cycle, but by
other rumours he shall be
dishonoured.

LOUIS PASTEUR, 1822–95.
FOUNDING OF INSTITUTE, 1889

Another fascinating quatrain which contains not only the name of
Pasteur but also a very specific dating although not apparent at
first. Pasteur's discovery that germs polluted the atmosphere was
one of the most important in medical history, and led to Lister's
theory of sterilization. The Encyclopaedia Britannica says that

Pasteur, the 'demi-Dieu', 'was now the acknowledged head of the greatest chemical movement of the time'. He founded his Institute Pasteur on 14th November 1889; the cycle of the moon ran from 1535 to 1889. The rumours that dishonoured him may mean the violent opposition to his methods which were roused among powerful members of the Academy, against the new practices of the Institute such as vaccines against hydrophobia etc.

26

Le grand du fouldre tumbe[1] d'heure diurne, *Mal & predict par porteur postulaire:* *Suivant presage tumbe[1] d'heure nocturne,* *Conflict Reims, Londres, Etrusque pestifere.*	The great man will be struck down in the day by a thunderbolt. An evil deed, foretold by the bearer of a petition. According to the prediction another falls at night time. Conflict at Reims, London, and pestilence in Tuscany.

ASSASSINATION OF J.F.K., 1963 AND R.F.K., 1968

The first three lines here may apply to the assassinations of the two Kennedy brothers. John F. Kennedy was shot down (thunderbolt) in broad daylight at Dallas, Texas on 22nd November 1963 by the psychopath, Lee Harvey Oswald. The other man linked with him who is killed at night, was his brother Robert F. Kennedy who was shot down on 5th June 1968 in the early morning while celebrating his victory in the presidential primary elections at an hotel. Line 2, the fact that the assassination had been told by the bearer of a petition may refer to the many death threats John F. Kennedy and his brother received during their terms of office. The troubles in France, England and Italy would refer to the world repercussions to these assassinations. See VIII. 46, 77.

27

Dessouz de chaine[2] Guien du ciel frappé, *Non loing de là est caché le tresor:* *Qui par longs siecles avoit esté grappé,* *Trouve mourra, l'oeil crevé de ressort:*	Beneath the oak tree of Gienne, struck by lightning, the treasure is hidden not far from there. That which for many centuries had been gathered, when found, a man will die, his eye pierced by a spring.

[1] *tumbe—tombe* = fall.

[2] *chaine*—O.F., *chene*, but could possibly mean *chaine* = a chain of mountains.

There are several puzzling quatrains linking the finding of a tomb, a man dead for many centuries, and a treasure, see quatrain IX. 7, but none of them make much sense. Guienne was an ancient province of South-west France, therefore this quatrain cannot refer to the opening of Nostradamus' tomb, which was done during the Revolution when his remains were transferred to the chapel of Notre Dame in the church of St. Laurent, as Salon is not in that province. *Guien* could stand for *gui*, meaning mistletoe, which alters the first line to 'beneath the mistletoe covered oak tree etc.'. However, this gets us no further in solving the quatrain, or the riddle of the spring guarding the tomb. I wonder whether the treasures could be the many antiquarian treasures of southern France, most of which were not seriously excavated until the end of the 19th Century.

28

La tour de Boucq craindra fuste[1] *barbare*	Tobruk will fear the barbarian fleet for a time, then much
Un temps, long temps apres barque hesperique:[2]	later the Western fleet. Cattle, people, possessions, all will be
Bestail, gens, meubles tous deux feront grand tare[3]	quite lost. What a deadly combat in Taurus and Libra.
Taurus & Libra quelle mortelle picque?[4]	

TOBRUK. SECOND WORLD WAR, 1941

It is possible that Tour de Boucq was the nearest Nostradamus could get to the place name Tobruk. The first line refers to Tobruk's chequered history as a trading port between Greeks and Libyans until the Italians became interested in it for strategic reasons. Tobruk then suffered the British invasion of 1941. Hesperique is a difficult word to interpret in the Centuries. It can mean either Western or Spanish, but I feel it cannot here mean Spain, and therefore is more applicable to America. Although it was the British Army which was fighting the Italians at Tobruk in January 1941, the attack upon Pearl Harbour occurred in November of that year in the same month as Tobruk was retrieved, and so Hesperique can refer to the American fleet. Rommel reached

---

[1] *fuste* = a low draught galley with sails and oars.
[2] *hesperique*—Spanish, Western or American.
[3] *tare* = loss.
[4] *?* —printers' error for *!*, if necessary at all.

Tobruk on 8th April (Taurus) and besieged it until November 1941, when it was relieved by British reinforcements. Libra is October, so Nostradamus was a month out in his calculations.

29

Quand la poisson terrestre & aquatique,
Par forte vague au gravier sera mis:
Sa forme estrange sauve & horrifique,
Par mer aux mure bien tost les ennemis.

When the fish that travels over both land and sea is cast up on to the shore by a great wave, its shape foreign, smooth and frightful. From the sea the enemies soon reach the walls.

POLARIS OR SUBROC

This is a perfect description of a Polaris ballistic missile fired from a submerged submarine, causing an enormous upheaval of water. Alternatively it describes the American equivalent, SUBROC, which although fired under water flies through the air to its target.

30

La nef estrange par le tourment marin,
Abourdera pres de port incogneu:
Nonobstant signes de rameau palmerin,[1]
Apres mort pille bon avis tard venu.

Because of the storm at sea, the foreign ship will approach an unknown port. Notwithstanding the signs of the palm branches, afterwards there is death and pillage. Good advice comes too late.

A very general quatrain. The rameau palmerin means palm branches indicating peaceful intent which is later reversed. It appears that the ship suffers the damage rather than the port, which lures it in feigning peaceful intentions.

31

Tant d'ans les guerres en Gaule dureront
Outre la course du Castalon[2] monarque:
Victoire incerte trois grands couronneront,
Aigle, coq, lune, lion, soleil en marque.

The wars in France will last for so many years beyond the reign of the Castulon kings. An uncertain victory will crown three great ones, the Eagle, the Cock, the Moon, the Lion, the Sun in its house.

[1] palmerin—Latin, palmarius = of a palm tree.
[2] Castulon = ancient Iberian city, standing for Spain.

DOWNFALL OF THE SPANISH MONARCHY

There are many ingenious interpretations offered for this quatrain concerning the French Revolutionary struggles and the Spanish Empire after the death of Charles V. It seems to indicate a great war in France after the downfall of the Spanish monarchy. Although some Spanish monarchs resigned and others were deposed, the real downfall of the monarchy must be dated from the founding of the Spanish Republic in 1923. This brings us to the 1930–40s, the period of the Second World War in which France was totally involved in *guerres en Gaule*. The three great powers who won an uncertain victory are America (Eagle), France (Cock), and Britain (Lion). The final capitulation of the Japanese which ended the war was proffered on 12th August (in Leo the Sun sign).

32

Le grand empire sera tost translaté,[1]	The great Empire will soon be
En lieu petit, qui bien tost viendra croistre:	exchanged for a small place, which soon will begin to grow.
Lieu bien infime d'exigue comté,	A small place of tiny area in the
Ou au milieu viendra poser son sceptre.	middle of which he will come to lay down his sceptre.

NAPOLEON I. ELBA AND ST. HELENA

The great Empire of the Imperial Napoleon (note the use of the word empire, not kingdom) is soon changed into the tiny island of Elba. However, on Napoleon's escape and the victorious 100 Days his empire begins, but only begins, to grow again. From here he is sent to an even smaller realm of no account, St. Helena, where he finally relinquishes all claims to power. This is one of the better quatrains, succinct and moving in its simplicity.

33

Pres d'un grand pont de plaine spatieuse,	Near a great bridge near a spacious plain the great lion
Le grand lion par forces Cesarees:[2]	with the Imperial forces will
Fera abbattre hors cité rigoureuse,	cause a falling outside the aus-
Par effrai portes lui seront reserées.[3]	tere city. Through fear the gates will be unlocked for him.

[1] *translaté*—Latin, *translatus* = transferred, exchanged.
[2] *Caesareus*—Latin = imperial.
[3] *reserées*—Latin, *reseratus* = unlocked.

The austere city of line 3 is probably Geneva, home of Calvinism. The plain may be Lombardy, and the Lion the commander of the Imperial forces. But if Nostradamus hoped for the fall of Geneva through the pressures of the Holy Roman Empire he was grievously wrong. The bridge is probably to be interpreted as a mountain pass. One must remember Nostradamus' strong pro-Catholic, anti-Huguenot feelings which seem to come out periodically in the prophecies.

34

L'oiseau de proie volant à la semestre,[1]
Avant conflict faict aux François pareure:[2]
L'un bon prendra l'un ambigue sinistre,
La partie foible tiendra par bon augure.

The bird of prey flying to the left, before battle is joined with the French, he makes preparations. Some will regard him as good, others bad or uncertain. The weaker party will regard him as a good omen.

HITLER AND FRANCE. c. 1938/40

Nostradamus is describing one of the great warmongers of all time, Hitler, as a bird of prey, which name he also gives to Napoleon. The former seems more appropriate here however. The left would mean nothing to Nostradamus other than in a geographical sense, that is the Low Countries. Hitler invaded France through Holland and Belgium having made his preparations (*pareure*) well in advance. The third line refers to the corruption and uncertainty rife among French politicians in the early days of the war, culminating in the Pétainists who accept Hitler's authority and the Vichy cabinet (*partie faible*).

[1] semestre—Latin, sinistre = left.
[2] pareure—O.F. = preparation.

Le lion jeune le vieux surmontera,	The young lion will overcome
En champ bellique par singulier	the older one, in a field of
duelle:	combat in single fight: He
Dans caige d'or les yeux lui	will pierce his eyes in their
crevera,	golden cage; two wounds in
Deux classes une, puis mourir,	one, then he dies a cruel death.
mort cruelle.	

DEATH OF HENRI II, 10th JULY 1559

This quatrain was understood in France during Nostradamus'
lifetime, and was one of the verses that caused Catherine de'
Medici to send for Nostradamus to interpret it. The Italian
prophet Luc Gauric had warned Henri II that both the beginning
and the end of his reign would be marked by a duel. The first took
place soon after his accession, so it seems strange that the king did
not take more care in the tournaments held in honour of the
double marriage of his sister Elizabeth to Philip II of Spain, and
Marguerite his daughter to the Duke of Savoy in the summer of
1559. During the festivities, which lasted for three days, the king
joined in the competitions in the lists at the rue St. Antoine. He was
victorious for the first two days, but on the third rode against
Montgomery, the captain of the Scottish guard. Henri failed to
unseat his opponent and insisted on refighting the bout. On the
third try they splintered lances successfully, but Montgomery failed
to pull up his lance in time, and the splintered shaft pierced the
king's gilt helmet and entered his head just above the eye. Some
reports say that he suffered a second wound in the throat. Henri's
end was cruel indeed, he lay in agony for ten days before death
released him. Montgomery was seven years younger than Henri
who was forty when he died. Henri sometimes used the lion as his
emblem. The word *classes* is understood here to come from the
Greek *klasis* meaning a break, or fracture, rather than the Latin
classis, a fleet.

Tard la monarque se viendra repentir	Too late the king will repent that he did not put his adversary to death. But he will soon come to agree to far greater things which will cause all his line to die.
De n'avoir mis à mort son adversaire:	
Mais viendra bien à plus hault consentir,	
Que tout son song par mort fera deffaire.	

HENRI III. DEATH OF GUISE BROTHERS
AT BLOIS 1588. LOUIS XVI?

This is a quatrain which seems to fit two historical events equally well. The first and most probable interpretation is that it refers to Henri III and his determination to quash the influence of the Guise family in French politics. The king caused both the Duke and his brother Louis to be murdered at Blois on 25th December 1588. However he did not kill the third brother, the Duc of Mayenne, the real ringleader, and was forced to further action to eliminate their power (*à plus hault consentir*). Other commentators prefer to interpret it as describing Louis XVI and his brother and adversary, the Duke of Orléans. Certainly Orléans intrigued against the king and was a sworn enemy of the Queen, Marie Antoinette. At one point he debated joining up with the revolutionaries. Here line 3 then refers to the constitutional monarchy that Louis was forced to accept and the later imprisonment of himself and his family, leading to their deaths on the guillotine. But Louis' brother did not die, *tout son sang*: he returned to France in 1814 as Louis XVIII so this is rather a less satisfactory interpretation.

Un peu devant que le soleil s'excuse,	Shortly before sun set, battle is engaged. A great nation is uncertain. Overcome, the sea port makes no answer, the bridge and the grave both in foreign places.
Conflict donné grand peuple dubiteux:	
Profliges, port marin ne faict response,	
Pont & sepulchre en deux estranges lieux.	

I cannot explain this quatrain but offer these possible clues to the ingenuity of the reader. *Pont* in line 4 often stands for Pontifex, Pope, in Nostradamus. If it is so in this case, one might connect the

Pope who died away from Rome in a foreign grave, with Pius VI, who died at Valence in 1799, captured by the French. His death occurred in August so could the first line mean the summer? The French nation were still *dubiteux* in 1799; the Directoire had suffered defeats both in Italy and Germany and Napoleon's Egyptian campaign was by no means completed. I can only suggest a reference to French naval action in Egypt for line 3; it cannot refer to the British fleet which were scouring the seas for Napoleon's ships.

38

Le sol & l'aigle an victeur paroistront	The Sun and the Eagle will appear to the victor. An empty answer is assured to the defeated. Neither bugle nor shouts will stop the soldiers. Liberty and peace, if achieved in time through death.
Response vaine au vaincu l'on asseure:	
Par cor ne cris harnois n'arresteront,	
Vindicte paix par mors si acheve à l'heure.	

WATERLOO, 1815

This quatrain probably followed on I. 23 in the original. It continues the vivid description of Waterloo with Napoleon, the Imperial Eagle, coming out of the mist into the sun to attack the victor, Wellington. Both sides knew this was a fight to the finish, but for Napoleon it was the final stand after the frantic 100 Days. No reasonable terms awaited him if he lost (*response vaine*), nothing but life exile on St. Helena. Once the men joined in battle they could not be stopped. Napoleon's Grenadiers fought until the last man dropped, and refused to retreat. Freedom and peace can once again come to Europe but only by means of the bloody slaughter of battle, and possibly also Napoleon's end, his political, if not actual, death.

De nuict dans lict le suspresme[1]
    estrangle,
Par trop avoir sejourné, blond
    esleu:
Par trois l'empire subrogé[2] exanche,[3]
A mort mettra carte, et pacquet ne
    leu.[4]
	At night the last one will be
	strangled in his bed because
	he became too involved with
	the blond heir elect. The
	Empire is enslaved and three
	men substituted. He is put
	to death with neither letter nor
	packet read.

DEATH OF LOUIS BOURBON CONDÉ, 1830

The last of the Condés, Louis, was found strangled one night in
1830, not however in his bed, but hanging in his bedroom. He was
probably murdered for the support he gave to the cause of the
Duke of Bordeaux, the Comte de Chambord, whom Nostradamus
rightly describes as *esleu* as he was the grandson of Charles X and
heir to the French throne. The three who usurped power can be
interpreted either as the three regimes which followed Charles X,
Louis Philippe, the Republic and then the Bonapartes, or it could
refer more specifically to the three men who intrigued against the
Condé family, Charles X, the Duke of Angoulême and the Duke of
Bourgogne. Le Pelletier says that Condé was fair-haired and had
written a will (*carte et pacquet*) in favour of the Duke of Bordeaux.
This is said to have been replaced by an earlier will written in
favour of the Duke of Aumale, son of Louis Philippe who became
king in 1830.

40

La trombe[5] fausse dissimulant
    folie,
Fera Bisance[6] un changement de
    loix:
Istra d'Egypte qui veut que l'on
    deslie,
Edict changeant monnaies & alois[7].
	The false trumpet concealing
	madness will cause Byzantium
	to change its laws. From
	Egypt there will go forth a man
	who wants the edict withdrawn,
	changing money and standards.

[1] *supresme* = either great or last, both meanings possible here.
[2] *subrogé*—Latin, *subrogatus* = substitute.
[3] *exanche*—Latin, *exancilatus* = enslaved.
[4] *leu.*—O.F., lu = read.
[5] *trombe*—Misprint, *trompe* = trumpet.
[6] *Bisance* = Byzantium.
[7] *alois* = alloy, standard (of metal).

I cannot interpret the first line. The quatrain seems to refer to a political situation between the Ottoman Empire (Bisance) and Egypt. Some commentators think that the last two lines refer to Napoleon's return from Egypt and the establishment of totally new values in France under the Directoire of money, laws, the Church, etc.

41

Seige en cité est de nuict assaillie, *Peu eschapés non loin de mer conflict:* *Femme de joie,*[1] *retours fils defaillie,* *Poison & lettres cachees dans le plic.*	The city is besieged and assaulted by night; few have escaped; a battle not far from the sea. A woman faints with joy at the return of her son, poison in the folds of the hidden letters.

This quatrain has been given many explanations by commentators who either refer it to the French invasion of Italy in 1556–47 or even to Dunkirk, 1940, where the Third Republic becomes the woman, the prostitute, and the poison the constitution (*lettres*) of the Nazi doctrines. None of these appears at all convincing.

42

Le dix Kalende[2] *d'Avril de faict Gothique,* *Resuscité encor par gens malins:* *Le feu estainct assemblé diabolique,* *Cherchant les os du d'Amant & Pselin.*	The tenth day of the April Calends, calculated in Gothic fashion is revived again by wicked people. The fire is put out and the diabolic gathering seek the bones of the demon of Psellus.

INSTITUTION OF THE GREGORIAN
CALENDAR SYSTEM, 1582. DIVINATION

It is believed that the last line should read '*cherchant les os du Demon et Psellus*', but that Nostradamus suppressed it for fear that the authorities might accuse him of magic practices. There is a description of a similar evocation of spirits in Michael Psellus' book *De Demonibus*. Nostradamus seems to have understood the change of the Calendar from the old style to the Gregorian system, which took place (after his death) in 1582. The tenth day of the Kalends

---

[1] *Femme de joie* = either a woman (fainting) with joy, or a prostitute.

[2] *Kalende*—Calend = 1st day of Roman month.

of April would be 10th April, as the Calends was the first day of the Roman month. When the Gregorian system was introduced ten days were removed, so possibly Nostradamus means 1st April, new style. Good Friday was regarded as the best day for magical evocations, and it is possible that Nostradamus is implying that this was the day on which he started using these methods to inspire the prophecies. Psellus mentions the use of a bowl of water 'which seems to boil over and a faint voice murmurs words which contain the revelation of future events'. Nostradamus may therefore have begun writing the Prophecies on a Good Friday which fell on 10th April, old style.

43

Avant qu'advienne le changement d'Empire	Before the Empire changes a very wonderful event will take place. The field moved, the pillar of porphyry put in place, changed on the gnarled rock.
Il adviendra un cas bien merveilleux:	
Un champ mué, le pillier de paphire[1]	
Mis translaté sur le rocher noilleux.	

Line 1 probably places this quatrain before 1789. There is another reference to a pillars of porphyry in IX. 32.

44

En bref seront de retour sacrifices,	In a short time sacrifices will be resumed, those opposed will be put (to death) like martyrs. There will no longer be monks, abbots or novices. Honey shall be far more expensive than wax.
Contrevenans seront mis à martyre:	
Plus ne seront moines, abbez, ne novices,	
Le miel sera beaucoup plus cher que cire.	

THE CULT OF REASON, 10th NOVEMBER 1793. ABOLITION OF CLERGY

The French Revolutionary government abolished the worship of God in 1793. The sacrifices in line 1 mean a restoration of paganism. On 10th November the Cult of Reason was established and in 1794 this was followed by a Festival of the Supreme Being, 8th June. The Constitution of 1790 declared the dissolution of the Clergy (no more monks) and of ecclesiastical orders. Many who refused to embrace the new ideology' were persecuted, and all

---

[1] *paphire* = porphyry—a type of red or white crystallized feldspar.

priests who refused to accept the Civil Constitution of the Clergy were expelled. The last line is a generalization implying that lack of demand for beeswax for church candles makes its price less than that of the honey it holds, a new state of affairs in France.

45

Secteur de sectes grand peine au delateur,	A founder of sects, much trouble for the accuser: A
Beste en theatre, dresse le jeu scenique,	beast in the theatre prepares the scene and plot. The author
Du faict antique ennobly l'inventeur,	ennobled by acts of older times; the world is confused by schis-
Par sectes monde confus & schismatique.	matic sects.

This is probably a tirade against Calvinism, like I. 33.

46

Tout aupres d'Aux, de Lestoure & Mirande,	Very near Auch, Lectoure and Mirande a great fire will fall
Grand feu du ciel en trois nuicts tumbera:	from the sky for three nights. The cause will appear both
Cause adviendra bien stupende & mirande,	stupefying and marvellous; shortly afterwards there will be
Bien peu aupres la terre tremblera.	an earthquake.

All three towns mentioned are in the Departement of Gers in south-western France. Perhaps Nostradamus is referring to a hail of meteorites, which make the earth tremble, or which are followed by a minor earthquake?

47

Du lac Leman¹ les sermons fascheront,	The speeches of Lake Leman will become angered, the days
Les Jours seront reduicts par les sepmaines:²	will drag out into weeks, then months, then years, then all
Puis mois, puis an, puis tous deffailliront,	will fail. The authorities will condemn their useless powers.
Les magistrats damneront leurs loix vaines.	

¹ *Leman* = Lake Geneva.
² *sepmaines—semaines* = weeks.

44

LEAGUE OF NATIONS, 1919-47

Geneva was important as the setting of the League of Nations whose first assembly was held there on 15th November 1920. The quatrain describes vividly the years of fruitless argument and failure until the final formal disbandment after the war in August 1947, although in fact it ceased to be effective after early 1940. See also V. 85.

48

Vingt ans du regne de la lune passez,	When twenty years of the Moon's reign have passed
Sept mil and autre tiendra sa monarchie:	another will take up his reign for seven thousand years. When
Quand le soleil prendra ses jours lassez,	the exhausted Sun takes up his cycle then my prophecy and
Lors accomplit & mine ma prophetie.	threats will be accomplished.

DATE OF PUBLICATION AND COMPLETION OF PROPHECIES

According to Roussat the cycle of the Moon lasted from 1535–1889, which places the date of the first line as 1555, the publication date of the first part of the Centuries. Nostradamus seems to envisage another 7,000 years from that date to the cycle of the sun when all will be accomplished. According to astrologers we have now entered the reign of Aquarius. This quatrain is interesting in that it gives the date of publication and associates this with the completion of the prophecies. It is as though Nostradamus believes the Centuries are written at the start of a new era lasting 7,000 years. It was a commonly held theory in the Middle Ages that the world would come to an end at the beginning of the seventh millennium. This information originated from the book of Enoch which was general reading during the first and second centuries but removed by the Church from the Canon in AD 300. Nostradamus also refers to 7,000 years in quatrain X. 74, but no commentator is able to agree on the date from which to start calculating, and this theory does not agree with the statements of some of the other prophecies.

Beaucoup avant telles menees,
Ceux d'orient par la vertu lunaire:
L'an mil sept cens feront grands
emmenees,
Subjugant presque le coing Aquilo-
naire.[1]

Long before these happenings
the people of the East, influenced by the Moon, in the
year 1700 will cause many to
be carried away, and will
almost subdue the Northern
area.

EVENTS AROUND 1700

The astrologer Roussat also believed the year 1700–2 would show
the start of great upheavals, but this seems a prophecy where both
he and Nostradamus are wrong. It could apply to various invasions
in the North (*Aquilonaire*). In February 1700, August II invaded
Livania. Peter the Great took Azov and Kouban from the Turks;
Charles XII occupied Iceland and Peter the Great then declared
war on Sweden, but none of these actions reduced the North
sufficiently in the sense Nostradamus means it.

50

De l'aquatique triplicité[2] *naistra.*
D'un qui fera le jeudi pour sa feste:
Son bruit, loz,[3] *regne, sa puissance*
croistra,
Par terre & mer aux Oriens
tempeste.

From the three water signs will
be born a man who will
celebrate Thursday as his
holiday. His renown, praise,
rule and power will grow on
land and sea, bringing trouble
to the East.

THIRD ANTICHRIST?

This describes a person with the three water signs of Aries, Cancer
and Aquarius dominant in his birth chart, presumably not a
Christian, *jeudi pour sa feste*, whose power becomes so great that he
brings trouble to countries in the East.

It may refer to the Third Antichrist. See II. 5, 62, 89, IV. 50,
VI. 33, VIII. 77, X. 66, 72, 74, 75.

[1] *Aquilonaire*—Latin, *aquilonaris* = northern.
[2] *aquatique triplicité* = the three water signs of the Zodiac.
[3] *loz*—Latin, *laus* = praise.

Chef d'Aries, Jupiter & Saturne,	The head of Aries, Jupiter
Dieu eternel quelles mutations?[1]	and Saturn. Eternal God, what
Puis par long siecle son maling[2]	changes! Then the bad times
temps retourne	will return again after a long
Gaule, & Italie quelles emotions?[1]	century; what turmoil in
	France and Italy.

13th DECEMBER 1702. WAR OF SPANISH SUCCESSION, AND FRANCE, 1802

The conjunction of Jupiter and Saturn in Aries took place on 13th December 1702 during the War of the Spanish Succession under Louis XIV. The great changes of line 2 are the French Revolution which will occur before the century mentioned in line 3 is completed. By 1802 France is embroiled in the Italian campaign and it was in January of that year that Napoleon was declared President of the Italian Republic. The next time this conjunction occurs will be 2nd September 1995.

52

Les deux malins de Scorpion con-	Two evil influences in con-
joinct,	junction in Scorpio. The great
Le grand seigneur meutri dedans sa	lord is murdered in his room.
salle:	A newly appointed king per-
Peste à l'Eglise par le nouveau roy	secutes the Church, the lower
joinct	(parts of) Europe and in the
L'Europe basse & Septentrionale.	North.

DEATH OF SULTAN SELIM III, 1807/8, AND NAPOLEON'S CONQUESTS

The two evil influences in Scorpio are Mars and Saturn, but this conjunction has occurred fourteen times since 1555. It happened in 1807 when Selim III of Turkey, one of whose titles incidentally was Seignior, was deposed in 1807, although he was not murdered until the following year. The troubles suffered by the Church are those caused by Napoleon who, having restored the Catholic hierarchy in France, at the same time held Pius VII prisoner. By this period, Napoleon had defeated Austria and Prussia (lower Europe) and Russia (Septentrionale) and France was at the height of her powers.

[1] *?* printers' error for *!*
[2] *maling—malin*, old spelling.

Las qu'on verra grand peuple tourmenté,	Alas, how we will see a great nation sorely troubled and the
Et la loi saincte en totale ruine:	holy law in utter ruin. Christ-
Par autres loix toute la Christienté,	ianity (governed) throughout
Quand d'or, d'argent trouve nouvelle mine.	by other laws, when a new source of gold and silver is discovered.

DISESTABLISHMENT OF CLERGY, 1790.
CREATION OF ASSIGNATS, 1789

This quatrain again tells of the disestablishment of the French Clergy, 14th July 1790, and of its subsequent persecution during the Revolution. The laws other than Christian that governed France were those of the Cult of Reason, see quatrain I. 44. The last line is interesting. In 1789 the National Assembly passed a decree on 19th December creating an issue of 400 million assignats. This currency was in fact based on the confiscated goods of the clergy which were used as security for the notes, and was certainly a new source of wealth on which the country could draw.

54

Deux revolts faicte du maling[1] falcigere,[2]	Two revolutions will be caused by the evil scythe bearer mak-
De regne & siecles faict permutation:	ing a change of reign and centuries. The mobile sign thus
Le mobil signe[3] à son endroit si ingere,[4]	moves into its house: Equal in favour to both sides.
Aux deux egaux & d'inclination.	

TWO REVOLUTIONS AND WAR
STARTING IN AUSTRIA

The evil scythe bearer is Saturn, and the two great Revolutions occurring in different centuries due to his malign influence are of course the French Revolution at the end of the 18th Century and the Russian Revolution in the early 20th Century. The mobile sign is Libra, the Balance, which governs Austria according to the

[1] *maling*—O.F. spelling = malin.

[2] *falcigere*—Latin, *falcam gerens* = bearing a scythe; the scythe was a sign of Saturn.

[3] Libra = the balance.

[4] *ingere*—Latin, *ingerere* (*se*) = to enter, penetrate. The *si* may be a misprint for *se*.

astrologers. Apparently the influence of Libra was not strong enough to tip the balance in favour of Austria (*aux deux egaux*) and so the malign influence of Saturn is able to cause war in that country following on the second revolution. Nostradamus is referring to the assassination of the Arch Duke Ferdinand at Sarajevo, 1914 and its consequence, the First World War.

55

Soubs l'opposite climat Baby- *lonique,* *Grand sera de sang effusion:* *Que terre & mer, air, ciel sera* *inique,* *Sectes, faim, regnes, pestes, con-* *fusion.*	In the land with a climate opposite to Babylon there will be great shedding of blood. Heaven will seem unjust both on land and sea and in the air. Sects, famine, kingdoms, plagues, confusion.

This is a very obscure quatrain, the only point of interest being the use of the word *air* in line 3. Nostradamus obviously comprehends that man will move in this dimension in the future, see quatrains I. 63, 64, II. 29, III. 69 etc.

56

Vous verrez tost & tard taire *grand change,* *Horreurs extremes, & vindications:* *Que si la lune conduicte par son* *ange,* *Le ciel s'approche des inclinations.*	Sooner and later you will see great changes made, dreadful horrors and vengeances. For as the moon is thus led by its angel the heavens draw near to the Balance.

Another astrological quatrain promising disaster in Libra, either the country, Austria, or using the sign as a date. It may follow on from the last verse, I. 55.

57

Par grand discord la trombe[1] *tremblera* *Accord rompu dressant la teste au* *ciel:* *Bouche sanglante dans le sang* *nagera,* *Au sol la face ointe[2] de laict &* *miel.*	The trumpet shakes with great discord. An agreement broken: lifting the face to heaven: the bloody mouth will swim with blood; the face anointed with milk and honey lies on the ground.

[1] *trombe = trompe*, trumpet.
[2] *ointe*—Latin, *unctus* = anointed.

EXECUTION OF LOUIS XVI.
21st JANUARY 1793

In 1793 amidst the horrors and discords of the Revolution Louis XVI accepted the constitution decreed by the National Assembly, (*accord rompu*). As Louis went to his execution he is recorded as having recited the Third Psalm—*exaltus caput meum* (*dressant la tête*). When a victim is guillotined the blood rushes out through the mouth of the corpse. Nostradamus is nothing if not meticulous about detail. Louis is described as anointed with milk and honey because he was actually so anointed as part of the coronation service. See also VI. 89.

58

Tranche le ventre, naistra avec deux testes,	Through a slit in the belly a creature will be born with two heads and four arms: it will survive for some few years. The day that Alquiloie celebrates his festivals Fossana, Turin and the ruler of Ferrara will follow.
Et quatre bras: quelques ans entiers vivra:	
Jour qui Alquiloie¹ celebrera ses festes,	
Fossen, Turin, chef Ferrare suivra.	

Through a slit in the belly a creature will be born with two heads and four arms: it will survive for some few years. The day that Alquiloie celebrates his festivals Fossana, Turin and the ruler of Ferrara will follow.

NAPOLEON AND THE BOURBONS

This is an involved quatrain dealing with both Napoleon and the Bourbon family. It is possible to interpret the first line literally as a Caesarian section, but it is more likely to refer to Louis XVI as the belly. *Tranche* is the same adjective that Nostradamus uses for the king's death elsewhere, from whom come the two comparatively short ruling heirs, Louis XVIII and Charles X (*deux testes*). The four arms are understood to be the Dukes of Angoulême, Normandy, Berry and Bordeaux. Alquiloie, the rule of the Eagle, connects them with Napoleon by whom the family was deposed, and the ruler of Ferrare was the Pope who 'followed' Napoleon back to France as a prisoner; the rest of Italy Fossana and Turin followed metaphorically, in that they were captured by the French. This is one of the quatrains in which Nostradamus has reversed the time sequence.

¹ *Alquiloie* = (a) *Aquila lex*, the rule of the eagle. (b) *Aquilene*, one of the great cities of the Roman Empire.

Les exilez deportez dans les isles,	The exiles deported to the
Au changement d'un plus cruel monarque	islands at the advent of an even more cruel king will be mur-
Seront meurtris:[1] *& mis deux les scintiles,*[2]	dered. Two will be burnt who were not sparing in their
Qui de parler ne seront estez parques.[3]	speech.

Nicollaud ascribes this to the events of the Coup d'Etat in 1857, when many members of French secret societies were deported to the Cayenne Islands. The new king was Napoleon III, who caused people who spoke against the regime (*ne seront estez parques de parler*) to be imprisoned and deported. All the lines fit, but I am not convinced by the interpretation. Some commentators, such as Roberts, ascribe it to the cremation of the Jews, but this is impossible if one reads the line (*mis deux les scintiles*); not even Nostradamus would reduce six million tragedies to two.

Un Empereur naistra pres d'Italie	An Emperor will be born near
Qui a l'Empire sera vendu bien cher:	Italy, who will cost the Empire very dearly. They will say,
Diront avec quels gens il se ralie,	when they see his allies, that he
Qu'on trouvera moins prince que boucher.	is less a prince than a butcher.

NAPOLEON I, 1769–1821

This is one of the famous quatrains predicting Napoleon, the Emperor born near Italy in Corsica. He cost France dearly in both manpower and strength. The third line may be a reference to the Creole origins of his first wife, Josephine, or to his own brothers whom he raised to positions of great honour, kings of Naples and Spain, Holland and Westphalia. The reference to butchery also covers the enormous number of men who died in the Napoleonic campaigns.

[1] *meutrir*—O.F. = to kill.
[2] *scintiles*—Latin, *scintilla* = sparks, flames.
[3] *parques*—Latin, *parcus* = sparing, economic.

La republique miserable infelice[1]	The wretched, unfortunate
Sera vastee[2] *de nouveau magistrat:*	republic will again be ruined
Leur grand amus de l'exile male-	by a new authority. The great
fice,	amount of ill will accumulated
Fera Sueve[3] *ravir leur grand*	in exile will make the Swiss
contracts.	break their important agree-
	ment.

The fourth line makes this quatrain difficult to interpret. Sueve is derived from the Latin Suevi, the German Swiss, which is hard to connect with a French republic devastated by a new government, characterized by the sending of many people into exile. The nearest to this is the rule of the Prince-President Louis Bonaparte III, 1852–70. If Sueve, the Swiss, can be understood as German/Prussian, then the reference may be to the Franco-Prussian war which started in the year of Napoleon III's deposition, 1870.

Le grande parte las que feront les	Alas! what a great loss there
lettres,	will be to learning before the
Avant le cycle de Latona[4] *parfaict:*	cycle of the Moon is completed.
Feu grand deluge plus par ignares	Fire, great floods, by more
sceptres,	ignorant rulers; how long the
Que de long siecle ne se verra	centuries until it is seen to be
refaict.	restored.

Nostradamus visualizes scholarship as suffering a great loss before the end of the Moon's cycle (1889). This may be open to two interpretations. First, that a work of scholarship becomes lost before that date, and reappears after many calamities after a century or so (*de long siecle*); second, a more general meaning that Nostradamus regarded scholarship as becoming vulgarized by the changing of scholastic standards and its availability to what he would have called the common people. Like all scholars of his time, Nostradamus regarded himself as one of an élite.

[1] *infelice*—Latin, *infelix* = unhappy.
[2] *vastee*—Latin, *vastatus* = ruined devastated.
[3] *Sueve*—Suevi = German Swiss tribe.
[4] *Latona* = mythological mother of Apollo and Diana; the Moon.

Les fleurs[1] passés diminue le monde,
Long temps la paix terres inhabitées:
Seur marchera par ciel, serre, mer & onde:
Puis de nouveau les guerres suscitées.

Pestilences extinguished, the world becomes smaller, for a long time the lands will be inhabited peacefully. People will travel safely through the sky (over) land and seas: then wars will start up again.

AIR TRAVEL. 20th CENTURY

It is not clear whether the age of pestilence refers to disease or war, but it is remarkable that Nostradamus envisages the world as a smaller place, presumably because of the ease of air travel mentioned in line 3 as well as more orthodox means by land and sea. Air travel specifically puts this quatrain into the 20th Century, and we are told that war will break about again after a long interlude of peace. This may be the third Great War of this century, which Nostradamus prophecies to follow the Hitler wars. The prophecies are mostly concerned with Europe and the last twenty-seven years are the longest era of peace it has known this century. If for nothing else, this and the following quatrain are noteworthy for their reference to air travel.

De nuict soleil penseront avoir veu,
Quand le pourceau demi-homme on verra:
Bruict, chant, bataille, au ciel battre aperceu:
Et bestes brutes à parler lon orra.

At night they will think they have seen the sun, when they see the half pig man: Noise, screams, battles seen fought in the skies. The brute beasts will be heard to speak.

AIR BATTLE. 20th CENTURY

This seemingly nonsensical quatrain is one of the most interesting. Nostradamus describes a vivid picture of a battle in the air. The sun, appearing at night, is the searchlight piercing the sky, or possibly bombs exploding. The pig-like man, which no commentator to date has ever deciphered, seems a clear picture in silhouette of the pilot in oxygen mask, helmet and goggles. The oxygen breathing apparatus would look just like a pig's snout to Nostradamus. The air battle is a remarkable enough description for the 16th Century, and the screams may be the sound of the

[1] *fleurs*—read *fléaux* = plague, pestilence.

dropping bombs as they whine to earth. The battle is watched by people on the ground (*aperceu*) and it is important to understand the wording of the last line. The pilots (*brutes bestes*) are heard talking to others; could this be a forecast of radio? This quatrain convinces me that Nostradamus' inspiration was certainly partly visual and he describes as best he can in his limited vocabulary the puzzling glimpses of a future he didn't always understand.

65

Enfant sans mains jamais veu si grand faudre,	A child without hands, never so great a thunderbolt seen,
L'enfant royal au feu d'oesteuf blessé:	the royal child wounded at a game of tennis. At the well
Au pui[1] brises[2] fulgures[3] allant mouldre,	lightning strikes, joining together three trussed up in the
Trois souz les chaines[4] par le milieu troussés.[5]	middle under the oaks.

A definite quatrain about a specific event and a deformed royal child which has not been realized to date.

66

Celui qui lors portera les nouvelles,	He who then carries the news,
Apres un peu il viendra respirer	after a short while will (stop)
Viviers, Tournon, Montferrand & Pradelles,	to breath: Viviers, Tournon, Montferrand and Pradelles;
Gresle & tempestes les fera soupirer.	hail and storms will make them grieve.

67

La grande famine que je sens approcher,	The great famine which I sense approaching will often
Souvent tourner, puis estre universelle:	turn (in various areas) then become world wide. It will be
Si grand & long qu'un viendra arracher,	so vast and long lasting that (they) will grab roots from the
Du bois racine & l'enfant de mamelle.	trees and children from the breast.

[1] *pui*—well, or possible O.F. *puy* = hill? It does not help to interpret the quatrain.
[2] *brises*—O.F., *briser* = to fracture, break.
[3] *fulgures*—Latin, *fulgur* = flash of lightning.
[4] *chaines*—Either oak tree or *chaine* = chain of hills.
[5] *troussés*—Some interpreters translate this as carry off.

The shortage of food throughout the world and particularly in the underdeveloped countries seems clear to Nostradamus. He describes local famines, however dreadful, whether those of France, 1709, Ireland, 1846, Biafra, 1969, India, 1971, as appearing small in comparison with the problem of world hunger which will develop and become universal.

68

O quel horrible & malheureux tourment,
Trois innocens qu'on viendra à livrer:
Poison suspecte, mal garde tradiment,[1]
Mis en horreur par bourreaux enivrez.

O to what a dreadful and wretched torment are three innocent people going to be delivered. Poison suggested, badly guarded, betrayal. Delivered up to horror by drunken executioners.

69

La grand montaigne ronde de sept stades,[2]
Apres paix, guerre, faim, innondation:
Roulera loin abismant grands contrades,[3]
Mesmes antiques, & grand fondation.

The great mountain, seven stadia round, after peace, war, famine, flooding. It will spread far, drowning great countries, even antiquities and their mighty foundations.

This probably describes a flood in southern France which may reveal many Graeco-Roman archaeological treasures sited somewhere near a mountain. Sites such as Glanum near the mountains of Les Beaux, very near Salon, may be indicated.

70

Plui, faim, guerre en Perse non cessée,
La foi trop grand trahira le monarque:
Par la finie en Gaule commencee,
Secret augure pour à un estre parque.

Rain, famine and war will not cease in Persia; too great a faith will betray the monarch. Those (actions) started in France will end there, a secret sign for one to be sparing.

[1] *tradiment*—O.F. = treason, betrayal.
[2] *stade*—Latin, *stadium* = measure roughly a furlong in length, seven stades would be just under a mile in circumference.
[3] *contrades*—Provençal, *contrad* = country.

France and Persia have been at war, with France an ally of Turkey, on several occasions, but it is difficult to relate this to a specific incident.

71

La tour marine trois fois prise & reprise,	The marine tower will be captured and retaken three

La tour marine trois fois prise & reprise,
Par Hespagnols, Barbares, Ligurins:[1]
Marseilles & Aix, Arles par ceux de Pise,
Vast,[2] feu, fer, pillé Avignon des Thurins.

The marine tower will be captured and retaken three times by Spaniards, barbarians and Ligurians. Marseilles and Aix, Arles by men of Pisa, devastation, fire, sword, pillage at Avignon by the Turinese.

This is an irritating quatrain because it appears to be indecipherable despite all the proper names given. The main problem is the identity of the marine tower, which could then be related to conflict between the French and the Italians. Could it refer to the Tour de Bouq I. 78. ?

72

De tout Marseille des habitants changee,
Course & poursuitte jusqu'au pres de Lyon,
Nalbon[3] Tholoze par Bordeaux outragee,
Tuez captifs presque d'un million.

The inhabitants of Marseilles completely changed, fleeing and pursued as far as Lyons. Narbonne, Toulouse angered by Bordeaux; the killed and captive are almost one million.

FRANCE AND CASUALTIES. SECOND WORLD WAR

The enormous number of dead places this quatrain in modern times, possibly in the last war, for which the official casualty lists give a figure of 675,000 Frenchmen dead or wounded. This sum does not include the Allies who fought alongside the French, so Nostradamus' total may be nearer the mark. When the German army entered Paris, June 1940, the French Government fled to Bordeaux. Narbonne, Toulouse and Lyons were all cities under the puppet Vichy régime. Marseilles, under German occupation, certainly had its *habitants changees*.

[1] *Ligurins* = people of Liguria in Italy.
[2] *vast*—Latin, *vastus* = laid waste.
[3] Apocope for Narbonne.

France à cinq pars[1] *par neglect assaillie,*[2]	France shall be accused of neglect by her five partners.
Tunis, Argel[3] *esmuez par Persiens:*	Tunis, Algiers stirred up by the Persians. Leon, Seville and
Leon, Seville, Barcelonne faillie	Barcelona having failed, they
N'aura la classe[4] *par les Venetiens.*	will not have the fleet because of the Venetians.

FRANCE AND COMMON MARKET.
LIBYAN REVOLUTION, 1969

Line 1 may refer to France during the end of de Gaulle's presidency, when she was under pressure from her five Common Market partners. This agrees in time with the trouble in North Africa, the 1969 Revolution in Libya which deposed King Idris. The reference to Persia is interesting. In Nostradamus' day Persia was part of the Ottoman Empire, an area which is now part of the U.S.S.R., and so, by implication, the Soviets are involved in the Middle Eastern troubles. The last two lines are unclear.

Apres sejourné vogueront en Epire	After a rest they will travel to
Le grand secours viendra vers Antoche:	Epirus, great help coming from around Antioch. The
Le noir[5] *poil crespe tendra fort à l'Empire,*	curly haired king will strive greatly for the Empire, the
Barbe d'aerain se roustira en broche.	brazen beard will be roasted on a spit.

Both Epirus and Antioch were part of the Turkish Empire until the 19th Century. As the footnote states, *'noir'* is continually used as an anagram of *'roi'*, king, in the Centuries. This dark-haired king recurs in other quatrains as does the red-bearded man. There was a family of Algerian corsairs named Barbarossa, whose plunderings were contemporary to Nostradamus. Other commentators refer this to Philip II of Spain who had a blondish beard, but his enigmatic fate is incomprehensible.

[1] *pars*—Used throughout Nostradamus to mean partner, rather than part. *See* IX. 20.

[2] *assaillir*—Literally assault. France has only been attacked on five sides once in 1813/4 and then by the European allies.

[3] *Argel*—Anagram or misprint for Alger = Algiers.

[4] *classe*—Latin, *classis* = fleet.

[5] *noir*—Anagram for *roi*. IX. 20 etc.

Le tyran Sienne occupera Savone,	The tyrant of Siena will
Le fort gaigné tiendra classe	occupy Savona, having won the
marine:	fort he will restrain the marine
Les deux armees par la marque	fleet. Two armies under the
d'Ancomme,	standard of Ancona: the leader
Par effrayeur le chef s'en examine.	will examine them in fear.

Siena was a free town and held out with French help against the
Florentine states until April 1555. Savena was a protectorate of the
Genoese Republic, and Ancona was part of the Papal States.

D'un nom farouche tel proferé sera,	This man will be called by a
Que les trois soeurs[1] *auront fato*[2]	barbaric name that three sisters
le nom:	will receive from destiny. He
Puis grand peuple par langue &	will speak then to a great
faict dira	people in words and deeds,
Plus que nul autre bruit & renom.	more than any other man will
	have fame and renown.

NAPOLEON BONAPARTE

This verse is always interpreted as fitting Bonaparte, because of the
derivation of his name from the Greek NEAPOLLUON, which
means destroyer or exterminator. The name was still spelt in this
way during his lifetime, as the inscription of 1805 in the Place
Vendôme shows, NEAPOLIO. IMP AUG. Napoleon was barbaric in a more general sense, being the younger son of a Corsican
family whose language and standards were not those of Parisian
society. He was also renowned for the great speeches made to his
troops (*par langue dira*) before battle.

Entre deux mers dressera pro-	A promontory stands between
montaire,	two seas: A man who will die
Que plus mourra par le mords du	later by the bit of a horse;
cheval:	Neptune unfurls a black sail for
Le sien Neptune pliera voille	his man; the fleet near Gib-
noire,	raltar and Rocheval.
Par Calpre & classe aupres de	
Rocheval.	

[1] The three Fates. In classical mythology they spin the web of a man's
destiny.

[2] *fato*—Latin, *fatum* = fate, destiny.

BATTLE OF TRAFALGAR, 21st OCTOBER 1805

The promontory separating the seas is Gibraltar between the Mediterranean and the Atlantic. The French and English fleets fought the battle of Trafalgar between Gibraltar and Cape Roche (Rocheval), Trafalgar itself being a point between two bays. The leader of the French fleet, Admiral Villeneuve, was reputedly strangled by one of Napoleon's Mamelukes with the bridle of a horse at an inn in Rennes in 1806, when he returned to France having been taken prisoner by the English. When Nelson was mortally wounded his ship raised a black sail on its return voyage to England. Rocheval may just be an anagram for *roche*, rock, which is the name given to mean Gibraltar.

78

D'un chef naistra sens hebeté	To an old leader will be born
Degenerant par savoir & par armes:	an idiot heir, weak both in
Le chef de France par sa soeur	knowledge and in war. The
redouté,	leader of France is feared by
Champs divisez, concedez aux	his sister, battlefields divided,
gendarmes.	conceded to the soldiers.

This has been referred to Marshal Pétain, who took over the government of France from Reynaud in 1940, but the sister is unsatisfactory and the whole quatrain too general.

79

Bazaz, Lestore, Condon, Ausch,	Bazas, Lectoure, Condom,
Agine,	Auch and Agen are troubled by
Esmens par loix querelle &	laws, disputes and monopolies.
menopole:	Carcassonne, Bordeaux, Tou-
Car[1] *Bourd, Toulouze Bay*[2] *mettra*	louse and Bayonne will be
en ruine.	ruined when they wish to renew
Renouveller voulant leur tauro-	the massacre.
pole.[3]	

All these towns are in the south-west of France. It may contain a reference to a trading dispute and the granting of rights to monopolies in the locality. The massacre or sacrifice is unclear.

[1] *Car*—Either apocope of Carcassonne, or *car* = because.
[2] *Bay*—Bayonne, as above.
[3] *tauropole*—Latin, *Taurobolium* = sacrifice of a bull; metaphorically, massacre, slaughter.

*De la sixieme claire splendeur
   celeste,
Viendra tonner si fort en la Bourgongne:
Puis naistra monstre de treshideuse
   beste,
Mars, Avril, Mai, Juin grand
   charpin[1] & rongne.*

From the sixth bright celestial light it will come to thunder very strongly in Burgundy. Then a monster will be born of a very hideous beast: In March, April, May and June great wounding and worrying.

Saturn being the sixth planet, apparently these portents will occur during the time governed by him. Some commentators date it as spring 1918.

*D'humain troupeau neuf seront mis
   à part,
De jugement & conseil separez:
Leur sort sera divisé en depart,
Kappa,[2] Thita,[3] Lamda,[4] mors
   bannis esgarez.*

Nine will be set apart from the human flock, separated from judgment and advice. Their fate is to be divided as they depart. K. Th. L. dead, banished and scattered.

This has been applied by at least one commentator to the death of the three Soviet cosmonauts. It is very obscure.

*Quand les colomnes de bois grande
   tremblee,
D'Auster conduicte couverte de
   rubriche:
Tant videra dehors grand assemblee:
Trembler Vienne & le Pays
   d'Austriche.*

When the great wooden columns tremble in the south wind, covered with blood. Such a great assembly then pours forth that Vienna and the land of Austria will tremble.

AUSTRIA, 1914–18

In the autumn of 1918, when the trees trembled in the wind, Austria was overturned and the new revolutionary (rubriche) rule replaced the autocratic order of the Habsburgs. The great

[1] *charpin*—O.F., rags to dress wounds. Wounds.
[2] Letter of the Greek alphabet K.
[3] Letter of the Greek alphabet Th.
[4] Letter of the Greek alphabet L.

assembly of the world Powers, which troubles Austria is the Triple Entente. Austria's troubles first started in the south (Auster) in Turkey and the Balkan States.

83

La gent estrange divisera butins,	The alien nation will divide the
Saturne en Mars son regard furieux:	spoils. Saturn in dreadful aspect in Mars. Dreadful and foreign
Horrible estrange aux Tosquans & Latins,	to the Tuscans and Latins,
Grecs qui seront à frapper curieux.	Greeks who will wish to strike.

ITALIAN OCCUPATION OF GREECE, 1940
The last two lines seem to refer to the Greek struggles with the Italian occupying forces of 1940. The booty taken by the Germans was proverbial; it is still reappearing in sale rooms throughout the world, *divisera butins*. Mars is the God of War, and Saturn indicates a bad aspect, which indeed it was for the Italians who allied themselves with the losing side.

84

Lune obscurcie aux profondes tenebres	The moon obscured in deep gloom, his brother becomes
Son frere passe de couleur ferrugine:[1]	bright red in colour. The great one hidden for a long time in
Le grand caché long temps soubs les tenebres,	the shadows will hold the blade in the bloody wound.
Tiedera[2] *fer dans la plaie sanguine.*	

MURDER OF THE DUKE DE BERRY.
13th FEBRUARY 1820
The Count of Artois is the man obscured, he was in exile, whose brother Louis XVI died (*passe*) in blood on the guillotine. D'Artois remained in exile for a long time before his return as Charles X, with his family. His son, the Duke de Berry, was attacked and fatally stabbed at the Opera on the night of 13th February 1820. As he died, he clutched the hilt of the knife and is reputed to have said, 'I am murdered. I am holding the hilt of the dagger.' See C. III. 96, IV. 73.

[1] *ferrugine*—Latin, *ferruginus* = rusty, blood-coloured.
[2] *Tiedera*—Read, *tiendra*.

Par la response de dame Roi troublé,
Ambassadeurs mespriseront leur vie:
Le grand ses freres contrefera doublé,
Par deux mourront ire, haine, ennui.

The king is troubled by the queen's reply. Ambassadors will fear for their lives. The greater of his brothers will doubly disguise his action, two of them will die through anger, hatred and envy.

MURDER OF THE DUKE DE GUISE AND HIS BROTHER, 1588

Catherine de' Medici, the Queen Mother, was furious at her son Henri III's action in killing not only the Duke de Guise, but also his brother the Cardinal because of their political power. The *Ambassadeurs* are probably the Estates whom the king assembled to meet him at Blois and who remonstrated strongly about the murders. The greater brother who survives was the Duke de Mayenne who then led the Catholic League, and became Lieutenant-General of France, *contrefera doublé*.

La grande roine quand se verra vaincue,
Fera excés de masculin courage:
Sus cheval, fleuve passera toute nue,
Suite par fer: à foi fera outrage.

When the great queen sees herself conquered, she will show an excess of masculine courage. Naked, on horseback, she will pass over the river pursued by the sword: she will have outraged her faith.

FLIGHT OF MARY QUEEN OF SCOTS, 1568

This is a very close description of the flight of Mary Queen of Scots, in May 1568, when having been defeated a second time by Murray she fled to England possessing nothing but the clothes she wore, *toute nue*. Mary crossed the river by ferry, but fled on horseback, and had outraged her faith, whether the Catholics, or the Scots, by her behaviour with Bothwell.

Ennosigee[1] feu du centre de terre.
Fera trembler au tour de cité neufue:
Deux grands rochiers long temps feront la guerre,
Puis Arethuse[2] rougira nouveau fleuve.

Earthshaking fire from the centre of the earth will cause tremors around the New City. Two great rocks will war for a long time, then Arethusa will redden a new river.

ATTACK ON NEW YORK?

An explosion in the centre of the city of New York making the land tremble, or could *tour* here mean towers or skyscrapers? The two great rocks are the immutable great powers who will eventually open war. Ingenious commentators interpret Arethusa as coming from Ares, God of War, and U.S.A. The new river is presumably blood see X. 49.

88

Le divin mal surprendra le grand prince,
Un peu devant aura femme espousee.
Son appuy & credit à un coup viendra mince,
Conseil mourra pour la teste rasee.

The divine wrath overtakes the great Prince, a short while before he will marry. Both supporters and credit will suddenly diminish. Counsel, he will die because of the shaven heads.

CHARLES I AND PARLIAMENT

Divine wrath overtook Charles I of England when he was sentenced by his own Court, but the trouble with Parliament broke out originally around the time of his marriage in 1625 to Henrietta Maria of France. On his actual wedding day, Charles directed that persecution of the Catholics should cease. Parliament refused this and demanded subsidies for the war against Spain. This led to his death, demanded by the Roundheads (*teste rasee*) in 1649. *See* IX. 49.

[1] *Ennosigaeus*—Greek = earth-shaking, a name given to Neptune.
[2] *Arethusa* = a Greek nymph who in one legend changed into a stream.

Tous ceux de Ilerde[1] seront dans la Moselle,
Mettant à mort tous ceux de Loire & Seine:
Le cours[2] marin viendra pres d'haute velle,
Quand Espagnols ouvrira toute veine.

Those of Lerida will be in the Moselle, killing all those from the Loire and Seine. The seaside track will come near the high valley, when the Spanish open every route.

PENINSULAR WARS, 1808–14

This seems to be a general quatrain about the Peninsular Wars when Wellington pushed up through Spain and Portugal across the Pyrenees to Bordeaux. James Laver suggests that *haute velle* is Nostradamus groping towards the name of Wellington.

90

Bourdeaux, Poitiers au son de la campane,
A grand classe ira jusques à l'Angon:
Contre Gaulois sera leur tramontane,
Quand monstre hideux naistra pres de Orgon.

Bordeaux and Poitiers at the sound of the bell will go with a great fleet as far as Langon. A great rage will surge up against the French, when an hideous monster is born near Orgon.

This specifies an invasion by the French, great resistance, and the birth of a monstrous child near Organ, probably like the two-headed one Nostradamus saw and described in another book. In *The Times*, 20th November 1971, a report was given of the birth of a two-headed boy, so that Nostradamus is not completely in the realms of fantasy.

91

Les dieux feront aux humains apparence,
Ce qu'il seront auteurs de grand conflict:
Avant ciel veu serein espee & lance
Que vers main guache sera plus grand affict.

The gods will make it appear to mankind that they are the authors of a great war. Before the sky was seen to be free of weapons and rockets: the greatest damage will be inflicted on the left.

[1] *Ilerde* = Lerida, city in Spain.
[2] *cours* = path, progress.

FUTURE WAR AFFECTING AMERICA?

Nostradamus declares that we will not know which side starts the next world war although in later quatrains he places blame for the start of the war upon China. After a peaceful interlude (I.63) the air will be full of weapons and fighting, rockets pointing like lances to the skies. The left hand side of the world on a map is America and the country will suffer great losses. However in IV. 95, he states that the victor will be born in America.

92

Sous un la paix par tout sera clamee	Under one man peace will be proclaimed everywhere, but not long after will be looting and rebellion. Because of a refusal, town, land and sea will be broached. About a third of a million dead or captured.
Mais non long temps pillé & rebellion:	
Par refus ville, terre, & mer entamee,	
Mors & captifs le tiers d un million.	

FRANCE AND THE FRANCO-PRUSSIAN WAR, 1870–1

The universal peace described here is the French Empire, bearing in mind Napoleon's statement, '*L'Empire, c'est la paix*'. The Franco-Prussian war is depicted in the rest of the quatrain, starting with the King of Prussia's refusal to agree to the humiliating French demands. The Encyclopaedia Britannica gives the figures of dead and wounded in this war as 299,000 which is very close to Nostradamus' estimate of 333,000.

93

Terre Italique pres des monts tremblera,	The Italian lands near the mountains will tremble. The Cock and the Lion not strongly united. In place of fear they will help each other. Freedom alone moderates the French.
Lyon & coq non trop confederez:	
En lieu de peur l'un l'autre s'aidera.	
Seul Catulon[1] & Celtes moderez.	

NAPOLEON'S ITALIAN CAMPAIGN, 1795

The mountains are the Alps and this is Napoleon's Italian Campaign which started in 1795. After capturing Toulon he set out on the Italian wars and France (*Coq*), saw the start of enmity which grew up between her and England (*Lion*). This is followed by a period of mutual alliance, after the accession of Louis XVIII, the French (*Celtes*) regaining their freedom from tyranny.

[1] *Castulon* = Liberty.

Au port Selin le tyran mis à mort,
La Liberté non pourtant recouvree:
Le nouveau Marc par vindicte & remort
Dame par force de frayeur honnoree.

The tyrant Selim will be put to death at the harbour but Liberty will not be regained, however. A new war arises from vengeance and remorse. A lady is honoured through force of terror.

BATTLE OF LEPANTO, 1571

At the battle of Lepanto fought on 7th October 1571 Ali Pasha, the Admiral of the Turkish fleet, was killed while on board his ship. Selim II was not killed himself but his aggression in the Mediterranean was finally crushed by the defeat at Lepanto. However, Liberty was not regained as had been hoped by the crusade of Christian countries to put down Turkish influence—this continued for some centuries. See IX. 42. The Pope formally ascribed the victory of Lepanto to the intercession of our Lady, line 4.

Devant moustier[1] trouvé enfant besson,[2]
De heroic sang de moine & vestutisque:[3]
Son bruit par secte langue & puissance son,
Qu'on dira fort esleue ie vopisque.

In front of a monastery will be found a twin infant from the illustrious and ancient line of a monk. His fame, renown and power through sects and speech is such that they will say the living twin is deservedly chosen.

Apparently the twin son of a monk will grow to be an important leader. Many commentators refer this to the Man in the Iron Mask who was possibly the son of Queen Anne and Cardinal Mazarin.

Celui qu'aura la charge de destruire
Templus, & sectes, changez par fantasie:
Plus aux rochiers qu'aux vivans viendra nuire,
Par langue ornee d'oreilles ressasie.

A man will be charged with the destruction of temples and sectes, altered by fantasy. He will harm the rocks rather than the living, ears filled with ornate speeches.

[1] moustier—Provençal = monastery.
[2] besson—Provençal = twin.
[3] vestutisque—Latin, vestutus = old.

A man will come whose religious destiny is concerned with people rather than the buildings, temples, bricks and mortar of accepted religions. It is possible that the rock in line 3 is the Rock of Peter, the Vatican, in which case this revival would harm the Catholic church.

97

Ce que fer, flamme n'a sceu paracheuer,	That which neither weapon nor flame could accomplish will
La douce langue an conseil viendra faire:	be achieved by a sweet speaking tongue in council. Sleeping,
Par repos, songe, le Roy fera resver,	in a dream, the king will see the enemy not in war or of
Plus l'ennemy en feu, sang militaire.	military blood.

ASSASSINATION OF HENRI III, 1589

Henri III was killed not while at war but in council. The monk, Jacques Clément came to the king at St. Cloud saying he had a secret letter, and leaning towards Henri, as though to speak confidentially, he stabbed him in the stomach. Henri died the next day. The fact that he had dreamed of his death is well authenticated; he told his courtiers three days before his death that he saw the royal regalia, his blue cloak, two crowns, sceptre, sword and spurs all trodden underfoot by monks and the populace. An example of double precognition; by Nostradamus and the victim himself. Is the *douce langue* in line 2 a play on words on the name Clément? It would be a typical Nostradamus double meaning, as the two words mean the same in French.

98

Le chef qu'aura conduit peuple infiny	The leader who will conduct great numbers of people far
Loing de son ciel, de meurs & langue estrange:	from their skies, to foreign customs and language. Five
Cinq mil en Crete & Thessalie fini	thousand will die in Crete and Thessaly, the leader fleeing in
Le chef fuyant, sauvé en marine grange.[1]	a sea going supply ship.

NAPOLEON'S EXPEDITION TO EGYPT, 1798/9

When Napoleon left Egypt, he successfully eluded the British Navy to land in France, leaving behind for the Turks an army

[1] *grange*—Fr. = literally, barn.

reduced to around 5,000 men. The Turks ruled Thessaly and Crete at this time, and Napoleon did flee in a wooden ship. This fact prevents the prophecy applying to the British Expeditionary forces in Crete and Thessaly in 1940, when ships were made of metal and the figures were also much greater.

99

Le grand monarque que fera com-
    pagnie,
Avec deux rois unis par amité:
O quel soupir fera la grand
    mesgnie,[1]
Enfans Narbon à l'entour quel
    pitié.

The great king will join with two kings, united in friendship. How the great household will sigh: around Narbon what pity for the children.

100

Longtemps au ciel sera veu gris
    oiseau,
Aupres de Dole & de Touscane
    terre:
Tenant au bec un verdoyant
    rameau,
Mourra tost grand & finera la
    guerre.

For a long time a grey bird will be seen in the sky near Dôle and the lands of Tuscany. He holds a flowering branch in his beak, but he dies too soon and the war ends.

COMTE DE CHAMBORD, 1820

The grey bird is both the dove of peace and the Comte de Chambord, son of the Duchess de Berry and last legitimate heir to the French throne. At his birth he was called the dove of peace, but unfortunately he was usurped by the Orléans family and exiled to Venice, near Dôle, and Modena, near Tuscany. He also married the daughter of the Duke of Tuscany in 1846. He died without regaining the French throne, but he and the Comte de Paris, Duke d'Orléans, the pretender, were reconciled when the latter was also sent into exile by the new republic. The death of the Comte de Chambord saved the possibility of another war between republicans and monarchists.

[1] mesgnie—O.F. = household, court.

CENTURY II

77
78
79*   Battle of Lepanto, 1571?
80
81F?
82
83*   Lyons, 1795
84
85   Napoleon?
86*   Napoleon in Egypt
87*   Accession of George I, 1714
88**   Seven children of Catherine de Valois and accession of
            Henri IV, *c.* 1590
89**F?   America, Russia and Third Antichrist?
90*   Hungarian Revolution, 1956
91*F?   Attack on U.S.A. or Russia?
92*   Napoleon III, 1870
93F?
94*   Napoleon
95F?   Kennedys?
96
97*   1799. Death of Pius VI
98
99*   Napoleon's Campaign in Russia, 1812
100

   KEY: * = of interest. F? = possibly future.

Vers Acquitaine par insuls Britan-niques	Towards Aquitaine, by British assaults, and by them also
De pars eux mesmes grands incur-sions	great incursions. Rains and frost make the terrain unsafe,
Pluies gelées feront terroirs uniques,	against Port Selin they will
Port Selin fortes fera invasions.	make mighty invasions.

THE DARDANELLES. FIRST WORLD WAR, 1915

An important quatrain. When France (Aquitaine) and Britain were deadlocked on the Western Front during 1915, Winston Churchill persuaded the Allies to open a new front against Turkey (Port Selin is Constantinople, and Turkey, by extension). It was planned to attack the Dardanelles in order to reach Constantinople. The dreadful weather suffered by troops during the First World War is referred to in line 3.

La teste bleu fera la tete blanche	The blue leader will inflict
Autant de mal que France a faict leur bien,	upon the white leader as much damage as France has done
Mort à l'anthene grand pendu sus la branche,	them good. Death from the great antenna hanging from
Quand prins des siens le Roy dira combien.	the branch, when the king will ask how many of his men have been captured.

Obscure but interesting in that the antenna may be understood as an aerial from which the King obtains information; an attempt to describe radio communications or something similar?

Pour la chaleur solaire sus la mer	Because of heat like that of the
De Negrepont les poissons demi cuits:	sun upon the sea the fish around Negrepont will become half
Les habitans les viendront entamer,[1]	cooked. The local people will
Quand Rhod, & Gannes leur faudra le biscuit.	eat them when in Rhodes and Genoa there is a lack of food.

ATOMIC EXPLOSION?

To produce such heat on the sea surface implies a very strong explosion, possibly of atomic force, somewhere in the Aegean sea,

---

[1] *entamer*—Literally to cut up, therefore = to eat.

as Negrepont is the Italian name for the Island of Ruboea. The second implication that in Italy and other parts of Greece people are starving, indicates either conditions of famine or war. Nostradamus mentions this explosion again in V. 98, when he says its source comes from the sky.

4

Depuis Monach[1] jusque aupres de Sicile
Toute la plage demourra desolée:
Il n'y aura fauxbourg, cité ne ville,
Que par Barbares pillé soit & volée.

From Monaco as far as Sicily all the coast will remain deserted. There will be no suburbs, cities nor towns which have not been pillaged and robbed by barbarians.

This may be a continuation of the last quatrain, II. 3. extending the area of the disaster through Italy to France. Nostradamus would describe as barbarian either Arab, Negro, Russian or Chinese, but from later quatrains the latter is the most likely interpretation.

5

Qu'en dans poisson, fer & lettres enfermée,
Hors sortira qui puis fera la guerre:
Aura par mer sa classe[2] bien ramée,
Apparoissant pres de Latine terre.

When weapons and documents are enclosed in a fish, out of it will come a man who will then make war. His fleet will have travelled far across the sea to appear near the Italian shore.

THE THIRD WAR, 1996? AND ITS ORIGINATOR

The fish is interpreted as a submarine rather than a ship as a fish travels under water; this one carries weapons and important papers as well as the man who is responsible for starting a new war. He is described as actually coming out (hors sortira) of the fish as are the hostile soldiers in I. 29, where the submarine is also called a fish by Nostradamus. The fleet brought by this unnamed man has travelled a great distance to appear in either the Mediterranean or Adriatic sea. It is tempting to link him with the man Nostradamus calls the Third AntiChrist whom he believes will start a third war in this century. The date may actually be given to us, because the first line contains a second, astrological meaning, 'When Mars and Mercury are in conjunction in Pisces'. According to Norab the

[1] Monach—Latin, Monoceus = Monaco.
[2] classe—Latin, classis = fleet.

next time this occurs is 23rd March 1996. and Nostradamus dates the war as starting around 1995 in I. 51, in 1993 in II. 41, and mentions it indirectly in I. 16, all of which are uncomfortably close and consistent.

6

Aupres des portes & dedans deux cités	Near the harbour and in two cities will be two scourges, the like of which have never been seen. Hunger, plague within, people thrown out by the sword will cry for help from the great immortal God.
Seront deux fléaux & oncques n'apperceu un tel:	
Faim, dedans peste, de fer hors gens boutés,	
Crier secours au grand Dieu immortel.	

THE BOMBINGS OF NAGASAKI AND HIROSHIMA; 1945
Both Nagasaki and Hiroshima are on the sea and experienced the plague of radiation which had never been seen before on earth. Two bombs were dropped (deux fléaux) and the survivors would have looked very similar to victims of the plague in Nostradamus' day, which turned them black, and for this was known as 'le charbon'. Radiation burns turn black too, and there was hunger among the miserable survivors who were thrown out of the cities by the sword of war. The last line speaks for itself.

7

Entre plusieurs aux isles déportés,	Among many people deported to the islands will be a man born with two teeth in his mouth. They will die of hunger having stripped the trees. A new king will pass new laws for them.
L'un estre nay à deux dents en la gorge:	
Mourrant de faim les arbres esbrotés,	
Pour eux neuf Roy, nouvel edict leur forge.	

The islands are either the French penal colonies such as Ile du Diable in South America or those along the south coast of France which are used for the detention of dangerous criminals. It is quite common for children to be born with some teeth already formed. The last line may predict the closing of the penal settlements; most of the tropical ones are no longer in use.

Nostradamus seemed greatly worried by the fate of the Catholic Church and its priests during the French Revolution and there are many references to it. The eyes of the people were closed to Christianity and the Cult of Reason was established in 1793. In 1789 the wearing of ecclesiastical costume was suppressed. The monarch can be interpreted either as Louis XVI, who had already helped despoil the monasteries, or as Napoleon, who continued to do so with great vigour until the time of his Coronation when he needed the Pope and found it necessary to restore the Roman Catholic religion to France.

13

Le corps sans ame plus n'estre en sacrifice. *Jour de la mort mis en nativité:* *L'esprit divin fera l'ame felice,* *Voyant le verbe en son eternité.*	The body without a soul no longer at the sacrifice. At the day of death it is brought to rebirth. The divine spirit will make the soul rejoice seeing the eternity of the word.

RELIGIOUS BELIEFS

This is an ambiguous statement of Nostradamus' religious beliefs. Once dead, he can no longer communicate with the spirits, whether he means the Mass or some magical rite by the word sacrifice is impossible to say. His soul will be reborn at his death into happiness. The word ('*verbe*') is either Christ as is used in the Christmas Gospel, *the word was made flesh*, or may be a promise made to Nostradamus in his magic studies which he expects to be fulfilled eternally at his death. If there is any occult meaning in this quatrain it is very deliberately hidden. Nostradamus foretold his own death to his confessor, Frère Vidal, and to his pupil, Chavigny, but he may have been able to do this by a medical diagnosis. He died on 1st July 1566.

14

A Tours, Gien, gardé seront yeux penetrans, *Descouvriront de loing la grand seraine:* *Elle & sa suitte au port seront entrans.* *Combat, poussez, puissance souveraine.*	At Tours and Gien watchful eyes will be guarded, they will spy far off the serene Highness. She and her suite will enter the harbour, combat joined, sovereign power.

Tours and Gien are both on the Loire. This probably refers in general terms to the regency of Catherine de' Medici and the wars of religion which troubled France from 1562–98. The Queen died in 1599 having seen her three sons predecease her, as predicted.

15

Un peu devant monarque trucidé[1]
Castor, Pollux en nef, estre crinite[2]
L'erain[3] public par terre & mer
* vuidé,*
Pise, Ast, Ferrare, Turin, terre
* interdicte.*

A short while before a king is murdered, Castor and Pollux in the ship, a bearded star. Public treasure emptied on land and sea, Pisa, Asti, Terrara and Turin are forbidden lands.

The second line of this quatrain gives a form of dating. Castor and Pollux, the twins, stand for Gemini, the ship is for Argo, and the bearded star is a comet. Linked with these is an assassinated king, a great war effort, money being raised on land and sea, and the Italian states being placed under interdict. This last thing has never happened since publication, and seems unlikely now to be fulfilled.

16

Naples, Polerme, Sicille, Syracuses,
Nouveau tyrans, fulgures[4] feux
* celestes:*
Force de Londres, Gand, Bruxelles,
* & Suses,*
Grand hecatombe, triomphe faire
* festes.*

In Naples, Palermo, Sicily and Syracuse new tyrants, thunder and lightning in the skies. A force from London, Ghent, Brussels and Susa: a great massacre, then triumph and festivities.

ITALY'S PART IN SECOND WORLD WAR

The new tyrants in the Italian towns are the Mussolini régime of the Fascisti. The thunder and lightning become the sound of war in Italy. London goes out in force against them, allied to Brussels, and wins the war after great slaughter.

---

[1] *trucidé*—Latin, *trucidare* = to slaughter.
[2] *crinite*—Latin, *crinitus* = bearded.
[3] *erain*—Latin, *eranus* = public fund.
[4] *Fulgures*—Latin, *fulgur* = lightning.

78

Le camp du temple de la vierge vestale,	The field of the vestal virgin's temple is not far from Ethne and the Pyrenees. The great one led is hidden in a trunk. In the North, the rivers overflow and the vines destroyed.
Non esloingé d'Ethne & monte Pyrenées:	
Le grand conduict est caché dans la male[1]	
North[2] getez fleuves & vignes mastinées.[3]	

Ethne is probably a greek anagram for Elne, *th* in Greek being one letter. Elne lies near the Pyrenees between the Tech and the Réart which flow into the Mediterranean. I cannot decipher this quatrain further.

Nouvelle & pluie subite impeteuse,	News; unexpected and heavy rain will suddenly prevent two armies. Stones and fire from the skies will make a sea of stones. The death of the seven suddenly by land and sea.
Empechera subit deux excercites:	
Pierre ciel, feux faire la mere pierreuse,	
La mort de sept terre & marin subites.	

HENRI III 1587–9

The clue to this quatrain lies in the last line, the death of the seven, the Valois children of Catherine de' Medici. When Henri III left Paris in 1587 the city was invaded by 35,000 German and Swiss troops. The Duc de Guise rushed with his troops of the League to Montargis, but the decisive battle was prevented by a violent rainstorm. In the following year, 1589, Henri III, the last of the Valois kings was assassinated; his death was the direct result of his clash with the Leaguers and the assassinations of the two Guise brothers.

[1] *male*—(a) *malle* = trunk, or possibly, (b) *mal* = evil.
[2] *North* = very rare use of English by Nostradamus.
[3] *mastiner*—O.F. = to bruise, destroy.

*Nouveau venus lieu basti sans
    defence.
Occuper la place par lors inhabit-
    able:
Pres, maisons, champs, villes
    prendre à plaisance,
Faim, Peste, guerre arpen[1] long
    labourable.*

Newcomers will build a place
without defences, occupying a
place inhabitable until then.
Meadows, houses, fields, towns
will be taken with pleasure.
Famine, plague, war, extensive
arable land.

20

*Freres & soeurs en divers lieux
    captifs,
Se trouveront passer pres du
    monaique;
Les contempler ses rameaux[2] enten-
    tifs,
Desplaisant voir menton, front,
    nez, les marques.*

Brothers and sisters captives
in differing places will find
themselves passing before the
monarch. His attentive offspring will look at them, dis-
pleased to see the signs on
their chins, foreheads and noses.

HENRI II 1557

The commentator Jaubert applies this to an event which occurred
soon after publication. In September 1557 some Huguenots were
captured in Paris during a raid and Henri II went to see them,
taking his children. The King is reputed to have been angry that
the captives had been wounded and bruised. But it is so general
that it may apply to other similar events.

21

*L'ambassadeur envoyé par biremes,
A mi-chemin d'incogneus repoulsez:
De sel renfort viendront quatre
    triremes,
Cordes & chaines en Negre pont
    troussez.*

The ambassador sent by the
biremes is repulsed half way by
an unknown man. Four tri-
remes come reinforced with salt;
he is bound with cords and
chains to Negrepont.

Biremes are oared galleys with two bridges, and triremes larger
ones with three. Salt in the Centuries often stands for taxation,
because of the famous French salt tax, the gabelle, or for wisdom
in the Biblical sense. Negrepont is the Italian name for Euboea
which belonged to the Turks until 1831, when it became part of
Greece.

[1] *arpen*—O.F. = measure of land, just under 1 acre.
[2] *rameaux*—Literally branches, therefore offspring.

Le camp Ascap[1] d'Europe partira,	The aimless army will depart
S'adjoignant proche de l'isle sub-	from Europe and join up close
mergée:	to the submerged island. The
D'Arton[2] classe[3] phalange pliera,	NATO fleet folds up its stan-
Nombril du monde plus grand voix	dard, the navel of the world in
subrogée.[4]	place of a greater voice.

NATO FLEET OFF BRITAIN

Nostradamus writes of the submerged island again in IX. 31
where it is identified with Britain. The army is described as aimless; could this mean that it, just like the NATO fleet, had no
warlike intent as they were both only on exercises? This view is
reinforced by the fact that the fleet folds up its standards showing
no signs of war. The navel of the world, and its centre, may be
understood as Italy, presumably the centre of the direction of
operations. But again, Nostradamus implies that NATO will be
taken over (*subrogée*) by a more powerful agency. European countries do combine at the present time to hold naval and military
exercises both in Europe and in the English Channel under the
auspices of NATO.

Palais, oiseaux, par oiseau des-	Birds at the palace, chased out
chassé,	by a bird very soon after the
Bien tost apres le prince parvenu:	upstart prince. How many of
Combien que hors fleuve ennemi	the enemy are repulsed beyond
repoulsé,	the river, the upheld bird
Dehors sousi trait d'oiseau soustenu.	seized from without by a trick.

This is very vague. Probably the birds are courtiers or supporters
of one prince where power is taken by an upstart who is finally
captured by a trick. Some interpret line 4 as 'captured outside, a
shaft held by a bird', i.e. by an arrow.

[1] *Ascop*—Greek, *askopos* = incredible, aimless.
[2] *Arton*—Either anagram for NATO or Greek, *artos* = bread.
[3] *classe*—Latin, *classis* = fleet.
[4] *subrogée*—Latin, *subrogatus* = substituted.

Bestes farouches de faim fleuves tranner,[1]	Beasts wild with hunger will cross the rivers, the greater part of the battlefield will be against Hitler. He will drag the leader in a cage of iron, when the child of Germany observes no law.
Plus part du champ encontre Hister sera.	
En caige de fer le grand fera treisner,	
Quand rien enfant de Germain observera.	

HITLER

One of Nostradamus' most remarkable series of quatrains, with the name Hitler given in anagram as Hister. There can be little doubt that Hitler is implied; who else could be so well described by the last line, the German who observed no law? In 16th-Century handwriting the resemblance is even closer with the use of the long *s*, Hifter. Commentators before 1930 understood the Hister to be the river Danube, from its latin name Ister. But Hitler recognized himself in these quatrains by the mid 1930s and Goebbells made great propaganda out of them in the pre-war party years. Evidence for this is found in many sources, chiefly Ellic Howe's book 'Nostradamus and the Nazis'. During the first year of the Second World War the development of the war was to a great extent dependent upon the rivers crossed by the Germans who came into Europe in a never-ending stream looting and pillaging (*farouches de faim*).

25

La garde estrange trahira forteresse	The foreign guard will betray the fortress the shadowy hope of an important marriage. The guard deceived, the fort taken in the crush. Loire, Saône, Rhône, Garonne outraged to death.
Espoir & umbre de plus hault mariage:	
Garde deçeue,[2] *fort prince dans la presse,*	
Loire, Son, Rosne. Gar à mort oultrage.	

CAPITULATION OF METZ, 1870

The defender of a fortress who betrays his trust chasing the illusion of a higher post (*plus hault mariage*) may be Bazaine who in 1870 handed over the fortress of Metz and his troops to the Germans,

---

[1] *tranner*—Latin, *tranare* = to swim across.

[2] *deçeue* = deceived, or Latin, *decisus* = to cut down.

and thus allowed them into the French interior during the Franco-Prussian War.

26

Pour la faveur que la cité fera,
Au grand qui tost prendra camp de bataille,
Puis le rang Pau Thesin versera
De sang, feux mors noyés de coup de taille.

Because of the fervour that a city will show towards a great man who later loses on the battlefield, the ranks will flee, rushing into the Po and the Tessin, blood, firing, dead men drowned and slashed.

27

Le devin verbe sera du ciel frappé,
Qui ne pourra proceder plus avant:
Du reserant[1], le secret estoupé[2]
Qu'on marchera par dessus & devant.

The divine voice will be struck by heaven and he will not be able to proceed further. The secret is hidden with the revelation so that people will walk over and ahead.

One of the several quatrains which indicate some secret locked up with the grave. Someone over whom one can walk (*par dessus & devant*) in French means to be buried at the foot of a wall, or chained in an underground cell. Some person will be struck down and not be able to reveal his information. He may be a theologian or religious man (*le divin verbe*).

28

Le penultiesme du surnom du prophete,
Prendra Diane pour son jour & repos:
Loing vaguera par frenetique teste,
Et delivrant un grand peuple d'impos.[3]

The last but one of the prophets' name, will take Monday for his day of rest. He will wander far in his frenzy delivering a great nation from subjection.

NAME BEGINNING HO, HAN OR DA

Is Nostradamus referring to Mahomet or Mohamed, or even to himself, Nostradamus? A man whose name begins with one of these sets of initials will apparently declare Monday, the day of Diana the moon, his Sabbath or day of rest. Could this be related

---

[1] *reserant*—Latin *resarare* = to unlock.
[2] *estoupé*—O.F. = to shut up.
[3] *impos*—O.F., *impost* = taxation.

to the next quatrain 29? One is not given any indication as to which nation this new leader will free from subjection.

29

L'Oriental sortira de son siege,	The man from the East will
Passer les monts Apennins voir la Gaule:	come out of his seat and will cross the Apennines to see France. He will cross through
Transpercera le ciel les eaux & neige,	the sky, the seas and the snows
Et un chacun frappera de sa gaule.	and he will strike everyone with his rod.

MAN FROM THE EAST?

This is a curious verse. The word *sortira* for *ira* indicates that the Easterner does not usually leave his country; could this refer to the North Vietnamese talks in Paris? France (*la Gaule*) to which he comes, was one of the few countries to maintain diplomatic relations with China until its acceptance into United Nations in October 1971. The third line seems to indicate air travel—he goes through the air to his destination. The last line is very ambiguous. The word *gaule* means a stick or rod, it could mean a weapon, it also means France and might be an indirect reference to the name of de Gaulle, which would certainly date the quatrain. There is a curiously threatening quality in the last line, as though no one is expecting any harm to come from the visitor. See also V. 54.

30

Un qui des dieux d'Annibal infernaux,	A man who revives the infernal Gods of Hannibal, the terror
Fera renaistre, effrayeur des humains:	of mankind. Never more horror nor the papers tell of worse in
Oncq' plus d'horreur ne plus dire journaulx,	the past, then will come to the Romans through Babel.
Qu'avint viendra Babel aux Romains.	

The infernal Gods of Hannibal imply North Africa and the near Middle East, from which a man will bring trouble to the world. The word for newspapers is interesting as there were none in Nostradamus' time; this line is a definite reading from the first edition of Benoist Rigaud, 1568. Pamphlets existed, of course, and the word may be used in this sense. Babel implies a confusion of languages and is also the Hebrew word for Babylon which some commentators feel that Nostradamus uses when he means Paris.

The quatrain may describe a relapse into paganism which brings terror to Rome and the Catholic Church.

31

En Campanie le Cassilin[1] fera tant,
Qu'on ne verra que d'aux des champs couvers:
Devant apres le pluie de long temps,
Hors mis les arbres rien l'on verra de vert.

In Campanie the Cassilin (river) will do so much that one will see only fields covered in water. Before and after the long lasting rain nothing green will be seen except for the trees.

This general quatrain predicts a flood of the Volturno river, perhaps of the town of Capua itself, in that it was built on the ruins of the Roman town of Casilinum.

32

Laict, sant grenouilles escoudre[2] en Dalmatie,
Conflict donné, peste pres de Balennes
Cri sera grand par toute Esclavonie,
Lors naistra monstre pres & dedans Ravenne.

Milk, blood, frogs will be prepared in Dalmatia: battle engaged, plague near Balennes. A great cry will go up throughout Slavonia, then will a monster be born near Ravenna.

This prophecy covers both sides of the Adriatic, but it is unclear what is to happen in the first line. Dalmatia is on the Eastern Adriatic, Balennes was Trebula Balliensis near Capua, Ravenna is in Central Italy. The former province of Slavonia is now part of Northern Yugoslavia and part of the Hungarian Empire.

33

Par le torrent qui descent de Veronne,
Par lors qu'au Pau guidera son entrée:
Un grand naufrage, & non moins en Garonne
Quand ceux de Gennes marcheront leur contree.

Through the torrent which pours down from Verona there where the entry is guided to the Po, a great wreck, and not less so in Garonne when the people of Genoa will march against their country.

This is similar to the last quatrain describing three 16th-Century states, France, Venice and Genoa. Verona is on the river Adige,

---

[1] *Cassalin* = a town on the Volturno river.
[2] *Escoudre*—Latin, *excudere* = to prepare.

which enters the Adriatic parallel to the Po about ten miles distant. The flood may be connected with II. 31.

34

L'ire insensee du combat furieux	The senseless rage of a furious
Fera à table par freres le fer luire:	struggle will cause the brothers
Les despartir, blessée, curieux,	to draw their weapons at table.
Le fier duelle viendra en France	A wounded man parts them,
nuire.	curious: the proud duel will
	bring harm to France.

The duel that affects France must occur between her princes or statesmen. Several French kings, including Henri III and Louis XIV have hated their brothers but none have actually duelled together.

35

Dans deux logis de nuict le feu	Fire will take hold in two houses
prendra,	at night, several people inside
Plusieurs dedans estouffes & rostis:	suffocated or burnt. It will
Pres de deux fleuves pour seul il	happen near two rivers for sure
adviendra:	when the sun, Sagittarius and
Sol, l'Arq & Caper tous seront	Capricorn are all diminished.
amortis.	

This event could occur on 22nd December of any year, for this is the day that the sun moves out of Sagittarius into Capricorn. It is difficult to distinguish a town on two rivers, there are so many. Commentators who lived *c.* 1600 all related it to a fire at Lyons in 1582, and this town is situated at the mouth of two rivers.

36

Du grand Prophete les lettres	The letters of the great prophet
seront prinses,	will be intercepted and fall into
Entre les mains du tyran deviendront:	the hands of the tyran. His
Frauder son Roy seront ses entre-	efforts will be to deceive his
prinses,	King, but soon his thefts will
Mais ses rapines bien tost le	trouble him.
troubleront.	

The Abbé Torné, a great interpreter of Nostradamus, believed this verse referred to him. It may just as well be Nostradamus talking of some personal vendetta of his own.

De ce grand nombre que l'on envoyera, *Pour secourir dans le fort assiegez,* *Peste & famine tous les devorera,* *Hors mis septante qui seront profligez.*[1]	Of the great number that are sent to relieve the besieged fort, disease and hunger will destroy them all except seventy who will be killed.

Des condamnez sera fait un grand nombre, *Quand les monarques seront conciliez:* *Mais l'un deux viendra si malencombre*[2] *Que guere ensemble ne seront reliez.*	There will be a great number of condemned people when the monarchs are reconciled. But one of them will be so unfortunate that they will hardly remain allies.

RUSSIA AND ALLIES?

This may be interpreted as a general quatrain about the alliance of Hitler and Stalin between the years 1939–41? Others apply it to the breakdown of the Yalta conference of 1945, and interpret line one as referring to the Nuremberg Trials and the misfortune as the commencement of the Cold War by Russia.

Un an devant le conflict Italique, *Germains, Gaulois, Hespaignols pour le fort:* *Cherra l'escolle maison de republique,* *Ou, hors mis peu, seront suffoque mors.*	A year before the war in Italy, Germans, French and Spanish will be for the strong one; the school house of the republic will fall, where, except for a few, they will suffocate to death.

EUROPEAN ATTITUDES TOWARDS GERMANY, *c.* 1939

This quatrain summarizes very succinctly the general situation in Europe during 1939, the year before Italy was involved in the Second World War, which she declared on 10th June 1940. The Spanish were certainly on the German side, and there was a definite pro-German element in France as was proved by the Vichy régime. The strong man was Hitler who had enormous support in Germany at this time. The school-house republic which falls and crushes so many of its people could be either

[1] *profligez*—Latin, *profligare* = to destroy, kill, ruin.
[2] *malencombre*—O.F., 13th Century, *malencontre* = misfortune.

France or Italy. It is difficult to understand the meaning of the adjective here. This quatrain seems to continue on to the following one with the claim that after these alliances between Germany, Spain and France there will be world battles on land and sea, which were part of the Second World War.

40

Un pres apres non point longue intervalle	Shortly afterwards, not a very long interval, a great tumult will be raised by land and sea. The naval battles will be greater than ever. Fires, creatures which will make more tumult.
Par mer & terre sera faict grand tumulte:	
Beaucoup plus grande sera pugne[1] navalle,	
Feux, animaux, qui feront plus d'insulte.[2]	

SECOND WORLD WAR

Should this quatrain be linked with II. 39 it becomes a continuation of the description of the Second World War. The importance of power at sea was obvious, submarines played a great part in the war game, and are probably described as the creatures of line 4, as in I. 29, II. 5 etc. *Feux* could be translated as firing, making them creatures with weapons.

41

La grand estoille par sept jours brulera,	The great star will burn for seven days and the cloud will make the sun appear double. The large mastiff will howl all night when the great pontiff changes his abode.
Nuée fera deux soleils apparoir:	
Le gros mastin fera toute nuict hurlera,	
Quand grand pontife changera de terroir.	

THIRD WORLD WAR, *c.* 1986–93?

There are several Popes who have changed their abode in the past, notably Pius VI who died in Valence, and Pius VII, who was forcibly detained by Napoleon before returning to Rome. However the reference to the two suns, plus the great star, which is probably a comet, may bring the quatrain to 1986 when Halley's comet will reappear and when the next Pope but one, predicted by Malachy, may well be in the Vatican whose motto is given as

[1] *pugne*—Latin, *pugna* = battle.
[2] *insulte*—O. Provençal = insult. Tumult, upheaval.

de laboris solis, the toil of the sun. Could this describe an atomic bomb which was referred to as a 'second sun' as early as 1947? This all fits in with Nostradamus' description of a Third World War towards the end of this century. The then Pope might well have to leave the Vatican, or even Europe, if this should arise. Perhaps the seven days stand for seven years, which brings Nostradamus to 1993, nearer the date given in other prophecies, *see* II. 46, 62, VIII. 59, 77, X. 49, 72, 74, 75.

42

Coq, chiens & chats de sang seront repeus	The cock, cats and dogs will be replete with blood when the tyrant is found dead of a wound in the bed of another, both arms and legs broken, he who was not afraid dies a cruel death.
Et de la playe du tyran trouvé mort.	
Au lict d'un autre jambes & bras rompus,	
Qui n'avait peur de mourir de cruelle mort.	

DEATH OF ROBESPIERRE, 1794

The cock is the emblem of France, and the dogs and cats the rabble who have had enough of the reign of Terror under the committee led by Robespierre. Between 12th–28th July 1,285 victims died on the guillotine. Robespierre was a tyrant but so were many others of his committee. On 26th July 1794, he said the Terror should be ended and the Committee of Public Safety renewed. Robespierre was arrested but freed by troops of the Commune who took him to the Hôtel de Ville (strange bed). Then the National Guard captured Robespierre; he was shot in the jaw (not arms and legs) and after a long night of agony he was executed without further trial on 29th July at the Place de la Revolution.

43

Durant l'estoille chevelue[1] apparente,	During the appearance of the bearded star, the three great princes will be made enemies. The shaky peace on earth will be struck from the skies, the Po, the winding Tiber, a serpent placed upon the shore.
Les trois grans princes seront faits enemis:	
Frappés du ciel paix terre tremulante,	
Pau, Timbre undans, serpent sus le bort mis.	

[1] *estoille chevelue* = comet.

TRIPLE ALLIANCE, 1881

Pope Leo XIII is given the motto 'Lumen in Caelo' by the prophet Malachy, and on his coat of arms was a comet (*estoille chevelue*). He is also referred to as this in VI. 6 by Nostradamus. During Leo XIII's reign the Triple Alliance (three great princes) was formed in 1881 by Germany, Austria and Italy against France. The fact that peace was disturbed is probably a reference to the Triple Entente, which ultimately led to the First World War. The snake which constricted the French leaders was that of the Triple Alliance.

44

L'aigle pousée entour de pavillions,
Par autres oiseaux d'entour sera chassée:
Quand bruit des cymbees, tubes & sonaillons,
Rendront le sens de la dame insensée.

The eagle driven back around the tents will be chased by other birds around him. When the sound of cymbals, trumpets and bells will restore sense to the senseless woman.

FRANCE, c. 1813–14

The Eagle is, as always, Napoleon, here driven back from Moscow and surrounded by the other birds of prey, Russia, Austria and Prussia. The last two lines may hold two separate interpretations. First, they may refer to the martial music of the armies which bring France back to her senses, that is, restore to her King Louis XVIII, or they refer to Napoleon's second marriage to Marie Louise of Austria and the grief and madness of the discarded Josephine (*dame insensée*). It was a common popular belief that Napoleon's luck deserted him when he discarded Josephine Beauharnais.

45

Trop le ciel pleure l'Androgyn[1] procrée,
Pres de ciel sang humain respondu:
Par mort trop tard grand peuple recrée,
Tard & tost vient le secours attendu.

The heavens weep too much for the birth of Androgeus, near the heavens human blood is spilt. It is too late for the great nation to be revived because of the death, soon, yet too late, comes the awaited help.

---

[1] *Androgyn* = (*a*) hermaphrodite. (*b*) Androgeus, son of Minos of Crete, killed by the young people of Athens because he won all the prizes at the Pantheon.

Androgin implies an hermaphrodite who causes some form of aerial warfare in the second line? The rest is very generalized.

46

Apres grand troche[1] humaine plus grand s'appreste,	After great misery for mankind an even greater approaches
Le grand moteur des Siecles renouvelle:	when the great cycle of the centuries is renewed. It will
Pluie, sang, laict, famine, fer & peste,	rain blood, milk, famine, war and disease: In the sky will be
Au ciel veu feu, courant long estincelle.	seen a fire, dragging a trail of sparks.

THIRD WORLD WAR, *c.* 1986?

The great catastrophe of war that Nostradamus predicts here is linked with a comet appearing at the end of a century. The most likely is Halley's comet, last seen in 1910 and due to reappear in 1986, which is consistent with the other dates given by Nostradamus. He is obviously not exactly clear when this war will break out and dates between the late 70s and 1999 are given. Comets were important to 16th-Century philosophers and had significance according to their place in the zodiac. It does not seem to apply to the 1910 dating, because Nostradamus specifies that a great war has already taken place before the comet appears. See I. 91, II. 41, 62, 91, IV. 97, VIII. 59, 77, X. 49, 72, 74, 75.

47

L'ennemi grand vieil dueil meurt de poison,	The enemy watches with grief the old man dead from poison;
Les souverains par infiniz subjugez	the kings are overcome by an immeasurable (number). It
Pierres plouvoir, cachez soubz la foison,	rains stones, hidden under the fleece; vainly articles are
Par mort articles en vain sont alleguez.	asserted by the dead man.

[1] *troche*—from the Greek, *trukos* = misery.

La grand copie[1] *qui passera les monts,*	The great army which will pass over the mountains when
Saturne en l'Arq tournant du poisson Mars:	Saturn is in Sagittarius and Mars moving into Pisces.
Venins caches soubs testes de saulmons,	Poison hidden under the heads of salmon, their chief in war
Leur chef pendu à fil de polemars.[2]	hung with a cord.

The conjunction mentioned in line 2 is rare and has apparently only occurred once since publication, 17th July 1751. Its next occurrence will be 13th July 2193. The mountains may be the Alps but the third line seems incomprehensible. A *saumon* in Provençal means a donkey head, but gets one no further.

Les conseilleurs du premier monopole,[3]	The advisers of the first conspiracy, the victors won over
Les conquerants seduits par la Melite:	on behalf of the Maltese; Rhodes and Byzantium opening
Rodes, Bisance pour leurs exposant pole,[4]	their towns for them, the pursuers in flight will need land.
Terre faudra les poursuivans de suite.	

The connection between Istanbul (Bizantium) Rhodes, Malta and a conspiracy is obscure. It almost certainly refers to an incident during the Ottoman Empire.

Quand ceux d'Hainault, de Gand[5] *& de Bruxelles,*[6]	When the people of Hainault, Ghent and Brussels see siege
Verront à Langres le siege devant mis:	laid before Langres: Behind their flanks will be dreadful
Derrier leurs flancs seront guerres cruelles	wars, the former wound being worse than their enemies.
La plaie antique fera pis qu'ennemis.	

[1] *copie*—Latin, *copia* = forces.
[2] *polemars* = (*a*) Greek *polemarches*, he who leads in war. (*b*) Provençal *polomar*, twine or thick string.
[3] *monopole*—Greek, *monopolum* = conspiracy.
[4] *pole*—Greek, *polis* = town.
[5] *Gand* = Ghent, chief city of Flanders.
[6] *Bruxelles* = Brussels, chief city of Brabent.

Hainault, Flanders (Ghent) and Brabant (Brussels) were the richest provinces of the 16th-Century Netherlands. Nostradamus sees them as involved with a siege upon Langres, which was an important city on the frontier during the Hapsburg wars. The third line then indicates the uprising of the Netherlands in 1568, but it is unclear what is meant by the 'former wound'; possibly some form of internal dissension?

51

Le sang de juste à Londres fera faulte,	The blood of the just will be demanded of London burnt
Bruslés par fouldres de vingt trois les six:	by fire in three times twenty plus six. The ancient lady will
La dame antique cherra de place haute,	fall from her high position, and many of the same denomina-
Des mesme secte plusieurs seront occis.	tion will be killed.

GREAT FIRE OF LONDON, 1666

The only fire in London occurring in a year '66 is the great one of 1666. This is one of Nostradamus' more interesting quatrains where he gets very close to giving an accurate dating that can be checked historically. The *'dame antique'* who falls is interpreted as the Cathedral of St. Paul's, which was destroyed, and the others of the same denomination, either the churches or their occupants. Many people did flee from their wooden homes hoping to escape the flames in the stone-built churches, but the heat was so intense that even these buildings did not escape. The blood of the just is understood to mean that the victims of the fire were undeserving of their fate. This quatrain is linked with II. 53, by the words *'sang de juste'* and *'dame antique'*.

52

Dans plusieurs nuicts la terre tremblera:	For several nights the earth will shake; in the spring two great
Sur le printemps deux efforts suite:	efforts in succession. Corinth
Corinthe, Ephere aux deux mers nagera,	and Ephesus will swim in the two seas; war will be stirred up
Guerre s'esmeut par deux vaillans de luit.[1]	by two valiant in combat.

[1] *luit*—Romance = fight, combat.

England was engaged in a naval war with the United Provinces from 1665-7, and if one can accept that they are represented by Corinth and Ephesus, even though the link is quite obscure, then this, the preceeding and following quatrains become a trio covering the same period.

53

La grande peste de cité maritime,	The great plague in the mari-
Ne cessera que mort ne soit vengée	time city will not stop until
Du juste sang par pris damné sans	death is avenged by the blood
crime,	of a just man taken and con-
De la grand dame par feincte	demned for no crime; the great
n'outragée.	lady is outraged by the pre-
	tence.

PLAGUE OF LONDON, 1665

Nostradamus clearly shows in the second line that he believes the Great Plague and Fire of London to be the result of the killing of Charles I; *see also* quatrain IX. 49, where it is predicted in detail. The maritime city is a description often used for London, and the plague broke out the year before the great Fire. It is suggested that the lady who is outraged, and was interpreted as St. Paul's Cathedral in II. 51, stands for the Church because soon after- wards Protestantism became re-established in England under William III, and Nostradamus was a fervent Catholic. His views towards all Protestant forms of religion are very hostile throughout his writings, probably a reflection of the development of Calvinism during his own lifetime. Again in this verse is the theme that the people suffering from the plague are those of '*juste sang*', the people of II. 51, who are described as being in London.

54

Par gent estrange, & Romains	By a foreign people, far from
lointaine,	the Romans, their great city
Leur grand cité apres eaue fort	will be greatly damaged by
troublée:	water. A girl without a greatly
Fille sans trop different domaine,	different estate taken by the
Prins chef, ferreure¹ n'avoir este	leader, the lock not having been
riblée.²	removed.

¹ *ferreure*—This may be read in variants as *serreure*.
² *riblée*—O.F., *ribler* = to rob, pillage.

This quatrain indicates that Rome will be attacked by a distant invader after or during a time of flooding. Whether the girl is to be understood literally or metaphorically is not clear.

55

Dans le conflict le grand qui peu valloit, *A son dernier fera cas merveilleux:* *Pendant qu'Hadrie verra ce qu'il falloit,* *Dans le banquet pongnale l'orgueilleux.*	In the conflict the great man who is of little worth will perform an astonishing deed at his end. While Hadrie sees what is needed, during a banquet he stabs the proud.

FRANCE, 1594

By 1594 the revolutionary ideas of the Paris Seize (Peoples' Parliament) were becoming too strong for the League to cope with, and the Duke de Mayenne, claimant to the throne through the House of Guise, carried out a *coup d'état*. He invited all the leaders of the Seize to a banquet in order to lull their suspicions and had them all killed on the following night. Mayenne hoped that he would be able to hold Paris for the Catholic league but Henri IV (Hadrie) realizing the situation, saw that he had to become Catholic and thus unite France.

56

Que peste & glaive n'a sceu definer,[1] *Mort dans le puis sommet du ciel frappé:* *L'abbé mourra quand verra ruiner,* *Ceux du naufrage l'escueil voulant grapper.*	One whom neither plague nor sword could kill will die on the top of a hill, struck from the sky. The abbot will die when he sees the ruin of the people in the shipwreck trying to hold on to the reef.

57

Avant conflict le grand tombera, *Le grand à mort, mort, trop subite & plainte,* *Nay imparfaict: la plus part nagera,* *Aupres du fleuve de sang la terre tainte.*	Before the battle the great man will fall, the great one to death, death too sudden and lamented. Born imperfect, he will go the greater part of the way; near the river of blood the ground is stained.

[1] *definer*—O.F. = die, finish, decide.

Mort, trop subite probably implies an assassination, and *nay imparfaict* a leader born with a deformity. If it were not for the deformity I would apply this to J. F. Kennedy's stand against Khrushchev over Cuba. The Russian fleet did come 'the greater part of the way', and it was after this confrontation that Kennedy was killed at Dallas *trop subite & plainte*.

58

Sans pied ne main dend aiguë & *forte,* *Par Globe¹ au fort de port & lainé* *nay:* *Pres du portail desloyal transporte,* *Silene² luit, petit grand emmené.*	Without either foot or hand, with strong and sharp teeth through the crowd to the fortified harbour and the elder born. Near the gates, treacherous, he crosses over; the moon shines but little, great pillage.

Some interpret the last line as 'the moon shines, the great little man is carried off' meaning Napoleon. They apply the same interpretation to '*petit grand*' in II. 85.

59

Classe Gauloise par appuy de *grande garde,* *Du grand Neptune, & ses tridens* *souldars:* *Rongée Provence pour soustenir* *grand bande,* *Plus Mars Narbon, par javelots &* *dards.*	The French fleet with the support of the main guard of great Neptune and his trident warriors; Provence scrounged to sustain this great band, moreover, fighting at Narbonne with javelins and arrows.

Neptune apparently refers to Turkey, the dominant power in the Mediterranean during Nostradamus' lifetime. The trident warriors are probably French allied troops. Toulon was used as a base against the Habsburgs during the 1540s but not later, and there does not seem to have been any trouble in Narbonne at this period.

¹ *Globe*—Latin, *globus* = a crowd, throng.
² *Silene*—Greek, *selene* = moon, but the spelling *selin* is more normal for Nostradamus, so this may be an anagram.

La foy Punicque en Orient rompue	Faith with Africa broken in the
Grand Jud.[1] & Rosne, Loire &	East, Great Jordan, Rosne,
Tag[2] changeront.	Loire & Tagus will change.
Quand du mulet la faim sera repue,	When the hunger of the mule is
Classe espargie,[3] sang & corps	sated, the fleet is scattered and
nageront.	bodies swim in blood.

At the time of some discord between Africa and an Eastern country the rivers Jordan in Palestine, Rosne and Loire in France, Tagus, Spain and Portugal will change. This may mean the borders of the parent countries change, and is in some way allied with a great naval disaster. Line three is completely obscure.

Euge,[4] Tamins,[5] Gironde & la	Bravo, men of the Thames,
Rochele,	Gironde and la Rochelle; O
O sang Troyen Mort ay port de la	Trojan blood killed by an
flesche:	arrow at the harbour. Beyond
Derrier le fleuve au fort mise	the river the ladder put against
l'eschele,	the port, flashes of fire, great
Pointes feu grand meutre sur la	slaughter in the breach.
bresche.	

The French Royal Family is referred to by Nostradamus as being of Trojan blood, see I. 19, but it did not exist by the time that Englishmen fought side by side with Frenchmen. There is no record of a prince of the blood being killed or wounded at a harbour.

Mabus puis tost alors mourra,	Mabus will then soon die and
viendra,	there will come a dreadful
De gens & bestes une horrible	destruction of people and
defaite:	animals. Suddenly vengeance
Puis tout à coup la vengeance on	will be revealed, a hundred
verra,	hands, thirst and hunger, when
Cent, main, soif, faim, quand	the comet will pass.
courra la comete.	

[1] *Jud*—Short for Jordan.
[2] *Tag*—Short for Tagus.
[3] *espargie*—O.F., *espargier* = to sprinkle.
[4] *Euge*—Latin = bravo!
[5] *Tamins*—Syncope of Tamisiens = people of the Thames?

Again we have the reference to a comet. If this is the same comet as in II. 41 and 46, this could be a reference to a future war. It is possible that Mabus is an anagram of the leader's proper name Nostradamus as a doctor would know that most diseases do not kill people as well as animals, yet in this verse he specifically says it will happen. It has been suggested that he is referring to atomic fallout which kills all living creatures equally dreadfully (*horrible defaite*).

63

Gaulois, Ausone[1] bien peu sub-jugera,	The French will subdue Ausonia in a little, while Pau
Par, Marne & Seine fera Perme l'vrie:	Marne and Seine Perme will make drunk. He who raises the
Qui le grand mur contre eux dres-sera,	great wall against them, the great one will lose his life from
Du moindre au mur le grand perdra la vie.	the least at the wall.

BATTLE OF IVRY, 1590

There does not seem to be much connection between Parme in Russia and this quatrain. However, if line 2 reads *Parme l'vrie* there is a most interesting possibility. In 1590 the Duke of Parma was ordered to France from the Netherlands to help the Catholic Leaguers against Henri of Navarre. Parma was defeated by Henri at the Battle of Ivry, 1590. However he did not die until 1592 from wounds received at another battle.

64

Seicher de faim, de soif, gent Genevoise,	The people of Geneva will dry up with thirst and hunger,
Espoir prochain viendra au defaillir:	hope at hand will come to failure; the law of the Cevennes
Sur point tremblant sera loi Geben-oise.[2]	will be at breaking point, the fleet cannot be received at the
Classe au grand port ne se peut acuillir.	great port.

CEVENNES, c. 1685

After the revocation of the Edict of Nantes 1685 by Louis XIV, the people of the Cevennes revolted, so deeply rooted was their

[1] *Ausone*—Ausonia, Southern Italy.
[2] *Gebenoise*—Cevennes mountain chain in Switzerland.

Calvinist faith. Presumably the fleet would be bringing supplies across Lake Geneva.

65

Le parc enclin grande calamité.	In the feeble lists, great cala-
Par l'Hesperie & Insubre fera:	mity through America and
Le feu en nef peste et captivité,	Lombardy. The fire in the
Mercure en l'Arc Saturne fenera.	ship, plague and captivity;
	Mercury in Sagittarius, Saturn
	warning.

7th DECEMBER 2044?

According to Wöllner the next date for this configuration is 7th December 2044, the last being 1839. Insubria is definitely either Milan or Lombardy but the dangers to it and America (Hesperie I. 28) are not clear.

66

Par grans dangiers le captif eschapé,	The captive escaped great dangers, his fortune greatly
Peu de temps grand a fortune changée:	changed in a short time. The people are trapped in the
Dans le palais le peuple est attrapé,	palace, by good omen, the besieged city.
Par bon augure la cité assiegée.	

NAPOLEON'S 100 DAYS, 1st MARCH–28th JUNE 1815

The captive who escapes great dangers and whose fortune changes so dramatically in a short time, is Napoleon after his escape from Elba on 1st March 1815. The line can also be read inversely with the meaning that the good fortune will very soon change back again, meaning the defeat at Waterloo on 18th June. The third line is interesting. On Napoleon's victorious return to Paris after his escape, the Parisian mob invaded the palace and court of King Louis XVIII and carried their hero, Napoleon, on their shoulders into the private chambers once occupied by the king, and reinstated him themselves physically. Apparently the crowd was so enormous that no one could get in or out for some hours. The final line is interpreted as meaning that Paris, the city besieged by the Allies, will find its monarch restored (*par bon augure*) as he was on 8th July 1815.

Le blond an nez forchu viendra commettre,
Par le duelle & chassera dehors:
Les exilés, dedans fera remettre,
Aux lieux marins commettant les plus fors.

The blond one will come into conflict with the hooknosed one, in a duel and will drive him out. He will have restored the exiles committing the strongest to the marine places.

JAMES II AND WILLIAM III, 1688–9

The blond man was understood even by contemporary pamphlets to stand for William of Orange, who was in fact also fair-haired. William's party drives out James II in 1688, but the Stuart party (*les exilez*) decided to reinstate him and put all their efforts into a sea battle. James based himself in Ireland and was aided by the French fleet. In 1690 the Allies were badly beaten at sea off Beachy Head but on the same day William III won the Battle of the Boyne and James was forced to flee to France, from which he never returned. The British fleet did not finally subdue the French and assure her maritime supremacy for another two years at Cap la Hague in 1692.

68

De l'aquilon[1] les efforts seront grands.
Sus l'Occean sera la porte ouverte:
Le regne en l'isle sera reintegrand,
Tremblera Londres par voille descouverte.

In the North great efforts will be made, across the seas the way will be open. The rule on the island will be re-established, London fearful of the fleet when sighted.

JAMES II, *continued*

This seems to continue the last quatrain, and is one of the pairs that Nostradamus overlooked when he separated them to make interpretation more difficult. The great efforts made in the North are those of the invader, William III of Orange. The British fleet was so sluggishly commanded at this time by the Earl of Torrington that he lost several sea battles to the French and Stuart fleets, particularly Beachy Head and Bantry Bay, and it was only William's strength on land that kept him the throne. There could be a second interpretation of line 2; that the seas were open and undefended allowing William to cross to England. The island, in the singular, indicates Ireland where James II took refuge; Nostradamus usually refers to the British Isles in the plural.

[1] *aquilon*—Latin = North Wind, North.

James naturally re-established Stuart rule there until displaced by the Battle of the Boyne, 1690. The last line again refers to the bad government of the British fleet under Lord Torrington. After the defeat at Beachy Head he withdrew his remaining ships to London where he was courtmartialled for lack of agressiveness, but acquitted. However, the British paid heavily for his reluctance to act during the next two years. It may also refer to the occasion in 1667 before William III came to England when his Dutch fleet sailed up the Thames on a raiding party.

69

Le Roy Gaulois par la Celtique dextre,	A Gallic king from the Celtic right hand (side) seeing the
Voyant discorde de la grande Monarchie	discord of the great monarch will flourish his sceptre over
Sus les trois pars fera florir son sceptre	the three leopards against the king of the great Hierarchy.
Contre la Cappe¹ de la grand Hierarchie.	

The clue for this quatrain is in line 3, the use of the word *pars*. In another book of his called 'the Horapollo' Nostradamus translates this word as leopards, and these are the three leopards of England, as Napoleon called the English heraldic lions. Thus we seem to continue yet again the theme of James II and William III. William is the Celtic king from Northern Gaul (i.e. Holland) (dextre is the northern side on a map) who seeing England in trouble under James II takes over the kingdom. Note that Nostradamus makes no mention of war. It was not a bloody invasion but one of invitation, William having many supporters in Britain. Cappe, as in other quatrains, is Nostradamus' version of Capet, the line of the French kings. As has been explained in the last two quatrains the French bitterly opposed William's establishment in England and allied themselves with the deposed James II and supplied him with troops and naval aid.

¹ *Cappe*—Nostradamus' version of Capet. One of the names of the French royal line until the last of the Bourbons. *See also* IX. 20 etc.

Le dard du ciel fera son estendre,	The dart from heaven will
Mors en parlant: grande execution:	make its journey; Death while
La pierre en l'arbre la fiere gent	speaking; a great execution.
rendue,	The stone in the tree, the
Bruit humain monstre purge expia-	proud nation brought down;
tion.	rumour of a human monster,
	purge and expiation.

NAPOLEON, 1815

This is often interpreted as referring to Napoleon but it seems too general in its meaning for this to be satisfactory. The theory is that the scene is Waterloo 1815, and the dart from the sky is the vengeance of heaven. The next line refers to the carnage and slaughter, and the stone to an axe cutting down the Bonaparte dynasty. Then France surrenders, is expiated, and the monster, Napoleon, is removed to St. Helena. Very ingenious if one can accept it.

71

Les exilés en Sicile viendront,	The exiles will come to Sicily
Pour delivrer de faim la gent	in order to deliver the foreign
estrange:	nation from hunger. At day-
Au point du jour les Celtes lui	break the Celts will fail them,
faudront	life remains by reason; the
La vie demeure à raison: Roi se	king joins in alliance.
range.	

72

Armée Celtique en Italie vexée,	The French army will be
De toutes pars conflict & grande	troubled in Italy, on all sides
peste:	conflict and great loss. Flee
Romains fuis, ô Gaule repoulsé,	the Italians, O France repelled;
Pres du Thesin,[1] Rubicon pugne[2]	near the Tessin the battle at
incerte.	the Rubicon is uncertain.

A difficult quatrain, because it sounds so specific and yet has not occurred since 1555. It is best used as an example of retroactive prophecy, that is, describing an event occurring during the prophet's lifetime or earlier and which has sunk into his subsconcious. If this is so, the first 3 lines are a good description of the Battle of

---

[1] *Thesin*—River Ticino flows into the Po below Pavia.

[2] *pugne*—Latin, *pugna* = battle.

Pavia 1525, the third line describing the strategy of the Imperial forces. But even then the outcome of Pavia was a definite victory for the Italians, not an uncertain one.

73

Au lac Fucin[1] de Benac[2] le rivage,	The shore of Lake Garda to
Prins du Leman[3] au port de l'Orguion:[4]	Lake Fucino, taken from Lake Geneva to the harbour of Orguion. Born with three arms
Nay de trois bras predict bellique image	it foretells a warlike image with three kingdoms for the great
Par trois couronnes au grand Endymion.[5]	Endymion.

A large number of wild interpretations have been made for this quatrain including (Allen 1943) that Endymion is a metaphor for the U.S.A.! The three arms and crowns may well be the triple tiara of the Pope, linking it with the Vatican States, or a state containing three kingdoms probably set in Italy.

74

De Sens, D'Autun viendront jusques au Rosne,	From Sens, from Autun they will come as far as the Rhône
Pour passer outre vers les monts Pyrenées:	to cross over the Pyrenees. The people going out from the
La gent sortir de la Marque d'Anconne,	Marches of Ancona will follow in great trails over land and
Par terre & mer suivra à grans trainées.	sea.

This quatrain is very muddled. Leoni (1961) has a clever interpretation in which he suggests that the Pyrenees are a mistake for the Alps. This would certainly help the geography, as Sens and Autun are in North Eastern France, but the Rhône is not on the way to the Pyrenees. If we interpret the mountains as the Alps the quatrain describes an invasion of Italy. The Marches of Ancona stretch from Rimini to north of Guilianova.

[1] *Fucin*—Lake Fucino, drained in 1876, in Italy.
[2] *Benac*—Lake Garda, Italy.
[3] *Leman*—Lake Geneva, Switzerland.
[4] *Orguion*—? possibly Orgon in Southern France, or Orgiano in Lombardy, not deciphered.
[5] *Endymion*—Youth in Greek mythology loved by Selene the moon, and having the gift of eternal sleep.

La voix ouie de l'insolite oiseau,
Sur le carron de respiral estage:[1]
Si hault viendra du froment le
boisseau,
Que l'homme de l'homme fera
Antropophage.[2]

The call of the unwanted bird
being heard on the chimney
stack; bushels of wheat will
rise so high that man will
devour his fellow man.

GENERAL FAMINE

The unwanted bird on the chimney stack is an owl or similar
bird of ill omen bringing warning of famine and the high price
of corn, but one is given no indication as to what famine will be
so dreadful that men will become cannibals. Possibly refers to
the World Famine of I. 67.

Foudre en Bourgongne fera cas
portenteux,
Que par engin[3] oncques ne pourrait
faire,
De leur senat sacriste fait boiteux
Fera scavoir aux ennemis l'affaire.

Lightning in Burgundy will
reveal portentous events. A
thing that could never have
been done by trickery. The
lame priest will reveal matters
of the senate to the enemy.

TALLYRAND, 1754–1838

Charles Maurice de Talleyrand-Périgord fits this quatrain remarkably well. The starting point lies in the third line, the lame
priest. Talleyrand became lame at the age of nearly four years
when a chest of drawers fell on his foot injuring it permanently.
He was destined by his family for the Church and took orders in
1778 and was Bishop of Antin by 1789. By 1790 he was totally
identified with the Revolutionaries, and was banned by the Pope
in the following year. By 1807 however, he resigned his position
as Grand Chamberlain in Napoleon's service because he dis-
approved of the Emperor's policies, and secretly advised the
Emperor Alexander I of Russia not to pressure Austria as Napoleon
wished. By 1814 he was contemplating absolute treachery. When
Alexander I came to the Hôtel Talleyrand he was advised by
Talleyrand that the restoration of the Bourbons was the only
solution for the future of France, and on 1st April in the same year
he convened the senate (line 3) who pronounced Napoleon to have
forfeited his crown.

[1] The line literally means—on the pipe of the breathing floor.
[2] Antropophage—Greek, anthro-phagos = man-eating.
[3] engin—Latin, ingenium = genius, ruse, trickery.

*Par arcs feux poix & par feux
   repoussés,*
*Cris hurlements sur la minuit
   ouis:*
*Dedans sont mis par les remparts
   cassez*
Par cunicules[1] les traditeurs[2] fuis.

Repulsed by bows, burning pitch and fires, cries and shouts will be heard in the middle of the night. They will get in through the broken defences; the traitors escape through the underground passages.

A general verse concerning a city captured in the middle of the night, with its ramparts broken down, and the people who betrayed it escaping through underground passages.

*Le grand Neptune du profond de la
   mer,*
*De gent Punique[3] & sang Gaulois
   meslé:*
*Les isles à sang pour le tardif
   ramer,[4]*
Plus lui nuira que l'occult mal celé.

Great Neptune from the depths of the sea, of mixed African race and French blood, the islands remain bloody because of the slow one; it will harm him more than the badly concealed secret.

Neptune was used by Nostradamus in II. 59 to refer to the Turkish Moslem fleet, which brings line 2 into the Franco-Turkish agreements of Nostradamus' day. The famous Barbary pirates, whose leader Barbarossa is also referred to in I. 74 are probably the Punic people, as their base was in Northern Africa. The last two lines may apply to an event of 1558 when, according to Jaubert, the Turkish fleet attacked Minorca (*les isles*), and took Chidadela, killing and enslaving the entire population of the town. He also states that the Turks were bribed to delay co-operating with the French fleet (*tardif ramer*) and thus demoralize them instead of coming to their aid in an Italian raid.

[1] *cunicules*—Latin, *cuniculus* = rabbit, interpreted as burrow, passage, mine.
[2] *traditeurs*—Latin, *traditor* = traitor.
[3] *Punique*—adjective for Carthage in North Africa.
[4] *ramer*—Romance = to remain, stay.

La barbe crespe & noir par engin	The man with the curly, black
Subjugera la gent cruelle & fiere:	beard will subdue the cruel and
Le grand CHIREN ostera du	proud nation through skill. The
longin,[1]	great Chiren will take from afar
Tous les captifs par Seline[2] *bar-*	all those captured by the Turk-
riere.	ish banner.

LEPANTO, 1571?

This quatrain poses a problem. All commentators have interpreted CHIREN as an anagram for HENRIC, an alternative spelling for Henri. This verse is then ascribed to the Battle of Lepanto 1571 which freed over 1,500 Christian slaves from the Turkish fleet (line 4). But at the time of Lepanto, Charles X was on the French throne, and Henri III was not to follow until 1574. Perhaps Nostradamus is a few years out in his dates, or uses Henri as a symbol for France? At Lepanto the Christian powers formed the last crusade against the Turks (Seline, because of their crescent-shaped banners). Command was given to Don John of Austria who was dark and bearded. The third line may mean that France benefited from the final removal of Turkish naval power from the Mediterranean. The clue lies in a definitive interpretation of CHIREN.

80

Apres le conflit du lesé l'eloquence,	After the battle, the eloquence
Par peu de temps se trame faint	of the one left behind for a
repas:	short time brings a short
Point l'on n'admet les grands à	respite. None of the great will
delivrance,	be allowed to go free, they are
Des ennemis sont remis à propos.	left to their enemies at the
	proper time.

[1] *longin*—Provençal, *longinc* = far off, distant.
[2] *Seline*—Greek, Selene = moon, crescent.

Par feu du ciel la cité presque
*   aduste,*
L'urne[1] menace encor Ceucalion,[2]
Vexée Sardaigne par la Punique
*   fuste,[3]*
Apres que Libra lairra son Phaeton.

The city is almost burned down by fire from the sky, water again threatens Deucalion. Sardinia is vexed by the African fleet after Libra has left Leo.

This quatrain appears to be modern for the first line implies the destruction of a city from the air with fire, by bombing or something similar. This devastation is followed by flooding, as Deucalion was the Noah of Greek Mythology. Then follows an African raid on Sardinia or Italy, and line four gives us an astrological dating. Phaeton was the youth who drove the chariot of the sun, Leo, when struck down by Zeus. Libra usually stands for Austria in astrological geography.

Par faim la proye fera loup
*   prisonnier,*
L'assaillant lors en extreme detresse,
Le nay[4] ayant au devant le dernier,
Le grand n'eschappe au milieu de
*   la presse.*

Through hunger the prey will make the wolf prisoner, the attacker then in great distress; the elder having the younger in front; the great man cannot escape in the middle of the crowd.

It is possible to invert the translation of the first line but unfortunately this does not make the quatrain any more specific.

Le gros traffic d'un grand Lyon
*   changé*
La plus part tourne en pristine[5]
*   ruine.*
Proie aux soldats par pille ven-
*   dengé[6]*
Par Jura mont & Sueve[7] bruine.

The great trade of great Lyons changed, the greater part turns into early ruin. A prey to the soldiers through a harvest of pillage. Fogs through the mountains of Jura and Switzerland.

[1] *urne*—Metaphor for waters, flooding.
[2] *Ceucalion*—Misprint for Deucalion in other editions, see commentary above.
[3] *fuste* = a kind of low oared galley.
[4] Probably corruption of *l'aîné* = elder.
[5] *pristine*—Latin, *pristinus* = former, early, first.
[6] *vendengé*—O.F. = vendage, harvest.
[7] *Sueve* = Switzerland, from the Latin Suevi, the German Swiss.

Nicollaud gives as the basis for interpreting this quatrain the Memoirs of the Marquis de Beauregard who says that during October 1795, when troops of the Revolution were putting down an uprising at Lyons, 'we saw large crowds of peasants . . . who with great empty sacks rushed to Lyons to pillage the town'. This was after a two month long siege and many of the town's inhabitants had been massacred. The fog mentioned in the last line was not recorded.

84

Entre Campaigne, Sienne, Flora, Tustie,	Between Campania, Sienna, Florence and Tuscany, it will not rain a drop for six months and nine days. A foreign language will be spoken in Dalmatia, it will overrun the country, devastating all the land.
Six mois neuf jours ne ploura une goutte:	
L'estrange langue en terre Dalmatie,	
Courira sus: vastant la terre toute.	

When Nostradamus wrote, Dalmatia belonged to the Venetians, but was surrounded by the Ottoman Empire. Perhaps he thought it would be taken by the Turks (*estrange langue*)? It was not captured, nor has so specific a drought been recorded along the west coast of Italy.

85

Le vieux plain barbe soubs le statut severe,	Under the severe authority of the old man with the flowing beard, at Lyon it is put above the Celtic Eagle. The small great one perseveres too far; noise of weapons in the sky, the Ligurian sea is red.
A Lyon faict dessus l'Aigle Celtique:	
Le petit grand trop autre persevere,	
Bruit d'arme au ciel: mer rouge Ligustique.[1]	

NAPOLEON?

The small great man of line 3 is applied possibly to Napoleon in II. 58 and the theme may be continued here. During the 100 Days Napoleon arrived at Lyons on 10th March; the Eagle is certainly the French eagle since it is described as Celtic, which further develops the possibility. It cannot be identified with the Habsburg Imperial Eagle in this quatrain. But the stumbling block is line

[1] *Ligustique*—Ligurian, North Eastern Mediterranean.

one; who is the severe bearded man who accepts Napoleon at Lyons? Marshall Ney was not bearded, and he went over to Napoleon at Auserre. I leave this to the ingenuity of the reader.

Naufrage à classe[1] *pres d'onde Hadriatique,*	The fleet is wrecked near the Adriatic sea, the earth trembles,
La terre tremble esmeüe sus l'air en terre mis:	pushed into the air and falls again. Egypt trembles; Maho-
Egypte tremble augment Mahometi-que.	metan increase; the herald is sent to call out for surrender.
L'Herault soi rendre à crier est commis.	

1799. NAPOLEON IN EGYPT

In 1799 during Napoleon's Expedition to Egypt the British and French fleets met on the Nile and the latter were roundly defeated by the British led by Sir Richard Abercromby. It is suggested that the second line may refer to the French army who had disembarked but were frightened when they heard that the French Admiral's vessel had been blown up and the pieces strewn along the beaches. From this defeat Napoleon led his troops against the Turks at Acre, but during the siege his men were struck with the plague and so finally Napoleon decided to withdraw to Egypt, if he could not break down the Turkish resistance. A herald was sent to demand the surrender of Acre but this was refused and Napoleon was compelled to raise the siege.

Apres viendra des extremes con-treés	Afterwards there will come from a distant country a
Prince Germain, dessus le throsne doré:	German prince upon the golden throne. Servitude met from
La servitude & eaux rencontrées,	over the seas. The lady sub-
La dame serve, son temps plus n'adore.	ordinated, in the time no longer adored.

GEORGE I, 1714

This prediction probably applies to the accession of the Hanoverian George I to the throne of England in 1714. George came from Germany, a distant country, and was a German Prince. Should the word germain be used with the second meaning of

---

[1] *classe*—Latin, *classis* = fleet.

cousin or relative, he was also a cousin of the Queen Anne, but the use of the capital letter makes the first interpretation the most likely. However, it may be one of Nostradamus' famous double meanings. The English throne was a great prize and so is described as golden. Servitude refers to the fact that George was invited to accept the throne; it was not won in battle, while the final line is probably a reference to the Mother Church (Catholicism) which was no longer to be the main religion once the Hanoverians came to the throne.

88

Le circuit du grand faict ruineux,	The completion of the great disastrous action, the name of the seventh will be that of the fifth. Of the third (name) a greater, foreign warmonger, Paris and Aix will not be kept in Aries.
Le nom septiesme du cinquiesme sera:	
D'un tiers plus grand l'estrange belliqueux,	
Mouton, Lutece,[1] Aix ne garantira.	

THE CHILDREN OF CATHERINE DE VALOIS AND ACCESSION OF HENRI IV

An interesting and detailed quatrain which becomes very clear on study. The clue again is the seven children of Catherine de' Medici of whom the fifth will be the seventh and last king, Henri III (tiers), as his younger brother the Duke d'Alençon had died earlier, and his sister Marguerite had married the foreigner of the same name, Henri IV, who would become even greater through acts of war. Henri IV was considered a foreigner because he was Prince of Navarre, separate from France at this time. He had to besiege Paris before France capitulated and accepted his rule, and he started the siege in the sign of Aries (March, April) after the Battle of Ivry in February 1590. The first line probably refers to the massacre of St. Bartholomew which really sowed the seeds of final destruction for the Valois line (circuit) as it was partly because of this dreadful deed (faict ruineux) that Henri III was assassinated by the Jesuit Clément and left the throne free for Henri of Navarre.

[1] Lutece—Latin, Lutetia = Paris.

Un jour seront demis les deux grands maistres,	One day the two great leaders will be friends; their great
Leur grand pouvoir se verra augmenté:	power will be seen to grow. The new land will be at the height
La terre neufue sera en ses hauts estres,	of its power, to the man of blood the number is reported.
Au sanguinaire le nombre racompté.	

AMERICA, RUSSIA (?) AND THE MAN OF BLOOD.
To solve this quatrain one must first decide on the translation of
the word *demis* in the first line. Nearly all versions have the word
d'amis (friends) which is how I have translated it here, because to
understand *demis* as meaning halved would make nonsense of
line two. The power of the leaders cannot be seen to increase if
they are halved. The two great leaders sound as though they may
be the great powers, and line 3 (the New Land) links this with
America as Nouvelle Lande was one of the contemporary names for
America. If not, it may refer to the modern usage of the New
World. When America is at the height of its power and is allied
with another great power (Russia?), then the man of blood, the
third AntiChrist of Nostradamus will start assessing his position,
See VIII. 77 where the war is described, II. 50, III. 60 and IV. 50
where he seems to be placed in Asia. There are many other
references to him.

Par vie & mort changé regne d'Ongrie,[1]	Through life and death the rule in Hungary will be changed,
La loi sera plus aspre que service:	the law will become more bitter than servitude. Their
Leur grand cité d'hurlements plaincts & crie,	great city calls out with howls and laments, Castor and Pollux
Castor & Pollux[2] ennemis dans la lice.	are enemies in the field.

REVOLUTION IN HUNGARY, 1956
The life and death change in Hungary certainly occurred during
the Revolution of 1956 after Premier Nagy renounced the Warsaw
Pact on 1st November of that year, and found Russian troops

---

[1] *Ongrie* = Hungary.
[2] *Castor & Pollux*—Identified with Gemini or the twins.

advancing into his country on 4th November. The strictness of the régime that followed, from which many thousands fled to the West, is well known. There was a general policy of severe repression and there were many executions. The great city of Budapest was occupied and badly damaged by the fighting during the Revolution. The last line means that the pro-Russian Hungarians were fighting against their brother Hungarians, as indeed happened. I do not think this is intended as an indirect form of dating.

91

Soleil levant un grand feu l'on verra,	At sunrise a great fire will be seen, noise and light extending towards the North. Within the globe death and cries are heard, death awaiting them through weapons, fire and famine.
Bruit & clarté vers Aquilon tendants:	
Dedans le rond mort & cris l'on orra,	
Par glaive, feu, faim, mort las attendants.	

ATTACK ON U.S.A. OR RUSSIA?

This is a frightening quatrain if one applies it to the future. It seems to imply that a Northern Country, Russia or the U.S.A. will be bombed suddenly at sunrise, and this will be followed by a period of great devastation. In I. 92 Nostradamus states that America will suffer the greatest destruction. If we link this quatrain with I. 91, II. 5, 41 and 46, we are facing a very gloomy prospect.

92

Feu couleur d'or du ciel en terre veu,	Fire the colour of gold from the sky seen on earth, struck by the high born one, a marvellous happening. Great slaughter of humanity; a nephew taken from the great one; the death of the spectator, the proud one escapes.
Frappé du haut nay, faict cas merveilleux:	
Grand meutre humain; prinse du grand nepveu.	
Morte d'expectacles eschappe l'orgueilleux.	

NAPOLEON III, 1870

The clue to this quatrain is the word nephew in line three. There are several references to Napoleon III as the nephew of Napoleon and this quatrain describes the German artillery; the second line an incident on 2nd August 1870 when a bullet hit the ground by the Prince Imperial's feet, an event much publicized by the newspapers. Napoleon III was captured during the general French capitulation of September 1870.

93

Bien pres du Timbre presse la Lybitine:[1]	Very near the Tiber hurries death a short while before a great flood. The captain of the ship taken and put into the bilges, the castle and palace burnt down.
Un peu devant grand inondation:	
Le chef du nef prins, mis à la sentine,[2]	
Chasteau, palais en conflagration.	

The word Tiber, in Rome, linked with the captain of a ship (the Bark of St. Peter) implies that the latter is a Pope who comes to a dreadful end before a flood. The castle and palace would be St. Angelo and the Vatican.

94

GRAND Pau grand mal pour Gaulois recevra,	Great Po will receive great harm from a Frenchman, vain terror to the maritime Lion. An infinite number of people will cross the sea and a quarter of a million will not escape.
Vaine terreur du maritin Lyon:	
Peuple infini par la mer passera.	
Sans eschapper un quart d'un million.	

NAPOLEON IN ITALY AND EGYPT

As the first line says, Italy (the Po) suffered great harm from Napoleon who also terrified the maritime British lion, but vainly, because he did not manage to invade her. A great army did cross the seas to Egypt with Napoleon and certainly at least a quarter of a million men died during his campaigns.

95

Les lieux peuplez seront inhabitables:	The populated lands will become uninhabitable, great disagreement in order to obtain lands. Kingdoms given to men incapable of prudence. Then for the great brothers, death and dissension.
Pour champs avoir grand division:	
Regnes livrez à prudents incapables,	
Lors les grands freres mort & dissention.	

[1] *Lybitine*—Latin, *Libitina* = Goddess of Death.
[2] *sentine*—Latin, *sentina* = (a) bilges, (b) dregs.

This quatrain is extremely vague. Some commentators apply it to the present and near future, in which case Nostradamus' opinion of our politicians is not high. The last line might then refer to the Kennedy brothers. There is no other world-known group of brothers to link with this period. The first line would be yet another description of the third war he believes will devastate this century. See VIII 46 and 77.

96

Flambeau ardent au ciel soir sera veu,	A burning torch will be seen in the sky at night near the end and source of the Rhône. Famine and weapon; help provided too late, Persia will turn and invade Macedonia.
Pres de la fin & principe du Rosne:	
Famine, glaive: tard le secours pourveu,	
La Perse tourne envahir Macedoine.	

The last line of this quatrain, by far the most specific, seems to indicate that Nostradamus foresaw the Persians (never part of the Ottoman empire) inflicting a great defeat on the Turks (Macedonia) so as to open up the Balkans. The light in the sky if the verse is to be accepted will be seen from the source of the Rhône at the Furka Pass as far as the mouth of the river west of Marseilles.

97

Romain Pontife garde de t'approcher,	Roman pontiff beware of approaching a city watered by two rivers. You will spit blood in that place, both you and yours, when the roses bloom.
De la cité que deux fleuves arrouse,	
Ton sang viendras aupres de là cracher,	
Toi & tes tiens quand fleurira la rose.	

DEATH OF POPE PIUS VI AT VALENCE, 1799

The Pontiff in question is Pius VI who was imprisoned at Valence by the French after they had taken Rome in 1799. The two rivers are the Rhône and the Saône near by at Lyons. The Pope did die spitting blood, he suffered from an attack of severe vomiting in the summer (when the roses bloom) and died on 29th August 1799. His people referred to in the last line were the thirty-two priests who were imprisoned with the Pope. The word rose may have a typical Nostradamus double meaning of red, and therefore revolutionary, as well as of summertime. Both interpretations fit beautifully.

98

Celui de sang reperse[1] le visage,	He whose face is spattered with
De la victime proche sacrifiée,	the blood of a newly sacrificed
Tonant[2] en Leo augure par pre-	victim. Jupiter in Leo fore-
sage,	warns through prediction. He
Mis estra à mort lors pour la	will be put to death for the
fiancée.[3]	promise.

99

Terroir[4] Romain qu'interpretoit	Roman land that the augur
augure,	interprets, will be greatly
Par gent Gauloise par trop sera	molested by the French nation.
vexée:	But the French will come to
Mais nation Celtique craindra	dread the time of the North
l'heure,	wind having driven their fleet
Boreas,[5] classe[6] trop loing l'avoir	too far.
poussée.	

FAILURE OF NAPOLEON'S RUSSIAN CAMPAIGN, 1812

The Vatican States were taken into the French Empire in 1810, the French certainly molested Italy at this point. But soon afterwards, in 1812, Napoleon is suffering the defeat of his Russian campaign due to the cold weather (Boreas) and the folly of his general overcommitment. The fleet may refer to the earlier defeat at Trafalgar.

100

Dedans les isles si horrible tumulte,	Within the islands will be so
Bien on n'orra qu'une bellique	dreadful a tumult although
brigue	one only hears the warlike
Tant grand sera des predateurs	party. So great will be the
l'insulte,	threat of the plunderers that
Qu'on se viendra ranger à la grand	they will come to join in the
ligne.	great alliance.

[1] reperse—Latin, respergere = to sprinkle, splash.
[2] Tonant—standing for Jupiter Tonans, the Thunderer.
[3] fiancée = (a) marriage, bride. (b) Romance—promise or assurance.
[4] terroir—Latin, terra = land.
[5] Boreas—Latin = North wind.
[6] classe—Latin, classis = fleet.

Malta 1565, when all the great powers of Christendom sent reinforcements and aid, the 'Grand Succorso', to La Vallette in order to save Europe. The great alliance is probably the supranational order of Malta plus the Christian powers.

CENTURY III

1
2   Alchemy
3
4   1556/7
5   *continued*
6   Châteauneuf, 1819
7*   Occupied France, 1940
8*   Spanish Civil War, 1936
9
10   House of Grimaldi, Monaco
11*   Assassination of Henri IV, 1610
12   Flood
13*   Submarine fleet
14*   Louis XV
15*   Louis XV
16F?
17
18
19
20*   Spain, 1610
21
22
23
24
25*   Henri IV
26
27
28*   England and France, *c.* 1558
29
30*   Count of Montgomery, 1574
31*   Lepanto, 1571
32*   Second World War
33

```
34
35**    Hitler/Napoleon
36
37*     Napoleon, 1796
38
39
40
41*     Death of Louis de Condé, 1569
42      Famine
43
44*?    Wireless or electricity?
45*     Battle of Toulouse, 1814
46
47
48
49*F?   France
50*     Paris, 1588
51*     Murders of the de Guise brothers, 1588
52
53?
54*     Franco and Spanish Civil War
55*     Henri II and III of France
56
57**    England, 1603–1939
58**    Hitler
59*     French Revolution
60
61
62
63**    Italy and Germany, 1937
64
65*F?   Tomb of St. Peter and a new Pope.
66*     Jerôme Greslot, 1562–9
67      Protestant sects
68**    Franco and Mussolini
69
70**    Great Britain, 1604
71**    Blockade of Britain, 1939–45. Concentration camps
72
73**    Duke of Bordeaux, 1820–71
74
75*F?   Chemical warfare in Europe?
76      Protestant sects, 16th Century
```

77*** October 1727
78
79
80* Charles I
81* Cromwell and Pontefract
82*F? Invasion of France?
83* Louis XVIII
84* Sack of Rome under Pius VI
85
86
87* Sinking of French fleet, 1655
88* Marseilles, 1596
89* Cyprus and Enosis
90
91* Duke of Bordeaux
92*?
93
94
95**F? Rise of Communism.
96** 13th February 1820
97**F? The founding of Israel and eventual defeat of U.A.R.
98
99
100* General de Gaulle

KEY * of interest. F? Possibly referring to the future.

Apres combat & bataille navale,	After the combat and naval
Le grand Neptune à son plus haut	battle, great Neptune in his
befroi:	highest belfry; the red adver-
Rouge adversaire de peur deviendra	sary will become pale with fear,
pasle	putting the great ocean into a
Mettant le grand Ocean en effroi.	state of terror.

In II. 59 Nostradamus used Neptune as a synonym for the Turkish
Algerian fleets who were then ravaging the coasts. The red adversary would be the Spanish whose colour was red, but here the
quatrain fails. At the Battle of Lepanto 1571 the Spanish defeated
the Turks although the Barbary Corsairs continued to dominate
the Mediterranean for some time to come.

2

Le divin verbe donrra[1] à la sub-	The divine word will give to
stance,	the substance (that which)
Comprins ciel, terre, or occult au	contains heaven and earth,
laict[2] mystique:	occult gold in the mystic deed.
Corps, ame esprit ayant toute	Body, soul and spirit are all
puissance	powerful. Everything is beneath
Tant soubs ses pieds comme au	his feet, as at the seat of heaven.
siege Celique.[3]	

ALCHEMISTIC QUATRAIN

Although many commentators dismiss this verse I think it is a
rare and important description of Nostradamus' beliefs and experiences. The divine word which takes on substance is either
Nostradmus literally calling forth the spirit who inspires him to
prophecy, or an incantation which gives him divine powers, 'the
occult gold and the mystic deed'. He feels his body to be possessed
of great powers and possibly the last line indicates that during his
prophetic sessions he felt disembodied, that his soul was outside
his body looking down on himself, at the foot of the heavenly seat.
This is a common trance-like experience. Alternatively Nostradamus could mean that the spirit of inspiration came down to him
and is as much present beneath his feet, and therefore under his
control, as it is at its heavenly source.

[1] *donrra*—Form of *donnera* = will give.
[2] *laict*—Misprint for *faict*, deed, found in other editions.
[3] *Celique*—O.F. = celestial, heavenly.

Mars & Mercure & l'argent[1] *joint ensemble,* *Vers le midi extreme siccité:* *Au fond d'Asie on dira terre tremble,* *Corinthe, Ephese lors en perplexité.*	Mars, Mercury and the Moon in conjunction towards the south there will be a great drought. An earthquake will be reported from the depths of Asia, both Corinth and Ephesus then in a troubled state.

In quatrain II. 52 Corinth and Ephesus are understood to mean England and Holland; there is no other reference to these two countries linked together throughout the quatrains. At a time of drought in Southern France (Midi) and of earthquakes in Asia, there will be trouble in these two countries. However, it is all very general in outline; perhaps Corinth and Ephesus do mean Greece and Asia Minor in this quatrain? The first line is obviously a dating but I am unable to place it.

Quand seront proches de defaut des lunaires, *De l'un à l'autre ne distant grandement,* *Froid, siccité, danger vers les frontieres,* *Mesme ou l'oracle a prins commencement.*	When the downfall of the lunar ones is close they will not be very distant from each other. Cold, drought, danger around the frontiers even where the oracle had its source.

1556/7

Joubert understands the first line as meaning a year when the solar and lunar eclipse come close together and arrives at the year 1556. He states that there was no rain from April to August followed by a very severe winter in 1556–7. The danger at the frontier was the Spanish invasion of Picardy. The last line must refer either to Salon where Nostradamus lived, or to St. Rémy where he was born. At both towns there were local uprisings against the Huguenots by the peasantry, the Cabans, which continued well on into the 1560s. It is just possible that *lunaires* may mean 'people of the crescent', i.e. Mohammedans, and then the quatrain should be interpreted with regard to the contemporary struggles against the Ottoman Empire.

[1] *argent*—synecdoche for the moon. An alchemistic term used because of its colour.

Pres loing defaut de deux grands
   luminaires,
Qui surviendra entre l'Avril &
   Mars:
O quel cherté nais deux grans
   debonnaires,
Par terre & mer secourrant toutes
   pars.

Then, after the eclipse of the
two great stars which will occur
between April & March. Oh,
what a loss! but two great good
influences will help on all sides
by land and sea.

1556–7 continued

The quatrain almost certainly continues on from III. 4, but it is
unclear as to what might have happened between March and
April. Perhaps it is prevented by the influences of two good
planets or stars? Nostradamus may mean that the drought and
winter of 1556–7 would have been more severe but for their
influence.

6

Dans le temple clos le foudre y
   entrera,
Les citadins dedans leur fort
   grevez
Chevaux, boeufs hommes, l'onde
   mur touchera,
Par faim, soif, soubs les plus
   faibles armez.

Lightning will strike inside the
closed temple and will harm
the citizens inside their strong-
hold. Horses, cattle, men, the
flood will reach the walls;
through hunger and thirst
beneath the weakest armed.

CHATEAUNEUF 1819?

Lightning must have struck more than one church since 1555 when
Nostradamus published this verse. There is however a famous
occasion in 1819 at Châteauneuf when nine people were killed
and eighty-two injured among those present. But this does not
have any connection with a flood around this period, nor with
people and cattle retiring to a fortified place on high ground to
escape the waters. It is possible that the last two lines belong to
another verse, and that this is one of the 'split' verses I mention
in the Introduction.

Les fugitifs, feu du ciel sus les piques.
Conflict prochain des corbeaux s'esbatans,
De terre on crie aide secours celiques,
Quand pres des murs seront les combatants.

The fugitives, fire from heaven on to their weapons, the next conflict will be that of the crows. They call on earth for help and heavenly aid when the aggressors draw near the walls.

OCCUPIED FRANCE, 1940

The quatrain is usually understood as describing the Fall of France in 1940, when the French army and multitudes of refugees were driven back in confusion along the roads to Paris. The fire from the sky may mean the aerial attacks to which they were subjected, even the refugees were heavily bombed and strafed on the roads. The aggressors are the Germans about to enter Paris.

Les Cimbres joints avecques leurs voisins,
Depopular viendront presque l'Espaigne:
Gens amassez, Guienne & Limosins,
Seront en ligue, & leur feront compaigne.

The Cimbrians, allied with their neighbours will come to ravage almost all of Spain. People gathered in Guienne & Limousin will be allied, and join their company.

SPANISH CIVIL WAR, 1936

The Cimbrians were a North German tribe who vanished as early as 100 BC becoming intermixed with the Teutones. This verse may refer to Germany and her neighbour Italy who supported the Fascist cause in Spain and Franco's armies, during the bloody civil war of 1936–9. The last two lines may be a reference to the wide support for Hitler's policies that existed inside France at this period, or alternatively to the many Frenchmen who came to fight for the Insurgent armies in Spain, and to the fact that the Republican Spanish army after its defeat at Teruel in 1938 was actually driven into France for a time, followed by a mass exodus of Spanish refugees into France early in 1939. See IX. 16.

Bordeaux, Rouan, & la Rochelle joints,	Bordeaux, Rouen & la Rochelle allied, will hold all around the open seas; The English, Bretons and Flemish allied will drive them as far as Roanne.
Tiendront autour la grand mer Occeane,	
Anglois, Bretons, & les Flamans conjoints,	
Les chafferont jusque au pres de Rouane.	

Although this quatrain gives detailed names and places it remains quite obscure. Bordeaux and la Rochelle are near each other, but Rouen is to the North. Roanne is on the upper Loire.

10

De sang & faim plus grand calamité,	With blood and famine even greater calamity; seven times it approaches the sea shore. Monaco, from hunger, captured, in captivity. The great golden one caught, in an iron cage.
Sept fois s'appreste à la marine plage:	
Monech[1] de faim, lieu pris, captivité,	
Le grand mené croc[2] en ferree caige.	

HOUSE OF GRIMALDI, MONACO

Monaco was already a semi-independent state under the House of Grimaldi in Nostradamus' time. This general quatrain could refer to any disaster occurring to Monaco since then. The last line is particularly difficult to translate.

11

Les armes battre an ciel longue saison	The weapons fight in the sky for a long period; the tree fell in the middle of the city. The sacred branch cut, a sword opposite Tison, then the King Hadrie falls.
L'arbre au milieu de la cité tombé:	
Verbine,[3] rongne, glaive en face, Tison	
Lors le monarque d'Hadrie succombé.	

[1] *Monech*—Latin, *Moneceus* = Monaco.
[2] *croc*—(*a*) Latin, *croceus* = yellow. (*b*) O.F., *croquer* = to crunch. (*c*) Prov., *croc* = a hook.
[3] *verbine*—Latin, *verbene* = sacred branch.

Hadrie is one of Nostradamus' anagrams for Henri IV, which seems at first sight to clash with line one, which suggests a modern battle in the air. But apparently when Henri was assassinated by Ravaillac on 14th May 1610 according to Guynaud there appeared in the *Mercure Français* of 1619 the story of a ghostly army marching in the skies at the time of the killing. It may have been a similar phenomenon to the Angels of Mons. Henri is the tree chopped down in the centre of the city of Paris, and he is also the last of the direct Valois family tree, as Louis XIII was the son of his second wife Marie de' Medici. He is described as sacred because he was anointed at his coronation; he was actually stabbed with a knife in the rue Ferronnierre, not far from the corner of which runs the Rue Tison. Nostradamus gives us another obscure but graphic proper name which helps sort out the whole quatrain.

12

Par la tumeur de Heb, Po, Tag, Timbre & Rome[1]	Because of the overflow of the Ebro, Po, Tagus, Tiber and Rhone and by the lakes of Geneva and Arezzo the two great and chief cities of the Garonne taken, dead, drowned. Human booty divided.
Et par l'estang leman[2] *& Arentin*[3]	
Les deux grands chefs & citez de Garonne,	
Prins mors noyez. Partir humain butin.	

FLOOD

The flooding described in this quatrain is so vast that it covers Spain and Portugal (Ebro and Tagus), Italy (Po and Tiber) and France (Rhône). Lake Geneva is in Switzerland and Lake Trasimine is near Arezzo. The two chief cities of the Garonne are Bordeaux and Toulouse. There are other quatrains of this type predicting a vast general flood.

[1] *Rome*—Misprint for Rhône, although it may be the city that is intended.
[2] *leman*—Latin, *Lemannus* = Lake Geneva.
[3] *Arentin*—Latin, *Arentius* = now Arezzo.

Par fouldre en l'arche[1] or &	Through lightning in the box
argent fondu,	gold and silver are melted,
De deux captifs l'un l'autre	the two captives will devour
mangera:	each other. The greatest one
De la cité le plus grand estendu,	of the city stretched when the
Quend submergee la classe[2] nagera.	fleet travels under water.

SUBMARINE FLEET

The first two lines are probably alchemistic and Nostradamus is referring to a chemical process that would fuse the two metals together. Line three is very obscure; the fourth line certainly indicates a fleet of submarines although it is difficult to know whether the metal of the first two lines is linked with the ships as a weapon, or a separate process.

Par le rameau[3] du vaillant per-	Through the offspring of a
sonnage,	valiant personage, of weakened
De France infime, par le pere	France because of the unhappy
infelice:	father; honours, riches, labour
Honneurs, richesses, travail en son	in his old age, because he
vieil aage[4]	believed the counsel of an
Pour avoir creu le conseil d'homme	inexperienced man.
nice.[5]	

LOUIS XV AND FLEURY

Louis XV, son of the glorious Sun King, that valiant personage Louis XIV, caused the weakening of France. He came to the throne aged five, and the Duke of Orléans exerted total power during his Regency. France was in such a poor financial state that it led to her bankruptcy under John Law in 1721. The inexperienced man who brings trouble to the king, must be Fleury, tutor and priest who did not come to power until he was seventy-two in 1726. His policies helped the general unrest leading to the attempted assassination of Louis XV by Damiens in 1757.

[1] *arche*—Latin *arx* = box ark.
[2] *classe*—Latin, *classis* = fleet.
[3] *rameau*—literally branch.
[4] *aage*—O.F. spelling = age.
[5] *nice*—Romance = simple inexperienced.

Coeur, rigeur, gloire le regne changera,	The kingdom will change in heart, vigour and glory. On
De tous points contre ayant son adversaire,	all sides having its adversary opposed. Then through death
Lors France enfance par mort subjuguera,	a child will rule over France, the great Regent will then be
Un grand regent sera lors plus contraire.	very contrary.

LOUIS XV

This quatrain continues with the subject of Louis XV. Again we get a reference to the glory of the reign of Louis XIV (the great kingdom will change in glory etc.) and a reference to the Regent, Philippe, Duke of Orléans, who was the complete opposite both in public and private life, to his predecessor (*adversaire*). There has been no other male Regent of France since the publication of the Centuries. It is possible that in the words 'then through death a child will rule over France' there is a confirmation of popular opinion of the time which stated that both the Duke of Burgundy and the Duke of Bretagne, Louis XV's grandfather and father, had been poisoned by the Regent in order to obtain control over the throne.

Un prince Anglais Mars a son coeur de ciel,	An English prince, Mars has his heart in the heavens, will
Voudra poursuivre sa fortune pro-spere:	wish to follow his prospering fortune. In two duels, one will
Des deux duelles l'un percera le fiel,	pierce him in the gall bladder,
Hai de lui, bien aimé de sa mere.	hated by him, but well loved by his mother.

A quatrain which seems unfulfilled to date. There have been very few English princes, and even the Scottish ones do not satisfy this prediction. It seems unlikely that duels will take place in the future so this is probably a failure.

Mont Aventine brusler nuict sera veu,	Mount Aventine will be seen burning at night, the sky in Flanders will be suddenly obscured. When the King drives out his nephew their churchmen will commit scandals.
Le ciel obscur tout à un coup en Flandres:	
Quand le monarque chassera son nepveu,	
Leurs gens à Eglise commettront les esclandres.	

Mount Aventine is one of the seven hills of Rome and therefore probably stands for the city itself. The sudden obscurity of the sky in Flanders may mean an eclipse of the sun, but I am unable to link it with a king driving out his nephew plus atrocities being committed in the Church. It sounds vaguely Napoleonic but Napoleon did not actually drive out his nephew, Napoleon III, however, he was driven out from Holland as a child when his father, King Louis, abdicated. The church scandals would relate to the Cult of Reason during the Revolutionary excesses. Presumably the first line may refer to Napoleon I's troops and their successful sack of Rome?

Apres la pluie laict assez longuette	After the rather long milky rain, several places in Reims will be touched by lightning. Oh what a bloody battle is approaching them, fathers and sons' kings will not dare approach.
En plusieurs lieux de Reims le ciel touché:	
O quel conflict de sang pres d'eux s'appreste,	
Peres & fils Rois n'oseront approcher.	

The reference to a rain of milk is puzzling. It also occurs in the following quatrain, III. 19.

En Luques sant & laict viendra plouvoir,	In Lucca it will come to rain blood and milk, shortly before a change of governor. Great plague and war, famine and drought will be seen, far from where the prince and ruler dies.
Un peu devant changement de preteur:[1]	
Grand peste & guerre, faim & soif fera voir.	
Loing où mourra leur Prince recteur.[2]	

[1] *preteur*—Latin, *praetor* = governor.
[2] *recteur*—Latin = leader, governor, instructor, ruler.

Lucca was a duchy between Tuscany and Modena. It is impossible to try and identify the governor and the prince. Apart from the rain of milk we now also have a rain of blood, a favourite of Roman historians, but which can occur when red dust clouds meet rain clouds and the resultant drops fall red coloured. After the atomic bombs were dropped in 1945 the rain fell black, full of atomic dust.

20

Par les contrees du grand fleuve Bethique[1]	Through the lands of the great river Guadalquivir far from
Loing d'Ibere[2] *au royaume de Grenade:*[3]	Spain to the kingdom of Grenada; the cross spurned by
Croix repoussees par gens Mahometiques,	the Mohammedans, a man from Cordova will betray his
Un de Cordube trahira la contrade.[4]	country.

SPAIN

Grenada, the last Moorish outpost of Iberia, North Eastern Spain, was conquered in 1492. It is south of the Guadalquivir river. The Jews in this area were allowed to remain after the conquest provided they accepted Christianity. In 1610, the remainder of the Jewish colony were accused of lack of sincerity in their religious practices and turned out of Spain by Philip II, despite the fact that a contract had been drawn up by Ferdinand and Isabella of Spain with Gonsalvo Fernandez de *Cordova* who helped negotiate the treaty. Here is another proper name produced by Nostradamus.

21

Au Crustamin[5] *par mer Hadriatique,*	Near the (river) Conca by the Adriatic sea will appear an
Apparoistra un horrible poisson	horrible fish with human fea-
De face humaine & la fin[6] *aquatique,*	tures and an aquatic purpose, it will be caught without the
Qui se prendra dehors de l'amacon.	hook.

[1] *Bethique*—Latin, *Baetis* = Guadalquivir river.
[2] *Ibere*—Greek for Spaniards around river Ebro.
[3] *Grenada*—Southern Spain.
[4] *contrade*—Provençal = country.
[5] *Crustamin*—Latin, *Crustumius* flows into the Adriatic, now called river Conca.
[6] *fin*—Either means end or purpose.

Garencières (1672) says in his commentary that a mermaid-like creature, perhaps a manatee or dugong was seen near Rome in 1523 and by Rondeletius in 1531. But Edgar Leoni states in his commentary that the records of Cattolica, where the Conca flows into the Adriatic, shows no such event. Even Garencières seems to have been carried away by hearsay events in this case.

22

Six jours l'assaut devant cité donné:	Six days the assault is made in front of the city. It will be freed in a strong and bitter fight. Three will hand it over, and to them pardon, to the rest fire and bloody slaughter and slashing.
Livrée sera forte & aspre bataille:	
Trois la rendront & à eux pardonné,	
Le reste à feu & sang tranche traille.	

Too general to be specifically identified.

23

Si France passes entre mer ligustique,[1]	If, France, you cross the Ligurian sea, you will find yourself besieged among islands and seas. Mahomet against you, more so the Adriatic, you will gnaw the bones of horses and asses.
Tu te verras en isles & mers enclos:	
Mahommet contraire, plus mer Hadriatique,	
Cheveux & d'Asnes tu rongeras les os.	

Another general prediction of disaster for contemporary France, particularly where the Ottoman Empire was concerned.

24

De l'entreprinse grande confusion,	From the expedition great confusion, immense loss of men and treasure. You must never attempt to expand there again, France, try to remember my prediction.
Parte de gens, tresor innumerable:	
Tu n'y dois faire encore tension[2]	
France à mon dire fais que sois recordable.[3]	

This is almost certainly a continuation of the warnings contained in the preceding verse.

[1] *ligustique*—Latin, *ligusticus* = Ligurian.
[2] *tension*—Latin, *tensio* = extension.
[3] *recordable*—O.F. = memorable.

Qui au Royaume Navarrois parviendra,
Quand de Sicile & Naples seront
joints:
Bigore & Landres par Foix loron
tiendra,
D'un qui d'Espaigne sera par trop
conjoint.

He who attains the kingdom of Navarre when Sicily and Naples are allies; he will hold Bigorre and Landes through Foix and Oloron from one who will be too strongly allied with Spain.

HENRI IV

The man who inherits Navarre is Henri IV; Sicily and Naples were joined together sporadically for centuries but the title was only formalized three times, first by Philip of Spain when he was due to marry Mary Tudor in 1554, later by Joseph Buonaparte and Joachim Murat in the 19th Century. Henri became king of Navarre in 1562 and king of France in 1594. All the places mentioned in line 3 are in Navarre, and Bigorre has a double meaning as Bigorro was the rallying cry of the Huguenot armies. The person too strongly allied with Spain from whom Henri IV keeps Navarre, is presumably his cousin Elizabeth, daughter of Henri II who married Philip of Spain in 1558. A rather generalized quatrain in many ways.

26

Des Rois & Princes dresseront
simulacres,
Augures, cruez eslueuz aruspices:[1]
Corne, victime dorée, & d'azur,
d'acre,
Interpretez seront les extipices.[2]

They will raise up idols of kings and princes, augurers and hollow priests elevated. A victim, its horns gilded with gold, azure, dazzling, the entrails will be interpreted.

27

Prince libinique puissant en Occident,
François d'Arabe viendra tant
enflammer,
Scavans aux lettres sera conde-
scendant,
La langue Arabe en François
translater.

The Libyan prince will be powerful in the West, the French will become so enamoured of Arabia; learned in letters he will condescend to translate the Arab Language into French.

[1] aruspices = auspices.
[2] extispicus = soothsayer, inspector of animal's entrails.

Nostradamus seems to use the term Libyan very loosely for North Africa in general, and of course the French made great use of the Barbary corsairs of Tunis and Algeria in their fight against the Turks. The literature line is puzzling—the first French Arabic dictionary came out in 1505 and one cannot think of any other great work of literary merit that was translated under these conditions.

28

De ferre faible & pauvre paren-tele,[1]	One possessing few lands and of poor parentage through efforts and peace will attain to the empire. For a long time a young woman shall reign, never has a worse influence remained on the kingdom.
Par bout & paix parviendra dans l'Empire:	
Long temps regner une jeune femelle,	
Qu'oncques en regne n'en survint un pire.	

ELIZABETH OF ENGLAND, 1558, AND HENRI OF NAVARRE, 1594

This is regarded by most commentators as a 'split' quatrain referring to two different people. The first two lines refer to Henri of Navarre whose court was renowned for its poverty and simplicity. Elizabeth and Henri only reigned contemporaneously between the years of 1594 and 1601, but Elizabeth's confirmation of Protestantism would rate the epithet 'worse influence' from the pro-Catholic Nostradamus. Elizabeth ruled for nearly half a century which was an extremely protracted reign for that period. However, the first two lines could perhaps refer to the lowly origin of Anne Boleyn, Elizabeth's mother, and the poverty to which she was subjected to as a child.

29

Les deux nepveux en divers lieux nourris:	Two nephews will be brought up in different places, a naval battle, fathers fallen to the ground. They will be greatly elevated by making war, to avenge their injury, the enemies overcome.
Navale pugne,[2] terre peres tombez:	
Viendront si haut esluuez enguer-ris,[3]	
Venger l'injure ennemis succombez.	

[1] parentele—O.F. = parentage.
[2] pugne—Latin, pugna = battle.
[3] enguerroier—O.F. = to make war.

The nephews mentioned here may be two of one of the many Popes, or alternatively the nephews of the then Constable of France, Anne de Montmorency, Coligny, Chatillon and d'Andelot; however there is nothing to show which of them were intended here.

30

Celui qu'en luitte & fer au faict bellique,	He who in the struggle with a weapon in deed of war will have carried off the prize from one greater than he; At night six will bring harm to his bed, naked without his armour he will suddenly be surprised.
Aura porté plus grand que lui le prix:	
De nuict au lict six lui feront la pique,	
Nud sans harnois subit sera surprins.	

COUNT OF MONTGOMERY, 1574

The Count of Montgomery, Captain of Henri II's Scottish Guard, who unwittingly killed his king in a friendly joust, is the hero of this quatrain. Although Henri had pardoned him, Catherine demanded Montgomery's life, determined to avenge her husband. He fled to England as a Huguenot and came back to Normandy to lead the rebelling Protestants. After various successes, he was surrounded by the Marshal de Matignon at Domfront and compelled to yield. Under the terms of surrender his life was to be spared but Catherine secretly sent six men of the royal guard to arrest him. He was taken in his bedroom on 27th May 1574 and sent to the Conciergerie at Catherine's command. Note that Nostradamus does not mention his death, only the circumstances of his capture.

31

Aux champs de Mede, d'Arabe & d'Armenie,	On the (battle)fields of Media, Arabia and Armenia, two great armies will assemble three times; near the border of Araxum the establishment of great Suliman will fall to the ground.
Deux grans copies[1] trois fois s'assembleront:	
Pres du rivage d'Araxes la mesgnie,[2]	
Du grand Soliman en ierre tomberant.	

LEPANTO, 1571

A great deal has been written about this quatrain referring it to battles which had already occurred during Nostradamus' life-

[1] *copies*—Latin, *copiae* = forces.
  mesgnie—O.F. = household, establishment.

time, in particular to the Battle of Araxes of 1514 or to the fighting with the Turks in Armenia and Media—but not Arabia—which continued until the general peace of 1555. It appears more probable that James Laver's interpretation is the correct one. The Battle of Lepanto, fought in 1571 in which Don John of Austria crushed Selim II, the son of Soliman (part of his establishment). Lepanto was fought off Cape Papa, then known as Cape Araxum, in the Mediterranean.

32

Le grand sepulchre du peuple Aquitanique,	The huge grave for the French people will approach from the
S'approchera aupres de la Toscane:	direction of Italy. When war is
Quand Mars sera pres du coing Germanique,	near the German corner and
Et au terroir de la gent Mantuane.	in the lands of the Italian people.

SECOND WORLD WAR

A general quatrain, but one which can best be applied to the Second World War because of Nostradamus' insistence on the involvement of Italy and Germany in a war that would kill many Frenchmen. Aquitaine stands for France, as do Tuscany and Mantua for Italy.

33

En la cité où le loup entrera,	Into the city which the wolf
Bien pres de là les ennemis seront:	will enter, the enemies will be
Copie estrange grand pays gastera,	very close by; A foreign army
Aux murs & Alpes les amis passeront.	will devastate the great country, the friends will pass the walls and Alps.

A quatrain involving wars between Italy and France with a third friendly party, possibly crossing the Alps?

34

Quand le deffaut du Soleil lors sera.	Then when the eclipse of the
Sur le plain jour le monstre sera veu:	sun will be in broad daylight the monster will be seen. It will
Tout autrement on l'interpretera,	be interpreted quite differently;
Cherté n'a garde mil n'y aura pourveu.	they will not care about expense, none will have provided for it.

This quatrain is almost impossible to interpret because we are given no date for the eclipse of the sun, other than the coming of a monster which may be interpreted literally or metaphorically. The last line indicates an unexpected famine or drought for which no provision will have been made.

35

Du plus profond de l'Occident d'Europe
De pauvres gens un jeune enfant naistra:
Qui par sa langue seduira grande troupe,
Son bruit au regne d'Orient plus croistra.

In the deepest part of Western Europe a child will be born of poor family, who by his speech will entice many peoples. His reputation will grow even greater in the Kingdom of the East.

HITLER OR NAPOLEON

This is an excellent example of the ambiguous quatrain, one that seems to apply equally satisfactorily to two distinct historical events, here separated in time by over a century. Perhaps this is an example of history repeating itself? It seems that throughout history certain situations have recurred which appear very similar when described only in general terms. Therefore we may take this quatrain as describing either Hitler or Napoleon. I prefer the former interpretation as Austria is better described as in deepest Europe, i.e. almost at the limits of the continent; Corsica is less apt in this context although it is near the borders of Africa; one must translate *profond* as lowest, if Corsica is preferred. Hitler came of lowly stock, as did Napoleon. Both were renowned for their personal magnetism and their famous speeches to their armies. Where Hitler is concerned we can see examples of this in the Nuremberg rallies on contemporary films. The crowd were completely in his hand. It is the last line which convinces me that the German leader is described here. The kingdom of the East, Japan, joined Hitler as an ally and his reputation there was obviously held in great esteem. As far as Napoleon was concerned the East means the Middle East, Egypt, and refers to the fact that Napoleon came to power on the Coup d'État on the 18th Brumaire 1798, on his return to France.

Enseveli non mort apopletique,	Burned, apoplectic but not
Sera trouvé avoir les mains man-	dead, he will be found to have
gees:	his hands gnawed; when the
Quand la cité damnera l'heretique,	city will condemn the heretic
Qu'avoit leurs loix se leur sembloit	who, it seemed to them, had
changees.	changed their laws.

The word apoplectic obviously indicates a person in a state of
coma or stroke during which he is buried, believed dead. There
are several medical cases on record of this having occurred. Presumably the hands of the wretched person are chewed by rats
before he returns to consciousness, or bleed as he struggled to get
out of the coffin. This event is meant to occur when a city revolts
against its leader, but this is unfortunately not specific enough to
identify it.

Avant l'assaut l'oraison[1] pro-	Before the assault a speech is
noncee,	proclaimed; Milan, deceived
Milan prins d'aigle par embusches	by the ambush is captured by
decevez:	the Eagle. The ancient walls
Muraille antique par canons enfon-	are breached by cannon; in fire
cee,	and blood few receive quarter.
Par feu & sang à mercy peu	
receus.	

NAPOLEON DURING THE ITALIAN CAMPAIGN, 1796

Here again, Napoleon I is described as the Eagle, the rapacious
bird of prey. He took Milan twice, first on 15th May 1796, and
then on 2nd June 1800. However, the first attack is referred to
here, when Napoleon made that famous speech to his troops before
the battle which echoed around Europe. 'Soldiers, you are ill-fed
and half-naked. The government owes you much but can do
nothing for you . . . Soldiers of Italy, are you wanting in courage?'
This speech so rallied his men that the defending Austrians
retired without trying to hold the city. The last two lines may refer
to the following battle of Pavia whose inhabitants rose up against
the French. The city walls were bombarded and breached and the
city totally sacked.

[1] *oraison* = (a) Speech. (b) Prayer.

La gent Gauloise & nation estrange,	The French people and a foreign nation beyond the mountains will be captured, killed and overcome. In a different month, near harvest time, by the Lords they will be put back into order.
Outre les monts, morts prins & profligez:	
Au mois contraire & proche de vendage,[1]	
Par les Seigneurs en accord redigez.[2]	

This is accepted by Jaubert as describing the peace declared between the Pope and the Spanish in September 1557, which could be either harvest time itself, or a month later, the grape harvest. In this peace the interests of the troops of the Duke de Guise belonging to the Pope, who were mainly French and Swiss, were completely ignored.

Les sept en trois mois en concorde,	The seven are in agreement for three months to subjugate the Apennines. But the storm and the cowardly Ligurian destroy them in sudden ruin.
Pour subjuguer des Alpes Appenines:	
Mais la tempeste & Ligure couarde,	
Les profligent en subites ruines.	

This quatrain seems to refer to one of the leagues of 16th-Century Italy, probably the Holy League of 1576, and it implies that their agreement is upset by Genoa (Liguria).

Le grand theatre se viendra se redresser,	The great theatre will be raised up again, the dice thrown and the nets already cast. The great one who tolls the death knell will become too tired, destroyed by bows split a long time ago.
Les des jettez & les rets ja tendus:	
Trop le premier en glaz viendra lasser,	
Par ares prostrais[3] *de long temps ja fendus.*	

The second line referring to the dice and the nets is reminiscent of Ancient Rome but the quatrain remains completely obscure.

[1] *vendage* = either harvest time, or the time of the vintage.
[2] Alternative translation. Drafted in agreement?
[3] *prostrais*—Latin, *prostratus* = destroyed, ruined.

Bossu sera esleu par le conseil,
Plus hideux monstre en terre n'apperceu,
Le coup[1] voulant[2] crevera l'oeil,
Le traitre au Roi pour fidelle reçu.

The hunchback will be elected by the counsel, a more hideous monster on earth was never seen. The deliberate shot will pierce his eye, the traitor whom the king received as loyal.

DEATH OF LOUIS DE CONDÉ. 13th MARCH, 1569

This quatrain is one of Nostradamus' more notable successes and had been recognized by many commentators. Prince Louis de Condé was a hunchback and was proclaimed chief of the Huguenot Assembly in 1560. He was reconciled with the king several times (and made a public confession of his loyalty to Charles IX in 1560 and 1562) but continued to plot against him. He was eventually taken at the battle of Jarnac, 13th March 1569, and was deliberately shot by Montesquiou in the head, although a prisoner.

42

L'enfant naistra à deux dents en la gorge,
Pierres en Tuscie par pluie tomberont:
Peu d'ans apres ne sera bled ni orge,
Pour saouler ceux qui de faim failliront.

The child will be born with two teeth in his mouth; stones will fall like his rain in Tuscany. A few years later there will be neither wheat nor barley, to satisfy those who will weaken from hunger.

FAMINE

There is also a reference to famine and a person born with two teeth already formed in II. 7. Possibly it could refer to Louis XIV who reputedly was born with some of his teeth fully grown, as there were local famines during his reign?

43

Gens d'alentour de Tarn Loth, & Garonne,
Gardez les monts Apennines passer:
Vostre tombeau pres de Rome & d'Anconne,
Le noir poil crespe fera trophee dresser.

People from around the Tarn, Lot and Garonne, beware of crossing the Apennine mountains. Your tomb is near Rome and Ancona; the man with the dark, curly hair will set up a trophy.

---

[1] *coup* = (a) Blow. (b) Shot.
[2] *voulant* = deliberate. Variant, *volant* = flying.

There are two other references to the elusive *noir poil crespu* in I. 74, and II. 79, if one disregards the Aenobarbe quatrains. The Lot and Tarn are both tributaries of the Garonne, and Ancona is situated on the eastern coast of central Italy. In the two earlier quatrains the blackbeard applied very aptly to the Turks but they had no hold on central Italy which proved disastrous to the French.

44

Quand l'animal à l'homme domestique,	When the animal tamed by man begins to speak after
Apres grands peines & sauts viendra parler,	great efforts and difficulty, the lightning so harmful to the rod
De fouldre à vierge[1] sera si malefique,	will be taken from the earth and suspended in the air.
De terre prinse & suspendue en l'air.	

WIRELESS COMMUNICATION AND ELECTRICITY

It is possible that Nostradamus is trying to describe wireless communication in this quatrain. He often used the word 'animal' to describe machines which have some of the qualities of life, i.e. that move or make a noise. Perhaps the tamed animal here is the discovery of the sound waves and the wireless as a form of communication. The lightning that is hostile to the rod, implies that the rod is either a radio mast sending out electric charges, or that it is being threatened by some electrical force, and the mast contains this force in the air. Some forms of electrical charges during storms go from the earth to the sky, although it is normally the other way round. One could alternatively interpret the last two lines as implying that the rod is a lightning conductor. Franklin discovered electricity by means of iron conducting rods in 1752, nearly two hundred years later.

45

Les cinq estranges entrez dedans le temple	The five foreigners having entered the temple; their blood
Leur sang viendra la terre prophaner:	will desecrate the land. The example made of the Toulous-
Aux Tholousains sera bien dur example,	ians will be very hard, made by the man who comes to wipe
D'un qui viendra les lois exterminer.	out their laws.

[1] *vierge*—O.F. spelling; *verge* = rod or wand.

In this quatrain the five strangers are understood to be the five great powers who allied against Napoleonic France, England, Austria, Russia, Spain and Prussia. France is the land desecrated by their invasion. The battle of Toulouse fought by Wellington was very brutal and there were great casualties. The man who wipes out the laws is again the Allied Powers because they bring with them the end of Napoleon's reign.

46

Le ciel (de Plancus la cité) nous presage,	The heavens foretell, concerning the city of Lyons by means of clear skies and fixed stars, that suddenly the time of change approaches, neither for its good nor evil fortune.
Par clers insignes & par estoilles fixes:	
Que de son change subit s'aproche l'aage,	
Ne pour son bien ne pour ses malefices.	

Plancus is Lyons, so called after its foundation by Lucius Munatius Plancus in 43 BC. The quatrain is very general and similar to II. 83 in its prediction of a gloomy future.

47

Le vieux monarque dechassé de son regne	The old king chased out of his realm will go to seek help from the people of the East: For fear of the crosses he will fold his banner; he will travel to Mitylene by land and sea.
Aux Orients son secours ira querre:	
Pour peur des croix ployera son enseigne,	
En Mitylene ira par port & par terre.	

A specific quatrain which fits no event to date. An old king chased from his kingdom will seek aid from the East. He will fold his banner for fear of the cross and take refuge in Greece or on the island of Lesbos. Could the crosses possibly refer to the swastika rather than the Christian cross? It is a possibility.

Sept cens captifs estachez rude- *ment,* *Pour la moitié meurtrir, donné le* *sort:* *Le proche espoir viendra si prompte-* *ment,* *Mais non si tost qu'une quinziesme* *mort.*	Seven hundred captives roughly bound, the lots are drawn for half to be murdered; sudden hope will come so quickly, but not fast enough for about fifteen dead.

No definite information has come to light about this very general quatrain, despite the specific numbers of prisoners and dead involved.

Regne Gaulois tu seras bien changé, *En lieu estrange est translaté* *l'empire:* *En autres moeurs & lois seras* *rangé,* *Roan, & Chartres te feront bien* *du pire.*	Kingdom of France you will be greatly changed, the Empire expands to foreign places. You will be set up with other laws and customs; Rouen and Chartres will do their worst towards you.

FRANCE AS AN EMPIRE AND ITS FUTURE
This is important because Nostradamus here calls France an Empire rather than a kingdom and clearly sees a change in the future from one form of ruler to another. Rouen is in Normandy, Chartres in the Orléanais and it is implied that possible future trouble for France will come from these places. The last part of this prophecy may not yet be completed.

La republique de la grande cité, *A grand rigeur ne voudra consentir:* *Roi sortir hors par trompette cité.* *L'eschelle ay mur, la cité repentir.*	The people's government of the great city will not consent to severe repression. The king, summoned by trumpets to leave the city, the ladder at the wall, the city will repent.

JOURNÉE DES BARRICADES. 12th MAY 1588
The Leaguers in France took Paris into their power after the Day of the Barricades when the people drove out the King, Henri III, and his followers. Henri retaliated by joining up with Henri of

Navarre at St. Cloud and resolved to besiege Paris. Before he could do this he was assassinated by Jacques Clément.

51

Paris conjure un grand meurtre commettre,	Paris conspires to commit a great murder. Blois will ensure that it is fully carried out. The people of Orléans will want to replace their leader; Angers, Troyes and Langres will do them a disservice.
Blois le fera sortir en plain effect:	
Ceux d'Orleans voudront leur chef remettre,	
Angiers, Troye, Langres leur feront un meffait.	

THE MURDERS OF THE DUKE DE GUISE AND HIS BROTHER, 1588

Henri III murdered the two brothers de Guise on 23rd December 1588. He planned the assassination in Paris and it was carried out at Blois whence the Duke de Guise had fled. He was killed by the king's bodyguard outside the royal appartment and the Cardinal, his brother, was killed the next day. At the same period the town of Orléans rose up against the governor, Balzac d'Entragues, and Charles de Lorraine, a prominent Leaguer and supporter of the Guise cause, took over. The line is inaccurate; both Angers and Langres allied themselves with the League and Troyes remained neutral.

52

En la campaigne sera si longue pluie,	In Campania there will be rain for so long and such a great drought in Apulia; the cock will see the Eagle, its wing badly finished put into difficulties by the Lion.
Et en la Pouille si grand siccité:	
Coq verra l'Aigle, l'aesle mal accompli	
Par Lyon mise sera en extremité.	

The Cock stands for France; it was the emblem both of the Gauls and of the French Revolutionaries. The Eagle may refer either to the Hapsburg Empire or to Napoleon. If the latter version is acceptable then the Lion stands for Britain who causes Napoleon's downfall. The rain and drought are not recorded but may possibly be metaphorical references to Napoleon's conquest of Italy.

Quand le plus grand emportera le pris,	When the greatest man carries off the prize of Nuremburg,
De Nuremberg, d'Auspourg & ceux de Basle	of Ausburg and those of Basle,
Par Agrippine[1] chef Frankfort repris:	Frankfurt retaken by the leader of Cologne: they will go
Traverseront par Flamant jusqu'au Gale.	through Flanders as far as France.

The only factor the places mentioned have in common is that they are all part of the Holy Roman Empire. Did Nostradamus think that after a new Emperor was elected France would be invaded from the North through Belgium? It is just possible that this quatrain connects with Hitler through the Nuremburg rallies. At that time he became the leader of Germany and did invade France from the North.

L'un des plus grands fuira aux Espaignes	One of the great men will flee to Spain which will bleed with
Qu'en longue playe apres viendra saigner:	a great wound thereafter. Troops will pass over the high
Passant copies par les hautes montaignes,	mountains devastating everything, then he will reign in
Devastant tout & puis en paix regner.	peace.

GENERAL FRANCO AND THE CIVIL WAR IN SPAIN, 1936–9

In 1936 General Franco was exiled from Spain to the Canary Islands as military governor. He then flew (*fuira*) to Morocco and back to Spain to start the rebellion that led to the Spanish Civil War. The wound from which Spain suffered so much was the war, with its appalling casualties 611,000 men in all. The armies who crossed the Pyrenees, Spain's border, were the 50,000 Italians and 10,000 Germans who fought for Franco's Nationalist party, and the 20,000 Russian soldiers sent to support the Loyalist Republican army. It is ironic that after the Civil War Spain did, in a sense, remain in peace, in that she was neutral throughout the Second World War.

[1] *Agrippine*—Latin, *Colonia Agrippina* = Cologne.

En l'an qu'un oeil en France regnera,	In the year that France has a one-eyed king the court will be in very great trouble. The great man from Blois will kill his friend, the kingdom put into difficulty and double doubt.
La court sera à un bien facheux trouble:	
Le grand de Blois son ami tuera,	
Le regne mis en mal & doubte double.	

THE DEATH OF HENRI II AND THE REIGN OF HENRI III, 1559–89

This famous quatrain was understood by Nostradamus' contemporaries. The one-eyed king was Henri II killed in the duel of 1559 (see I. 35) being wounded in the eye by Montgomery and dying after ten days of agony. The last two lines describe his son Henri III, who assassinates the de Guise brothers at Blois and the general civil unrest which followed this action. *Doubte double* probably refers to the two factions, the Leaguers and the Royalists.

56

Montauban, Nismes, Avignon & Besier,	Montauban, Nîmes, Avignon and Béziers, plague, lightning and hail at the end of March. Of the bridge at Paris, the wall at Lyons and Montpellier, since six hundred and seven score three pairs.
Peste tonnere & gresle à fin de Mars:[1]	
De Paris pont, Lyon mur, Montpellier,	
Depuis six cens & sept vingts trois pars.[2]	

The dating of this verse from the last line, see footnote, is extremely difficult. All the towns in the first line are in Southern France, but there does not seem to be much connection between the bridge of Paris and the walls of Lyons.

[1] Or in the wake of war.
[2] There are several possible readings for this. As above, which is 746 i.e. 1746 or 2301 (1555 plus 746) or 'six hundred and seven twenty three pairs' which gives 1653, or 2208 if added to 1555.

Sept fois changer verrez gent Britannique	Seven times you will see the British nation change, dyed in
Taintz en sang en deux cents nonante an:	blood for two hundred and ninety years. Not at all free
Franche non point par appuy Germanique,	through German support, Aries fears for the protectorate of
Aries doubte son pole Bastarnien.	Poland.

BRITISH HISTORY 1603–1939

The great problem for this verse is to find the date from which to calculate the 290 years and the seven great changes which affect Britain. If the year 1603 is taken as the starting point, quite arbitrarily, the whole verse fits, including the last line which clearly links Poland (*Bastarnien*) with Britain in some manner connected with a war. Aries the first sign of the Zodiac rules the East. Nostradamus indicates that there will be a critical state of affairs in Poland at the same time as Britain faces a great crisis connected with Germany. It also implies that the royal family on the throne at that time will be the last British dynasty of any note.

1 1603. New Stuart Monarch, James I.
2 1649. Death of Charles I and declaration of a Republic.
3 1660. Restoration of the Stuarts in Charles II.
4 1689. Usurpment of Stuarts by William of Orange.
5 1702. Restoration of Stuarts under Queen Anne.
6 1714. Hanoverian accession to British throne under George I.
7 1939. Pronouncement of war after the German invasion of Poland.

Aupres du Rhin des Montaignes Noriques,	Near the Rhine from the Norican mountains will be
Naistra un grand de gens trop tard venu.	born a great man of the people, come too late. He will defend
Qui defendra Saurome & Pannoniques,	Poland and Hungary and they will never know what became
Qu'on ne sçaura qu'il sera devenu.	of him.

HITLER

Hitler was born in Noricum, that is Austria, and he was the son of simple parents. He came too late in Nostradamus' view because his type of Empire was outdated. The third line must be read as describing Hitler's motives, his so-called 'defensive' attacks on

Poland and Hungary to 'save' them from the Allies. The final line is interesting. Could Hitler possibly have escaped after all from the bunker at Berlin? Were the bodies found those of his mistress and himself? There has always been doubt about this question in many people's minds despite Hugh Trevor-Roper's very thorough research into the facts of Hitler's death at the end of the war.

59

Barbare empire par le tiers usurpé,	The barbarian empire is
Le plus grand part de son sang	usurped by a third, the greater
mettre à mort:	part of its people being put to
Par mort senile par lui le quart	death. The fourth man, senile,
frappé,	struck dead by his country, fears
Pour peur que le sang par le sang	lest the line of his blood be
ne soit mort.	dead.

THE FRENCH REVOLUTION. THE TIERS ÉTAT

The third is usually accepted as meaning the Tiers État of the French Revolution 1789, although one wonders why Nostradamus calls the Bourbons barbaric. There were also three Committees of Public Safety during the Reign of Terror, those of Danton, Robespierre and the Directoire. The fourth man is Napoleon who took over from the Directoire in 1799 and died a senile death, from old age, on Saint Helena. Napoleon always feared that his line would not be continued and made himself an hereditary monarch.

60

Par toute Asie grande proscription,	Throughout Asia there will be
Mesme en Mysie, Lysie, &	great proscription, also in
Pamphylie:	Mysia, Lycia and Pamphilia.
Sang versera par absolution,	Blood will flow because of the
D'un jeune noir[1] rempli de felonnie.	absolution of a young dark
	man, filled with evil doing.

The countries mentioned in line 2 are all to be found in Asia Minor which implies that Asia in line 1 is the East as we understand the word. The great proscription might describe China's military system very aptly—whereby everyone has to be in the army for a certain period of their lives—but the Eastern influence has not yet travelled to Asia Minor, that is Modern Turkey, Iran, Iraq, etc. It is probable that this quatrain has not yet been completed

---

[1] *noir* = (*a*) A young dark-haired man or a Negro. (*b*) The usual Nostradamus anagram for roi, king.

and the bloodshed and villainy of the last two lines have yet to come.

61

La grand band & secte crucigere,	The great following of the sect
Se dressera en Mesopotamie:	of the cross will arise in Meso-
Du proche fleuve compagnie legiere,	potamia. Light company of the
Que telle loi tiendra pour ennemie.	nearby river who will regard
	such a law as inimical.

The solution to this quatrain obviously lies in the identification of the *secte crucigere*. Did Nostradamus mean the Crusades or even the swastika, the *croix gammée,* as it was known in France. Mesopotamia is Iraq and the two rivers are the Tigris and the Euphrates. However some commentators insist that Mesopotamia stands for Paris between the rivers Seine et Marne and that this quatrain thus refers to the German occupation of France in 1940.

62

Proche del duero par mer Cyrrene close,	Near the Douro closed by the Cyrenian sea he will come to
Viendra percer les grands monts Pyrenées:	cross the great mountains of the Pyrenees. The shortest
La main plus courte & sa percee[1] gloze,[2]	hand and his opening noted he will take his followers to
A Carcassonne conduira ses menées.	Carcassonne.

The river Douro rises in the mountains around Burgos in Spain and the Cyrenian sea is the Mediterranean. Apparently some leader will come across Spain into France. The third line is practically untranslatable, see footnote, and the fourth could carry the second meaning 'He will hatch his plots at Carcassonne'. Perhaps by the shortest hand means that this leader crossed the Carcassonne by the shortest route?

63

Romain pouvoir sera du tout abas,	Roman power will be quite put
Son grand voisin imiter les vestiges:	down following the footsteps
Occultes haines civiles & debats,	of its great neighbour. Secret
Retarderont aux bouffons leurs folies.	hatreds and civil disputes will delay the crassness of these buffoons.

[1] *percee*—O.F., *perce* = stake pole, or opening.
[2] *gloze*—O. Provençal, *gloza* = commentary, notes.

This describes accurately the state of Italy under Mussolini and its relations with its great neighbour Hitlerian Germany after 1937, in whose footsteps Mussolini tried to follow. The name Mussolini literally means muslin maker—a craft regarded as the lowest of the low, and yet this man is dictator of Italy. The word 'buffoons' describes these two dictators horribly well with their histrionics and projects of Aryan purity and world domination. Hitler was certainly unbalanced and it is probable that Mussolini was also in his later years.

64

Le chef de Perse remplira grande Olchade,[1]
Classe Frireme contre gent Mahometique:
De Parthe, & Mede, & piller les Cyclades,
Repos long temps aux grand port Ionique.

The Persian leader will fill up great Spain. A fleet of triremes against the Mohammedans from Parthia and Media, he will pillage the Cyclades: then a long wait in the great Ionian harbour.

The trireme fleet is one with three banks of oars, probably Italian or Venetian. Parthia and Media are both parts of Persia, presumably they are the country of the invading leader who sacks the Greek islands of the Cyclades around Delos in the Aegean. The great harbour in which he shelters in the Ionian sea could be one of many—the sea lies between Greece and Sicily. It is unclear as to whether the trireme fleet is destroyed by the Persian before he retires to port or not.

65

Quand le sepulcre du grand Romain trouvé,
Le jour apres sera esleu Pontife:
Du Senat gueres il ne sera prouvé,
Empoisonné son sang au sacré scyphe.

When the tomb of the great Roman is found a pope will be elected the next day; he will not be approved of by the Senate, his blood poisonous in the sacred chalice.

THE TOMB OF ST. PETER AND A NEW POPE

This indicates that after the finding of a tomb, possibly that of St. Peter, a Pope will be elected who will turn out to be highly unsuitable, disliked by the Synod and possibly very wicked if his

[1] *Ochlades*—Latin = race living in Southern Spain near Cartagena.

blood was poison to the sacred chalice. Alternatively this line may indicate that this Pope will be poisoned. It also indicates that the tomb which was found recently and suggested to be that of St. Peter may not be so after all.

66

Le grand Baillif d'Orleans mis à mort,	The great Bailiff of Orleans is condemned to death by one
Sera par un de sang vindicatif.	vindictive for blood. He will
De mort merite ne mourra, ne par sort,	not die a deserved death, nor one by jurors; they will keep
Des pieds & mains mal le faisoit captif.	him captive inefficiently (bound) by his hands and feet.

JERÔME GRESLOT, 1562–9

The Bailiff of Orleans was an hereditary post for the Greslot family since 1530, so Nostradamus clearly intended it for someone of the family. A certain Jerôme Greslot was put to death having opened the gates of the town in April 1562, but he was not condemned to death for this until 1569. Presumably this is what Nostradamus means by his being inefficiently guarded, a gap of seven years between action and execution?

67

Une nouvelle secte de Philosophes,	A new set of philosophers
Mesprisant mort, or, honneurs & richesses:	despising death, gold, honours and riches will not be limited
Des monts Germains ne seront limitrophes,	by the mountains of Germany, in their following will be crowds
A les ensuivre auront appuy & presses.	and support.

PROTESTANT SECTS

Nostradamus is probably referring to the sects of the Anabaptists which had been almost wiped out around 1536, and it seems as though he is expecting a revival of these or some similar Protestant sects from the direction of Germany.

Peùple sans chef d'Espaigne &
d'Italie,
Morts, profligez[1] dedans le Cher-
ronesse:[2]
Leur dict[3] trahi par legiere folie,
Le sang nager par tout à la
traverse.

Leaderless people from Spain
and Italy dead and overcome
in the Peninsula. Their dictator betrayed by stupid folly,
blood will flow all about in the
area.

SPAIN AND ITALY IN THE 20th CENTURY

This is an interesting quatrain in that Nostradamus gives us the
two countries of Spain and Italy without their kings but with
dictators, so this verse definitely describes the 20th Century. The
dictator who is betrayed is Mussolini and a fascinating possibility
is that by *à la traverse*, he was referring to Mussolini's being
hanged. *La traverse* also means a cross roads, the usual place for a
gibbet and is a typical Nostradamus play on words.

69

Grand excercite conduict par jouven-
ceau,
Se viendra rendre aux mains des
ennemis:
Mais la vieillard nay au demi-
porceau,
Fera Chalon & Mascon estre amis.

The great army led by a young
man, will come to give itself
up into the enemy's hands. But
the old man born to the half
pig will make Châlon and
Mâcon into friends.

The half pig turns up also in I. 64 where Nostradamus describes
a man wearing an oxygen mask. Probably here it is derived from
the false etymology of Milan which according to legend derived
its name from the finding of an animal half sheep, half pig at its
foundation. Both Mâcon and Châlon are in Burgundy.

[1] *profliges*—Latin, *profligatus* = overcame.
[2] *Cherronesse*—From the Greek word meaning peninsula.
[3] *dict*—Alternative, *duict* = leader, but meaning remains unaltered.

La grande Bretagne comprinse l'Angleterre,	Great Britain, including England will be covered by very deep floods. The new league in Ausonne will make war so that they will ally against them.
Viendra par eaux si haut à inonder	
La ligue neufue d'Ausonne[1] fera guerre,	
Que contre eux ils se viendront bander.	

GREAT BRITAIN 1604–7

A very interesting quatrain. England did not become Great Britain until the unification of the English and Scottish thrones under James I. He assumed the title of King of Great Britain on 24th October 1604. In January 1607 there were great floods recorded around Bristol and in Somerset, the country being covered for an area of approximately ten leagues, or thirty miles. The last two lines then refer to the renewal of the Holy League in 1606, Ausonia standing for Italy.

Ceux dans les isles de longtemps assiegez,	Those besieged in the islands for a long time will take strong measures against their enemies. Those outside, overcome, will die of hunger, by such starvation as has never occurred before.
Prendront vigeur force contre ennemis:	
Ceux par dehors mors de faim profligez,	
En plus grand faim que jamais seront mis.	

BLOCKADE OF BRITAIN 1939–45. CONCENTRATION CAMPS

The blockading of Britain by the German navy during the Second World War is vividly portrayed in this verse, as are the strong countermeasures taken by her, described in line 2, which opened the Atlantic routes for supplies. Britain apparently never had more than six weeks of food supplies in the country at one time, and all that was strictly rationed. The two final lines indicate that while the British islanders did not starve there was great famine abroad. This refers to Europe and to the appalling concentration and labour camps of the Nazi régime where starvation was a matter of

[1] *Ausonne* = Ausonia. Southern Italy, especially Naples but also used poetically for the whole country.

policy and a convenient means of killing off those millions who did not go to the gas chambers.

72

Le bon vieillard tout vif enseveli,
Pres du grand fleuve par fausse souspeçon:
Le nouveau vieux de richesse ennobli,
Prins a chemin tout l'or de la rançon.

The good old man is buried while still alive, near a great river through false suspicion. The newcomer is old, ennobled by wealth, having taken all the ransom gold on the way.

The theme of someone being buried alive is also found in III. 36. but both quatrains are very obscure.

73

Quand dans la regne parviendra la boiteux,
Competiteur aura proche bastard:
Lui & le regne viendront si fort roigneux,
Qu'ains qu'il guerisse son faict sera bien tard.

When the lame man comes into the kingdom, a bastard, close to him will compete with him. Both he and the kingdom will be greatly trimmed before he recovers, so that his action will be too late.

THE DUKE OF BORDEAUX, 1820–71

This is an excellent quatrain full of interesting facts. The Duke of Bordeaux was the heir of Charles X of France. He became lame as the result of a riding accident in 1841. His close competitor was the Count Paris, who was the illegal pretender to the throne. The trimming away of the kingdom refers to the Franco-Prussian war, so that by the time the Duke came to an agreement with the French they had declared the Third Republic and would not accept his terms, and he died in exile, as did the Count of Paris.

74

Naples, Florence, Favence & Imole,
Seront en termes de telle fascherie:
Que pour complaire aux malheureux de Nolle
Plainct d'avoir faict à son chef moquerie.

Naples, Florence, Faenza and Imola will be on terms of such disagreement that to comply with the wretches of Nola they complain that they had mocked its chief.

Nothing can be made of this quatrain. Faenza and Imola were in the Papal States; Florence, the capital of Tuscany, and Naples of the Two Sicilies. Nola is some eighteen miles East of Naples.

75

Pau, Verone, Vicence, Sarragousse,	Pau, Verona, Vicenza, Saragossa, swords dripping with blood from distant lands. A very great plague will come with the great shell, relief near, but the remedies far away.
De glaives loings terroirs de sang humides.	
Peste si grance viendra à la grand gousse,[1]	
Proche secours, & bien loing les remedes.	

CHEMICAL WARFARE IN EUROPE

The cities here come from France, Italy and Spain, and Nostradamus implies that they will be invaded, possibly by the man from the East of the other quatrains. The third line is uncomfortably close to chemical warfare and perhaps the near relief is death, since help is far away.

76

En Germanie naistront diverses sectes,	Various sects will arise in Germany which will come near to a happy paganism. The heart captive, the returns small, they will return to pay the true tithe.
S'approchant fort de l'heureux paganisme,	
Le coeur captif & petites receptes,	
Feront retour à payer le vrai disme.	

PROTESTANT SECTS, 16th CENTURY

This is another of Nostradamus's obsessions, the many Lutheran, Anabaptist and Calvinist sects that were springing up in Northern Europe throughout the 16th Century. He seems to imply in the last line that they will return to the true faith, Catholicism, which hardly seems likely at the present.

77

Le tiers climat sous Aries comprins,	The third climate included under Aries, in the year 1727 in October the king of Persia, captured by those of Egypt: battle, death, loss: great shame to the cross.
L'an mil sept cens vingt & sept en Octobre:	
Le Roy de Perse par ceux d'Egypte prins;	
Conflit, mort, perte: à la croix grand approbre.	

[1] *gousse* = shell, scab, husk.

Here is a quatrain with not only the year, but the actual month and place! Nostradamus must have overlooked it when he went through the quatrains to make them more difficult to interpret. It is quite correct. In October 1727 a peace was concluded between the Turks and the Persians. Egypt belonged to the Ottoman Empire and stands for the Turks. The loss to Christianity is explained by the fact that the Shah Ashraf, in return for the recognition of his dynasty, gave the lands of Emvan, Tauris and Hamadan to the Turks and recognized the Sultan as legitimate successor to the Caliph. The Ottoman power continued in strength until this century, and no more Crusades were ever raised by the Christians.

78

Le chef d'Escosse avec six d'Alemaigne,	The leader from Scotland with six Germans will be captured by Eastern seamen. They will pass Gibraltar and Spain presented in Persia to the new dreadful king.
Par gens de mer Orienteaux captif:	
Traverseront le Calpre & Espaigne,	
Present en Perse au nouveau Roy craintif.	

79

L'ordre fatal sempiternal par chaisne,	The fatal and eternal order of the cycle will turn in due order. The chains of Marseilles will be broken, the city taken and the enemy at the same time.
Viendra tourner par ordre consequent:	
Du port Phocen[1] sera rompu la chaisne,	
La cite prinse, l'ennemi quant & quant.	

The first two lines are astrological and extremely obscure making it impossible to date the downfall of Marseilles.

80

Du regne Anglois l'indigne dechassé,	The unworthy man is chased out of the English kingdom. The counsellor through anger will be burnt. His followers will stoop to such depths that the pretender will almost be received.
Le conseiller par ire mis à feu:	
Ses adhera iront si bas tracer,	
Que le batard sera demi receux.	

[1] Phocen = Marseilles, after the Phocenses who founded the city.

Charles lost his kingdom mainly due to his own behaviour and irresponsibility towards Parliament. Of his counsellors Stafford was beheaded and Archbishop Laud burnt for treachery, the former in 1641, and the latter in 1645. His followers who stooped so low were the Scots who sold the king back to Parliament in 1646. The Pretender, or bastard, who is almost received in the kingdom is Oliver Cromwell, a man who has no true right to rule and who becomes Lord Protector, not king.

81

Le grand crier sans honte audacieux,	The great speechmaker, shame-
Sera esleu gouverneur de l'armee:	less and bold will be elected
La hardiesse de son contentieux,	governor of the army. The
Le pont rompu cité de peur pasmee.	boldness of his contention, the
	broken bridge, the city faint
	from fear.

PONTEFRACT AND CROMWELL

The key to this quatrain lies in the broken bridge. If one can accept this as Pontefract from the Latin pons, a bridge, fractus, broken, then we have a description of this town which held out for Charles I and suffered two severe sieges during the Civil War. The speechmaker who takes over the army is Cromwell, for whom Nostradamus has little liking, as is apparent in other quatrains.

82

Friens, Antibor, villes autour de Nice,	Frejus, Antibes, the towns around Nice will be greatly
Seront vastees fort par mer & par terre:	devastated by land and sea; the locusts, by land and sea,
Les saturelles terre & mer vent propice,	the wind being favourable, captured, dead, trussed up,
Prins, morts, troussez, pillés, sans loi de guerre.	plundered without law of war.

INVASION OF FRANCE?

An invasion of the coast of Southern France by air is probably implied by this quatrain. As we have seen, Nostradamus describes all his machines as types of animals, and locusts, if read literally, could not cause the death and destruction of the final line.

Les longs cheveux de la Gaule Celtique, *Accompaignez d'estranges nations:* *Mettront captif la gent Aquitanique,* *Pour succomber à Internitions.*[1]	The long-haired people of Celtic Gaul, joined by foreign nations will capture the people of Aquitaine in order that they should succumb to their plans.

LOUIS XVIII 1755–1824

Louis XVIII of France was known contemporarily as *le Chevelu*—the long-haired one, his long hair being a great contrast to the short cropped hair of the Revolutionaries and Bonapartists. The foreign nations who help him are the Allied Armies who defeat Napoleon. The last two lines are unclear. In IX. 6 Aquitaine means England or an English colony.

84

La grand cité sera bien desolee, *Des habitans un seul n'y demoura:* *Mur, sexe, temple & vierge violee,* *Par fer, feu, peste, canon peuple mourra.*	The great city will soon be quite deserted, not a single one of the inhabitants will remain. Wall, sex, temple and virgin violated, people will die from the sword, fire, plague and cannon shot.

SACK OF ROME UNDER PIUS VI, 1775–1799

If the word is *sexe* an abbreviation of Sextus, which it could well be, this verse then applies to the Sack of Rome by Napoleonic troops. Many commentators think the city is Paris.

85

La cité prinse par tromperie & fraude, *Par le moyen d'un beau jeune attrappé:* *Assaut donne Raubine pres de LAUDE,* *Lui & tous morts pour avoir bien trompé.*	The city is taken by trickery and deceit, captured by means of a handsome young man. An assault is made by Raubine near LAUDE, he and all of them dead, for having deceived so well.

The interpretation of this stanza is connected with the river Robine, a tributary of the Aude, and presumably the city which is taken lies upon either of these.

[1] *Internitions*—Read intentions in all other texts.

Un chef d'Ausonne aux Espaignes ira,
Par mer fera arrest dedans Marseille:
Avant sa mort un long temps languira
Apres sa mort on verra grand merveille.

A leader from Italy will go to Spain by sea and he will make a stop at Marseilles. He will linger a long time before dying, after his death great wonders will be seen.

This implies that a ruler of any Southern Italian state, or of the two Sicilies in particular, because that was the home of the Ausones in ancient times, will die a lingering death at Marseilles. This does not seem to have occurred.

Classe Gauloise n'approches de Corsegne,
Moins de Sardaigne tu t'en repentiras:
Trestout mourrez frustrez de l'aide grogne,
Sang nagera, captif ne me croiras.

French fleet, do not approach Corsica; even less Sardinia, you will regret it. You will all die, the help from the cape in vain, captive, swimming in blood you will not believe me.

SINKING OF PART OF FRENCH FLEET, 1655

In 1655 part of the French fleet, under the command of the Chevalier de la Ferrière, was sunk in the Gulf of Lyons while sailing past the islands of Sardinia and Corsica. Many were lost because they were unable to reach the nearby Cap de Porceau. This is an interesting double meaning. Grogne can mean a cape, or the snout of a pig. Nostradamus uses it to describe two things with extreme economy of words. Le Captif was the name of the pilot, Jean de Rian, who had been earlier captured and taken as a galley slave by the Algerian corsairs.

De Barcellonne par mer si grand armee,
Tout Marseille de frayeur tremblera:
Isles saisies de mer aide fermee,
Ton traditeur en terre nagera.

From Barcelona such a great army by sea, all Marseilles will tremble with terror. The islands seized, help cut off by sea, your traitor will swim on land.

On this day in 1596, Philip II of Spain sent a fleet to Marseilles under the command of Charles Doria to divide French interests between the Leaguers and the king. It occupied the islands of Château d'If and Ratonneau and thus prevented help coming into Marseilles by sea. A certain Charles de Casau tried to betray Marseilles to the Spanish but was found out and assassinated by Pierre Libertat; he was killed by the sword and literally drowned in his own blood.

89

Vieux trucidez, mais par mesles¹ & lyphres²	and supplications, the king is won over, the queen more
En ce temps là sera frustree Cypres,
De son secours de ceux de mer Egee:
Vieux trucidez, mais par mesles[1] *& lyphres*[2]
Seduict leur Roy, Royne plus outragee.

At that time Cyprus will be deprived of its help from those of the Aegean sea. Old men slaughtered, but by cannons and supplications, the king is won over, the queen more outraged.

ENOSIS AND CYPRUS

This quatrain may describe Cyprus during the Troubles of the 1950s, when union with Greece was the great political problem. The quatrain clearly shows that Cyprus will not attain complete union with Greece, that the King (Constantine?) will be misled, and the Queen, probably Frederika, greatly upset by their enforced exile.

90

Le grand Satyre & Tigre d'Hyrcanie,
Don presenté à ceux de l'Occean:
Un chef de classe istra de Carmanie,
Qui prendra terre au Tyrren Phocean.

The great Satyr and Tiger of Hyrcania; gift presented to the people of the Ocean: the leader of a fleet will come forth from Carmania and land at the Phocea of Tyre.

The key to this quatrain is in the last line. Phocea is Marseilles but it is not situated on the Tyrrhenian sea so Nostradamus is probably intending another seaport associated with the early Phoenician colonists of Tyre. Carmania and Hyrcania were both provinces of Persia but the expedition would have to cross by land as well

[1] *mesles*—Probably variant O.F., *masle* = cannon ball.
[2] *lyphres*—Possibly Greek, *lypros* = a supplication.

as sea, as there was no Suez canal at this period. An uncertain quatrain.

91

L'arbre qu'estoit par long temps mort seché, *Dans une nuict viendra à reverdir:* *Cron*[1] *Roy malade, Prince pied estaché,*[2] *Criant d'ennemis fera voile bondir.*	The tree which had been dead and withered for a long time will flourish again in one night. The Cronian king will be sickly. The prince with a damaged foot, fear of his enemies will make him hoist sail.

BIRTH OF THE DUKE DE BORDEAUX 1820, HIS EXILE & DEATH, 1838

The tree which sprouts again miraculously overnight is the line of the Bourbons, when the Duchesse de Berry gave birth to a son, the Duke de Bordeaux on 29th September 1820 seven months after her husband was assassinated. He was a sickly child and injured his foot in a fall from his horse in Austria which resulted in a permanent limp. He went into exile in 1830 with his grandfather Charles X and despite long negotiations with Republican France, did not succeed in regaining the throne.

92

Le monde proche du dernier periode, *Saturne encor tard sera de retour:* *Translat empire devers nation Brodde,* *L'oeil arraché à Narbon par Autour.*	The world is near its final period, Saturn will again be late on his return. The empire will shift towards the Brodde nation; An eye at Narbonne plucked out by a goshawk.

This is an astrological quatrain dealing probably with the future of the African nations, as *Brodde* in old French means either black or dark brown. It also contains the meaning of decadent. Nostradamus speaks several times of an '*Empire translaté*' when referring to Napoleon. Here he implies that more power will be given to African nations as is happening at the present, before the final cycle of the world occurs. It might also mean that French power

---

[1] *Cron*—From the Latin, *Cronus* = Saturn, an old man, in this case his grandfather.

[2] *estaché*—O.F. = stump, club foot.

shifts towards Africa—which it did until France left Algeria. In which case we are now approaching this final period.

93

Dans Avignon tout le Chef de l'empire
Fera arrest pour Paris desolé:
Tricast[1] tiendra l'Annibalique ire,
Lyon par change sera mel consolé.

In Avignon, the leader of all the Empire will make a stop because Paris is deserted. Tricast will contain the African anger, the Lion will be poorly consoled by the change.

The quatrain hints at a great enemy of France, possibly also of Rome, in that Avignon belonged to the Vatican until 1791. The British lion will dislike this enemy in Africa—there is a temptation to link this quatrain with the British campaigns in Africa during the Second World War.

94

De cinq cent ans plus compte l'on tiendra
Celui qu'estoit l'adornement de son temps:
Puis à un coup grand clarté donra,
Que par ce siecle les rendra tres contens.

For five hundred years more they will take notice of him who was the ornament of his age. Then suddenly a great revelation will be made which will make people of that (same) century well pleased.

This has been used by almost every interpreter of Nostradamus' quatrains to date as a guarantee of the inspired nature of their works. No further comment is needed. The commentator has not yet appeared.

95

La loy Moricque on verra deffaillir,
Apres un autre beaucoup plus seductive:
Boristhenes[2] premier viendra faillir,
Par dons & langue une plus attractive.

The Moorish law will be seen to fail, followed by another that is more pleasing. The Dnieper will be the first to give way through gifts and tongues to another more appealing.

[1] *Tricast→Tricasses* = city of Troyes.
[2] *Boristhenes*—Latin = the river Dnieper in the U.S.S.R.

RISE OF COMMMUNISM?

The prophecy states that a creed, founded near the river Dnieper in the U.S.S.R. will have a widespread success before it declines. In Nostradamus' own day this was one of the most backward areas of Europe. It is probable that he is forecasting the rise of Communism but interesting in that he also predicts its eventual failure.

96

Chef de Fosan aura gorge coupee,	The leader from Fossano will
Par le ducteur du limier &	have his throat cut by the man
laurier:	who exercised the bloodhounds
La faict patre par ceux de mont	and greyhounds. The deed will
Tarpee,	be committed by those of the
Saturne en Leo 13 de Fevrier.	Tarpean rock, when Saturn
	is in Leo on 13th February.

13th FEBRUARY 1820

To trace the leader from Fossano is difficult. If he is the Duke de Berry then he is called this because his maternal grandfather was King of Fossano in Sardinia. The rest of the quatrain fits very accurately. The assassin was Louvel, who worked in the royal stables. He was a Republican, hence the reference to the Tarpean rock from which Republican Rome threw her criminals. Saturn rules Aquarius, so when it is in the opposite sign of Leo it should be understood as maleficent. The Duke de Berry was stabbed on 13th Febrary 1820, as Nostradamus stated, when leaving the Opéra. See I. 84.

97

Nouvelle loi terre neufve occuper,	A new law will occupy a new
Vers la Syrie, Judee & Palestine:	land around Syria, Judea and
Le grand empire barbare corruer,	Palestine. The great barbarian
Avant que Phoebus son siecle	Empire will crumble before
determine.	the century of the sun is
	finished.

THE CREATION OF ISRAEL AND FINAL DEFEAT OF U.A.R. 20th CENTURY

The first two lines speak for themselves and describe the creation of the state of Israel. By barbarian Nostradamus means Arabic or non-Christian and implies here that Israel will eventually triumph over her Arab enemies before the end of the 20th Century—the century of the sun.

98

Deux royals freres si fort guerroierent,	Two royal brothers will fight so fiercely and the feud between them will be so deadly that both will live in fortified places. Their great quarrel will concern their lives and the kingdom.
Qu'entre eux sera la guerre si mortelle:	
Qu'un chacun places fortes occuperont,	
De regne & vie sera leur grand querelle.	

This is a fairly straightforward prophecy which suits the king of France, Henri III, and the Duc d'Alençon most closely (1574–84), but also fits Louis XIII and his brother the Duke of Orléans around the period 1632. A very good example of history, and prophecy, repeating themselves!

99

Aux champs herbeux d'Alein et du Vaineigne,	In the green fields of Alleins and Vernegues of the Luberon mountains near Durance, the fighting on both sides will be so bitter for the armies that Mesopotamia shall cease to be found in France.
Du mont Lebrou proche de la Durance,	
Camps de deux parts conflict sera si aigre	
Mesopotamie defaillira en la France.	

It is from the last line of this quatrain that commentators refer to Mesopotamia throughout the Centuries as referring to Paris. Both places in line one are villages near Salon, Nostradamus' home; the Luberon mountains are near the river Durance.

100

Entre Gaulois le dernier honnoré,	The man least honoured among the French will be victorious over his enemy. Strength and lands he explored in action, when suddenly the envious one dies from the shot.
D'homme ennemi sera victorieux:	
Force & terroir en mouvement exploré	
D'un coup de traict quand mourra l'envieux.	

GENERAL DE GAULLE?

This quatrain is normally applied to de Gaulle and the man who is assassinated is then identified as Admiral Darlan, who was killed on 24th December 1942. *Le traict* is the normal word for the shot of an arrow, but here may mean gunshot.

CENTURY IV

34
35
36
37*   Napoleon, 1800
38?   Machine?
39**   U.S.A. and U.A.R.
40*?   Bunker at Berlin, 1945
41
42
43?   Aerial warfare
44
45
46
47*   24th August 1572
48
49
50**F? America and Asia
51
52
53
54*   Napoleon
55
56
57
58
59?   Iran?
60
61*   Marshal Pétain, 1940–4
62*   Oliver Cromwell. Colonel Gadalfi of Libya.
63   France, 1702–4
64
65*   Napoleon III
66
67
68**   Tripartite Pact. Hitler and Mussolini
69
70*   Wellington. The Peninsular War
71
72?
73*   Assassination of the Duke de Berry, 1820
74
75**   Waterloo, 1815
76

166

77?
78
79
80*   Maginot Line. Second World War
81
82*   Retreat from Moscow, 1812–13
83
84?
85*   Louis XVI and French Revolution
86
87
88
89**   William III of England
90
91
92?   Radio Equipment
93**   The Count de Chambord, 1820
94
95F?   U.S.A. and War?
96**   William and Mary
97
98
99F?   Missiles or rockets?
100*   Franco-Prussian War, 1870–1

KEY: * Of interest F? Possibly referring to the future.

Cela du reste de sang non espandu,
Venise quiert secours estre donné,
Apres avoir bien long temps
attendu,
Cité livrée au premier cornet
sonné.

The remaining blood will not be spilt, Venice seeks for help to be given; Having waited for a very long time the city is handed over at the first trumpet blast.

This probably describes the Turkish attack on Cyprus (1560-73). Venice received very little help and Famagusta, the capital of Cyprus, fell to the Turks after a prolonged siege in 1571.

Par mort la France prendra voyage
à faire,
Classe par mer, marcher monts
Pyrenées,
Espaigne en trouble, marcher gent
militaire:
Des plus grand Dames en France
emmenées.

Because of a death France will undertake a journey, the fleet at sea, marching over the Pyrenean mountains. Spain will be troubled, an army will march, some of the greatest ladies brought into France.

WAR OF SPANISH SUCCESSION 1701-1713

This is a comparatively successful quatrain. Philip V, grandson of Louis XIV, inherited the Spanish throne from Charles II in 1700. This was not popular with Austria, England, Holland, Prussia and Savoy, who formed a coalition to support the pretensions of the Archduke Charles. The French fleet took to the sea, and her army crossed the Pyrenees. The war in Spain lasted for twelve years and it was all due to two Spanish princesses who married into the French line, the wives of Louis XII and Louis XIV respectively.

D'Arras & Bourges[1], de Brodes
grans enseignes,
Un plus grand nombre de Gascons
batre à pied,
Ceux long du Rosne saigneront les
Espaignes:
Proche du mont ou Sagonte s'assied.

From Arras and Bourges great banners from the Dark Ones, a greater number of Gascons fight on foot. Those along the Rhône will make the Spanish bleed. Near the mountain seat of Sagunto.

Brodes probably means dark-haired people, possibly the Spanish Moors in this context. If Bourges is understood as Bruges then line

[1] *Bourges* = possibly Bruges.

one describes another Hapsburg invasion from the North, probably that which resulted in the Battle of St. Quentin, in 1557. The last two lines suggest that the French invaded Spain, which they did not do for another fifty years or so. The importance of Sagunto is unclear.

4

L'impotent Prince faché, plaincts & querelles,	The powerless Prince is angered, complaints & quarrels, rape and pillage, by the cock and by the Libyans. It is great on land, at sea innumerable sails; Italy alone will be driving out the Celts.
De rapts & pille, par coqz & par Libiques:	
Grand est par terre par mer infinies voilles	
Seule Italie sera chassont Celtiques.	

The cock is the French symbol and the Libyans are the Algerian corsairs who allied with them. The Prince is therefore probably a Hapsburg, possibly Duke Cosimo, who was in charge of the defence of Elba and the surrounding lands. These territories were ravished in 1555. The last line is confusing suggesting that the French will be defeated by the Italians but successful everywhere else. Exactly the reverse occurred. The French held their own in Italy but were defeated in the North.

5

Croix paix, soubz un accompli divin verbe,	Cross, peace under one the divine word achieved. Spain and Gaul will be united. A great disaster is close, the fighting very ferocious, no heart so brave as will not tremble.
L'Espaigne & Gaule seront unis ensemble:	
Grand clade[1] *proche, & combat tresacerbe,*	
Coeur si hardi ne sera qui ne tremble.	

SPANISH SUCCESSION, 1701–1713

Spain and France were united for the short time that Louis XIV's grandson inherited the Spanish throne. Perhaps the revocation of the Edict of Nantes is hinted at in line one? Peace achieved under the divine word could be the Papal Bull Unigenitus which was issued in 1713, the year the war ended. The great disaster following upon the union of the countries is the War of the Spanish Succession of IV. 2, and the final line is self-explanatory, just used to fill up the quatrain.

[1] *clades*—Latin = disaster.

D'habits nouveaux apres faicte la
    treuve,[1]
Malice tramme & machination:
Premier mourra qui en fera la
    preuve,
Couleur venise insidation.[2]

After the truce is made, new clothes will be put on, malice, conspiracy and plotting. He who will prove it is the first to die, the colour of Venetian treachery.

A very obscure quatrain. Perhaps the new clothes imply a new order of monks, and there is a shade of yellow-brown called venetian red. Perhaps this is meant rather than the city.

Le mineur filz du grand & hai
    Prince,
De lepre aura à vingt ans grande
    tache,
De deuil sa mere mourra bien triste
    & mince,
Et il mourra là où tombe cher
    lache.

The younger son of a great and hated prince, will be greatly marked by leprosy by the time he is twenty. His mother will die of grief, very sad and thin, and he will die when the cowardly flesh falls (from his bones).

There is no record to date of a younger, or youngest, son of a Royal family dying of leprosy.

La grand cité d'assaut prompt &
    repentin,
Surprins de nuict, gardes inter-
    rompus:
Les excubies & vielles sainct
    Quintin,
Trucidés gardes & les pourtails
    rompus.

The great city will be surprised at night by a sudden and quick assault. The guards interrupted; the watch and guards of St. Quintin slaughtered, the guards and the gates broken down.

ST. QUENTIN, 1557

There was a Battle of St. Quentin in 1557 but the city was taken not in the way Nostradamus describes it, but by a seventeen-day siege. But at least the prediction of the town's capture is correct, see IV. 3.

[1] *treuve*—O.F., *treve* = truce.
[2] *insidation*—O.F. = snare, trap.

Le chef du camp au milieu de la presse,
D'un coup de fleche sera blessé aux cuisses,
Lors que Geneve eu larmes & detresse,
Sera trahi par Lozan & Souisses.

The leader of the army in the middle of the crowd is wounded in the thighs with an arrow. When Geneva in trouble and distress is betrayed by Lausanne and the Swiss.

Presumably another anti-Calvinist tirade by Nostradamus. He seems to foresee that Lausanne and Switzerland generally return to the Roman Catholic faith with only Geneva led by the wounded leader, holding out. A completely mistaken verse.

10

Le jeune prince accusé faulsement,
Mettra en trouble le camp & en querelles:
Meutri le chef pour le soustenement,
Sceptre appaiser: puis guerir escrou-elles.

The young Prince, falsely accused will put the camp into quarrels and trouble. The leader is murdered for his support to appease the crown: then he cures the king's evil.

This describes the leader of an army who supports a Prince but loses his life. A new King comes to the throne, line 4, because French and English kings were reputed to cure scrofula by their touch, particularly on the day of their coronation.

11

Celui qu'aura gouvert de la grand cappe,[1]
Sera induict à quelques cas patrer[2]
Les douze rouges viendront fouiller la nappe.
Soubz meutre, meutre se viendra perpetrer.

He who will have government of the great cloak will be led to execute in certain cases. The twelve red ones will come to spoil the cover, under murder, murder will be perpetrated.

A detailed quatrain, but one that has not yet materialized. A Pope will be forced into some rash action, and then be condemned by his twelve cardinals. It is implied that they connive at the Pope's murder or will commit further murders.

[1] *cappe* = (*a*) Cloak. (*b*) Cape, standing for Pope and Vatican.
[2] *patrer*—Latin, *patrare* = to perform, execute.

Le camp plus grand de route mis en fuite,	The greatest army on the march put to flight will
Guaires plus outre ne sera pourchassé:	scarcely be pursued further. The army reassembled and the
Ost recampé, & legion reducte,	legion reduced, they will then
Puis hors ses Gaules du tout sera chassé.	be driven out of France completely.

This is a very general quatrain and the German invasions of France in the last two wars fit it most accurately. However, there is nothing sufficiently explicit to go on.

De plus grand perte nouvelles raportées,	News of the great loss is brought; the report will
Le raport fait le camp s'estonnera:	astonish the camp. Bands unite
Bandes unies encontre revoltées,	against those revolting, the
Double phalange grand abandonnera.	double phalanx will forsake the great one.

1580, DUKE OF PARMA

This verse is normally applied to the 1580s when a rumour spread through the Duke of Parma's army of so great a defeat that they were quite demoralized and allowed the Dutch to capture Antwerp for a time. A phalanx was 800 men, so 1,600 men are understood to have revolted.

La mort subite du premier personnage.	The sudden death of the leading personnage will have
Aura changé & mis un autre au regne:	changed and put another to rule. Soon, but too late come
Tost, tard venu à si haut & bas aage,	to high position, of young age,
Que terre & mer faudre que on la craigne.	by land and sea it will be necessary to fear him.

J. F. KENNEDY

A general prophecy about a young leader who comes to power too late to alter the *status quo* of the country. It has fancifully been suggested that it may refer to J. F. Kennedy, succeeding the aged General Eisenhower, whose policies still could not lessen world tension. During the Cuba incident Kennedy's power was to be feared on land and sea.

D'où pensera faire venir famine, *De là viendra le rassasiement:* *L'oeil de la mer par avare canine* *Pour de l'un l'autre dorna huile,* *froment.*	From the place where he will think to bring famine, from there will come the relief. The eye of the sea, like a covetous dog; the one will give oil and wheat to the other.

GREAT BRITAIN 1939–45. SUBMARINES

This verse describes Britain's predicament during the Second World War very accurately. The German blockade tried to starve her out, see also III. 71, but instead, she received large quantities of American aid. 'The eye of the sea, like a covetous dog' is understood as meaning the periscope of the German U-boats, which certainly hunted down the British convoys in packs.

16

La cité franche de liberté fait serve,
Des profligés & resveurs faict
    asile:
Le Roy changé à eux non si pro-
    terve[1]
De cent seront devenus plus de mille.
	The free city of liberty is enslaved, it becomes the refuge of profligates and dreamers. The king changes and is not so ferocious towards them. From one hundred they will become more than a thousand.

Europe had many free cities when Nostradamus wrote. He may here be referring to Orange, which gave its name to the Dutch royal line, and did not belong to France until 1713. During Nostradamus' time it belonged to William the Silent, and line 2 may be intended as meaning that it had become a haven for Protestants, which it was.

17

Changer à Beaune, Nuy, Chalons &
    Dijon,
Le duc voulant amander[2] *la*
    Barrée[3]
Marchant pres fleuve, poisson, bec
    de plongeon,
Vers la queue; porte sera serrée.
	Changes at Beaune, Nuits, Chalon & Dijon, the Duke wishes to improve the Carmelites. Walking near the river, a fish, a diving (bird's) beak, towards the tail; the gate will be locked.

[1] *proterve*—Latin, *protervus* = violent.
[2] *amander*—O.F. = improve, to better.
[3] *Barrée*—This was the name for the Carmelite monks and nuns, from the O.F., *barré* = motley.

The first two lines may refer to St. Theresa who reformed the order of Carmelite nuns in Spain in 1562. But nothing can be made of the following lines.

18

Des - plus lettrés dessus les faits celestes Seront par princes ignorans re-prouvés: Punis d'Edit, chassez comme sceles-tes, Et mis à mort là où seront trouvés.	Some of the most learned men in the heavenly arts will be reprimanded by ignorant Princes; punished by an Edict, driven out as scoundrels and put to death wherever they are found.

Shades of the Inquisition linger over this verse, for in fact astrologers were never as grossly persecuted after Nostradamus' death as they were during the century before. However if he was also thinking of the witch hunts which bedevilled Europe they did not die out until somewhat later.

19

Devant Rouen d'Insubres mis le siege, Par terre & mer enfermés les passages: D'Haynault, & Flandres, de Gand & ceux de Liege, Par dons laenées[1] raviront les rivages.	The Insubrians lay siege in front of Rouen, the passages closed by land and sea. By Hainaut & Flanders, by Ghent and those of Liege, through cloaked gifts they will ravage the shores.

Rouen was first captured by the Duke of Parma who was helping de Guise against Henri of Navarre in 1592 but without much of a siege. Since Milan was part of his dominions there could have been Italians (Insubres) among his troops. Since then Rouen has never been captured by Italy, the Germans captured it in 1870 and 1940 and the Americans in 1944. All the other towns mentioned are in the Netherlands and Flanders. Although reasonably clear, this prophecy has not been fulfilled.

[1] laenées—Latin, laena = cloak, mantle.

Paix uberté¹ long temps lieu louera;
Par tout son regne desert la fleur de lis:
Corps morts d'eau, terre là lou apportera,
Sperants vain heur d'estre là ensevelis.

Peace and plenty for a long time the place will praise: the fleur de lis deserted throughout the kingdom. Bodies dead by water, *they* will be brought to land there, waiting in vain for the opportunity of being buried.

The fleur de lis was the emblem of many other families besides the French kings so this is not much help. The obvious time that it disappears throughout the kingdom is during the Revolution and the Empire. The last two lines would then be generalities about war and death.

21

Le changement sera fort difficile,
Cité, province au change gain fera:
Coeur haut, prudent mis, chassé lui habile,
Mer, terre, peuple son estat changera.

The change will be very difficult. Both city and province will gain by it. A prudent man highly placed, will be chased out by the cunning one. By land and sea people will change their estate.

FRANCE, 1940–4. DE GAULLE
The first two lines of this quatrain may refer to the fall of France and Marshal Petain's 'centralized decentralization'. The prudent man is de Gaulle, who is chased out to England and the last line refers to the general state of the country and the war.

22

La grand copie² qui sera deschasée,
Dans un moment fera besoing au Roi,
La foi promise de loing sera faulsée
Nud se verra en piteux desarroi.

The great army which will be driven out at one moment will be needed by the King. The faith promised from afar will be broken, he will see himself with nothing, in pitiful disorder.

This is a general type of quatrain that may have occurred several times. A king quarrels with an ally, and having dismissed its forces

¹ *uberté*—Latin, *ubertas* = abundance.
² *copie*—Latin, *copia* = army, troops.

suddenly finds he needs them again. But because one of them breaks a promise the king is left powerless.

23

La legion dans la marine classe,	The legion in the marine fleet
Calcine,[1] *Magnes*[2] *soulphre, &*	will burn, lime, magnesia,
paix bruslera:	sulphur and pitch. The long
Le long repos de l'asseuree place,	rest in a safe place; Port Selin,
Port Selyn,[3] *Hercle*[4] *feu les con-*	Monaco will be consumed by
sumera.	fire.

GREEK FIRE

This is a very strange quatrain. The second line appears to be giving a recipe for Greek fire, the famous 'secret weapon' of the Greeks and Byzantines. Nostradamus is quite correct because after much research, Lieut.-Colonel H. Hime said that it was the presence of quicklime which distinguished Greek fire from all other known incendiaries of the period. The mixture gave rise to heat on contact with water and thus took fire spontaneously when wetted, and was used with great success in sea battles. But again, Port Selin, if I am correct in identifying it with Genoa, and Monaco, have not been attacked since Nostradamus' day. But the port of Toulon was used by Barbarossa when he helped the French against the Emperor during the 1540s.

24

Oui soubs terre saincte dame voix	The faint voice of a woman is
fainte,	heard under the holy ground.
Humaine flamme pour divine voix	Human flame shines for the
luire:	divine voice. It will cause the
Fera les seuls de leur sang terre	earth to be stained with the
tainte,	blood of celibates and destroy
Et les saincts temples pour les	the holy temples for the wicked.
impurs destruire.	

PERSECUTION OF CLERGY

An impossible quatrain because of the many variants of the first line. To which word does *saincte* belong? *Dame* is also given as

[1] *Calcine*—Latin, *calcina* = lime.

[2] *Magnes*—Latin for loadstone or magnet. Also an abbreviation of Magnesie, used loosely to describe Greek fire.

[3] *Port Selyn*—Genoa was a crescent-shaped republic and Selene means crescent in Greek.

[4] *Hercle*—Latin, *Herculeis Monacei* = another name for Monaco.

d'ame, of the soul, and *fainte* as *sainte*. The general idea seems to be the persecution of the church, perhaps personified in the Holy Lady of the first line, and its most probable fulfilment was the abolition and persecution of the clergy during the French Revolution.

25

Corps sublimes sans fin à l'oeil visibles:	The heavenly bodies endlessly visible to the eye come to cloud (the intellect) for their own reasons. The body, together with the forehead, senses and head all invisible, as the sacred prayers diminish.
Obnubiler viendront par ses raisons:	
Corps, front comprins, sens chief & invisibles.	
Diminuant les sacrees oraisons.	

OCCULT QUATRAIN

Some commentators regard this as referring to the invention of the telescope (1610) bringing new worlds and ideas which will be hostile to religion. But I think that Nostradamus is here describing the sensation of 'bodilessness' which he experiences when in a predictive trance, when his mind and intellect are used by the heavenly beings for their own purposes. The prayers of the last line are the invocations to the spirits made by Nostradamus. As they finish, he is possessed. See also I. 1 and 2, and III. 2.

26

Lou grand eyssame se levera d'abelhos,	The great swarm of bees will arise but no one will know whence they have come, the ambush by night, the sentinel under the vines, a city handed over by five tongues not naked.
Que non sauran don te siegen venguddos:	
De nuech l'embousque, lou gach dessous las treilhos	
Cuitad trahido per cinq lengos non nudos.	

THE *COUP D'ÉTAT* OF EIGHTEENTH BRUMAIRE
(9th NOVEMBER 1779)

This is one of the few quatrains written entirely in Provençal. It describes Napoleon's *coup d'état* of 1799 very accurately. The swarm of bees is Napoleon's emblem—they can still be seen on the embroideries at Malmaison and Fontainebleau. The five men (literally babblers), who handed over Paris were the members of the Directory who were bribed (*non nudos*) to give way to Napoleon's Consulate; they were also wearing official clothes as members of

177

the Directory, as opposed to their everyday apparel. The coup was planned the night before it took place. Most commentators take *las treilhos* to be an anagram for the Tuileries into which Napoleon moved once he saw his action was successful. The exact French equivalent is *treilles*, but it is close enough and the quatrain fits very well in all other respects.

27

Salon, Mansol, Tarascon de SEX. l'arc,	Salon, Mansol, Tarascon, the arch of SEX: where the pyramid is still standing. They will come to deliver the Prince of Denmark, a shameful ransom to the temple of Artemis.
Ou est debout encor la piramide:	
Viendront livrer le Prince Dannemarc,	
Rachat honni au temple d'Artemide.	

The complicated first line stands for St. Rémy where Nostradamus was born, where there are two great historical monuments, a mausoleum with the inscription *SEX. L.M. JUILEI C.F. PARENTIBUS SUIS* and next to it a triumphal arch. *Mansol* is a misprint for Mausole, a priory just outside St. Rémy. The problem lies in connecting them with Dannemarc. The word may well be one of Nostradamus' better concealed anagrams which I cannot decipher.

28

Lors que Venus du Sol sera couvert,	When Venus will be covered by the Sun, under the splendour will be a hidden form. Mercury will have exposed them to the fire, by a rumour of war will be affronted.
Soubs l'esplendeur sera forme occulte:	
Mercure au feu les aura descouvert,	
Par bruit bellique sera mis à l'insulte.	

OCCULT

This, and the following quatrains IV. 29, 30, 31 and 33 are all occult quatrains and probably describe Nostradamus' attempts to discover the elusive philosopher's stone which transmutes all other metals into gold, here described as the sun.

Le Sol caché eclipse par Mercure,
Ne sera mis que pour le ciel
    second:
De Vulcan Hermes sera faicte
    pasture,
Sol sera veu pur, rutilant & blond.

The hidden Sun eclipsed by Mercury will be placed only second in the heavens. Hermes will be made the food of Vulcan, the Sun will be seen pure, shining and golden.

OCCULT
See IV. 28. Vulcan here stands for fire.

Plus onze fois Luna Sol ne voudra,
Tous augmenté & baissez de
    degré:
Et si bas mis que peu or on cendra,
Qu'apres faim, peste, descouvert le
    secret.

More than eleven times the Moon will not want the Sun, both raised and lessened in degree. Put so low that one will sew little gold: after famine and plague the secret will be discovered.

OCCULT
See IV. 28. The Moon here probably means silver.

La Lune au plain de nuict sur le
    haut mont,
Le nouveau sophe d'un seul cerveau
    l'a veu:
Par ses disciples estre immortel
    semond,
Yeux au midi, en seins mains,
    corps au feu.

The moon, in the middle of the night over the high mountain, the young wise man alone with his brain has seen it. Invited by his disciples to become immortal, his eyes to the south, his hands on his breast, his body in the fire.

OCCULT
In this quatrain it is suggested that the young sage who finally makes this great discovery either comes to a violent end or is racked by mental torment.

Es lieux & temps chair un poisson donra lieu, *La loi commune sera faicte au contraire:* *Vieux tiendra fort plus osté du millieu,* *Le Pánta chiona philòn mis fort arriere.*	In those times and places that meat gives way to fish the common law will be made in opposition. The old (order) will hold strong, then removed from the scene, then All Things common among Friends put far behind.

DECLINE OF COMMUNISM

Pánta chiona philòn is the Greek for all things held in common among friends, that is, Communism in its strictest sense. Nostradamus has already described this in the U.S.S.R. in quatrain III. 95, and seems definite that its appeal will fade and there will be strong attempts to revive the old order. One wonders whether this is associated with the theory that America and the U.S.S.R. will ally together against the East, probably China? See V. 78.

Jupiter joinct plus Venus qu'à la Lune, *Apparoissant de plenitude blanche:* *Venus cachée souz la blancheur Neptune* *De Mars frappée par la gravée branche.*	Jupiter joined more to Venus than to the Moon appearing in a white fullness. Venus hidden under the whiteness of Neptune struck by Mars by the engraved wand.

OCCULT

The translation of the last line is difficult. I take *gravée* to mean engraved, because *branche* is used by Nostradamus to refer to the ceremonial wand and tripod used in his predictions therefore that the wand is engraved with hieroglyphics. The rest is very obscure.

Le grand mené captif d'estrange terre, *D'or enchainé ay Roy CHYREN offert:* *Qui dans Ausone, Milan perdra la guerre,* *Et tout son ost mis à feu & à fer.*	The great man led captive from a foreign land, chained in gold, offered to King Chyren. He who in Ausonia, Milan, will lose the war and all his army put to fire and sword.

CHYREN is an almost definite anagram for the Old French spelling of Henri, *HENRYC*, but the great problem lies in deciding which Henri these verses refer to. Many commentators favour Henri IV, others of the 19th Century in particular, a new king of France yet to come. The quatrains are not completely favourable to either idea, so maybe they have yet to be fulfilled? See II. 79, VI. 27 and 70, VIII. 54, IX. 41 etc.

35

Le feu estaint, les vierges trahiront	The fire put out, the virgins will
La plus grand part de la bande nouvelle:	betray the greater part of the new band; lightning in sword,
Fouldre à fer, lance les seulz Roi garderont	lances alone will guard the king, Tuscany and Corsica, by
Etrusque & Corse, de nuict gorge allumelle.	night throats slit.

During the Empire, Tuscany and Corsica were both bothered by the French as Tuscany was an ally and Genoa owned Corsica.

36

Les jeux nouveau en Gaule redressés,	New games are set up in Gaul, after the victory of the Insu-
Après victoire de l'Insubre[1] champaigne:	brian campaign. The mountains of Hesperia the great ones
Monts d'Esperie, les grands liés, troussés:	tied and bound. Romania and Spain will tremble with fear.
De peur trembler la Romaigne & l'Espaigne.	

If *Romaigne* in line 4 stands for the Roman Empire, i.e. Germany, the best interpretation of France's victories in Spain and the north would be the Napoleonic campaigns.

37

Gaulois par saults, monts viendra penetrer:	The Gauls will penetrate the mountains in leaps and occupy
Occupera le grand lieu de l'Insubre:	the great seat of Insubria. He will make his army go deep
Au plus profond son est fera entrer,	(into the land), Genoa and Monaco will repulse the red
Gennes, Monech pousseront classe rubre.	fleet.

[1] *Insubre* = Italy, around Milan, Lombardy.

In the year 1800, Genoa was besieged by Austria, and surrendered on 4th June. The British fleet which had been helping with a blockade attacked Monaco on 23rd May. Earlier that month Napoleon made his incredible crossing of the St. Bernard pass with an army of 40,000 men, and took Milan (Insubria) on 2nd June. A very satisfactory quatrain.

38

Pendant que Duc, Roi, Royne occupera, *Chef Bizant du captif en Samothrace:* *Avant l'assault l'un l'autre mangera,* *Rebours ferré suivra du sang la trace.*	While the Duke occupies the King and Queen, the Byzantine leader is held captive in Greece. Before the attack one will devour the other. The metalled reverse will follow the trail of blood.

MACHINE?

Does the 'metalled reverse' indicate a type of machine similar to a Geiger counter, that will be able to follow a man's tracks?

39

Les Rhodiens demanderont secours, *Par le neglect de ses hoirs delaissée:* *L'Empire Arabe revalera son secours,* *Par Hesperies la cause redressée.*	The people of Rhodes will demand help, abandoned by the neglect of their heirs. The Arab Empire will assess its course, its cause revived again by the West.

U.S.A. AND U.A.R.

At a time of unrest in Greece, which could refer to the present regime, the U.A.R. will assess its position and be helped in some way by America. Possibly this last line refers to the attitude taken by the U.S.A. over Suez or to the complicated political pressures now being brought to bear on the Middle East?

40

Les fortresses des assiegés serrés, *Par poudre à feu profondés en abisme:* *Les prodeurs seront tous vifs serrés* *Onc aux sacristes n'advint si piteux scisme.*	The fortress of the beseiged shut up by gunpowder sunk into its depths; the traitor will be emtombed alive, never did so pitiful a schism happen to the sextons.

The clue to this verse lies in the last line. *Sacristes* translates as sextons, which is meaningless in this context. However, if Nostradamus meant Saxons, the Germans and this is associated with a schism, a breaking up of a party, this could refer to Hitler and those pitiful few of his followers who remained in the fortified bunker to be shelled by the Allies. See also III. 58.

41

Gymnique¹ sexe captive par hostage,	A female (sex) captive as a
Viendra de nuit custodes decevoir:	hostage will come by night to
Le chef du camp deceu par son	deceive the guards. The leader
langage:	of the camp deceived by her
Lairra à la gente, sera piteux à voir,	language will leave her to the
	people, it will be pitiful to see.

An unknown woman who is abandoned to a mob after tricking the guards; very general.

42

Geneve & Langres par ceux de	Geneva and Langres through
Chartres & Dole,	the people of Chartres and
Et par Grenoble captif au Montli-	Dôle, and Grenoble, captive at
mard:	Montelimar: Seysel, Lausanne,
Seysett, Losanne par fraudulente	through a fraudulent trick will
dole	betray them for sixty gold
Les trahiront par or soixante marc.	marks.

There are too many scattered place-names in both Switzerland and France to make this quatrain clear. A mark was 8 oz. of gold.

43

Seront ouis au ciel les armes battre:	Weapons will be heard fighting
Celui an mesme les divins ennemis:	in the skies: in the same year
Voudrant loix sainctes injustement	the divine are enemies: they
debatre,	will want unjustly to query the
Par foudre & guerre bien croyans	holy laws, through lightning and
à mort mis.	war many believers put to
	death.

AERIAL WARFARE?

The first line seems to indicate an air battle of some type but the divine enemies are difficult to decipher.

¹ *Gymnique*—Misprint for Greek, *gynique* = female.

Deux gros de Mende, de Rondés &
    Milhau,
Cahours, Limoges, Castres malo
    sepmano
De nuech l'intrado de Bourdeaux
    un cailhau,
Par Perigort au toc de la campano.

The two large ones of Mende, of Rodez and Milhau, Cahors and Limoges, Castres a bad week: by night the entry; from Bordeaux an insult, through Perigord at the peal of the bell.

A quatrain of mixed Provençal and French phrases. Unfortunately they seem to disguise little more than the names of a series of towns in South-west France.

Par conflit Roi, regne abandonnera,
Le plus grand chef faillira au
    besoing:
Mors profligés peu en rechapera,
Tous destranchés un en sera tes-
    moing.

Through a battle the king will abandon his kingdom, the greatest leader will fail in time of need. Dead, ruined, few will escape it all cut down, save one who will be a witness.

This quatrain is suggested as suitable for Napoleon I at Waterloo, Napoleon III at Sédan or Kaiser Wilhelm II. The reader can take his choice. A typical prophecy.

Bien defendu le faict par excellence,
Garde toy Tours de ta proche ruine:
Londres & Nantes par Reims fera
    defense
Ne passe outre au temps de la
    bruine.

The deed, through its excellence, strongly forbidden, Tours, beware of your approaching ruin. London and Nantes will make a defence through Reims. Do not go further afield at the time of the fog.

Le noir farouche quand aura
    essayé
Sa main sanguine par feu, fer,
    arcs tendus:
Trestout le peuple sera tant
    effrayé,
Voir les plus grans par col & pieds
    pendus.

When the ferocious king will have exercised his bloody hand through fire, the sword and the bended bow. All the nation will be so terrified to see the great ones hanging by their neck and feet.

In line 1 *noir* is the usual anagram for *roi*, King. The savage king was the mad Charles IX, who was reputed to kill for the sake of blood when out hunting, decapitating animals which came across his path. The fear of the people refers to the massacre of St. Bartholomew, of the French Huguenots on 24th August 1572, when Admiral Coligny was killed by the mob and hung from a gibbet by one foot.

48

Planure Ausonne fertile, spacieuse,
Produira taons si tant de sauter-
*   elles:*
Clarté solaire deviendra nubileuse,
Rouger le tout, grand peste venir
*   d'elles.*

The plains of Ausonia, rich and wide, will produce so many gadflies and grasshoppers, that the light of the sun will be clouded over. They will devour everything and a great pestilence will come from them.

Perhaps *sauterelles* could be translated as locusts in this context. But have they ever been found as far north as Naples (Ausonia)?

49

Devant le peuple, sang sera res-
*   pandu,*
Que de haut ciel ne viendra esloig-
*   ner:*
Mais d'un long temps ne sera
*   entendu,*
L'esprit d'un seul le viendra
*   tesmoigner.*

Blood will be spilt in front of the people, which will not go far from the high heavens. But for a long time it will not be heard, the spirit of a single man will bear witness to it.

Line 2 probably implies that the spilt blood was calling to the heavens for vengeance, but the bloody deed which caused it is not clarified.

50

Libra verra regner les Hesperies,
De ciel & terre tenir la monarchie:
D'Asie forces nul ne verra paries,
Que sept ne tiennent par rang le
*   hierarchie.*

Libra will be seen to reign in the West, holding the rule over the skies and earth. No one will see the strength of Asia destroyed until seven hold the hierarchy in succession.

According to this prediction, when Libra the Balance rules over America, that country will be at the height of its powers. But Asian strength will be equally strong until the seventh comes. Does this mean the seventh ruler in Asia, or the seventh decade? The last line may mean that a war between East and West may occur during the 7th decade of this Century. See II. 89, III. 60, IV. 95, VI. 21, etc. Equally it may refer to the Seven, the Common Market as it existed, until the four new members joined in 1973. See V. 40 etc.

51

Un Duc cupide son enemi ensuivre,	A Duke eager to follow his enemy will enter in, hindering the phalanx. Hurried on foot they follow so closely that the day of the battle is near Ganges.
Dans entrera empeschant la phalange:	
Hastez à pied si pres viendront poursuivre,	
Que la journee conflite pres de Gange.	

Ganges may be understood as a town in France near Montpellier, or the River Ganges. The former is more likely.

52

En cité obsesse aux murs hommes & femmes,	In the besieged city men and women at the walls, the enemy without, the leader ready to surrender; the wind will be strong against the armed men, they will be driven off by lime, dust and cinders.
Ennemis hors le chef prest à soi rendre	
Vent sera fort encontre les gendarmes,	
Chassez seront par chaux, poussiere, & cendre.	

53

Les fugitifs & bannis revoquez,	The fugitives and the banished are recalled, fathers and sons strengthening the deep wells. The cruel father and his followers suffocated; His most wicked son drowned in the well.
Peres & fils grand garnissant les hauts puits:	
Le cruel pere & les siens suffoquez,	
Son fils plus pire submergé dans le puits.	

Du nom qui onques ne fut au Roy
Gaulois,
Jamais ne fut un fouldre si craintif:
Tremblant l'Italie, l'Espaigne &
les Anglois,
De femme estrangiers grandement
attentif.

Of a name which never held by
a French king, never was there
so fearful a thunderbolt. Italy,
Spain and the English tremble;
he will be greatly attentive to
foreign women.

NAPOLEON I

This is a fascinating quatrain. Napoleon brought the new name of
Bonaparte to the line of French kings, for most kings had shared
the same names, i.e. Louis (6), Henri (2), Charles (2), Francis (1),
since Nostradamus' time. Napoleon's was the great reshaping of
the map of Europe and he was very enamoured of his two foreign
wives, Josephine the Créole, Marie Louise the Austrian, and
possibly it also refers to his Polish mistress, Marie Walewska. The
reference to his name being dreadful as a thunderbolt should be
compared with IV. 82, where Nostradamus calls him the Destroyer.

Quant la corneille sur tout de
brique joincte,
Durant sept heures ne fera que
crier:
Mort presagee de sang statue
taincte,
Tyran meutri, aux Dieux peuple
prier.

When the crow on a tower
made of brick will do nothing
but croak for seven hours; it
foretells death, a statue stained
with blood, a tyrant murdered,
people praying to their Gods.

Both the crow, and the statue weeping blood are common omens
of evil, the latter has been recorded even in this country. But the
results of these omens are too general to pinpoint the stanza.

Apres victoire de babieuse langue
L'esprit tempte en tranquil & repos:
Victeur sanguin par conflict faict
harangue,
Roustir la langue & la chair & les
os.

After the victory of the raging
tongue, the spirit tempted in
tranquil rest. Throughout the
battle the bloody victor makes
speeches, roasting the tongue,
the flesh and the bones.

Ignare envie au grand Roi sup-
portee,
Tiendra propos deffendre les
escripitz:
Sa femme non femme par un autre
tentee,
Plus double deux ne fort ne criz.

Ignorant envy supported by
the great king, he will propose
forbidding the writings. His
wife, not his wife, tempted by
another, no longer will the
double dealing couple protest
against it.

It has been suggested that Nostradamus is here referring to his own
writings and Henri II's cool reception of the Prophecies. The
mistress would be Diane de Poitiers. There is a similar reference in
VII. 9. The last line is very difficult to translate.

Soleil ardent dans le gosier coller,
De sang humain arrouser terre
Etrusque:
Chef seille¹ d'eaue, mener son fils
filer,
Captive dame conduicte en terre
Turque.

To swallow the burning sun in
the throat, the Tuscan land
sprinkled with human blood,
the leader leads his son away,
the pail of water, a captive
lady led into Turkish lands.

Deux assiegez en ardente ferveur,
De soif estaincts pour deux plaines
tasses:
Le fort lime, & un vieillart
resveur,
Au Genevois de Nira monstra
trasse.

Two besieged in a burning
heat, killed by thirst for want
of two full cups; the fort filed,
and an old dreamer will show
the tracks of Nira to the
Genevans.

IRAN?

Nira is one of the few unsolved enigmatic names in the Prophecies.
It may be a corruption of Jura, the Swiss mountain range, or imply
someone quite different. It is an anagram of modern Iran.

Les sept enfans en hostaige laissés,
Le tiers viendra son enfant trucider:
Deux par son filz seront d'estoc
percés,
Gennes, Florence, los viendra
encunder.²

The seven children left in
hostage, the third will come to
slaughter his child. Two will be
pierced by a hook because of
his son, he will come to strike
against Genoa and Florence.

¹ *seille*—O.F. = pail, bucket.
² *encunder*—Probably from the Latin, *incutiere* = to strike against.

It is not clear whether these seven children are the Valois children of Catherine de Medici; the rest of the quatrain does not clarify the position.

61

Le vieux mocqué & privé de sa
place,
Par l'estrangier qui le subornera:
Mains de son filz mangées devant
sa face,
Le frere à Chartres, Orl. Rouen
trahira.

The old man, mocked and deprived of his position by the foreigner who will suborn him. The hands of his sons are devoured before his face, he will betray his brother at Chartres, Orléans and Rouen.

MARSHAL PÉTAIN, 1940–4

Marshal Pétain's nickname during the Vichy régime was *Le Vieux*, and nothing could describe his position more clearly than line 2. The hands which are devoured in front of him are the forces of his régime which are destroyed. The brothers are the Allies who simultaneously reached the three towns here mentioned, Chartres, Orleans and Rouen on 19th August 1944. They were betrayed by Pétain to the Germans, who was deported to Sigmariggen on the very day of their liberation.

62

Un coronel machine ambition,
Se saisira de la plus grand armée,
Contre son prince fainte invention,
Et descouvert sera soubz sa ramée.

A colonel intrigues through ambition, he will seize the greater part of the army. Against his Prince a false invention; he will be discovered under his flag.

OLIVER CROMWELL

Most commentators accept this as a general quatrain about Oliver Cromwell, who took over the greater part of Charles I's armies and fought with them under the British flag. He certainly connived in the plotting and accusations laid against the king at his trial and execution. However it would apply very neatly to Colonel Qaddafi who overthrew King Idris of Libya in 1971.

L'armée Celtique contre les montaignars,	The Celtic army against the mountaineers, who will be
Qui seront sceus & prins à la lipée:	revealed and caught in a trap.
Paysans frais pousseront tost faugnars,	The fresh bracken will soon be pressed by the peasants, they
Precipitez tous au fil de l'espee.	will all perish on the sword's blade.

FRANCE 1702–4

This probably refers to Marshal Villar's fight against the Camisard rebels of the Cevennes who practised a very competent form of guerrilla warfare (1702–4).

Le deffaillant en habit de bourgeois,	The defaulter, dressed as a citizen will come to try the king
Viendra le Roi tempter de son offence:	with his offence; Fifteen soldiers, for the most part outlaws,
Quinze souldartz la plupart Ustagois,	the end of his life and the greater part of his estate.
Vie derniere & chef de sa chevance.	

Au deserteur de la grand forteresse,	To the deserter of the great fortress, after he will have
Apres qu'aura son lieu abandonné:	abandoned his post, his adversary will display such prowess
Son adversaire fera si grand prouesse,	that the Emperor will soon be condemned to death.
L'Empereur tost mort sera condamné.	

NAPOLEON III

Napoleon III, while still Louis Napoleon, was condemned to life detention in the fortress of Ham by the French, but on 25th May 1846 escaped from the castle to England. Louis Philippe abandoned his position as king of France in the 1848 Revolution and Louis Napoleon was voted Prince-President in December of the same year. He did not, however, display great skills as an Emperor, and his policies were responsible for the Franco-Prussian war and the consequent disaster to France. He died soon afterwards in 1873. The adversaries who are so powerful are, of course, the Prussians.

Soubz couleur faincte de sept testes
    raseés
Seront semés divers esplorateurs:
Puys & fontaines de poisons
    arrousées,
Au fort de Gennes humains devora-
    teurs.

Under the false colours of seven
shaven heads several spies will
be scattered. The wells and
springs will be sprinkled with
poisons, at the fort of Genoa,
they devour human flesh.

Shaven heads is sometimes used by Nostradamus to describe
Cromwell's roundheads.

L'an que Saturne & Mars esgaux
    combuste,
L'air fort seiché longue trajection:
Par feux secrets, d'ardeur grand
    lieu adust
Peu pluie, vent chault, guerres,
    incursions.

In the year that Saturn and
Mars are equally fiery, the air
is very dry, a long meteor.
From hidden fires a great place
burns with heat, little rain, a
hot wind, wars and raids.

The configuration of Saturn and Mars is a common one, so further
information is needed to understand this quatrain. The dating of
the comet or meteor is probably the key.

En lieu bien proche non esloigné de
    Venus,
Les deux plus grans de l'Asie &
    d'Affrique
Du Rhin & Hister qu'on dira sont
    venus,
Cris, pleurs à Malte & costé
    ligustique.

At a nearby place not far from
Venus, the two greatest ones
of Asia and Africa will be said
to have come from the Rhine
and Hitler; cries and tears at
Malta and the Ligurian coast.

HITLER AND MUSSOLINI. TRIPARTITE PACT

The word Venus is the clue to this quatrain. It probably stands for
Venice, thus linking Italy with Hitler. The two dictators met not
far from the city at the Brenner Pass to seal the Tripartite Pact
with Asia, that is, the Japanese. The last line refers to the blockade
of Malta by the Italians, and the trouble on the Ligurian coast,
to the Allied bombing of Genoa, and to the bombardments by
British battleships operating from Gibraltar.

La cité grande les exiles tiendront,
Les citadins morts meurtris &
*   chaffés:*
Ceulx d'Aquilee à Parme pro-
*   mettront,*
Monstrer l'entree par les lieux non
*   trassés.*

The exiles will hold the great city, the citizens are dead, murdered and driven out. The people of Aqualeia will promise Parma to show them the entrance by untrodden paths.

Aqualeia was a great city in ancient times, but nothing more than a village by the 16th Century. Parma belonged to the Papacy and became an hereditary duchy for the Pope's bastard in 1545.

Bien contigue des grans monts
*   Pyrenees,*
Un contre l'aigle grand copie
*   addresser:*
Ouvertes veines, forces exterminees,
Comme jusque à Pau le chef
*   viendra chasser.*

Very near the great mountains of the Pyrenees, a man will raise a great army against the Eagle. Veins will be opened, strength disappears; the leader will chase them as far as the Pau.

WELLINGTON'S CAMPAIGN IN THE PENINSULAR WAR

This describes Wellington's approach to France through Portugal and Spain where he is to confront the Eagle, Napoleon. The opened veins probably indicate the lost supply lines of the French when they were driven back as far as the Pau, despite the French victory at Toulouse, which was of uncertain value to Napoleon.

En lieu d'espouse les filles trucidées,
Meurtre à grand faulte ne sera
*   superstile:*[1]
Dedans le puys vestules inondées,
L'espouse estraincte par hauste
*   d'Aconite.*

Instead of a bride the girls are slaughtered, murder with such wickedness, there will be no survivors. The vestals are drowned in the wells, and the bride killed by a draught of Aconite.

Aconite is a classical poison distilled from monkshood and wolfs-bane. Otherwise the quatrain seems completely obscure.

[1] *superstile*—Misprint for *superstite* = survivor.

Les Artomiques par Agen & *l'Estore,* *A sainct Felix feront leur parlement:* *Ceux de Basas viendront à la* *mal'heure,* *Saisir Concon & Marsan prompte-* *ment.*	The Artomiques through Agen & Lectoure will hold their parliament at St. Felix. Those of Bazas will come at an unfortunate time to seize Condon & Marsan promptly.

What the Artomiques are is not certain. Artos in Greek means bread, but there is also a resemblance to the modern word atomic.

Le nepveu grand par forces prou- *vera,* *Le pache[1] faict du coeur pusillanime:* *Ferrare & Ast le Duc esprouvera,* *Par lors qu'au soir sera le panto-* *mime.*	The nephew shall prove by great strength the crime com- mitted by a cowardly heart. The Duke will try Ferrara and Asti; then when the comedy takes place in the evening.

ASSASSINATION OF THE DUKE DE BERRY, 1820

This event is described vividly by Nostradamus in I. 84 and III. 96 in which quatrain he gives the date as well. The Duke de Berry was killed leaving the Opéra on the evening of 13th February 1820. The nephew who benefits from this is Napoleon III who later succeeds to the throne because of the assassination of the male heir.

Du lac liman & ceux de Brannon- *ices,[2]* *Tous assemblez contre ceux d'Aqui-* *taine* *Germains beaucoup, encor plus* *Souisses,* *Seront defaictz avec ceux* *d'Humaine.[3]*	The people of Lake Geneva and of Mâcon, all gathered against the people of Aquitaine; many Germans, even more Swiss will be routed together with those of Maine.

It is just possible that by *Humaine* in the last line Nostradamus is referring to the Humanists whom he would regard as responsible for the Protestants Reformation in Switzerland.

[1] *pache*—O.F. = treaty. Variant, *peche* = crime.
[2] *Brannonices*—Latin = people from around Mâcon.
[3] *Humaine*—Variant, *ceux du Maine*.

Prest à combatre fera defection.	He who was ready to fight will
Chef adversaire obtiendra la	desert, the chief adversary will
victoire.	win the victory. The rear guard
L'arriere garde fera defension,	will make a defence, those
Les deffaillans mort au blanc	faltering, dying in a white
territoire.	country.

WATERLOO, 1815

Marshal Grouchy is the deserter of the first line. He was commander of the French cavalry whose orders from Napoleon were delayed for twelve hours, but even when he received them, Grouchy did not do as asked. Wellington is the great adversary of the French who is victorious. The famous stand of Napoleon's Imperial Guard who fought to the last man is described in the following line, while the white country may be an indirect reference to Napoleon's retreat from Moscow in 1812, and is a direct one to the sign of the white cockade of the Bourbons. It was said that after Napoleon's capture there were so many white cockades that Paris looked as though there had been a fall of snow.

Les Nictobriges[1] par ceux de	The people of Agen by those
Perigort,	of Perigord will be troubled as
Seront vexez tenant jusques au	far as the Rhône. The asso-
Rosne:	ciation of Gascons & Bigorre,
L'associé de Gascons & Begorne,	betrays the Church, the priest
Trahir le temple, le prebstre	giving his sermon.
estant au prosne.	

Both Agen and Perigord are about two hundred miles west of the Rhône. Bigorre was a Gascon town, but also a rallying cry of Henri de Navarre's Huguenots, and the verse is probably hinting at the Protestant, Catholic conflict in France in the 16th Century.

[1] *Nictobriges* = the people around Agen.

SELIN monarque l'Italie pacifique,	Selin king, Italy peaceful, king-
Regnes unis Roi chrestien du monde:	doms united by the Christian king of the world. When he
Mourrant voudra coucher en terre blesique[1]	dies, he will want to lie in Blois territory, having chased
Apres pirates avoir chassé de l'onde.	the pirates from the sea.

This is the quatrain upon which many 19th Century royalists built their hopes of a great French king who would come and change the face of Europe. The key to the quatrain is the word *SELIN*; it comes from the Greek *Selene*, the Moon or Diana. There is a strong possibility that Nostradamus went completely off the rails with this series of quatrains and intended them for Henri II and his mistress Diane de Poitiers. Henri II also adopted the moon as his device, but nevertheless these verses were not understood by his contemporaries. Perhaps they are a good example of retroactive history, as I explain in the introduction, of something that seems unlikely now ever to take place. The notion of a Christian king governing the world seems impossible, particularly when compared with the quatrains which describe the situation envisaged by Nostradamus between America and the Far East.

78

La grand armee de la pugne civile,	The great army of the civil war,
Pour de nuict Parme à l'estrange trouvée,	Parma taken at night by foreigners. Seventy-nine mur-
Septante neuf meurtris dedans la ville,	dered in the town, the foreign- ers all put to the sword.
Les estrangiers passez tous à l'espee.	

Parma was an Italian duchy and an ally of the French, so the Spanish army is the most likely interpretation for line 2.

[1] *blesique*—Med. Latin, *Blesa* = Blois.

Sang Royal fuis, Monhurt, Mas, Eguillon,	Flee, royal blood, Monheurt, Mas, Aiguillon, the Landes will be full of people from Bourdeaux. Navarre, Bigorre, points and spurs, deeply hungry they devour acorns of the cork oak.
Remplis seront de Bourdelois les landes,	
Navarre, Bigorre poinctes & eguillons,	
Profondz de faim vorer de liege glandes.	

All these places are in South-west France and have probably some connection with IV. 76, the struggle of the Huguenots and Henri de Navarre against the Catholics. As mentioned before, Bigorre was the rallying cry of the Protestants.

Pres du grand fleuve, grand fosse, terre egeste,	Near the great river, a great trench, earth excavated, the water will be divided into fifteen parts. The city taken, fire, blood, cries and battle given, the greater part concerned with the collision.
En quinze pars sera l'eau divisee:	
La cité prinse, feu, sang, cris conflict mettre	
Et la plus part concerne au collisee.[1]	

THE MAGINOT LINE

James Laver suggests that this is the quatrain which persuaded the Abbé Torné to insist that France erected the infamous Maginot line, which fell so quickly to the Germans. The River in line 1 is the Rhine. Hitler partially ignored the Maginot line and advanced from other directions thus fulfilling lines 3 and 4. The collision becomes the series of battles fought in France during the Second World War.

Pont on fera promptement de nacelles,	A bridge will quickly be built from boats, to cross the army of a great Belgian Prince. Poured forth inside not far from Brussels, having passed over, seven will be cut down by a pike.
Passer l'armee du grand prince Belgique:	
Dans profondres[2] & non loing de Brucelles,	
Outre passés, detrenchés sept à picque.	

[1] *collisee*—Latin, *collisus* = clash.
[2] *profondres*—Latin, *profondatus* = poured forth.

When Nostradamus wrote, the word Belgian was archaic and could only have referred to Philip II, who had been given the territory in 1554 by the Emperor Charles V. An attack on Northern France, crossing the River Scheldt was made in the 1560s.

82

Amas s'approche venant d'Escla-vonie, *L'Olestant vieux cité ruinera:* *Fort desolee verra sa Romanie.* *Puis la grand flamme estaindre ne sçaura.*	A mass of men will draw near, coming from Slavonia, the Destroyer will ruin the old city, he will see his Romania quite desolated, then will not know how to extinguish the great flame.

NAPOLEON'S RETREAT FROM MOSCOW, 1812–13
The grande armée retreated from Moscow during the bitter winter of 1812/13. The word Olestant means Destroyer and Nostradamus refers to Napoleon as this in IV. 54 when he calls him the dreadful thunderbolt. The old city is Moscow which was razed to the ground by fire. The word Romanie cannot refer to Rumania which did not exist in Nostradamus' time, but may well refer to Rome, as Napoleon's young son had just been made king of Rome, and his empire would not continue for much longer. The great flame is probably a metaphor for the war which Napoleon started and which gathered in momentum to finally defeat him.

83

Combat nocturne le vaillant capitaine, *Vaincu fuira peu de gens profligé:* *Son peuple esmeu, sedition non vaine,* *Son propre filz le tiendra assiegé.*	In a night battle the brave captain is overcome and flees, ruined by a few men. His people are moved, they agitate successfully, his own son will hold him besieged.

84

Un grand d'Auxerre mourra bien miserable, *Chassé de ceux qui soubs lui ont esté:* *Serré de chaines, apres d'un rude cable,* *En l'an que Mars, Venus, & Sol, mis en esté.*	An important man from Auxerre will die very wretchedly, driven out by the people who were under him. Bound in chains, then with a strong rope, the year that Mars, Venus and the Sun are in conjunction in the summer.

This is a very rare conjunction but has not brought forth an important man from Auxerre to date, so this quatrain may apply to the future.

85

Le charbon blanc du noir sera chassé,	The white coal is driven out by the black, made a prisoner, led to the tumbril: his feet are tied together like a rogue, when the last born will let slip the falcon.
Prisonnier faicte mené au tombereau:	
More[1] Chameau sus piedz entrelassez,	
Lors le puisné sillera l'aubereau.	

LOUIS XVI AND THE FRENCH REVOLUTION

Charbon is an anagram for Bourbon, *noir* the usual anagram for king and white the colour of the Bourbon standard. Louis XVI was the last Bourbon king before the Revolution. He was imprisoned in the Temple and dragged on a tumbril, with his feet tied, to his death on 27th January 1793. The last line probably implies that his heir, Louis XVII, about whom there has been so much speculation and doubt, may have escaped from the Temple and have lived quietly in Europe. Nostradamus refers to this theme eslewhere in the Prophecies. Louis was the second son, the last born son of the family. His elder brother Charles died in 1795.

86

L'an que Saturne en eau sera conjoinct,	In the year Saturn is in conjunction with Aquarius, and with the Sun, the very powerful king will be received and anointed at Reims & Aix. After conquests he will murder innocent people.
Avecques Sol, le Roi fort & puissant:	
A Reims & Aix sera reçeu & oingt,	
Apres conquestes meurtrira innocens.	

The astrological conjunction of lines 1 and 2 is again reasonably rare. Reims is the traditional coronation site for the French Kings and Aix that of the German and Holy Roman Emperors. No king has been crowned in both places since Nostradamus' time. This is another of the quatrains used by French Royalists to predict the return of the French royal line.

[1] *more*—Latin, *mos, moris* = custom, a practice.

Un filz du Roi tant de langues aprins,	The son of a king, having learnt many languages, different from his elder in the kingdom. His father-in-law understanding well the elder son, will cause the main adherent to perish.
A son aisné[1] au regne different:	
Son pere beau[2] au plus grand filz comprins	
Fera perir principal adherent.	

The quatrain implies that the younger son of a king will take over the kingdom, the elder, legitimate heir having been removed by his father (in law?).

Le grand Antoine du nom de faicte sordide	Anthony, great in name, in his actions base, at the end will be devoured by lice. One who is eager for lead, passing the harbour will be drowned by the elected one.
De Phthiriase[3] à son dernier rongé:	
Un qui de plomb voudra estre cupide,	
Passant le port d'esleu sera plongé.	

A difficult prophecy for someone named Anthony. Phthiriasis, pediculosis, is an illness caused by lice.

Trente de Londres secret conjureront,	Thirty Londoners will secretly conspire against their king; the enterprise on the sea. He and his courtiers will not like death, a fair king elected, native of Friesland.
Contre leur Roi sur le pont[4] entreprinse,	
Lui, satalites la mort degousteront.	
Un Roi esleu blonde, natif de Frize.	

WILLIAM III OF ENGLAND

This is a good prediction of the Glorious Revolution of 1688–9. William III insisted that those lords who supported him in England should sign a document. There were certainly a number of conspirators crossing the seas to Holland and back before William sailed with his fleet. The ones who dislike death are James II and his supporters who decide to flee rather than fight the matter out

[1] *aisné* = elder or predecessor.
[2] *pere beau* = father-in-law or handsome father.
[3] *Phthiriase*—*Phthisis* = consumption. Phthiriasis = suffering from lice.
[4] *pont*—Latin, *pontus* = sea, not a bridge in this context.

once the Duke of Marlborough, who led the army, deserted their cause. It is not certain whether William III was fair-haired but he did come from Friesland. What makes this prophecy so interesting is that there was no possible Dutch candidate for the English throne while Nostradamus was alive.

90

Les deux copies aux murs ne pourront joindre.
Dans cest instant trembler Milan, Ticin:[1]
Faim, soif doubtance si fort les viendra poindre,
Chair, pain, ne vivres n'auront un seul boucin.[2]

The two armies cannot join up at the walls. At that time Milan and Pavia tremble. Hunger, thirst and doubt will weigh upon them so much, they will not have a scrap of meat, bread nor supplies.

91

Au duc Gauloise contrainct battre au duelle,
La nef Mollele monech n'approchera,
Tort accusé, prison perpetuelle,
Son fils regner avant mort taschera.

For the French duke compelled to fight in a duel, the ship Mellele will not approach Monaco. Wrongly accused in perpetual prison his son will attempt to reign before his death.

Mellele may be a corruption of Melilla, a Moroccan sea port, but it does not fit into context very well. Perhaps this quatrain has some connection with IV. 83? The last lines are very similar.

92

Teste tranchee du vaillant capitaine,
Sera gettee devant son adversaire:
Son corps pendu de la chasse à l'antenne,
Confus fuira par rames à vent contraire.

The head of the brave captain cut off it will be thrown down in front of his adversary. His body hung from the masts of the ship, confused, he will flee using oars in a contrary wind.

RADIO OR RADAR EQUIPMENT?

It is interesting that Nostradamus used the word antenne here instead of mât for the ship's mast. Perhaps he was using this word to indicate complex equipment with which he was not familiar

[1] Ticin—Latin, Ticinum = Pavia.
[2] boucin—Provençal = mouthful, morsel.

but which he recognized to be scientific, such as a radio mast or radar equipment?

Un serpent veu proche du lict royal;	A serpent will be seen near the royal bed by a lady at night,
Sera par dame nuict chiens n'abayeront:	the watchdogs will not bark;
Lors naistre en France un Prince tant royal,	Then will be born in France a Prince so royal, that all the
Du ciel venu tous les Princes verront.	princes will see him as a gift from heaven.

THE COUNT DE CHAMBORD, 1820–83

The Duchesse de Berry gave birth to a son in 1820, seven months after he husband's assassination. The legitimacy of the birth was contested by the Duke of Orléans, the snake, who had right of entry as a member of the family and so the watchdogs were not alerted. This birth of a grandson to Charles X was the cause of great rejoicing to French monarchists and the child was called 'Dieudonné', a gift from heaven, as Nostradamus so aptly puts it.

94

Deux grans freres seront chassez d'Espaigne,	Two great brothers will be driven out of Spain, the elder
L'aisné vaincu sous les monts Pyrenees:	is beaten under the Pyrenean mountains. The sea is red-
Rougir mer, rosne, sang lemam d'Alemaigne,	dened, the Rhône, blood in Lake Geneva from Germany,
Narbon, Blyterre, d'Agath¹ contaminees.	Narbonne and Beziers contaminated by Agde.

A detailed qutrain containing five separate predictions:
1 Exile for two Spanish leaders.
2 Defeat for one of them near the Pyrenees.
3 A bloody naval battle.
4 An attack against Geneva from Germany.
5 A possible plague spreading from Agde, see also VIII. 21 to local towns.

¹ *Agatha*—Latin = Agde.

La regne à deux laissé bien peu tiendront,	The rule left to two, they will hold it a very short time. Three
Trois and sept mois passés feront la guerre.	years and seven months having passed they will go to war. The
Les deux vestales contre eux rebelleront,	two vestals will rebel against them; the victor then born on
Victor puis nay en Armorique terre.	American soil.

U.S.A. AND WAR?

If in this quatrain the two powers are understood to be world powers, it implies that 3 years and 7 months after the Russian/American alliance, which Nostradamus predicts elsewhere, has taken place they will go to war against Asia. *Vestales* in line 3 is probably a corruption of *vassals*—two smaller countries disagree with this decision and perhaps stay neutral. The final victory lies in the West, with America. But see also III. 60 and IV. 50 for a possible dating in the 70s etc.

96

La soeur aisnée de l'isle Britannique,	The elder sister of the island of Britain will be born fifteen
Quinze ans devant le frere aura naissance:	years before her brother. Because of his promise proving to
Par son promis moyennant verrifique,	be true, she will succeed to the kingdom of the Balance.
Succedera au regne de balance.	

WILLIAM AND MARY

Mary was the elder sister of James III, who never came to the English throne, but she was in fact twenty-six, not fifteen years older than her brother. Mary acceded to the throne through her own, and her husband William of Orange's, promises to the English parliament. The Balance is Libra, the zodiacal sign, which Nostradamus seems here to apply to England although many astrologers apply it to Austria and Savoy. It also governs a trading nation, which the British certainly are. Note that again Nostradamus speaks of the British Isles and not of England which immediately dates the quatrain later than 1603.

L'an que Mercure, Mars, Venus retrograde,	In the year that Mercury, Mars and Venus are retrograde, the
Du grand Monarque la ligne ne faillit:	family line of the great King will not fail. Elected by the
Esleu du peuple l'usitant[1] pres de Gagdole,[2]	Portuguese people near Cadiz, who in peace will grow very old
Qu'en paix & regne viendra fort envieillir.	in his kingdom.

This quatrain seems to describe the Portuguese succession and is limited in time by the conjunction of line 1. It seems also to imply that the Portuguese king is elected in Spain, which never happened. But Philip II of Spain seized the Portuguese throne and ruled it until 1621, followed by his son Philip III, until the Portuguese revolted against the Spanish in 1640. However, Nostradamus did appear to understand the Spanish seizure of the Portuguese throne.

Les Albanois, passeront dedans Rome,	The people of Alba will cross into Rome, by means of
Moyennant Langres demipler[3] affublés,	Langres the multitude are weakened. The Marquis and
Marquis & Duc ne pardonnes à l'homme,	the Duke will spare no man, fire, blood and smallpox, no
Feu, sang, morbilles[4] point d'eau, faillir les bleds.	water, the crops will fail.

The word *Albanois* is hard to interpret. It probably stands for the troops of the Duke of Alba, but Albania is a possibility. The many disasters are obscure. *Langres* is in Champagne, so possibly it is the same person as in VII. 4?

[1] *usitant*—Misreading for *Lusitans* = Portuguese.

[2] *Gagdole*—Probable misprint for *Gades* = Cadiz, as the present reading doesn't even rhyme and is obviously incorrect.

[3] *demipler*—A word invented by Nostradamus, probably from the Greek, *demis-pleres* = mob-full or multitude.

[4] *morbilles*—O.F. = smallpox.

L'aisné vaillant de la fille du Roy,	The brave eldest son of a king's
Repoussera si profond les Celtiques:	daughter will drive the Celts
Qu'il mettra foudres, combien en	back very far. He will use
tel arroi	thunderbolts, so many in such
Peu & loing puis profond és	an array, few and distant, then
Hesperiques.[1]	deep into the West.

MISSILES OR ROCKETS?

The Celts referred to here are the French who are driven back by an unidentified leader. He fights with such fearful and far-reaching weapons that they can even penetrate as far as Spain or America, implying either mortar shells, missiles or possibly rockets with warheads.

De feu celeste au Royal edifice,	Fire will fall from the sky on to
Quant la lumiere de Mars defail-	the royal building when the
lira:	light of war is weakened. For
Sept mois grand guerre, mort gent	seven months a great war,
de malefice,	people dead through evil,
Rouen, Eureux au Roi ne faillira.	Rouen and Evreux will not fail
	the king.

FRANCO-PRUSSIAN WAR, 1870–71

During the siege of Paris the royal palace, the Tuileries, was destroyed by cannon fire. The glory of the Bonaparte family was weakened and almost ended by this war. Napoleon III was to die two years later, and France remained a republic from then on. The Franco-Prussian war did last for seven months, July 1870 to February 1871, an accurate prediction. The last line refers to towns in Normandy, which part of France remained loyal to the king and wanted to restore the monarchy through the National Assembly.

[1] *Hesperiques*—As always, either the Western lands of Spain and Portugal, or the U.S.A.

CENTURY V

34?
35
36
37
38*   Louis XV
39*   Count de Chambord
40**   U.S.A., France and the Common Market
41
42*   Return of Savoy to France
43
44
45*   Battle of Sedan, 1940
46?   New Pope?
47
48
49?   Future Pope from France
50
51**   Second World War. The Allies
52
53
54*F? Man from East?
55
56*   New Pope
57**   Montgolfier balloon, 1783
58*   1627
59
60*   Cromwell
61*   Eugène de Beauharnais
62
63
64
65
66
67*   France and the Vatican
68?
69*   Louis Philippe, 1830
70
71
72   Edict of Poitiers, 1577
73
74
75
76

206

77
78**F Alliance between U.S.A. and U.S.S.R.?
79*   Napoleon
80
81*? Berlin Wall?
82
83
84
85*   League of Nations
86   France and Turkey
87
88*   1815. Savona
89
90*F? Chemical Warfare in Greece and Balkans?
91
92*   Future of the Vatican
93*   The Young Pretender
94*   Hitler and Russia
95
96
97   Man in the Iron Mask
98
99   Napoleon and the last of the Stuarts
100

KEY: * Of interest. F? Possibly referring to the future.

Avant venu de ruine Celtique,	Before the ruin of France, there
Dedans le temple deux parlementer- *ont*	will be parliamentary discussions about the second. Stabbed
Poignard coeur, d'un monté au *coursier & pique,*	to the heart by one riding on a charger with a lance, they will
Sans faire bruit le grand enter- *reront.*	bury the great one secretly.

THE MURDER OF LOUIS XVII (1785–95?)

There has always been much speculation about the fate of Louis XVII, the second son and heir of Louis XVI and Marie Antoinette. The King and his family were housed in the Temple in 1792, when the Revolutionary mobs appeared to be getting out of hand. The fate of the whole family was debated by the newly formed French Legislative Assembly (*parlementeront*). It is not known how Louis XVII died but Nostradamus indicates clearly that he was killed in line 4. The third line describes his killer as an unidentified soldier. He was appallingly ill-treated in prison, separated from his mother and sisters and kept in the dark for months on end, like a wild beast. In May 1795 he was declared to be seriously ill and his death was announced on 8th June. Several pretenders came forward during the next forty years claiming to be the young Prince, but if Nostradamus is correct he was buried at the Church of St. Marguerite on 10th June, as was officially announced, without even a stone to mark the spot '*sans faire bruit*'.

2

Seps conjurés au banquet feront *luire,*	Seven conspirators at a banquet will cause their weapons to flash
Contre les trois le fer hors de navire:	against the three who come
L'un des deux classes au grand fera *conduire*	from the ship. One of the two will take the fleet to the leader
Quand par le mail. Denier au front *lui tire.*	when the other will shoot him in the forehead through his armour.

Le successeur de la Duché viendra,
Beaucoup plus outre que la mer de
  Tosquane:
Gauloise branche la Florence tiendra,
Dans son giron d'accord nautique
  Rane.[1]

The successor to the Duchy will
come from far beyond the sea of
Tuscany. A French branch will
hold Florence, in its wake a
nautical agreement (with the
frog?).

DUKE OF LORRAINE, 1737

Florence was the capital of the Duchy of Tuscany from the rule of
Alessandro de' Medici in 1531 until the death of Gian Gastone in
1737 when the Duchy was assigned to Francis, Duke of Lorraine, a
Frenchman, and remained in the Lorraine family until 1859,
except during the French Revolution. The reference to a nautical
agreement and a frog is unclear. It may refer to the myth in which
the earliest inhabitants of Tuscany were turned into frogs by
Bacchus.

Le gros mastin de cité deschassé,
Sera fasché de l'etrange alliance,
Apres aux champs avoir le cerf
  chassé
Le lous & l'Ours se donront
  defiance.

The great mastiff is driven out
of the city, angered by the
foreign alliance. Later having
chased the stag to the field, the
wolf and the bear will defy each
other.

SECOND WORLD WAR

The other name for a mastiff in French is le dogue anglais, and
England is probably intended in line 1. Angered by a foreign
treaty England chases the stag to the battlefield where the wolf
(Italy) and the Bear (Russia) are defying each other. This appears
to refer to the Second World War when the Russians entered the
war as British Allies.

Souz ombre faincte d'oster de
  servitude,
Peuple & cité l'usurpera lui
  mesmes:
Pire fera par fraux de jeune pute,
Livré au champ lisant le faux
  proesme.

Beneath the faint pretext of re-
moving servitude, the people
and the city will themselves
usurp power. He will do worse
because of the trickery of a
young whore, delivered in the
field, reading the false promise.

[1] *Rane*—Latin, *rana* = a frog, possible misprint for *rame*=oar, which
is more suitable.

LOUIS XVI AND MARIE ANTOINETTE

This describes the French Revolution, which replaced Louis XVI's rule with one just as autocratic. The people of Paris took over government of their city, after the revolt of the Bastille, 14th July 1789. The woman who makes things worse by her double dealing is Marie Antoinette, by her general extravagance and in particular by the affair of the diamond necklace from which her popularity never recovered. When she and Louis were later caught trying to go to St. Cloud in 1792, the family were turned back by the crowds who said to Louis XVI, 'we love you alone'. The false promises were those given by the king when he promised not to try to escape from the Temple where he and his family had been placed to protect them from the people. They fled to Varennes in 1792 and were caught. See IX. 20, and IX. 34.

6

Au roi l'Augur sur le chef la main mettre,
Viendra prier pour la paix Italique:
A la main gauche viendra changer le sceptre
De Roi viendra Empire pacifique.

The Augur will put his hand on the king's head and pray for peace in Italy. The sceptre will be changed to his left hand, from king he will become a peaceful Emperor.

NAPOLEON III

The Pope was godfather by proxy to the son of Louis Napoleon, later Napoleon III. He was not too successful in his dealings with Italy and the Vatican because the Roman Revolutionaries felt he was too accommodating. The changing of the sceptre probably refers to Napoleon III's underhand manipulation of the Revolution in France of 1848 and to the fact that he declared himself Emperor on 2nd December 1851. Nostradamus views him as a peaceful monarch, which ties in well with the famous statement Napoleon III made on acquiring power. *'L'empire, c'est la paix.'* The art of Empire is peace.

7

Du Triumvir seront trouvé les os,
Cherchant profond thresor aenigmatique:
Ceux d'alentour ne seront en repos.
Ce concaver marbre & plomb metallique.

The bones of the Triumvir will be found by those searching for a deep and enigmatic treasure. Those around will not be peaceful. This hollowing of marble and metallic lead.

LOUIS PHILIPPE

This describes Louis Philippe's attempt to revive his waning popularity when he brought back Napoleon's ashes from St. Helena and interred them in the Invalides. Triumvir is the key word; after the *coup d'état* of 18th Brumaire Napoleon reduced the five members of the Directory to three, and made himself first Consul. The treasure Louis Philippe was searching vainly for was Napoleon's popular appeal, some of which he hoped to gain by honouring Napoleon's ashes. The restless people are the Bonapartistes who were politically encouraged by this and insisted on helping in the task of burying the ashes. The coffin itself was of lead.

8

Sera laissé le feu vif, mort caché,	There will be let loose living fire
Dedans les globes horrible espou- *vantable,*	and hidden death, fearful inside dreadful globes. By night
De nuict à classe cité en poudre *lasché,*	the city will be reduced to rubble by the fleet, the city on
La cité à feu, l'ennemi favorable.	fire, helpful to the enemy.

The dreadful object Nostradamus visualizes here is certainly no cannonball but some sort of bomb containing explosive material. Ships appear to bombard a city which, once on fire, is a landmark probably helpful to enemy aircraft.

9

Jusques au fonds la grand arq *demolue,*	At the foot of the great fallen arch, the friend is captured
Par chef captif, l'ami anticipé:	forestalled by the leader. A
Naistra de dame front face chevelue,	woman will bear a son whose
Lors par astuce Duc à mort *attrapé.*	face and forehead are covered with hair; then through cunning the Duke escapes death.

ASSASSINATION ATTEMPT ON NAPOLEON III, 1858

The first two lines are thought to refer to Napoleon III who had been involved in the Italian revolutionary movement when a young man. After some years of power in France the Italians felt he had betrayed their cause and four of them attempted to assassinate him as he left the Opéra on the night of 14th January 1858. The plot was led by Count Orsini—the building was damaged but did not collapse as Nostradamus describes it, although several bystanders were killed. The captured friend was Pieri, a friend of Orsini's, who was arrested before the explosion. Napoleon III was only slightly hurt. The third line is obscure but the last implies that Napoleon III escaped death through foreknowledge, probably due to Pieri's arrest. This quatrain appears to lead straight on to the next one, presumably Nostradamus forgot to separate them.

10

Un chef Celtique dans le conflict blessé,	A French leader wounded in the struggle sees his subjects
Aupres de cave voyant siens mort abbatre:	struck dead near the theatre. Hustled by enemies with bloody
De sang & plaies & d'ennemis pressé,	wounds, he will be saved from the four by unknown people.
Et secourus par incognus de quatre.	

ASSASSINATION ATTEMPT, NAPOLEON III
(continued)

As stated in V. 9. Napoleon III was slightly wounded when Italian revolutionaries attempted to kill him with a bomb outside the Opéra. (*Cavea* is the Latin word for theatre). The ordinary people standing around him saved him by shielding him from the blast. The four conspirators were Orsini, Pieri, Gomez and Rudio.

11

Mer par solaires seure ne passera,	Those of the sun will not cross
Ceux de Venus tiendront toute l'Affrique:	the sea in safety, the people of Venus will hold the whole of
Leur regne plus Saturne n'occupera,	Africa. Then Saturn occupies
Et changera la part Asiatique.	their kingdom no longer and the part of Asia will change.

SECOND WORLD WAR. ITALY AND
THE EAST, 1941–3

Japan's flag is a sun; her ships will not be safe once she has entered the war, and caused Asian politics to change, as China then joined with the Allied Powers in 1941. The people of Venice (Venus is a common corruption for this city throughout the Prophecies) which stands for Italy, are fighting with Rommel in North Africa. The malign influence of Saturn on Italian affairs causes them to withdraw from the war in 1943.

Aupres du lac Leman sera conduite,	Near Lake Geneva he will be
Par garse estrange cité voulant	led by a foreign woman who
trahir:	wants to betray the city. Before
Avant son meutre à Auspourg la	her death a great retinue will
grande suitte,	come to Augsburg. They will
Et ceux du Rhin la viendront	come to invade the people of
invahir.	the Rhine.

THIRTY YEARS WAR, 1636

The Battle of Augsburg, during the Thirty Years War forced the retreat of Bernhard, Duke of Saxe Weimar, across the Rhine. This left Southern and Central Germany exposed to the attacks of the Habsburg armies of the Holy Roman Emperor, Ferdinand II. Augsburg fell to Ferdinand as did other towns along the Rhine near the Swiss border. The use of the word Auspourg by Nostradamus is probably a typical pun, containing the two key words of the Habsburg and Augsbourg. The only puzzle is the young woman.

Par grand fureur le Roi Romain	In a great rage the Roman king
Belgique	will wish to trouble Belgium
Vexer vouldra par phalange bar-	with barbarian warriors. In a
bare:	gnashing fury he will chase the
Fureur grinsseant chassera gent	Libyan peoples from Hungary
Libyque	as far as Gibraltar.
Despuis Pannons[1] jusques Hercules	
la hare.[2]	

THIRTY YEARS WAR

The Holy Roman Emperor Ferdinand II and Philip of Spain were allied together against Denmark, Norway and Sweden. In 1648 the Treaty of Westphalia recognized the republic of the United Netherlands, part of which is now modern Belgium. The barbarian warriors are the German Protestant powers. The Thirty Years War started as a revolt in Bohemia and spread as far as Gibraltar when Spain and France refused to recognize the 1648 treaty and continued to fight until the Treaty of the Pyrenees in 1659.

[1] *Pannons*—Latin, *Pannonia* = now Hungary.
[2] *hare*—Misprint for *bare* = pillars of Hercules, or Gibraltar.

Saturne & Mars en Leo Espagne captifve,
Par chef Libyque au conflict attrapé,
Proche de Malthe, Heredde prins vive,
Et Romain sceptre sera par coq frappé.

Saturn and Mars in Leo, Spain is captive, taken in battle by a Libyan leader. Near when Malta and (the knights of) Rhodes are captured alive, and the Roman power smitten by the cock.

NAPOLEON'S CAMPAIGNS, 1797–1807/8

The only time that Spain can be considered as captive is during the Peninsular War of 1807/8, when Napoleon's troops occupied both Spain and Portugal. The resistance of Spanish patriots led the British to send in an army under General Sir Arthur Wellesley, who succeeded in driving out the French after five years of fighting. The rest of the quatrain refers to events ten years earlier. In 1797 the first action of Napoleon's Egyptian campaign was the capture of Malta held by the Knights of Rhodes, Heredde being an anagram. Finally at the Treaty of Tolentino the Pope ceded part of the Vatican and Church states to the cock, the symbol of France.

En navigant captif prins grand pontife,
Grans aprets faillir les clercz tumultuez:
Second esleu absent son bien debise,
Son favori bastard à mort tué.

While sailing, the great Pope will be captured; great preparations by the troubled clerics fail. The second elected absent, his power declines, his favourite bastard, put to death.

PIUS VII AND NAPOLEON, 1808

Pius VII was taken prisoner by the French in 1808 having travelled to crown Napoleon in Paris in 1804. He is the second Pope to be materially hurt by Napoleon, the first was Pius VI who died in exile at Valence. The trouble among the clergy describes the great religious discontent in France after the abolition of the established Church. The bastard of the final line is usually interpreted as Napoleon inheriting a crown that was not rightfully his, who having received the favours of the Pope, sacks Rome in 1808 and imprisons the Pope, although he doesn't kill him.

A son hault pris plus la lerme sabee,
D'humaine chair par mort en cendres mettre,
A l'isle Pharos par croisars perturbee,
Alors qu'à Rodes paroistra dur espectre.

The Sabine tears will no longer be of value, human flesh through death is burnt to ashes; the island of Pharos disturbed by (man of) the cross, when at Rhodes a dreadful sight is seen.

SECOND WORLD WAR. AFRICA AND GREECE

This quatrain seems to implicate Italy with the appalling deaths of Jews and others in the German concentration camps. It is important to remember that cremation was anathema to a 16th-Century man such as Nostradamus, and condemned not only by the Church but also socially. Pharos is an island opposite Alexandria and is probably used by Nostradamus to indicate Tobruk which is not far from there. It was disturbed several times by the men of the cross, the Nazis, as the battles in the African desert between the Allies and Rommel waged back and forth. The dreadful sight at Rhodes would be the invasion of Greece by Mussolini in 1940, followed by the Germans in 1941. Despite British evacuations, the Germans claimed 270,000 prisoners. In fact about 70,000 people were believed to have died.

De nuict passant le roi pres d'une Andronne,
Celui de Cypres & principal guette:
Le roi failli la main fuict long du Rosne,
Les conjurés l'iront à mort mettre.

The king, passing at night through a narrow lane, the man from Cyprus is the main guard; the king dies, the hand flees the length of the Rhône: the conspirators will put him to death.

Cyprus belonged to Venice until 1571, but the place of this conspiracy is obscure.

De deuil mourra l'infelix profligé,
Celebrera son vitrix l'hecatombe:
Pristine loi franc edict redigé,
Le mur & Prince au septiesme jour tombe.

The wretched man, destroyed, will die of grief. His victorious consort will celebrate the ceremonies. Former laws, free edicts drawn up, both the Prince and the wall fall on the seventh day.

This quatrain implies that a man is destroyed by his actions, whereas his wife celebrates his death and brings an end to an oppressive régime. The wall may refer to the legal repressions, or may be understood literally. There is a hint that the wife may have helped towards his death. The seventh day means either a Sunday or, more literally, that the Prince took seven days to die.

19

Le grand Royal d'or, d'aerain augmenté,	The great golden Royal, augmented by brass breaks the covenant; war is started by a young man. The people are afflicted by a lamented leader, the land will be covered with barbarian blood.
Rompu la pache,[1] par jeune ouverte guerre:	
Peuple affligé par un chef lamenté	
De sang barbare sera converre terre.	

20

Dela les Alpes grand armée passera,	A great Army will cross over the Alps. A short while before a wretched monster will be born. In a strange way, suddenly, the great Tuscan will return to his native land.
Un peu devant naistre monstre vapin:	
Prodigieux & subit tournera,	
Le grand Tosquan à son lieu plus propin.	

NAPOLEON III, 1859

Napoleon III crossed the Alps against Austria in 1859. The evil monster is the Italian Revolution; it is interesting to note that one of the first results of the 1859 campaign was to drive the Grand Duke of Tuscany, Leopold II, from Florence. He was a Habsburg and retired to Austria to escape the Italians, thus fulfilling line 4 in retiring to his native land. The wretched monster is understood to refer to Garibaldi.

21

Par le trespas du monarque latin,	By the death of a Latin king. Those people whom he will have assisted during his reign; the fire glows, the booty is shared out; public death for the bold incursors.
Ceux qu'il aura par regne secouruz:	
Le feu luira, divisé le butin,	
La mort publique aux hardis incoruz.	

The Latin monarch is difficult to interpret. If it stands for the ruler of Latium it means the Pope. It could possibly refer to Mussolini and the Fascists.

[1] pacha—Provençal = treaty, covenant.

Avant qu'à Rome grand aie rendu l'ame,	Before the great man gives up his soul at Rome, there is much
Effrayeur grande à larmée estrangere:	fear among the foreign army. The ambush by the squadrons
Par Esquadrons, l'embusche pres de Parme,	takes place near Parma, then the two red ones will feast to-
Puis les deux rouges ensemble feront chere.	gether.

While a Pope lies dying some trouble occurs in Parma, in Northern Italy. At the same time two revolutionary leaders will be meeting each other in a festive way. It may continue in the next quatrain.

Les deux contens seront unis ensemble,	The two contented men are united together when most
Quand la pluspart à Mars seront conjoinct.	(planets) are conjunct with Mars. The African leader
Le grand d'Affrique en effrayeur & tremble:	trembles in terror. The twin alliance scattered by the fleet.
DUUMVIRAT par la classe desjoinct.	

TWO ALLIES

If the two mentioned here are a continuation of the two revolutionaries of V. 22, they are very soon involved in war with most other nations. Africa is troubled by the alliance which is finally broken through naval strength.

Le regne & lois souz Venus eslevé,	The kingdom and law raised
Saturne aura sus Jupiter empire:	under Venus, Saturn will domi-
La loi & regne par le Soleil levé,	nate Jupiter. Law and empire
Par Saturnins endurera le pire.	raised by the Sun, will endure the worst through those of Saturn.

This verse is similar to V. 11, but the meanings of Saturn and Venus are unclear. Nostradamus is probably using a configuration for dating purposes. The Sun could also stand for Charles V, or the Catholic Church. It is a very difficult quatrain to decipher.

Le prince Arabe Mars, Sol, Venus, Lyon,	The Arab Prince, Mars, the Sun, Venus and Leo, the rule of
Regne d'Eglise par mer succombera:	the Church will succumb to the
Devers la Perse bien pres d'un million,	sea. Towards Persia very nearly a million men will invade Egypt
Bisance, Egypte, ver. serp.[1] invadera.	and Byzantium, the true serpent.

1987?

When Mars, the Sun and Venus are in conjunction with Leo, the following predictions are forecast about a new Arabian Empire. It will attack Persia, Egypt, Constantinople (Byzantium) and the navies of Christendom. According to the commentator Lee McCann (1942) this conjunction will take place on 21st August 1987. This must therefore in some way link up with the quatrains about the uprising in Asia.

26

La gent esclave par un heur martial,	The Slav people, through fortune in war, will become ele-
Viendra en haut degré tant esleuee:	vated to a high degree. They
Changeront prince, naistre un provincial,	will change their Prince, one born a provincial; an army
Passer la mer copie aux monts levee.	raised in the mountains to cross over the sea.

KING CONSTANTINE OF GREECE, 1917–20

The word *esclave* may mean either slave of Slav. The Russians were not regarded as Slavs in Nostradamus' day, this word was used to describe the Balkan peoples. The Greeks, partially Slav, rose against the Turks and landed troops at Smyrna in 1919 and stayed there until 1922. They also changed their king at this time as Nostradamus predicted. King Constantine, who was exiled in 1917, was recalled in 1920 but exiled again in 1922. Although of German origins Constantine was born in Athens. His rival was Premier Venizelos from Crete.

[1] *ver. serp.*—Suggested interpretation, *vera serpens* = true serpent.

Par feu & armes non loing de la marnegro,	With fire and weapons, not far from the Black Sea, he will
Viendra de Perse occuper Trebisonde:	come from Persia to occupy Trebizond. Pharos and Mytil-
Trembler Phatos Methelin, Sol alegro,	ene tremble, the Sun is bright, the Adriatic sea covered with
De sang Arabe d'Adrie couvert onde:	Arab blood.

Does this quatrain link up with V. 25? It is not clear whether the conquerors are the Arabs or Persians. Pharos is an island off Alexandria and Mytilene is the Greek island of Lesbos. Perhaps *Sol alegro* has a connection with a victorious crusade, which afterwards degenerates into a fight among the victors.

Le bras pendu & la jambe liée,	His arm hung and his leg
Visage pasle au seing poignard caché:	bound, with pale face and a dagger hidden in his breast:
Trois qui seront jurez de la meslee,	Three who will be sworn in the
Au grand de Gennes sera le fer lasché.	scuffle, against the great one of Genoa will the blade be drawn.

ASSASSINATION OF KING UMBERTO
OF ITALY, 1900

King Umberto was assassinated on 29th July 1900 by an unemployed smith called Acciarito. Genoa belonged to Savoy after 1815. Nostradamus seems to imply that the assassin had an arm in a sling, which was not the case in this instance. It is therefore possible that another assassination is referred to here.

La liberté ne sera recouvree,	Liberty will not be regained; it
L'occupera noir fier vilain inique:	will be occupied by a black, proud, villainous and unjust
Quand la matiere du pont sera ouvree,	man. When the matter of the Pope is opened by Hitler, the
D'Hister, Venise faschée la republique.	republic of Venice will be vexed.

HITLER, MUSSOLINI AND THE PAPACY

This quatrain describes Mussolini's intrigues to secure an alliance with Hitler between the years 1934–8. Hitler and Mussolini met at Venice—by this time a republic with Mussolini as its dictator. Note how accurate Nostradamus' details are. The adjective black probably refers to the Fascisti—the blackshirts. The matter of the Pope (Pontifex) refers to the Concordat drawn up between Mussolini and the Pope in 1928, which line 4 infers will bring trouble or war to Italy, as indeed it did.

30

Tout à l'entour de la grand Cité,	All around the great city sol-
Seront soldats logez par champs &	diers will be billeted in fields
villes:	and towns. Paris will make the
Donner assaut Paris, Rome incité,	assault, Rome incited: there
Sur le pont lors sera faicte grande	will be great pillage made
pille.	against the Pont(iff).

SACK OF ROME, 1797/1808

This verse describes Rome being sacked by the French which occured twice, in 1797 and 1808. The great pillage refers to the fact that the Pope was made to cede part of the Papal States in 1797, and in 1809 they were incorporated into the republic of France.

31

Par terre Attique chef de la sapience,	From the land of Attica, source
Qui de present est la rose du monde:	of all wisdom which at the
Pont ruiné & sa grand pre-	present is the rose of the world:
eminence,	the Pont(iff) ruined, its great
Sera subdite & naufrage des undes.	pre-eminence will be subjected
	and wrecked beneath the
	waves.

Apart from commentating that this is the third successive verse with the word Pont possibly implying the Papacy, I cannot decipher this verse. Attica if taken literally means South-eastern Greece, north of the Peloponnesus. It is not clear what ruins the Papacy.

Où tout bon est tout bien Soleil & *Lune,* *Est abondant sa ruine s'approche:* *Du ciel s'advance vaner ta fortune,* *En mesme estat que la septiesme* *roche.*	Where all is good, all well abun- dant, in Sun and Moon its ruin approaches. It comes from heaven as you boast of your fortune, in the same state as the seventh rock.

FRANCO-PRUSSIAN WAR, 1870–1

James Laver suggests that this refers to the Franco-Prussian war.
The use of *ta fortune,* the second person singular is applied only to
France by Nostradamus. When Paris is at the height of her fortune,
the Exposition Universelle of 1867, etc; then the Prussians will
declare war, as they did on 19th July 1870. The seventh rock is
understood as a reference to the desolation of the seventh rock in
the Apocalypse.

Des principaux de cité rebellee *Qui tiendront fort pour liberté* *ravoir:* *Detrencher masles, infelice meslee,* *Cris hurlemens à Nantes piteux* *voir.*	Some of the principal citizens of the rebellious city who will try hard to regain their liberty; the men are cut up, unhappy confusion; Cries, groans at Nantes pitiful to see.

ATROCITIES AT NANTES, 1793

During the excesses of the Revolution, Nantes suffered a series of
appalling atrocities known as the Noyades. In 1793 its principal
citizens had allied themselves with neighbouring districts and
declared a Central Assembly of Resistance to Oppression. The
National Convention quickly broke this counter-Revolution. Over
1,000 citizens were guillotined (cut up); others were tied, two
together, face to face, naked, and placed in boats which were
rowed to the middle of the river Loire and scuttled. The wretched
victims were watched by their executioners as they drowned in a
threshing mob of bodies.

Du plus profond de l'occident *Anglois.* *Où est le chef de l'isle Britannique:* *Entrera classe dans Gironde par* *Blois,* *Par vin & sel, feux cachez aux* *barriques.*	From the deepest part of the English West where is the leader of the British Isles; a fleet will enter Gironde through Blois, through wine and salt, fires hidden in casks.

It is unlikely that this quatrain refers to the West of England although these are the traditional lands of the heir to the English throne, c.f. Prince of Wales and the Duchy of Cornwall. Some interpret it as suggesting the Anglicization of North America, or even the Hundred Years War when the English held the West Coast of France for some decades. The wine and salt are suggested as metaphors for taxation, like the gabelle or salt tax. The fires in casks may be weapons. This quatrain is possibly still to be fulfilled.

35

Par cité franche de la grand mer Seline,	For the free city of the great crescent sea, which still carries the stone in its stomach, an English fleet will come in under the mist to seize a branch, war opened by the great one.
Qui porte encores à l'estomac la pierre:	
Angloise classe viendra soubs la bruine	
Un rameau prendre, du grand ouverte guerre.	

This quatrain may connect with the preceding one and refer to a series of protracted encounters with English invaders. The crescent sea may have the usual meaning of Genoa, but is a rare theatre of operations for a British fleet.

36

De soeur le frere par simulte faintise,	The sisters' brother through feigned deceit will come to mix dew into the mineral. On the cake given to the slow old woman who dies tasting it, she will be simple and rustic.
Viendra mesler rosee en mineral:	
Sur la placente[1] donne à vielle tardifve,	
Meurt, le goustant sera simple & rural.	

The only information I can offer here is that the *rosee*, dew, in the second line may stand for a Latin poison, *rosarius*, which was extracted from the laurel rose.

[1] *placente*—Latin, *placenta* = a cake.

Trois cents feront d'un vouloir &
  accord,
Que pour venir au bout de leur
  attaincte:
Vingt mois apres tous & records,
Leur Roi trahi simulant haine
  saincte.

Three hundred will be of one agreement and accord to come to the execution of their end; twenty months later, after all remembrance, their king is betrayed pretending a feigned hatred.

Ce grand monarque qu'au mort
  succedera,
Donnera vie illicite & lubrique,
Par nonchalance à tous concedera,
Qu'à la parfin faudra la loi
  Salique.

He who succeeds upon the death of a great king will lead an illicit and debauched life. Through carelessness he will give way to all so that in the end Salic law will fail.

LOUIS XV

Louis XV succeeded to his great grandfather Louis XIV (great in both senses) and led a life of great debauchery and irresponsibility. An example of this was his famous *seraglio* at the Parc des Cerfs, and, of course, the influence of Madame de Pompadour. The *Encyclopaedia Britannica* says that it is difficult to find a European king whose life shows such a record of vulgar vice. His carelessness in state affairs was partially responsible for the troubles which were to come to a head under the Revolution. Salic law forbade the accession of women to the throne. Louis was succeeded by his son. Could the line possibly mean that France was effectively ruled by the mistresses and wives of both these men—Mme de Pompadour, Mme du Barry and finally (Louis XVI) by Marie Antoinette? Some historians would accept this view.

Du vrai rameau de fleur de lys issue
Mis & logé heretier de Hetrurie:
Son sang antique de long main tissu
Fera Florence florir en l'armoirie.

Issued from the true branch of the fleur de liys, placed and lodged as heir to Etruria, his ancient family line woven by many hands, will make the armorial bearings of Florence flower.

COUNT DE CHAMBORD

The Count of Chambord was the heir to Charles X and his legitimacy was questioned by the Duke of Orléans at his birth (see IV.

93). His mother the Duchess of Berry took her son into exile with her to Venice, Etruria standing for Italy. Here in 1846 he married the daughter of Duke Francis IV of Florence. The fleur de lis is part of the coat of arms of the house of Florence as well as the French royal line, and their marriage caused their united family lines to flower.

40

Le sang royal sera si tresmeslé,	The Royal blood will be very
Contrainct seront Gaulois de l'Hes-	mixed, the French will be re-
perie:	strained by the West. They will
On attendra que terme soit coulé,	wait until his term of office has
Et que memoire de la voix soit	ended, and the memory of his
perie.	voice has perished.

AMERICA, FRANCE AND THE COMMON MARKET

The first line probably indicates that the Royal blood in France is no longer truly royal, i.e. is not a ruling power, which brings the quatrain into the 20th Century. The restraint put on France by America (*Hesperie*) may well refer to the pressures to allow England to join the Common Market. Once de Gaulle's term of office has ended through his death, his policy, the famous '*Non*' is soon forgotten.

41

Nay souz les umbres & journée	Born beneath the shadows on a
nocturne	dark day, he will be sovereign
Sera en regne & bonté souveraine:	in ruling and in goodness. He
Fera renaistre son sang de l'antique	will cause his blood to revive
urne,	the ancient urn, renewing the
Renouvellant siecle d'or pour	century of gold for one of brass.
l'aerain.	

42

Mars esleue en son plus haut befroi,[1]	A warlike man raised to the
Fera retraire les Allobrox[2] *de*	heights will bring about the
France:	return of Savoy to France. The
La gent Lombarde fera si grand	people from Lombardy will
effroi,	cause such great fear to those of
A ceux de l'aigle comprins souz la	the Eagle included under the
Balance.	Balance.

[1] *befroi*—Literally a belfry.
[2] *Allobrox*—The Allobroges were a tribe that occupied what is present day Savoy.

Napoleon III and Cavour of Italy agreed between them that in return for French assistance for driving the Austrians (the Eagle) out of Italy (Libra), Savoy should be returned to France, which occurred on 22nd March 1860.

43

La grande ruine des sacrez ne s'esloigne,	The great ruin of the clergy is not far off, Provence, Naples,
Provence, Naples, Sicille, Seez & Ponce:	Sicily, Sees and Pons. In Germany at the Rhine and
En Germanie, au Rhin & la Cologne,	Cologne, vexed to death by those of Maine.
Vexez à mort par ceux de Magonce.[1]	

In this far-reaching quatrain Nostradamus is probably inferring that Mainz and the other places would turn Protestant, possibly because Mainz was the centre of Gutenberg's city and the original centre of printing with all its inherent dangers. If so, a totally unsuccessful quatrain.

44

Par mer le rouge sera prins de pirates,	On the sea the red one will be taken by pirates and because of
La paix sera par son moyen troublee:	him peace will be troubled. He
L'ire & l'avare commettra par fainct acte	will reveal anger and greed through a false act; the army of
Au grand Pontife sera l'armee doublee.	the great Pontiff will be doubled.

This prophecy was probably a contemporary one because it implies that a Cardinal (*le rouge*) will be captured by pirates— probably the corsairs of the Mediterranean. During the 16th Century Popes still had real armies. There is no record of its being fulfilled.

45

Le grand Empire sera tost desolé	The great Empire will soon be
Et translaté pres d'arduenne silve:	desolated and changed near the
Les deux bastardz par l'aisné decollé,	forest of Ardennes. The two bastards will be beheaded by
Et regnera Aenodarb, nez de milve.	the oldest, Aenodarb, will rule, the hawk-nosed one.

[1] *Magonce*—Maguntiacum = Mainz or Mayenze.

The whole of the French empire was lost to the Germans in 1940 and there were great battles around the Ardennes forests, both then and in 1944/5. The two bastards may be the two 'unworthy' French generals who let the German advance through after the Battle of Sedan, André Georges Corap of the French 9th Army and the second-in-command, Henri Giraud, who was taken prisoner. The commander-in-chief, Maxime Weygand (*l'aisné*) then took over, but the battle was already lost for the Allies. The hawk-nosed man may refer to General de Gaulle. He was the only French general who, with the 4th Armoured Division, put up any real opposition to the Germans at Montcornet May 17th–19th. Dunkirk followed upon this crushing defeat.

46

Par chapeaux rouges querelles & mouveaux scismes	Quarrels and new schisms by the red hats when the Sabins
Quand on aura esleu le Sabinois:	will have been elected. They
On produira contre lui grans sophismes,	will produce great sophisms against him and Rome will be
Et sera Rome lesse par Albanois.	injured by those of Albania.

THE PAPACY

The red hats are the Cardinals who become divided among themselves when they elect a Pope from the land of the Sabines, north-east of Rome. The Albanians are a problem. Perhaps they cannot connect with this verse in that they are a people with strong links with Communist China which disturbs the Vatican?

47

Le grand Arabe marahera bien avant,	The great Arab will march well to the fore, he will be betrayed
Trahi sera par les Bisantinois:	by the Byzantians: ancient
L'Antique Rodes lui viendra au devant,	Rhodes will come forward to meet him and greater harm
Et plus grand mal par autre Pannonois.	through the other Hungarians.

The Byzantines are the Turks, since their capital was originally Byzantium. Nostradamus seems to imply that Rhodes in Greece will be the base for an operation against the Arabs. The Turkish conquest of Hungary is referred to in the final line. Probably a retroactive prophecy.

Apres la grand affliction du sceptre,
Deux ennemis par eux seront de-
*   faictz:*
Classe d'Afrique aux Pannons
*   viendra naistre,*
Par mer & terre seront horribles
*   faictz.*

After the great affliction of the sceptre two enemies will be defeated by them. A fleet from Africa will come forth to the Hungarians; dreadful deeds will occur on land and sea.

This is almost certainly a continuation from the last quatrain. The fleet may be going to Fiume, now *Rijeka*, which used to belong to the Holy Roman Empire.

Nul de l'Espaigne mais de l'antique
*   France*
Ne sera esleu pour le tremblant
*   nacelle,*
A l'ennemi sera faicte fiance,[1]
Qui dans son regne sera peste
*   cruelle.*

Not from Spain but from ancient France will he be elected for the trembling ship. He will make a promise to the enemy who will cause great plague during his reign.

FUTURE POPE

Since Nostradamus' day there have only been Italian Popes so this prediction may lie in the future. It indicates that there will be two main candidates for the Papacy, one Spanish and one French, when the Church is doing badly, 'trembling ship'. The French candidate will be elected and will try to compromise with his enemy, presumably Communism, with remarkably little success. See V. 46.

L'an que deux freres du lys seront en
*   aage,*
L'un d'eux tiendra la grand
*   Romanie:*
Trembler les monts, ouvert Latin
*   passage*
Pache macher, contre fort d'Armenie.

The year that the brothers of the lily come of age one of them will hold great Romania. The mountains tremble, a Latin passage is opened; a treaty to march against the fort of Armenia.

The brothers of the lily are presumably sons of the French royal house. Romania is probably the Holy Roman Empire, and the

---

[1] *fiance*—O.F. = assurance, promise.

mountains, the Alps crossing to Rome. Armenia is difficult to interpret. In V. 94 it connects with Hitler and the Second World War.

51

La gent de Dace,[1] d'Angleterre & Polonne	The people of Dacia, England and Poland and Czechoslovakia
Et de Boesme[2] feront nouvelle ligue:	will form a new alliance. In
Pour passer outre d'Hercules la colonne	order to pass beyond the straights of Gibraltar the
Barcins,[3] Tyrrens[4] dresser cruelle brique.	Spanish and the Italians will hatch a cruel plot.

ALLIED ALLIANCE. SECOND WORLD WAR, 1939
One of Nostradamus' more interesting predictions. In March 1939 Britain allied with the Balkan countries. Her support of Poland started the war in September 1939. It was essential to keep the Mediterranean open for shipping for allied troops and supplies. The Italians were allied to Germany and the Spanish were technically neutral, their plot presumably the aid given to Hitlerian Germany.

52

Un Roi sera qui donra l'opposite,	There will be a king who will
Les exilez esleuez sur le regne:	give opposition, the exiles elec-
De sang nager la gent caste[5] hyppolite,[6]	ted over the kingdom. The chaste, poor ones swim in blood
Et florira long temps soubs telle enseigne.	and he will flourish for a long time under this standard.

Line 3 probably refers to an order of mendicant Friars; otherwise this quatrain is unclear.

[1] Dacia—Now part of modern Rumania.
[2] Boesme—Modern Czechoslovakia.
[3] Barcins—Latin, Barcino = Barcelona; therefore Spanish.
[4] Tyrrens—Latin, Tyrrheni = the ancestors of the Tuscans and therefore Italians.
[5] castus—Latin = chaste, pure.
[6] hyppolite—Greek, hypolitos = poor, mean, little.

La loi du Sol, & Venus contendens,
Appropiant l'esprit de prophetie:
Ne l'un ne l'autre ne seront entendus,
Par Sol tiendra la loy du grand
*   Messie.*

The law of the Sun contending with Venus, appropriating the spirit of prophecy. Neither the one nor the other will be understood; the law of the great Messiah retained through the Sun.

The Sun may stand here for Christianity and Venus for Islam. This is a repetition of Nostradmus' belief that eventually Christianity would rule the world: unfortunately this is another of those prophecies which now seem unlikely to reach fulfilment.

Du pont Euxine, & la grand
*   Tartarie,*
Un roi sera qui viendra voir la
*   Gaule*
Transpercera Alane & l'Armenie,
Et dans Bisance lairra sanglante
*   Gaule.*

From beyond the Black Sea and great Tartary, there will be a king who will come to see France. He will pass through Alania and Armenia and leave his bloody rod in Byzantium.

THE MAN FROM THE EAST

Nostradamus says elsewhere that the Third Anti-Christ of this century will come from Asia, and this quatrain seems to confirm this view, as he will come from beyond Tartary, that is from China. His route to France lies through Alania, Southern Russia, and Armenia round the Balkan peninsula to Constantinople. The mention of a bloody rod occurs also in connection with a man from the East and France in II. 29. It may be intended as a weapon of some sort.

De la felice Arabie contrade,[1]
Naistra puissant de loi Mahome-
*   tique:*
Vexer l'Espaigne conquester la
*   Grenade,*
Et plus par mer à la gent Ligus-
*   tique.*[2]

In the fortunate country of Arabia will be born one powerful in the laws of Mahomet. He will trouble Spain and conquer Grenada and most of the Ligurian nation from the sea.

[1] *contrade*—Provençal, *contrada* = country.
[2] *Ligustique*—The Ligurians come from around Genoa.

Nostradamus seems to envisage a reconquest of Spain and Grenada by the Arabs who will extend their rule into Italy. Grenada was lost to the Moors in 1492.

56

Par le trespas du tres vieillart pontif,	Through the death of the very old Pope will be elected a
Sera esleu Romain de bon aage:	Roman of good age. It will be
Qu'il sera dict que le siege debisse,	said of him that he weakens the
Et long tiendra & de picquant ouvrage.	(Holy) Seat, but he will hold it long and with stinging effort.

NEW POPE

Instead of the usual aged Pope, one will be elected who is comparatively young and who, despite his detractors, reigns very effectively for a long time.

57

Istra du Mont Gaulfier & Aventin,	There will go forth from Montgaulfier and the Aventine one,
Qui par trou avertira l'armée:	who through a hole will warn
Entre deux rocs sera prins le butin,	the army. The booty will be
De SEXT. mansol faillir le renommee.	taken between two rocks. The renown of Sextus the celibate will fail.

MONTGOLFIER BALLOON AND THE BATTLE OF FLEURUS, 1794

The hot air balloon was invented by the Montgolfier brothers in 1783 and was used on a scouting party at the Battle of Fleurus 1794. The French victory at Fleurus was the turning point in the first coalition phase of the Revolutionary Wars paving the way for the sack of Rome and the Aventine. The word *mansol* is derived from *manens solus*—he who remains alone. Elsewhere Nostradamus calls monks and priests *les seuls*. *Sext.* is short for Sextus, and Pius VI who was captured by Napoleon, is the only Pope since Nostradamus' day, apart from the present one, Paul VI, to have this number. By the Treaty of Tolentino 1797, the Pope was deprived of much of his lands, the rocks on which his power was based.

De l'acqueduct d'Uticense,[1] *Gardoing,*
Par la forest & mont inaccessible,
En mi du pont sera tasché au poing,
Le chef nemans & qui tant sera terrible.

By the aqueduct of Uzès by Gard, through the forest and inaccessible mountain; in the middle of the bridge he will be cut in the hand, the chief of Nîmes who will be very terrible.

1627

There is a famous Roman aqueduct in France which extended from Uzès to Nîmes. In 1627 the Duke de Rohan tried to support his fellow Calvinists who were besieged at Nîmes. He moved his artillery in by means of the aqueduct. Line 3 is interpreted as some of his soldiers cutting some of the supports of the bridge at Gard to widen the path for the cannons to be brought up. When Rohan arrived at Nîmes he was put in command. An impressive quatrain.

59

Au chef Anglois à Nimes trop sejour,
Devers l'Espaigne au secours Aenobarbe:
Plusieurs mourrant par Mars ouvert ce jour,
Quand an Artois faillir estoille en barbe.[3]

The English chief stays too long at Nîmes, towards Spain Aenobarbe to the rescue. Many will die through war started on that day, when a bearded star falls in Artois.

60

Par teste rase viendra bien mal eslire,
Plus que sa charge ne porte passera:
Si grand fureur & raige fera dire,
Qu'à feu & sang tout sexe trenchera.

Through the shaven heads he will be seen to have been wrongly elected. Burdened with a load he cannot carry. He will be made to proclaim with such great fury and rage that all one sex will be cut to pieces by fire and blood.

CROMWELL

Although many commentators interpret this verse as applying either to Napoleon or to the Popes, whose heads were shaven as

[1] *Uticense*—Castrum Uceciense, Uzès.
[2] *nemans*—Nemansus = Nîmes.
[3] *estoille en barbe* = comet or meteorite.

monks, I think it is more appropriately applied to Cromwell. Nostradamus says that Cromwell is elected to power, he did not rule by divine right. The fury and rage that cover Britain refers to the Civil War between Cavaliers and Roundheads (*testes rases*) which was a war both of politics and religion. A great number of men (*tant un sexe*) lost their lives during this time. There were comparatively few atrocities committed on women and children.

61

L'enfant du grand n'estant à sa naissance, *Subjugera les hauts monts Apennis:* *Fera trembler tous ceux de la balance,* *Et de monts feux jusques à mont Senis.*	The child of the great man, not through his birth, will subjugate the high Apennine mountains. He will make all those under the Balance tremble, fire from the mountains as far as Mount Cenis.

EUGÈNE DE BEAUHARNAIS

The nearest person to fulfil this quatrain to date is Eugène de Beauharnais, the son of Josephine. It states that the adopted son of a French ruler will vex the Habsburgs (Libra) in Spain and Italy and conquer Italy. Unfortunately it was Napoleon who conquered. Eugène only acted as ruler.

62

Sur les rochers sang on les verra plouvoir, *Sol Orient, Saturne Occidental:* *Pres d'Orgon guerre, à Rome grand mal voir,* *Nefs parfondrees & prins le Tridental.*[1]	Blood will be seen to rain on the rocks, Sun in the East, Saturn in the West. War near Orgon, a great evil seen near Rome, ships sunken and the trident taken.

One of Nostradamus' detailed but unintelligible quatrains. The Sun is probably Christianity and Saturn the Antichrist. Tridental refers to general sea power.

[1] *Tridental* = One who holds the trident: i.e. power of the seas.

232

De vaine emprise l'honneur indue plaincte,	From the useless enterprise honour and undue complaint,
Galiotz errans par Latins froit, faim, vagues	boats wandering among the Latins, cold, hunger, waves;
Non loing du Timbre de sang la terre taincte.	Not far from the Tiber the land stained with blood and there
Et sur humains seront diverses plagues.	will be several plagues upon mankind.

Les assemblés par repos du grand nombre,	Those assembled through the calm of the great number,
Par terre & mer conseil contre-mandé:	countermanded by land and sea; near Autonne, Genoa, the
Pres de l'Autonne Gennes, Nice de l'ombre	shadow of Nice, revolution against the leader through fields
Par champs & villes le chef contre-bandé.	and towns.

Autonne is one of Nostradamus' unsolved anagrams, written Antonne in some editions. The nearest equivalents phonetically are Nentone or Antibes (Antipolis) but do not clarify the meaning.

Subit venu l'effrayeur sera grande,	Suddenly appeared, the terror will be great, hidden by the
Des principaux de l'affaire cachés:	ringleaders of the affair. The
Et dame en braise plus ne sera en veue	women on the charcoal will no longer be seen; thus, little by
Ce peu à peu seront les grans fachés.	little, the great ones will be angered.

Soubs les antiques edifices vestaulx,	Under the ancient buildings of the vestals not far from the ruin
Non esloignez d aqueduct ruine:	of the aquaduct. There will be
De Sol & Lune sont les luisans metaulx,	the glittering metals of Sun and Moon, the golden lamp of
Ardante lampe Traian d'or burine.	Trojan burning, pillaged.

It has been suggested by Jaubert that the convent of St.-Sauveur-de-la-Fontaine at Nîmes was built on the site of a temple of Diana and that a lamp of gold and silver will eventually be dug up.

Quand chef Perouse n'osera sa tunique	When the great head of Perugia dare not risk his tunic, without
Sens au couvert tout nud s'expolier:	any cover and strip himself
Seront prins sept faict Aristocratique,	quite naked. The seven aristocrats will be taken, father and
Le pere & fils mors par poincte au colier.	son dead through a wound in the throat.

VATICAN AND FRANCE, 1585-9

The head of Perugia was the Pope, in this case Sixtus V who, in 1585, had excommunicated Henri de Navarre and was therefore reluctant to do the same to Henri III and risk losing France (stripping himself naked). When he was eventually forced to do so in 1589, he did not release his Catholic subjects from their oath of allegiance, because the Papacy had already lost the revenues of England and Northern Europe. The seven are again the children of Catherine de' Medici. Their father was already dead from a wound in the throat and his last ruling son, Henri III was to die from stab wounds, not in the throat but in the stomach in 1589. Possibly Henri's assassin Jacques Clément meant to get the king in the throat but missed.

Dans le Danube & du Rhin viendra boire,	The great Camel will come to drink of the Danube and the
Le grand Chameau ne s'en repentira:	Rhine, and will not repent of it. Those of the Rhône tremble
Trembler du Rosne & plus fort ceux de Loire,	and even more so those of the Loire; near the Alps the cock
Et pres des Alpes coq le ruinera.	will ruin him.

The great Camel also appears in IV. 85 and VI. 55. Nostradamus probably means an Arabian leader, or less possibly, a hunchback. Although this person sweeps aside German opposition, he will get his comeuppance in France.

Plus ne sera le grand en faux sommeil,	The great one will no longer be in a false sleep; unease will take
L'inquietude viendra prendre repoz:	the place of repose. The
Dresser phalange d'or, azur, & vermeil,	phalanx of gold, blue and vermillion to subdue Africa and
Subjuger Affrique la ronger jusques oz.	gnaw it down to the very bone.

Louis Philippe usurped his nephew's French crown in 1830, having waited for an opportune moment, line 2. He was the first legitimate Bourbon to accept the tricolour of red, white and blue. The French conquest of Algeria took place in the same year that he snatched the throne. Nostradamus says the flag is gold, red and blue. James Laver makes a charming comment, 'the old eyes of the prophet may be pardoned for being slightly colour blind'.

70

Des regions subjectes à la Balance,	Some of the regions subject to
Feront troubler les monts par grand guerre.	the Balance will trouble the mountains with a great war.
Captifz tout sexe deu & tout Bisance,	The entire sex will be captured, enthralled, and all Byzantium,
Qu'on criera à l'aube terre à terre.	so that at dawn they will call from land to land.

The Balance, Libra, as always is astrologically either Austria and Savoy, and sometimes England by Nostradamus' own reckoning. It appears that this country will overthrow the Ottoman empire. Possibly Austria's troubles in the Balkans in the early 1900s are hinted at in this verse?

71

Par la fureur d'un qui attendra l'eau,	By the fury of one who will wait for the water, by the great rage
Par la grand raige tout l'exercite esmeu:	that moves all the army; seventeen boats loaded with nobles,
Chargé des nobles à dix sept bateaulx,	the messenger comes too late along the Rhône.
Au long du Rosne, tard messagier venu.	

This quatrain has been tentatively applied to every would-be invader of Britain. Napoleon, Hitler etc.

72

Pour le plaisir d'edict voluptueux,	For the pleasure of an edict of
On meslera la poison dans l'aloy:	vice, poison will be mixed with
Venus sera en cours si vertueux,	the law. At Court, Venus will
Qu'obfusquera du soleil tout à loi.	be so virtuous, that all the glory of the sun will be obscured.

Nostradamus considered that the edict of Poitiers encouraged vice because it allowed the clergy to marry and legalized Calvinism. Henri III's court was very depraved; his openly flaunted homosexuality offended the country and his mignons were notorious for the fantastic wealth they acquired. The King was reputed to be a sorcerer with a familiar named Tarragon. Is the reference to the sun an oblique reference to the Roi Soleil, Louis XIV of the next century?

73

Persecutee sera de Dieu l'eglise,
Et les sainctz temples seront expoliez:
L'enfant la mere mettra nud en chemise,
Seront Arabes aux Polons raliez.

The Church of God will be persecuted, and the holy temples will be pillaged; the mother will put out the child, naked in a shift. The Arabs will ally with the Poles.

74

De sang Troyen[1] naistra coeur Germanique
Qu'il deviendra en si haute puissance:
Hors chassera gent estrange Arabique
Tournant l'Eglise en pristine preeminence.

Of Trojan blood he will be born with a German heart and will rise to very great power. He will drive out the foreign, Arabic nation and return the Church to her early glory.

75

Montera haut sur le bien plus à dextre,
Demourra assis sur la pierre quarree:
Vers le midi posé à la fenestre,
Baston tortu en main, bouche serree.

He will rise high over his wealth, more to the right, he will remain seated on the square stone; towards the south placed at the window, a crooked staff in his hand, his mouth sealed.

A typically convoluted Nostradamus quatrain. A crooked staff normally refers to a bishop's crook.

[1] sang Troyen—Refers to the myth by which the French royal line were descended from Francus, son of Priam of Troy.

En lieu libere tendra son pavillon, *Et ne voudra en citez prendre place:* *Aix, Carpens l'isle volce, mont* *Cavaillon,* *Par tous ses lieux abolira sa trasse.*	In a free place he will pitch his tent, he will not want to stay in the cities. Aix, Carpentras, L'Ile Vaucluse, Montfavet, Cavaillon, in all these places he will abolish his trace.

All these places are quite close to Salon in Provence.

Tous les degrez d'honneur Eccle-
  siastique
Seront changez en dial¹ quirinal.²
En Martial quirinal flaminique,
Puis un Roi de France le rendre
  vulcanal.
	All degrees of ecclesiastical honour will be changed to Jupiter and Quirinus. A priest of Quirinus in martial guise then a king of France will make him a man of Vulcan.

Les deux unis ne tiendront longue-
  ment,
Et dans treize ans au Barbare
  Satrappe:
Au deux costez seront tel perdement,
Qu'un benira le Barque & sa
  cappe.
	The two will not remain allied for long; within the thirteen years they give in to barbarian power. There will be such a loss on both sides, that one will bless the bark (of Peter) and its leader.

ALLIANCE BETWEEN U.S.A. AND U.S.S.R.?

The alliance between the USSR and the USA, see II. 9, created because of Eastern developments will not last for more than thirteen years, maybe less. Then the barbarian hordes will cause them to fight. The scale of modern warfare makes Nostradamus' comment quite mundane, but it is interesting to see that he expects a Pope to play a singular and important part towards world peace. The prophecies of Malachy give four more Popes until the end of the world, and the name for the third is Gloria Olivae—the olive branch, which is traditionally a sign of peace. Most Popes are old men when elected. If we allow each an average of ten years this would bring us to the 1990s. The alliance should therefore occur in the late 1970s.

---

¹ *dial*—Latin, *Dialis* = of Jupiter.
² *Quirinus*—Sabine = Mars, identified with Romulus.

La sacree pompe viendra baisser les aisles,	The sacred pomp will come to lower its wings at the coming of
Par la venue du grand legislateur:	the great law giver. He will
Humble haulsera vexera les rebelles,	raise the humble and trouble
Naistra sur terre aucun aemulateur.	the rebellious; his like will not again appear on earth.

NAPOLEON

This is a general quatrain but the generalities do apply particularly well to Napoleon. He treated the Church and the Popes with arbitrary power. He originated the Code Napoléon, France's legal system. He made aristocrats from the lowly, and stamped out rebellion brutally. Line 4 may be an exaggeration, but he was a great man.

Logmion[1] grande Bisance approchera,	Ogmios will approach great Byzantium, the barbarian
Chasse sera la barbarique ligne:	league will be driven out. Of
Des deux loix l'une l'estinique[2] lachera,	the two laws the pagan one will fail, barbarian and freeman in
Barbare & franche en perpetuelle brigue.	perpetual struggle.

L'oiseau royal sur la cité solaire,	The royal bird over the city of
Sept mois devant fera nocturne augure:	the sun will give a nightly warning for seven months; the wall
Mur d'Orient cherra tonnerre esclaire,	in the East will fall, thunder
Sept jours aux portes les ennemis à l'heure.	and lightning, in seven days the enemies directly to the gates.

FRANCE. BERLIN WALL?

The royal bird is probably an eagle which flying over Paris or Rome will warn of a disaster to come. The wall in the East has been identified with the fall of France, the Maginot line and the Blitzkrieg, the seven days being 5th–11th June 1940. However, it may refer to the Berlin wall, and indicate that it will come down eventually, although other disasters will follow in its wake.

[1] *L'Omigon* was the Celtic Hercules.
[2] *l'estinique*—Latin, *ethnicus* = pagan.

238

Au conclud pache hors de la for- *teresse,* *Ne sortira celui en desespoir mis:* *Quand ceux d'Arbois, de Langres,* *contre Bresse,* *Auront monts Dolle, bouscade¹* *d'ennemis.*	At the conclusion of the treaty outside the fortress he will not go who is overcome with despair. When the people of Arbois, Langres, against Bresse, will have an enemy ambush at the mountains of Dôle.

Ceux qui auront entreprins sub- *ventir,* *Nompareil regne puissant & in-* *vincible:* *Feront par fraude, nuictz trois* *advertir,* *Quant le plus grand à table lira* *Bible.*	Those who will have an undertaking to subvert an unparalleled kingdom, powerful and invincible. They will deceive, warn for three nights, when the greatest one is reading his Bible at the table.

The propaganda mentioned here could have many applications in this century.

Naistra du gouphre & cité im- *mesuree,* *Nay de parents obscure & tene-* *breux:* *Qui la puissance du grand roi* *reveree,* *Voudra destruire par Rouen &* *Evereux.*	Born of the gulf and the immeasurable city, born of parents both obscure and dark. He who will wish to destroy the power of the great, revered king through Rouen and Evereux.

Rouen and Evereux are linked also in IV. 100 as loyal to Napoleon III and the monarchy.

Par les Sueves² & lieux circon- *voisins,* *Seront en guerre pour cause des* *nuees:* *Gamp marins locustes & cousins,* *Du Leman fautes seront bien* *desnuees.*	Through the Swiss and surrounding areas they will war because of the clouds. A swarm of marine locusts and gnats, the faults of Geneva will be laid quite bare.

¹ *bouscade*—embuscade = ambush.
² *Sueves*—Latin, Suevi = ancestors of German Swiss.

LEAGUE OF NATIONS AND THE
SECOND WORLD WAR

This quatrain describes very accurately the failure of the League of Nations and the commencement of the Second World War. See also I. 47.

86

Par les deux testes, & trois bras separés,	Divided by the two heads and three arms, the great city will be troubled by water. Some of the great men among them, wandering in exile; Byzantium is hard pressed by the leader of Persia.
La cité grande par eaux sera vexee:	
Des grands d'entre eux par exile esgarés,	
Par teste perse Bisance fort pressee.	

PARIS, PERSIA AND TURKEY
17th AND 18th CENTURIES

This probably describes Paris flooded by the Seine, which occurred reasonably frequently during the early 17th Century when the Turks (Byzantium) were hard pressed by Persia. There was further fighting in the East during the first half of the 18th Century.

87

L'an que Saturne hors de servage,	In the year that Saturn is freed from servitude the Frankish territory will be inundated by water. His marriage will be of Trojan blood and he will be closely encircled by the Spaniards.
Au franc¹ terroir sera d'eau inundé:	
De sang Troyen² sera son mariage,	
Et sera ceur d'Espaignols circundé.	

The only clear factor here is that a French prince (or princess) will marry a Spaniard at the time of a great flood.

88

Sur le sablon par un hideux deluge,	Through a dreadful flood on the sand a marine monster will be found from other seas. A refuge will be made near the place, holding Savona the slave to Turin.
Des autres mers trouvé monstre marin:	
Proche du lieu sera faict un refuge,	
Tenant Savone esclave de Turin.	

¹ *franc*—Either Frank, probably *Franche Comté*, or free.

² *sang Troyen*—Again the reference to the French royal line and its mythical descent from Francus, son of Priam.

In 1815 Savona, which was part of the State of Genoa, was given to the House of Savoy to whom Turin also belonged. The sea monster was not recorded.

89

Dedans Hongrie par Boheme, Navarre,	Into Hungary through Bohemia, Navarre and by the
Et par banniere fainctes seditions:	banner feigned sedition. The
Par fleurs de lys pays portant la barre,	country of the fleur de lis carrying the bar; they will
Contre Orleans sera emotions.	cause disturbances against Orléans.

The fleur de lis with a diagonal bar to each corner was the arms of the Bourbon family. The junior branches such as the Vendômes, who got the throne, and the Condés, just had a diagonal bar in the centre. It appears that Nostradamus is describing an expedition into Bohemia and Hungary led by one of the French royal line, possibly a Bourbon Vendôme of Navarre? It is all very obscure, and appears to be unfulfilled.

90

Dans les cyclades, en perinthe & larisse,	In the Cyclades, in Perinthus and Larissa, in Sparta and all
Dedans Sparte tout le Peloponnesse:	of the Peloponnesus; a very
Si grand famine, peste par faux connisse,[1]	great famine, plague through false dust: it will last nine
Neuf mois tiendra & tout le chevronesse.	months throughout the whole peninsula.

CHEMICAL WARFARE IN GREECE AND THE BALKANS?

It is possible that by the words 'false dust' Nostradamus is trying to imply that the plague and famine described here are artificially induced? It appears to be a widespread disaster throughout the whole of Greece and the southern Balkans. This quatrain may tie in with the ones that predict trouble in the Middle East.

[1] *connisse*—Difficult, possibly Greek, *Konis* = dust, or Latin, *connissus* = exerted.

Au grand marché qu'on dict des mensongiers,	At the great market, called that of the liars, of all Torrent and the field of Athens: they will be surprised by the light armed horses, by the Albanians, when Mars is in Leo, and Saturn in Aquarius.
Du tout Torrent[1] & champ Athenien:	
Seront surprins par les chevaux legiers,	
Par Albanois Mars, Leo, Sat. un versien.[2]	

Again a reference to an attack from the Albanians.

Apres le siege tenu dix sept ans,	After the See has been held seventeen years, five will change within the same period of time. Then one will be elected at the same time who will not be too agreeable to the Romans.
Cinq changeront en tel revolu terme:	
Puis sera l'un esleu de mesme temps,	
Qui des Romains ne sera trop conforme.	

THE VATICAN AND ITS FUTURE

Nostradamus says that after a Pope rules for seventeen years there will be five Popes within the next seventeen years. If he is slightly out in his calculations this could apply to Pius XII who reigned for nineteen years. It is interesting to note that the Irish prophet, Malachy, with whom Nostradamus seems to agree to a remarkable degree, gives only another five Popes before the Final Coming. John XXIII ruled for five years, the present Paul VI has been in the Vatican since 1963 and is 75 years old. This allows a very short life span for the next three Popes but since most are elected as old men it may just be possible.

Soubs le terroir du rond globe lunairs,	Under the land of the round moonlike globe, when Mercury is at the height of his powers. The island of Scotland will produce a leader, who will put the English into confusion.
Lors que sera dominateur Mercure:	
L'isle d'Escosse fera un luminaire,	
Qui les Anglois mettra à deconfiture.	

[1] *Torrent*—It is unclear whether this is a proper name or not.
[2] *versien*—*Verseau* = Aquarius.

THE YOUNG PRETENDER

Most commentators apply this to Charles I, because he was born in Scotland in 1600 before the Stuarts came to the throne. But it seems more applicable to Bonnie Prince Charlie who did put the English into confusion for a while when he marched as far south as Derby.

94

Translatera en la grand Germanie,
Brabant & Flandres, Gand,
Bruges & Bolongne,
La traifue fainte, le grand duc
d'Armenie,
Assaillira Vienne & la Coloigne.

He will change into the Greater Germany, Brabant and Flanders, Ghent, Bruges and Boulogne. The truce feigned, the great Duke of Armenia will assault Vienna and Cologne.

HITLER AND RUSSIA, 1939/40

The Greater Germany is, of course, the Third Reich. Hitler assimilated all the places mentioned in the quatrain during his march across Europe. The feigned truce probably describes the invasion of Poland under the guise of help, which Nostradamus elsewhere calls 'similé secours'. The Duke of Armenia stands for Russia, who moved troops southwards into Germany.

95

Nautique rame invitera les umbres
Du grand Empire lors viendra con-
citer
La mer Aegee des lignes les en-
combres,
Empeschant l'onde Tirreme defflo-
tez.

The nautical oar will invite the shadows and then come to provoke the great Empire. In the Aegean sea the remains of (bits of) wood, obstruct the Tyrrhenian sea and impede it.

This seems to describe a few ships 'nautical oars', which grow in power into a mighty fleet and trouble the Empire, whether French or Roman is not clear. The end result is a devastating sea battle and great destruction in Italy.

96

Sur le milieu du grand monde la
rose,
Pour nouveaux faicts sang public
espandu:
A dire vrai on aura bouche close,
Lors au besoing viendra tard
l'attendu.

The rose upon the middle of the world, because of new deeds, public blood is shed; to speak the truth they will have closed mouths, then, at time of need the awaited one will come late.

Le nay defforme par horreur suf-
    foqué,
Dans la cité du grand Roi habi-
    table:
L'edict severe des captifs revoqué,
Gresle & tonnere, condon inestim-
	One born deformed, suffocated through horror in the city inhabited by the great king. The severe edict of the captives is revoked, hail and thunder, Condom too great.

THE MAN IN THE IRON MASK

It has been suggested that the first two lines refer to the man in the Iron Mask, reputed son of the Queen and Cardinal Mazarin. Line 3 is taken as a reference to the Edict of Nantes, 1685.

A quarante huict degré climaterique,
A fin de Cancer si grande seicheresse:
Poisson en mer, fleuve, lac cuit
    hectique,
Bearn, Bigorre par feu ciel en
    destresse.
	At the forty-eighth degree of the climacteric, the end of Cancer there is a very great drought. Fish in the sea, river and the lake boiled hectic, Bearn and Bigorre in distress from fire in the sky.

The 48° of the climacteric may mean 48° latitude, which runs through France near Rennes, Orléans and Langres. The drought is predicted as occurring after 22nd July when the sun leaves the sign of Cancer; there is another reference to fish cooking in the heat in II. 3. Fire in the sky is probably some form of freak electrical storm or an attack by bombs or rockets.

Milan, Ferrare, Turin & Aquil-
    laye,
Capne Brundis vexés par gent
    Celtique:
Par le Lion & phalange aquilee
Quant Rome aura le chef vieux
    Britannique.
	Milan, Ferrare, Turin & Aquileia, Capua and Brindisi vexed by the Celtic nation: by the lion and his eagle-like phalanx, when Rome will have the old British chief.

NAPOLEON AND THE LAST OF THE STUARTS, 1807

The cities mentioned cover all regions of Italy showing how complete was Napoleon's conquest. It is specifically dated to the time of Napoleon because it was in 1807 that Cardinal York, the last of the Stuarts, died in Rome.

Le boutefeu par son feu attrapé, *De feu du ciel à Carcas & Co-* *minge:* *Foix, Aux, Mazere, haut veillart* *eschappé,* *Par ceux de Hasse, des Saxons &* *Turinge.*	The incendiary trapped in his own fire; fire from the sky at Carcassonne and Comminges: Foix Auch & Mazeres, the important old man escaped, through those of Hesse and Thuringia and some Saxons.

Yet another reference to fire in the sky, perhaps a battle, this time in South-western France. Not many Germans got as far South as this even during the Second World War, so this verse may still be unfulfilled.

CENTURY VI

248

77
78   Retroactive prophecy?
79*   Battle of Lodi, 1796
80**F? War in Middle East. The Third Antichrist
81
82
83   Philip of Spain with France and Netherlands
84
85
86
87*   Emperor Ferdinand, 1558–62
88
89
90
91
92**   Death of Louis XVI
93
94
95
96
97*F?   Bombing of New York?
98
99
100*   Incantation against stupid critics

KEY: * Of interest. F? Possibly referring to the future.

Autour des monts Pyrenees grans amas,
De gent estrange secourir roi nouveau:
Pres de Garonne du grant temple du. Mas,
Un Romain chef le craindra dedans l'eau.

Around the Pyrenean mountains a great throng of foreign people will help the new king. Near the great temple of Mas by the Garonne, a Roman leader will fear him on the water.

Le Mas d'Agenais has many famous Roman antiquities which Nostradamus would have seen when he lived at Agen. The Roman chief is unclear.

En l'an cinq cens octante plus & moins,
On attendra le siecle bien estrange:
En l'an sept cens, & trois cieux en tesmoings.
Que plusieurs regnes un à cinq feront change.

In the year five hundred and eighty more or less one will await a very strange century. In the year seven hundred and three, the skies as witness that several kingdoms, one to five, will make a change.

1580 AND 1703

A daring quatrain with two dates, both of which seem accurate. In 1580, Nostradamus nearly always leaves out the thousand for reasons of scansion, France was torn by the Civil War called the Seventh War and had little to look forward to. But by 1703 Louis XIV was defying Europe and fighting the war of the Spanish Succession. The five kingdoms were probably the Two Sicilies, Milan, the Netherlands, the Americas and Spain which were inherited by the French grandson of Louis XIV, Philip V.

Fleuve qu'esprouve le nouveau nay Celtique,
Sera en grande de l'empire discord:
Le jeune prince par gent ecclesiastique,
Ostera le sceptre coronel de concorde.

The river that the newborn French heir attempts; there will be great discord among the empire. The young prince, because of the ecclesiastics will remove peace from crown and sceptre.

There is a legend that in former times new-born heirs to the French throne were put on a target and made to swim up the Rhine to see if they were lawfully begotten or not. (*Garancières*).

4

Le Celtiq fleuve changera de rivaige,	The French river will change
Plus ne tiendra la cité d'Agripine:[1]	course and no longer surround
Tout transmue ormis le vieil lan-	the city of Agrippina; all
gaige,	changed except the old lan-
Saturne, Leo, Mars, Cancer en	guage, Saturn in Leo, Mars
rapine.	plundering in Cancer.

CHANGES OF FRENCH BORDER
After the Franco-Prussian war and the surrender of Alsace and Lorraine to the Germans the Rhine—the French river—was no longer the border between France and Germany. The old language that remained was German; everything else will be changed by war.

5

Si grand Famine par unde pestifere.	A very great famine (caused) by
Par pluie longue le long du pole	a pestilent wave will extend its
arctique,	long rain the length of the
Samarobrin cent lieux de l'hemi-	Arctic pole. Samarobrin one
sphere,	hundred leagues from the hemi-
Vivront sans loi exempt de polliti-	sphere; they will live without
que.	law, exempt from politics.

MANNED SPACE STATION? FALLOUT OR BACTERIAL WARFARE
This quatrain has caused more comment than most in the Prophecies. It seems to indicate that a great pestilence, caused perhaps by fallout or bacterial warfare, will cover the Northern pole of the earth, and that it appears to come from the unidentified Samarobrin which is circling above at a height of approximately two hundred and seventy miles. Could Nostradamus possibly have foreseen a manned space station? The word Samarobrin may be the nearest he can get to its name. This quatrain may well fit the decade of the 1970s. Already there have been space stations manned for long periods sent up by both Russia and the U.S.A.

[1] *Agripine*—Colonia Agrippina = Cologne.

Apparoistra vers la Septentrion,	He will appear towards the
Non loin de Cancer l'estoille	North, not far from the bearded
chevelue:	star in Cancer; Susa, Siena,
Suze, Sienne, Boece, Eretrion,	Boetia, Eretria, the great man
Mourra de Rome grand, la nuict	of Rome will die, the night
disparue.	dispersed.

POPE LEO XIII

The great man of Rome was Pius IX who died in February 1878. He was succeeded by Pope Leo XIII whose family arms have a comet, a bearded star, and who is also called Lumen in Caelo, light in the sky, by the prophet Malachy.

7

Norneigre & Dace, & l'isle	Norway and Dacia and the
Britannique,	British Isles, will be troubled
Par les unis freres serong vexeés:	by the united brothers. The
Le chef Romain issue' de sang	Roman leader, came from
Gallique,	French blood; the forces thrust
Et les copies au forestz repoulsées.	back into the forests.

HITLER AND MUSSOLINI

This quatrain is similar to V. 51. Hitler and Mussolini are the united brothers or allies who trouble Norway, Dacia (Rumania) and Great Britain during the Second World War. The forces in the forests are the famous Resistance Movements, which so troubled the Nazis.

8

Ceux qui estoient en regne pour	Those who were in the kingdom
scavoir,	for knowledge will become
Au Royal change deviendront apouv-	impoverished by a royal
ris:	change. Some exiled without
Uns exilez sans appui, or, n'avoir,	support, having no gold,
Lettrez & lettres ne seront à grand	neither learning nor the learned
pris.	will be held of much value.

A general comment on Nostradamus' belief that learning would decline during a period after his death.

Au sacrez temples seront faicts escandales,
Comptez seront par honneurs & louanges.
D'un que on grave d'argent, d'or les medalles,
La fin sera en torments bien estranges.

In the sacred temples scandals will be committed, they will be thought of as honours and praiseworthy. By one whom they engrave on silver, gold and medals; the end will be in very strange torments.

10

Un peu de temps les temples de couleurs
De blanc & noir des deux entre-meslee:
Rouges & jaunes leur embleront les leurs
Sang, terre, peste, faim, feu, d'eau affollee.

In a short time the colours of temples; with black and white, the two will be intermingled. The red and yellow ones will carry off their (possessions), blood, earth, plague, hunger, fire, maddened by thirst.

11

Des sept rameaux à trois seront reduicts,
Les plus aisnez seront surprins par mort,
Fraticider les deux seront seduicts,
Les conjurez en dormans seront morts.

The seven branches will be reduced to three, the elder ones will be surprised by death. Two will be attracted towards fratricidal (strife): the conspirators will die while asleep.

FRANCE 1575–88

A good quatrain. When Catherine de' Medici's seven children have been reduced to three, which occurred in 1575 when only Henri III, François d'Alençon and Marguerite of Navarre were alive, then Henri and his brother were involved in a series of complicated plots. François allied himself with the Leaguers, led by the Duc de Guise, and hoped to succeed to the throne. Both the de Guise brothers were murdered at Blois in the early morning on Henri's orders. See II. 18, III. 51 etc.

Dresser copies pour monter à l'Empire,	To raise forces to ascend to Empire from the Vatican the
Du Vatican le sang Royal tiendra:	Royal blood will hold fast.
Flamans, Anglois, Espaigne avec Aspire,[1]	Flemish, English, Spain with Aspire: he will fight against
Contre l'Italie & France contendra.	France and Italy,

EUROPE?

This is interesting because Europe is visualized in modern, not medieval, terms. Italy did not exist as such until 1870, and the Flemings were a Habsburg dependency until modern Belgium was created. The prophecy states three main points. The first will be an attempt to gain the Imperial throne. The second, a French Pope (possibly of Royal Blood). The third, the Habsburgs and English will ally against France and Italy, which occurred during the Napoleonic wars, as did the first point. We have not yet had a French Pope who occurs also in V. 49.

Un dubieux ne viendra loing du regne,	A doubtful one will not come far from the kingdom the
La plus grand part le voudra soustenir:	greater part will wish to support him. A Capitol will not
Un Capitole[2] *ne voudra point qu'il regne,*	want him to reign: he will not be able to bear his great
Sa grande charge ne pourra maintenir.	burden.

This has been generally applied to the fall of the House of Savoy, the rulers of Italy.

Loing de sa terre Roy perdra la bataille,	Far from his country, a king will lose the battle; quickly
Prompt eschappé poursuivi suivant prins,	escaped, he is followed and taken. The ignorant one taken
Ignare prins soubs la doree maille.	under the golden chain-mail
Soubs fainct habit & l'ennemy surprins.	under a false garment, and the enemy surprised.

[1] *Aspire*—Uncertain, possibly Speyer or Spires?
[2] *Capitole*—Probably the Pope, as the Capitol was the Roman citadel.

Here is another quatrain to support a romantic theory, such as V. 1. King Sebastian of Portugal decided to raise a Crusade despite the objections of the Pope and the Spanish king. He crossed to Morocco in 1578 and attacked the Army of the King of Fez and was obliterated at the Battle of Kasr Al-Kabir. He was reported killed but there were persistent rumours that he had escaped. Nostradamus seems to believe that he did so by changing armour with one of his followers. Although the Moors discovered this they did not reveal the news for political reasons. Nostradamus gives us a new slant on history!

15

Dessoubs la tombe sera trouvé le Prince,	Under the tomb will be found a Prince, who will have taken
Qu'aura le pris par dessus Nuremberg:	him above Nuremberg. The Spanish king, Capricorn thin,
L'Espaignol Roi en Capricorne mince,	deceived and betrayed by the great Wittemberg.
Fainct & trahi par le grand Uvitemberg.	

16

Ce qui ravi sera du jeune Milve,	That which the young hawk will carry off, by the Normans
Par les Normans de France & Picardie:	of France and Picardy. The black ones of the temple at the
Les noirs du temple du lieu de Negrisilve	Black wood will make an inn and fire at Lombardy.
Feront aulberge & feu de Lombardie.	

The black ones are almost certainly the Benedictines, sometimes known as the Black monks, who had a monastery at Harrenalb in the Black Forest. The rest is obscure.

17

Apres les limes[1] brusler les asiniers,[2]	After the penances are burned the ass drivers will be forced to
Contraints seront changer habits divers:	change into different clothing.
Les Saturnins bruslez par les meusniers,	Those of Saturn burnt by the millers, except the greater part
Hors la plupart qui ne sera convers.	which will not be covered.

[1] *limes*—O.F. = penance.
[2] *asniers*—Some texts have rasniers but both readings are doubtful.

Par les phisiques le grand Roy delaissé,
Par sort non art de l'Ebrieu est en vie,
Lui & son genre au regne hault poussé.
Grace donnee à gent qui Christ envie.

The great king deserted by the physicians lives through chance not the skill of the Jew. He and his people placed high in the realm, pardon given to the race which denies Christ.

An interesting quatrain which unfortunately does not seem to have occurred. But it is worth remembering Nostradamus' Jewish background and beliefs. It does not sound as though he had relinquished them in this verse.

La vraie flamme engloutira l a dame,
Que voudra mettre les Innocens à feu:
Pres de l'assaut l'excercite s'enflamme,
Quant dans Seville monstre en boeuf sera veu.

The true flame will swallow up the woman who will want to put the Innocents to the fire. Near the assault, the army is inflamed, when in Seville a monstrous ox will be seen.

The ox and Seville are probably a reference to bull fighting, although the fanatic queen's identity is not clear.

L'union faincte sera peu de durée,
Des uns changés reformés la pluspart:
Dans les vaissaux sera gent endurée,
Lors aura Rome un nouveau liepart.

The feigned union will last a short time, some changed, the greater part reformed. People will be suffering in the vessels, then when Rome has a new Leopard.

In heraldry a Leopard is a lion walking to the left with its head turned left to face the spectator. So possibly when a Pope has a Leopard in his coat of arms there will be great changes. It could equally refer to the English heraldic lion.

Quant ceux du polle artiq unis
ensemble,
En Orient grand effrayeur &
crainte:
Esleu nouveau, soustenu le grand
tremble,
Rhodes, Bisance de sang Barbare
taincte.

When those of the Northern
pole are united together in the
East will be great fear and
dread. A new man elected,
supported by the great one
who trembles, both Rhodes and
Byzantium will be stained with
Barbarian blood.

ALLIANCE OF U.S.A. AND U.S.S.R.

This quatrain must be linked with VI. 5 which describes the
people of the northern pole as devastated by a possibly man-
induced plague. Nostradamus does seem to indicate that the
U.S.A. and U.S.S.R. will finally unite to form a new geopolitical
group and that this will cause the East, China, to worry at the
shift in the balance of power. This is followed by war, particularly
in the Middle East. See V. 78, VI. 80.

Dedans la terre du grand temple
celique,
Nepveu à Londres par paix faincte
meutri:
La barque alors deviendra scis-
matique,
Liberte faincte sera au corn & cri.

In the land of the great
heavenly temple, a nephew at
London is murdered through a
false peace. The ship will then
be schismatic, false liberty will
be shouted abroad.

The above quatrain appears to describe England as the land of
the great heavenly temple. The nephew of a ruler is asked to
come to London on a peace treaty, and then murdered, so this
rules out the two Pretenders. At the same time there will be
trouble and schism in the Vatican. Some commentators have seen
the death of Darnley, Mary Queen of Scots' second husband, in
this verse. It is one of the most frustrating in all the Prophecies.

D'esprit de regne munismes des-
criées,
Et seront peuples esmuez contre leur
Roi:
Paix, faict nouveau, sainctes loix
empirées,
Rapis onc fut en si tres dur arroi.

Defences undermined by the
spirit of the kingdom people
will be stirred up against their
king. A new peace is made, holy
laws become worse, never was
Paris in such great trouble.

FRENCH REVOLUTION

Rapis is Nostradamus' standard anagram for Paris. This verse is full of generalities which best apply to the French Revolution, new peace and new laws, with religious observations being controlled by the state, and Paris in a state of anarchy.

24

Mars & le sceptre se trouvera conjoinct, *Dessoubz Cancer calamiteuse guerre:* *Un peu apres sera nouveau Roi oingt,* *Qui par long temps pacifiera la terre.*	Mars and the sceptre will be in conjunction, a calamitous war under Cancer. A short time afterwards a new king will be anointed who will bring peace to the earth for a long time.

21st JUNE 2002

The sceptre here stands for Jupiter and, according to Wölner, the only time the conjunction will occur is on 21st June 2002. There will be a terrible war; this may be the war Nostradamus has already predicted for the end of this century, followed by a long era of peace.

25

Par Mars contraire sera la monarchie, *Du grand pecheur en trouble ruineux:* *Jeune noir[1] rouge prendra la hierarchie,* *Les prodideurs iront jour bruineux.*	With Mars adverse the monarchy of the great fisherman will be in ruinous trouble. The young red king will take over the government. The traitors will act on a misty day.

VICTOR EMMANUEL AND ITALIAN REVOLUTION

The Vatican will be in trouble when its troops are defeated. This happened in 1796–1815 against Napoleon and again in 1860–70. The young king with politically socialist leanings probably stands for Victor Emmanuel and the Italian Revolution.

[1] Anagram for king as elsewhere.

Quatre ans le siege quelque bien peu tiendra,
Un surviendra libidineux de vie:
Ravenne & Pise, Veronne soustiendront,
Pour eslever la croix de Pape envie.

For four years the seat will be held for some little good, one will acceed to it who is libidinous in life: Ravenna and Pisa, Verona will support him, desirous of elevating the Papal Cross.

JOHN XXIII

A good Pope will die after four years to be succeeded by a worldly one. This might possibly refer to John XXIII who was Pope for just under four and a half years. He was probably a more popular Pope than any for several centuries. The present Paul VI appears more sophisticated and withdrawn.

Dedans les isles de cinq fleuves à un,
Par le croissant du grand Chyren Selin:
Par les bruines de l'aer fureur de l'un,
Six eschapés, cachés fardeaux de lin.

Within the islands of five rivers to one, by the crescent of the great Chyren Selin. Through the mists in the air the fury of one; six escaped, hidden in bundles of flax.

Although connected with the other Chyren Selin quatrains this remains undeciphered.

Le grand Celtique entrera dedans Rome,
Menant amas d'exilés & bannis:
Le grand pasteur mettra à mort tout homme,
Qui pour le coq estoient aux Alpes unis.

The great Celt will enter Rome, leading a crowd of exiled and banished. The great Pastor will put to death every man who was united over the Alps for the Cock.

PIUS VII

The Great Celt may refer to Napoleon's conquering of Rome and the subsequent return of the Pope Pius VII with his clergy who had been imprisoned in France. But the third line is totally incorrect as Pius VII was extraordinarily kind to his ex-captors and their adherents until his death in 1823.

La veuve saincte estendant les nouvelles,	The holy widow hearing the news of her offspring in trouble
De ses rameaux mis en perplex & trouble:	and distress: He who will be led to calm the quarrels by his
Qui sera duict appaiser les querelles,	pursuit will make the shaven heads pile up.
Par son pourchas des razes fera comble.	

CATHERINE DE' MEDICI AND HER SONS

Catherine de' Medici will learn of the problems and troubles of her children, in particular the massacre of St. Bartholomew and the murder of the Duke de Guise and of his brother by her son, Henri III. These actions all increased civil unrest and led to the eventual civil war between the Leaguers and the Huguenots.

Par l'apparence de faincte saincteté,	By the appearance of fake holiness, the seat will be betrayed
Sera trahi aux ennemis le siege:	to the enemies, in the night
Nuict qu'on cuidoit dormit en seureté,	when they thought to sleep safely; the people of Liège will
Pres de Braban marcheront ceux du Liege.	march near Brabant.

Liège was a province east of Brabant in the Netherlands. Normally the word seat in Nostradamus indicates the Vatican but here it is difficult to be sure.

Roi trouvera ce qu'il desiroit tant,	The King will find that which he desires so greatly; when the
Quand le Prelat sera reprins à tort.	Prelate will be wrongfully
Responce au duc le rendra mal content,	taken. The reply to the Duce will make him angry; in Milan
Qui dans Milan mettra plusieurs a mort.	he will put several to death.

MUSSOLINI

The king of Italy, gets what he desires when he angers the Duce, Mussolini. The executions at Milan probably refer to the deaths of Ciano and others. The Pope being wrongfully taken is understood as the Vatican, a neutral city, being completely surrounded by a hostile Fascist Italy.

Par trahison de verges à mort battu,
Prins surmonté sera par son desordre:
Conseil frivole au grand captif sentu,
Nez par fureur quant Berich viendra mordre.

Beaten to death by rods for treason; captured he will be overcome because of his disorder. Frivolous advice is handed to the great captive, when Berich comes to bite his nose in a rage.

The name of Berich, possibly an anagram, remains unsolved to this day.

Sa main derniere par Alus sanguin-aire
Ne se pourra par la mer guarantir:
Entre deux fleuves craindre main militaire,
Le noir[1] l'ireux le fera repentir.

His hand finally through the bloody Alus, he will be unable to protect himself by sea. Between two rivers he will fear the military hand, the black and angry one will make him repent of it.

NAME OF THIRD ANTICHRIST?

Alus is another unsolved mystery. I wonder whether it connects with the fearsome Mabus of II. 62? There is the repetition of the word main in connection with both. It may be an approximation of name of the third Antichrist tying up with the cryptic quatrain (II. 28) where Nostradamus seems to be trying to spell the letters of his name. See I. 50, II. 89, VIII. 77, X. 72.

Du feu volant la machination,
Viendra troubler au grand chef assiegez:
Dedans sera telle sedition,
Qu'en desespoir seront les profligez.

The machine of flying fire will come to trouble the great, besieged chief. Within there will be such sedition that those abandoned will be in despair.

BOMBING OR ROCKETS

A general quatrain describing the situation of any place besieged by modern weapons. However, the first line is very striking.

[1] noir—Possible anagram for king—roi.

Pres de Rion[1] *& proche à la blanche laine,*
Aries, Taurus, Cancer, Leo, la Vierge,
Mars, Jupiter, le sol ardra grand plaine,
Bois & citez, lettres cachez au cierge.

Near the Bear and close to the white wool, Aries, Taurus, Cancer, Leo, Virgo, Mars, Jupiter the Sun will burn the great plain, woods and cities; letters hidden in the candle.

The white wool is probably the Milky Way, but Nostradamus has produced too many constellations for one to be sure what he intended apart from a drought on a great plain.

Ne bien ne mal par bataille ter- restre,
Ne parviendra aux confins de Perousse:
Rebeller Pise, Florence voir mal estre,
Roi nuict blessé sur mulet à noire house.

Neither good nor evil from the earthly battle will come to the borders of Perugia. Pisa to rebel, Florence seen to be in bad (times): a king on a mule, wounded by night, to the black covering.

L'oeuvre ancienne se parachevera,
Du toict cherra sur le grand mal ruine:
Innocent faict mort on accusera:
Nocent caiché taillis à la bruine.

The ancient work will be accomplished and from the roof evil ruin will fall on to the great man. Being dead, they will accuse an innocent of the deed, the guilty one hidden in the misty woods.

Although this is a detailed prophecy and seems likely to have occurred, I do not know of its ever having been fulfilled.

[1] *Rion*—Misprint for *Trion*, from Latin, Triones = the Bear Con- stellation.

Au profligez de paix les ennemis,
Apres avoir l'Italie superee:
Noir[1] sanguinaire, rouge sera com-
mis,
Feu, sang verser, eaue de sang
couloree.

The enemies of peace, the dis-
solute ones, having overcome
Italy the bloody black one, red
will be seen, fire, bloodshed,
water coloured with blood.

The exposure of the colour red presumably means revolution
although the colour did not contain this sense until the late 18th
Century. Before that it referred to the Spanish or to Cardinals of
the Church. Some of Nostradamus' concepts are surprisingly
modern.

L'enfant du regne par paternelle
prinse,
Expolié sera pour delivrer:
Apres du lac Trasimen l'azur
prinse,
La troupe hostaige pour trop fort
s'enivrer.

The child of the kingdom,
through his father's capture,
will be deprived to deliver him;
near Lake Trasimene the azure
captive, in order that the
hostage troop may become very
drunk.

Grand du Magonce[2] pour grand
soif estaindre,
Sera privé de sa grand dignité:
Ceux de Cologne si fort le viendront
plaindre,
Que le grand groppe[3] au Rin sera
getté.

To quench the great thirst the
great one of Mainz will be
deprived of his great dignity.
Those from Cologne will come
to complain so strongly that
the great rump will be thrown
into the Rhine.

HOLY ROMAN EMPIRE, 1806

The Archbishop of Mainz was one of the Electors of the Empire.
Mainz was captured by the French during the Revolution and
ceded by the Treaty of Campoformio to the French. However, the
Elector held his title until the formal end of the Holy Roman
Empire in 1806. The Archbishop of Cologne was also an elector,
whose office was abolished three years early in 1803, so he had the
right to complain.

[1] *Noir*—either black or king, the usual anagram.
[2] *Magonce*—Latin, *Maguntiacum* = Mainz or Mayence.
[3] *groppe*—Low Latin, *groppa* = haunches, rump.

Le second chef de regne d'Anne-marc,
Par Ceux de Frise & l'isle Britannique,
Fera despendre plus de cent mille marc,
Vain exploicter voyage en Italique.

The second leader of the kingdom of Annemarc, through those of Frisia and the British Isles, will spend more than one hundred thousand marks, attempting in vain a voyage to Italy.

A difficult quatrain made interesting by the fact that when Nostradamus wrote, England and Frisia had the same ruler, Philip of Spain, husband to Mary of England and ruler of all the Netherlands. In IV. 89. Nostradamus foresees William of Orange, a Frisian, attaining to the English throne. A problem remains in the uninterpreted Annemarc, also in IV. 27.

A lomygon[1] sera laissé le regne,
Du grand Selin qui plus fera de faict:
Par les Italies estendra son enseigne,
Regi sera par prudent contrefaict.

To Ogmios the kingdom of the great Selin will be left, who will do even more. He will extend his banner throughout Italy and it will be ruled by careful forgery.

Ogmios also appears in V. 80, VIII. 44, IX. 89, but his identity is not certain.

Long temps sera sans estre habitée,
Ou Signe & Marne autour vient arrouser:
De la Tamise & martiaux tentée,
Decevez les gardes en cuidant repouser.

For a long time it will remain uninhabited around where the Seine and Marne come to gush forth. Tried by Tamise and soldiers, the guards deceived in believing it rebuffed.

Paris is the city between the Seine and Marne which Nostradamus seems to envisage here as uninhabited. The Tamise can mean the river Thames in London, or a town of that name near Antwerp.

[1] *lomygon*—Misprint for Ogmios, the Celtic Hercules.

De nuict par Nantes L'Iris appa-
  roistra,
Des artz marins susciteront la
  pluie:
Arabique goulfre grand classe par-
  foudra,
Un monstre en Saxe naistra d'ours
  & truie.

By night the rainbow will
appear near Nantes, the marine
arts will raise up rain. In the
Arabian Gulf a great fleet will
flounder: in Saxony a monster
will be born of a bear and a
sow.

20th CENTURY?

This quatrain may apply to the 20th Century. In 1947 the scien-
tists discovered how to produce artificial rain (line 2). At a time
when a rainbow appears at Nantes a fleet will meet disaster either
in the Red Sea, since there is no actual Gulf of Arabia, or in the
Arabian sea, which lies to the south, or the Persian Gulf to the
east.

Le gouverneur du regne bien
  scavant,
Ne consentir voulant au faict
  Royal:
Mellile classe par le contraire vent,
  Le remettra à son plus desloyal.

The very learned governor of
the kingdom does not wish to
consent to the Royal deed. The
fleet at Melilla, by a contrary
wind, will deliver him back to
his most disloyal one.

Melilla is in Spanish Morocco; from this some commentators
apply the quatrain to the Spanish Civil War.

Un juste sera en exile renvoyé,
Par pestilence aux confins de
  Nonseggle,
Response au rouge le fera desvoyé,
Roi retirant à la Rane & à
  l'aigle.

A just one will be sent back into
exile through pestilence to the
confines of Nonseggle. His reply
to the red one will mislead him,
the king withdrawing to the
Frog and the Eagle.

Nonseggle remains an unsolved proper name or anagram. The
frog reappears here as in quatrains V. 3, and V. 95. The first
line may refer to Louis XVIII during the Hundred Days but the
rest is completely obscure.

Entre deux monts les deux grans assemblés	The two great ones, assembled between two mountains will
Delaisseront leur simulté[1] secrette:	give up their secret quarrel.
Brucelle & Dolle par Langres acablés,	Brussels and Dôle overcome by Langres in order to execute
Pour à Malignes executer leur peste.	their pestilence at Malines.

Brussels and Dôle and Malines were all in the Spanish Netherlands. This quatrain may therefore predict their being conquered by France, Langres.

La saincteté trop faincte & seductive,	The holiness, too false and too attractive accompanied by an
Accompaigné d'une langue diserte	eloquent tongue: The old city,
La cité vieille & Parme trop hastive,	Parma too hasty, they will make Florence and Siena even
Florence & Sienne rendront plus desertes.	more deserted.

De la partie de Mammer[2] grand Pontife,	The great Pontiff by the warlike party who will subjugate
Subjugera les confins du Danube:	the borders of the Danube. The
Chasser les croix par fer raffe ne riffe,	cross pursued by hook or by crook; captives, gold, jewels,
Captifz, or, bagues plus de cent mille rubes.	more than one hundred thousand rubies.

THE SWASTIKA?

The cross is described as *ne raffe ne riffe*, an expression which can mean by hook or by crook, but also, by extension, crooked. The crooked cross can only be the swastika. Hitler's party originated in Austria, the Danube. The last line is horribly reminiscent of the millions of pounds of personal jewellery, gold and possessions the Nazis stole from their victims, most of whom ended up in the concentration camps. The position of the Pope in the verse is not clear but Pius XII was criticized for not taking a stronger line

[1] *simulté*—O.F. = quarrel.

[2] *Mammer* = (a) Mamers, Sabine name for Mars. (b) Mamertini. People of Messina, Sicily.

against the Nazis and for allowing them refuge in the Vatican city
after the war.

50

Dedans le puys seront trouvés les oz.
Sera l'incest conmis par la maratre:[1]
L'estat changé on querra bruict & loz,
Et aura Mars attendant pour son astre.

The bones will be found inside the wells; it will be incest committed by the stepmother. The state changed he will seek renown and praise and will have Mars attendant as his star.

51

Peuple assemblé, voir nouveau expectacle,
Princes & Rois par plusieurs assistans:
Pilliers faillir, murs, mais comme miracle
Le Roi sauvé & trente des instants.

The people gathered to see a new sight; Princes and Kings among many onlookers. The pillars, walls, fall, but as if by a miracle the King and thirty of those present are saved.

HITLER?

It would be curious to speculate whether this was the verse that
caused Ernst Krafft, who worked on Nostradamus for Goebbels'
Propaganda Ministry, to warn Hitler against an assassination
attempt that was made upon him in November 1939. The bomb
was hidden in a pillar behind the rostrum and it was by sheer
chance that Hitler and some of his Party members left for Berlin
unexpectedly early. The notoriety gained by Krafft after this was
to eventually cost him his life.

52

En lieu du grand qui sera condemné,
De prison hors son ami en sa place:
L'espoir Troien en six mois joinct, mortnay,
Le Sol à l'urne seront prins fleuves en glace.

In the place of the great one who will be condemned he is outside prison, his friend in his place. The Trojan hope for six months joined, the born, dead; the Sun in Aquarius, the rivers will be frozen.

[1] maratre—more likely stepmother than mother-in-law because of the
incest theme.

Another tantalizing quatrain in which Nostradamus contradicts the little that is known of an historical mystery, the fate of Louis XVII, see V. I. Here he implies that another child dies in prison in 1795 in his place, the Trojan blood always referring to French royal blood because of the legend of Francus, son of Priam of Troy. Line 3 is difficult to interpret. Does it refer to the death of the fake king after six months, or to the death of the real king six months after his escape? The Sun in Aquarius applies from mid-February to mid-March. The Dauphin was reported dead on 8th June 1795, but this prophecy must refer to the earlier months.

53

Le grand Prelat Celtique à Roi suspect,
De nuict par cours sortira hors du regne:
Par duc fertile à son grand Roi, Bretaigne,
Bisance à Cipres & Tunes insuspect.

The great French Prelate suspected by the king by night will flee from his realm; through a Duke fertile to his great King, Britain, Byzantium to Cyprus and Tunis undiscovered.

This quatrain appears to indicate that a French Cardinal or Bishop will flee to England and from there to Tunis via Constantinople and Cyprus. Very confused.

54

Au poinct du jour au second chant du coq,
Ceulx de Tunes, de Fez, & de Bugie,
Par les Arabes captif le Roi Maroq,
L'an mil six cens & sept, de Liturgie.

At daybreak at second cockcrow, those of Tunis, Fez and of Bougie; the Arabs captured by the king of Morocco in the year sixteen hundred and seven by the Liturgy.

1607?

This quatrain seems to be one of Nostradamus' total failures. He appears to see the fall of the Ottoman Empire through a new European king, and also in Asia through new Persian and Arab Empires in the year 1607. The only point in Nostradamus' favour is that no commentator can agree about what is meant by 'the Liturgy'. This may alter the date as it now appears, but how is not clear. It could simply be an equivalent of Anno Domini, but Nostradamus was usually more convoluted than that.

55

Au chalme Duc, en arrachant l'esponce,	The calmed duke drawing up the contract, the Arabian sail
Voile Arabesque voir, subit descouverte:	is seen, a sudden discovery. Tripolis, Chios and those of
Tripolis Chio, & ceux de Trapesonce,	Trabzon; the Duke captured, the Black Sea and the city
Duc prins, Marnegro & la cité deserte.	deserted.

All one can say with certainty about this verse is that the action takes place in Asia Minor, the Black Sea and the Aegean (Chios).

56

La crainte armee de l'ennemi Narbon,	The dreaded army of the Narbonne enemy will greatly
Effrayera si fort les Hesperiques;[1]	terrify the Hesperians. Perignan
Parpignan vuide par l'aveugle darbon,[2]	empty, through the blind one of Arbon, then Barcelona by
Lors Barcelon par mer donra les piques.	sea will take up her weapons.

SIEGE OF PERPIGNAN, 1597

In this quatrain it appears that the Spaniards are being terrified by the French from Narbonne. Narbonne was only forty miles north of Perpignan, while Barcelona, sending supplies and relief, lies about one hundred miles to the south. Perpignan was besieged for a short while by the French in 1597.

57

Celui qu'estoit bien avant dans le regne,	He who was well to the front in the kingdom, having a red
Ayant chef rouge proche à la hierarchie:	chief close to the seat of power. Harsh and cruel he will make
Aspre & cruel, & se fera tant craindre,	himself most greatly feared; he will succeed to the sacred
Succedera à sacré monarchie.	monarchy.

[1] *Hesperiques*—(*a*) Spanish or Western. (*b*) American.
[2] *Arbon* (?) may be geographical. If so either in France or Switzerland.

A cruel cardinal will succeed to the Papacy. It is difficult to know if Nostradamus had any particular one in mind. The quatrain is very general.

58

Entre les deux monarques esloin-guez,	Between the two distant monarchs when the clear Sun is lost by Selin; great enmity between two indignant ones, so that liberty is restored to the Islands and to Siena.
Lors que Sol par Selin clair perdue:	
Simulté grande entre deux indignez,	
Qu'aux Isles & Sienne la liberté rendue.	

PHILIP II AND HENRI II

This was a quatrain contemporary with Nostradamus' lifetime. The sun and the chariot of Apollo were the devices of Philip II of Spain. The moon was that of Henri II of France, partly to honour his mistress, Diana of Poitiers, *Selin* meaning the Moon, line 2. Nostradamus seems to think France will conquer the Habsburgs. Siena was held by the French at this time and they were also trying to conquer Corsica. Does the restoration of Liberty mean the coming or the withdrawal of the French? Nostradamus is usually more patriotic than this.

59

Dame en fureur par rage d'adultere,	The lady, furious, in an adulterous rage, will come to conspire not to speak to her Prince. But the culprit will soon be known so that seventeen will be martyred.
Viendra à son Prince conjurer non de dire:	
Mais bref cogneu sera le vitupere,	
Que seront mis dix sept à martyre.	

60

Le Prince hors de son terroir Celtique	The Prince, outside his French territory will be betrayed, deceived by the interpreter. Rouen, La Rochelle, by those of Brittany at the port of Blaye deceived by monk and priest.
Sera trahi, deceu par l'interprete:	
Rouan, Rochelle par ceux de l'Armorique	
Au port de Blaue deceus par moine & prebstre.	

Le grand tappis plié ne monstrera,
Fois qu'à demi la pluspart de
l'histoire:
Chassé du regne loing aspre
apparoistra
Qu'au faict bellique chascun le
viendra croire.

Folded, the great carpet will
not show except by halves,
the greater part of its history.
Driven far out of the kingdom
he will appear harsh, so that
each one will believe in his
warlike act.

Trop tard tous deux les fleurs seront
perdues,
Contre la loi serpent ne voudra
faire:
Des ligueurs forces par gallots[1]
confondues,
Savone, Albinque par monech grand
martyre.

Too late both of the flowers will
be lost, the snake will not want
to act against the law; the
forces of the leaguers con-
founded by the French, Savona,
Albenga through Monaco great
martyrdom.

AN ERRONEOUS QUATRAIN

Nostradamus seems to intend a league against the French in this
verse in which the French triumph. But Monaco was bound to the
Spanish by treaty and Savona and Albenga belonged to Genoa.
Nostradamus probably had one of the 16th-Century Italian
leagues in mind, but in this case, wrongly.

La dame seule au regne demuree,
L'unic estaint premier au lict
d'honneur:
Sept ans sera de douleur exploree,
Puis longue vie au regne par grand
heur.

The lady left alone in the
kingdom, her only (spouse)
first dead on the bed of honour.
For seven years she will be
weeping with grief, then a long
life for the good fortune of the
kingdom.

CATHERINE DE' MEDICI

Nostradamus may have been prejudiced in this quatrain when he
describes Catherine de' Medici as living for the good of her kingdom. Equally, knowing the prophet's writings she may have gone
out of her way to fulfil the prediction. Catherine left off mourning
for her husband on 1st August 1566, seven years after his death.
She lived on until 1589 as Regent under Francis II and Charles IX,
but lost most of her power under Henri III.

[1] *gallots*—O.F., *gallot* = Gallic or French.

On ne tiendra pache aucune arresté,
Tous recevans iront par tromperie:
De paix & trefve, terre & mer
  protesté'.
Par Barcelone classe prins d'indus-
  trie.

They will not keep any peace agreed upon, all the receivers will go through deceit. In peace and truce land and sea having protested, the fleet is seized with skill by Barcelona.

Gris & bureau[1] demie ouverte
  guerre,
De nuict seront assaillis & pillez:
Le bureau prins passera par la
  serre[2]
Son temple ouvert, deux au plastre
  grillez.

Grey and brown in half declared war, at night they will be besieged and pillaged. The captured brown one will pass through the prison, his temple opened, two slipped in the plaster.

It is likely that Nostradamus was describing a feud between two monastic orders. The Franciscans wore grey habits, although some were brown in subsidiary orders.

Au fondement de la nouvelle
  secte,
Seront les os du grand Romain
  trouvés,
Sepulchre en marbre apparoistra
  couverte,
Terre trembler en Avril, mal
  enfouetz.

At the founding of a new sect the bones of the great Roman will be found. A sepulchre covered in marble will appear: the earth will quake in April, badly buried.

It appears that an April earth tremor may reveal the sepulchre of an important Roman, probably a Pope. This is also mentioned in III. 65. The sect is presumably Protestant.

[1] *bureau*—variant of *burel*. O.F. = brown.
[2] *serre*—Literally lock, or saw.

Au grand Empire parviendra tout un aultre	Quite a different man will attain to the great Empire, distant from kindness, more so from happiness. Ruled by one not long come from his bed, the kingdom rushes to great misfortune.
Bonté distant plus de felicité:	
Regi par un issue non loing du peaultre,	
Corruer regnes grande infelicité.	

There are two interpretations of the third line, either that the new Emperor is but a child having left the bed where he was born, or, that he leads a debauched life because *peaultre* can also mean a brothel. Possibly the Emperor Napoleon ruled by Josephine.

68

Lors que soldatz fureur seditieuse,	When the soldiers in a treacherous fury at night rise up and fight against their leader. The enemy of Alba with furious hand then troubles Rome and wins over the principals.
Contre leur chef feront de niuct fer luire:	
Ennemi d'Albe soit par main furieuse,	
Lors vexer Rome & principaux seduire.	

THE DUKE OF ALVA

This prediction was probably meant for the near future, i.e. 16th Century and the Duke of Alva (Alba). Nostradamus foresees him trying to suppress a revolt in the Spanish army, which he had to do soon afterwards in the Netherlands.

69

La pitié grande sera sans loing tarder,	The great pity will arrive before very long: those who gave will be forced to take. Naked, starving with cold and thirst, they band together to cross the mountains causing a great scandal.
Ceux qui donoient seront contrains de prendre.	
Nudz affamez de froit, soif, soi bander,	
Les monts passer commettant grand esclandre.	

DISBANDING OF THE CLERGY, *c.* 1792

Once France had declared the disestablishment of the Clergy in 1792 many priests found themselves in wretched circumstances. Instead of keeping themselves through their duties to their parishes they were constrained to beg to stay alive. Many did band together to cross the Alps and take refuge in the Vatican. Their plight naturally caused a scandal.

70

Au chef du monde le grand Chyren sera,	The great Chyren will be chief of the world, after 'Plus oultre' loved, feared and dreaded. His fame and praise go beyond the heavens and he will be greatly satisfied with the sole title of victor.
Plus oultre[1] apres aimé, craint, redoubté:	
Son bruit & loz les cieux surpassera,	
Et du seul titre victeur fort contenté.	

The implication of line 2 is that the new hero Chyren will be greater in every way than the Emperor Charles V. It is tempting to equate Chyren with Henri IV of Navarre, the word being the obvious anagram from the old spelling of Henri, HENRYC. But the other Chyren quatrains will not bear this interpretation. Perhaps Nostradamus foresaw several great men named Henri?

71

Quand on viendra le grand roi parenter	When they will come to give the last rites to the great king, before he has quite given up his soul, he who will come to lament him the last, through lions the cross and crown of the eagles sold.
Avant qu'il ait du tout l'ame rendue,	
Celui qui moins le viendra lamenter,	
Par Lions, d'aigles, croix, couronne vendue.	

This general description could apply to the deaths of many kings. Presumably the last line indicates the armorial bearings of those involved.

72

Par fureur faincte d'esmotion divine,	Through feigned fury of a divine emotion the wife of the great one will be badly violated. The judges wishing to condemn such a doctrine, the victim is sacrificed to the ignorant people.
Sera la femme du grand fort violee:	
Juges voulans damner telle doctrine,	
Victime au peuple ignorant imolee.	

[1] *'Plus oultre Carol Quint'* was the device of Charles V. It is in capitals in the 1605 edition which clarifies the reading.

Many modern commentators see in this verse a reference to the manner in which Rasputin dominated the wife of the Czar. The word violated should be taken metaphorically although rumours certainly went around the Russian Court that the Priest was the Czarina's lover. The whole family became victims of their ignorant people, when they refused to understand the doctrines of the times, which led eventually to their deaths.

73

En cité grande un moine & artisan,	In a great city a monk and an
Pres de la porte logés & aux murailles:	artisan are lodged near the gate and the walls; speaking vainly
Contre Modene secret, cave disant,	and secretly against Modena,
Trahis pour faire souz couleur d'espousailles.	betrayed for acting under the guise of a marriage.

74

La deschassee au regne tournera,	She who was cast out will return
Ses ennemis trouvés des conjurés:	to reign, her enemies found
Plus que jamais son temps triomphera,	among conspirators. More than ever will her time be trium-
Trois & septante à mort trop asseures.	phant, at three and seventy to death very sure.

ELIZABETH I

Elizabeth was certainly rejected during her childhood and was the victim of conspiracies during her sister's reign. England rose to new heights during her reign. She died in her seventieth year in 1603. Most commentators want to insert a comma between *trois et septante*, indicating the first number as the year she died, 1603, and the second as her age. I leave it to the reader to decide.

75

Le grand pilot par Roi sera mandé,	The great pilot will be com-
Laisser la classe pour plus haut lieu attaindre:	missioned by the King to leave the fleet to attain to higher
Sept and apres sera contrebandé,	rank. Seven years later he will
Barbare armée viendra Venise craindre.	be in rebellion, Venice will come to fear the barbarian army.

De Coligny was made Henry II's Admiral of the fleet (grand pilot) in 1552 and resigned the post seven years later, 1559, after the King's death to join up with the Calvinist party. He was one of the principal instigators of the Huguenot/Catholic wars in France. These events occurred at the same time that Venice was suffering the attacks of the Sultan Selim II, who took Cyprus from them in 1570.

76

La cité antique d'antenoree[1] forge.	The ancient city created by
Plus ne pouvant le tyran supporter:	Antenor is no longer able to
Le manchet[2] fainct au temple couper gorge,	support the tyrant; a false one-armed man in the temple will
Les siens le peuple à mort viendra boucher.	cut the throat, the people will come to put his followers to death.

Padua belonged to Venice which, as I have mentioned earlier, was governed by an hereditary office of podestas. But there does not seem to be any record of a murder in a church followed by the further killings of followers.

77

Par la victoire du deceu fraudulente,	Through the fraudulent victory
Deux classes une, la revolte Germaine:	of the deceived, two fleets in one, the German revolt. The
Le chef meurtri & son filz dans la tente	chief murdered with his son in the tent. Florence and Imola
Florence, Imole pourchassés dans Romaine.[3]	pursued into Romania.

During the 16th and 17th Centuries there were many revolts against the authority of the Emperor. *Romaine* is most likely to be Romagna because Imola is located there.

[1] *antenoree*—Anteor was the legendary founder of Padua.

[2] *manchet*—O.F. = one armed.

[3] *Romania* = (a) Romagna, (b) The Holy Roman Empire, or (c) The Papal States.

Crier victoire du grand Selin croissant,[1]
Par les Romains sera l'Aigle clamé,
Ticcin, Milan, & Gennes n'y consent,
Puis par eux mesmes Basil[2] grand reclame.

To shout aloud the victory of the great crescent moon the Eagle will be proclaimed by the Romans. Pavia, Milan and Genoa will not agree to it: then the great Lord is claimed by themselves.

RETROACTIVE PROPHECY?

This quatrain obviously refers to the Ottoman and Holy Roman Empires whose particular emblems were the crescent moon and the Eagle. The Sultan was known in Europe as the Grand Seignior, but not one has been captured by the Roman Empire since Nostradamus' day. The last was the Sultan Jem in the 15th Century, so this is possibly a retroactive prophecy.

Pres du Tesin les habitans du Loire,
Garonne & Saonne, Seine, Tain, & Gironde:
Outre les monts dresseront promontoire,
Conflict donné Pau granci,[3] submergé onde.

Near the Ticino the inhabitants of the Loire, Garonne and Saône, the Seine, Tain and Gironde: Beyond the mountains they will build a promontory; conflict engaged, Pau seized, submerged by the wave.

BATTLE OF LODI, 10th MAY 1796

Many interpreters accept the word Pau in the last line as a shortened form of Napoleon, see VIII. 1. If so, this is a very precise description of an accident which befell Napoleon at the Battle of Lodi. While the bridge over the Adda was being stormed, Napoleon fell into the water (submerged by the wave) but was pulled out before he could drown.

[1] croissant = (a) Growing. (b) Crescent moon.
[2] Basil—Greed, Basilous = Lord, king, captain.
[3] granci—Either grancito, Tuscan for snatched, seized; or erratum for grandi.

De Fez le regne parviendra à ceux d'Europe,	From Fez the kingdom will stretch out to those of Europe.
Feu leur cité, & lame trenchera:	The city blazes, the sword will slash; the great man of Asia with a great troop by land and sea so that blues, perse, he will drive out the cross to death.
Le grand d'Asie terre & mer à grand troupe,	
Que bleux, pers,¹ croix, à mort dechassera.	

WAR IN MIDDLE EAST. THE THIRD ANTICHRIST

Nostradamus stated in VI. 54 that the King of Fez might be captured by the Arabs, but I think this quatrain fits into a more modern context. There is constant repetition of the theme of War in the Middle East, connected with the man from Asia, who is tentatively identified with Nostradamus' Third Antichrist.

Pleurs, cris & plaincts, hurlement effrayeur,	Tears, cries and wailing, howls and terror, an inhuman cruel heart, black and cold. Lake Geneva, the Islands, the main people of Genoa; blood pours, hunger for wheat, mercy to none.
Cœur inhumain, cruel, noir & transi:	
Leman, les isles de Gennes les majeurs,	
Sang epancher, frofaim² à nul merci.	

This may continue the horrors of the last quatrain, with the war spreading to Switzerland, Italy and the Mediterranean islands.

Par les desers de lieu, libre & farouche,	Through the deserts of the free, wild place, the nephew of the Great Pontiff will wander. Killed by seven with a heavy club, by those who will afterwards occupy the chalice.
Viendra errer nepveu du grand Pontife:	
Assommé à sept avecques lourde souche,	
Par ceux, qu'apres occuperont le cyphe.	

¹ *perse*—A colour, either blue or blue green.
² *frofaim*—A Nostradamus word possibly from *froment-faim* meaning hunger for wheat?

Celui qu'aura tant d'honneur & caresses	He who will have so much honour and affection at his
A son entree de la Gaule Belgique:	entry into Belgian Gaul; a
Un temps apres fera tant de rudesses,	while after he will act as crudely and will be very bellicose to-
Et sera contre à la fleur tant bellique.	wards the flower.

PHILIP OF SPAIN, FRANCE AND THE NETHERLANDS

When Charles V abdicated, Philip of Spain was well received in the Netherlands until his bigotry alienated the people to such a degree that they revolted in 1558. Then Francis Duke of Alençon was invited by the Netherlands to be their Protector in 1580 but stupidly he attempted to regain control of Antwerp and lost the loyalty of his subjects. The flower in the last line is presumably the fleur de lis of France, against which Philip went to war during 1589–98, against Henri of Navarre.

Celui qu'en Sparte Claude[1] ne peut regner,	The lame man who could not rule in Sparta, he will do much
Il fera tant par voie seductive:	seductive ways. That by the
Que du court, long, le fera araigner,	long and the short of it he will
Que contre Roi sera sa perspective.	be accused of aiming his objectives against the king.

The first line merely refers to the fact that the Spartans killed any children who were born imperfect. Then one must look for famous lame men in history; perhaps Talleyrand if one may read Emperor for king, or Lord Byron working with the Greek Freedom fighters?

La grand cité de Tharse par Gaulois	The great city of Tarsus by the Gauls will be destroyed, all
Sera destruite, captifs tous à Turban:	captured at Turban. Help from the sea from the great Portu-
Secours par mer du grand Portugalois,	guese; the first day of summer,
Premier d'esté le jour du sacre Urban.	Urban's consecration.

[1] *Claude*—Latin, *claudus* = lame.

Nostradamus seems to envisage a French army capturing Tarsus in Asia Minor and continuing on into Asia. Portugal was one of the greatest sea powers in Nostradamus' day, and he envisages them as allies of the French. The dating of the last line is obscure. There are two main saints called Urban, one is celebrated on 25th May, the other on 23rd January: there are twelve other minor saints with this name but the first is most likely as summer begins on 21st June.

86

Le grand Prelat un jour apres son songe,	One day the great Prelate, after his dream interpreted the opposite to its meaning; from Gascony a monk will come to him who will cause the great Prelate of Sens to be elected.
Interpreté au rebours de son sens:	
De la Gascogne lui surviendra un monge,	
Qui fera eslire le grand Prelat de sens.	

87

L'election faite dans Frankfort,	The election made in Frankfurt will not be valid, Milan will oppose it. The closest follower will seem so very strong that he will drive him out beyond the Rhine into the marshes.
N'aura nul lieu Milan s'opposera:	
Le sien plus proche semblera si grand fort	
Que outre le Rhin és mareschz chassera.	

EMPEROR FERDINAND, 1558–62

The election at Frankfurt probably refers to the coronation of Ferdinand as Holy Roman Emperor which took place there in 1558. Philip, who was Ferdinand's rival had been given Milan by his Uncle Charles V before his death in 1542. Philip tries to drive Ferdinand out of Germany, line 4, and into the Netherlands. In fact he was not at all successful in this, but he did continue to intrigue against Ferdinand for the succession until 1562.

88

Un regne grand demourra desolé,	A great kingdom will remain desolate, near the Ebro they will be gathered in assemblies. The Pyrenean mountains will console him when in May there will be earth tremors.
Aupres del Hebro se feront assemblees:	
Monts Pyrenees le rendront consolé,	
Lors que dans Mai seront terres tremblees.	

Entre deux cymbes[1] piedz & mains estachés,
De miel face oingt & de laict substanté:
Guespes & mouches, fitine[2] amour fachés,
Poccilateur[3] faucer, Cyphe[4] tempté.

Feet and hands bound between two boats, the face anointed with honey and touched with milk. Wasps and flies, fatherly love angered, the cupbearer lies, the goblet tried.

The fact that the face is anointed with milk and honey indicates that the victim was a crowned king for these are part of the Coronation service. The wasps may be an indirect reference to Napoleon's emblem of bees.

L'honnissement puant abhominable
Apres le faict sera felicité,
Grand excusé, pour n'estre favourable,
Qu'à paix Neptune ne sera incité.

The stinking and abominable shame, after the deed he will be congratulated. The great one excused for not being favourable, that Neptune cannot be tempted towards peace.

Someone gets away with a deed of such skullduggery that it is almost incredible; and yet he is unsuspected and congratulated despite the fact that he cannot arrange for a naval peace. Presumably he was in communication with the enemy?

Du conducteur de la guerre navale,
Rouge effrené, severe horrible grippe,
Captif eschappé de l'aisné dans la baste:
Quant il naistra du grand un filz Agrippe.

Of the leader of the naval war, the red one unbridled, severe, horrible quarrel; captive escaped from the older one in the saddle, when the great Agrippa bears a son.

The Naval commanders in Nostradamus' time were the Baron de la Garde, and M. de la Mole, but the rest of the quatrain is obscure.

[1] *cymbe*—O.F. = boat.
[2] *fitine*—Gk., *phitus* = father.
[3] *Poccilateur*—Latin, *poccilator* = cup-bearer.
[4] *Cyphe*—Latin, *scyphus* = cup, goblet.

Prince de beauté tant venuste,
Au chef menee, le second faict
trahi:
La cité au glaive de poudre face
aduste,
Par le trop grand meutre le chef du
Roi hai.

The Prince of such handsome beauty, intrigues against his person, betrayed to the second rank. The city put to the sword, consumed with a powder that burns. By this, so great a murder, the head of the king is hated.

LOUIS XVI's DEATH

Louis XVI was considered to be very handsome as a youth. He finds intrigues (*menees*) directed against him and will be deposed to the second rank of a constitutional king. Then he is betrayed. The line '*poudre face aduste*' has been most interestingly interpreted by James Laver from the Latin, *fax*, a torch, and *adustus*, burned, as consumed by a powder that burns. It was into quicklime that the hated head of the King was thrown from the wicker basket after his execution on the guillotine. The third line '*cité au glaive*', is an excellent description of revolutionary Paris.

Prelat avare d'ambition trompé.
Rien ne sera que trop viendra
cuider:
Ses messagiers, & lui bien attrapé,
Tout au rebours voir, qui le bois
fendroit.

The greedy prelate deceived by ambition, he will think that nothing is too great (for him). He and his messengers, completely trapped, the man who cuts the woods sees all in reverse.

Un Roi iré sera aux sedifragues,[1]
Quant interdicts seront harnois de
guerre:
La poison taincte au succre par les
fragues[2]
Par eaux meutris, mors, disant
serre serre.

A king will be angry with the sedifragues[1] when warlike arms are prohibited; the poison tainted with sugar in the strawberries, murdered by waters, death, saying, close, close.

[1] *sedifragus*—A Nostradamus word; possible compounded from *sedem frangere*—which literally means to break a seat.
[2] *fragues*—Latin, *fraga* = strawberries.

The see breakers, if one has understood Nostradamus correctly, probably refer to the Protestants who broke up the unity of the See of Rome.

95

Par detracteur calumnie à puis nay.
Quant istront faicts enormes &
   martiaux:
La moindre part dubieuse à l'aisney
Et tost au regne seront faicts
   partiaux.

Calumny against the younger born by the detractor, when enormous, martial deeds will occur. The least part doubtful for the elder one, and soon in the kingdom there will be partisan actions.

96

Grande cité à soldatz abandonné,
Onques n'y eut mortel tumulte si
   proche,
O quel hideuse calamité s'approche,
Fors une offense n'y sera pardonnée.

A great city abondoned to the soldiers, there was never a mortal tumult so close; Oh what a dreadful calamity approaches; except for one offence it will not be forgiven.

This quatrain is so general that it could be applied to the sack of any city. Commentators are particularly fond of applying it to the sack of St. Quentin (1557) or Paris during the Revolution.

97

Cinq & quarante degrés ciel
   bruslera,
Feu approcher de la grand cité
   neufve,
Instant grand flamme esparse
   sautera,
Quand on voudra des Normans faire
   preuve.

The sky will burn at forty-five degrees, fire approaches the great New City. Immediately a huge, scattered flame leaps up when they want to have proof of the Normans.

BOMBING OF NEW YORK?

New York county lies between 40° and 45° parallel in the U.S.A. There are other references to it as the cité neufve. It appears that the attack is very widespread (scattered flame). The position of France when this occurs is unclear, but France is also involved in a similar quatrain, see X. 49 in particular and I. 91, IX. 92.

Ruine aux Volsques[1] de peur si fort
   terribles,
Leur grand cité taincte, faict
   pestilent:
Piller Sol, Lune & violer leurs
   temples:
Et les deux fleuves rougir de sang
   coulant.

Ruin for the Volcae, so very terrible with fear, their great city stained by a pestilential deed. To plunder the Sun and Moon and violate their temples and to redden the two rivers running with blood.

The sun and moon plundered are gold and silver. The capital city of Languedoc would probably be Toulouse.

L'ennemi docte se tournera confus,
Grand camp malade, & de faict
   par embusches,
Monts Pyrenees & Poenus[2] lui
   seront faicts refus
Proche du fleuve decouvrant antiques cruches.

The learned enemy will turn around confused, the great camp sick and defeated by ambushes. The Pyrenean Mountains and the Pennines will be refused to him, near the river discovering ancient urns.

LEGIS CANTIO CONTRA INEPTOS CRITICOS

Quos legent hosce versus maturè
   censunto,
Profanum vulgus & inscium ne
   attrectato:
Omnesq; Astrologi Blenni,[3] Barbari procul sunto,
Qui alter facit, is ritè, sacer esto.

INCANTATION OF THE LAW AGAINST INEPT CRITICS.

May those who read this verse think upon it deeply, let the profane and ignorant herd keep away. Let all astrologers, idiots and barbarians stay far off, he who does otherwise, let him be priest to the rite.

This verse is odd. Line 4 sounds vaguely like a threat or curse. If the verses were originally written in Latin, as I believe they were, this gives the reader a good idea of the type of construction and vocabulary used by Nostradamus. Why does Nostradamus include Astrologers among the people he damns? Is this yet another example of his trying to bluff the authorities?

[1] Volsques—People of Languedoc. Southern France.
[2] Poenus—Latin, Alpes Poeninae = the Pennine Alps.
[3] Blenni—Greek, Blennos = simpleton, idiot.

CENTURY VII

34*	France, 1940 *continued*
35*	Henri III
36	
37	
38*	Death of Prince Ferdinand
39	
40	
41?	A haunted house?
42	

An incomplete Century.

KEY: * Of interest. F? Possibly referring to the future.

L'arc du thresor par Achilles deceu, *Aux procrées[1] sceu la quadrangu-* *laire:* *Au faict Royal le comment sera sceu,* *Cors veu pendu au veu du populaire.*	The arc of the treasure deceived by Achilles, the quadrangule known to the procreators. The invention will be known by the Royal deed; a corpse seen hanging in the sight of the populace.

There are only two well-known Achilles in French history. The first was Achille de Harlay, President of the Parlement de Paris who contributed to the downfall of the Queen Regent's favourite, Concini, who was assassinated in 1517. The other was Achille Bazaine, a Marshal of France whose incapacity and defeatism led to the fall of France in 1870.

Par Mars ouvert Arles ne donra *guerre.* *De nuict seront les soldartz* *estonnés:* *Noir, blanc à l'inde dissimulés en* *terre,* *Sous la faincte umbre traistres* *verez & sonnés.*	Arles opened up by war will not offer resistance, the soldiers will be astonished by night. Black and white concealing indigo on land under the false shadow you will see traitors sounded.

Apres de France la victoire navale, *Les Barchinons, Saillinons,[2] les* *Phocens,* *Lierre d'or, l'enclume serré dedans* *la basle,* *Ceux de Ptolon[3] au fraud seront* *consens.*	After the naval victory of France, the people of Barcelona the Saillinons and those of Marseilles; the robber of gold, the anvil enclosed in the ball, the people of Ptolon will be party to the fraud.

Even the proper names are obscure in this quatrain. France is clear and the Phocens who were from Marseilles. The Barchinons may be from Barcelona. The Saillinons and Ptolons are unclear. Garencières suggests that Ptolons should be from Toulon. It is

[1] *procrées*—There is a variant *procès* which would give a better reading of 'in the documents'.

[2] *Saillinons*—Not identified.

[3] *Ptolon* = Either the land of Ptolomy, Egypt, or Acre, earlier called Ptolemais.

possible that the name could be contorted like this by Nostradamus.

4

Le duc de Langres assiegé dedans Dolle,	The Duke of Langres besieged at Dôle accompanied by people from Autun and Lyons.
Accompaigné d'Ostun & Lyonnais:	
Geneve, Auspour, joinct ceux de Mirandole,	Geneva, Augsburg allied to those of Mirandola, to cross the
Passer les monts contre les Anconnois.	mountains against the people of Ancona.

THE DUKE DE GUISE

This complicated verse describes the Duke de Guise (*Langres*) with soldiers from Autun and Lyons being besieged in Dôle during an attack on the Spanish. At the same time armies of the Empires from Geneva, Augsburg and Northern Italy will invade the Papal States (Ancona belonged to the Pope).

5

Vin sur la table en sera respandu	Some of the wine on the table will be spilt, the third will not have that which he claimed. Twice descended from the black one of Parma, Perouse will do to Pisa that which he believed.
Le tiers n'aura celle qu'il pretendoit:	
Deux fois du noir[1] de Parme descendu,	
Perouse à Pize fera ce qu'il cuidoit.	

Pisa belonged to Tuscany, Perugia and Parma to the Vatican, the latter being given to his bastard son Pierluigi Farnese by Pope Paul III in 1545. When the Farnese family died out Parma passed to the Bourbons. I cannot decipher this verse further.

6

Naples, Palerme, & toute la Secille,	Naples, Palerma and all of Sicily will be uninhabited through Barbarian hands. Corsica, Salerno and the island of Sardinia, hunger, plague, war the end of extended evils.
Par main barbare sera inhabitee,	
Corsicque, Salerne & de Sardeigne l'isle,	
Faim, peste, guerre fin de maux intemptee.[2]	

[1] *noir*—The usual second meaning of *roi*, king, is possible here.

[2] *intemptee*—Latin, *intentatus* = extended, stretched.

288

This general verse predicts that Sicily and Southern Italy as well as Corsica and Sardinia will be ravaged by invasions of the Barbary pirates. There were many raids in the 16th Century both before and after Nostradamus wrote the Prophecies, so this may be a retroactive verse.

7

Sur le combat des grans cheveux, legiers,	Upon the struggle of the great, light horses, it will be claimed
On criera le grand croissant confond.	that the great crescent is destroyed. To kill by night, in the
De nuict tuer monts, habits de bergiers,	mountains, dressed in shepherds' clothing, red gulfs in the
Abismes rouges dans le fossé profond.	deep ditch.

The crescent moon was the emblem of the Turks and apparently Nostradamus sees them as suffering a great defeat. The third line suggests that some soldiers dress up as shepherds when attacking. The red gulfs almost certainly stand for rivers of blood.

8

Flora fuis, fuis le plus proche Romain,	Florence, flee, flee the nearest Roman, at Fiesole will be
Au Fesulan[1] sera conflict donné:	conflict given: blood shed, the
Sang espandu les plus grands prins à main,	greatest ones taken by the hand,
Temple ne sexe ne sera pardonné.	neither temple nor sex will be pardoned.

The quatrain seems to predict that Florence will suffer a severe attack by Vatican troops. Fiesole is only a few miles away and would naturally suffer the same fate.

9

Dame à l'absence de son grand capitaine,	The lady in the absence of her great master will be begged for
Sera priee d'amours du Viceroi,	love by the Viceroy. Feigned
Faincte promesse & malheureuse estraine,[2]	promise and misfortune in love, in the hands of the great Prince
Entre les mains du grand Prince Barrois.	of Bar.

[1] *Fesulan*—Latin, *Faesulae* = Fiesole.
[2] *estrenne*—O.F. = success in love, luck.

DUKE DE GUISE AND DIANE DE POITIERS

France has never had a Viceroy, the only comparable offices are those of the Constable, or the Lieutenant-General, which de Guise held when Nostradamus wrote. The title Duke de Bar was that given to the eldest son of the Duke de Lorraine. As the Duke was a child there was no holder at that period. It is unlikely that Dame refers to the Queen, Catherine de' Medici, but it may well describe Henri II's influential mistress, Diane de Poitiers, who would be in her late fifties.

10

Par le grand Prince limitrophe du Mans	By the great Prince bordering le Mans, brave and valliant
Preux & vaillant chef de grand excercite:	leader of the great army; by land and sea with Bretons and
Par mer & terre de Gallotz & Normans,	Normans, to pass Gibraltar and Barcelona to pillage the island.
Caspre passer Barcelone pillé isle.	

DUKE D'AUMALE, 1526–1573

Le Mans used to be the main city of Maine in North Western France, whereas Mayenne the next most important city, belonged to de Guise. In Nostradamus' lifetime it was held by de Guise's brother Claude, whose titles were Marquess of Mayenne and Duke d'Aumale. The latter did fight at Metz in 1552 and later at Calais, St. Denis, Dreux and Montcontour, but he never invaded Spain or North Africa. Nostradamus seems to have foreseen a much greater future for him that that which actually happened.

11

L'enfant Royal contemnera la mere,	The royal child will scorn his
Oeil, piedz blessés, rude, inobeissant,	mother, eye, feet wounded rude disobedient; strange and very
Nouvelle à dame estrange & bien amere,	bitter news to the lady; more than five hundred of her people
Seront tués des siens plus de cinq cens.	will be killed.

This quatrain seems to refer to the quarrels of a Queen Regent with her son. Since Nostradamus' lifetime there has been one notable example between Louis XIII and his mother Marie de' Medici. In the ensuing battle Garencières states that more than five hundred of the Queen's supporters were killed.

Le grand puisné fera fin de la guerre,
Aux dieux assemble les excusés:
Cahors, Moissac iront long de la serre,
Reffus Lestore, les Agenois razés.

The great younger son will make an end of the war, he assembles the pardoned before the gods; Ahors and Moissac will go far from the prison, a refusal at Lectoure, the people of Agen shaved.

A cadet or younger son was usually used to refer to the younger brother, or descendent of a younger brother of a king or ruler. This may refer to a son of the Guise family which were cadets of the Dukedom of Lorraine, all the towns being quite close together in Gienne, South-western France.

De la cité marine & tributaire,
La teste raze prendra la satrapie:
Chasser sordide qui puis sera contraire
Par quatorze ans tiendra la tyrannie.

From the marine tributary city, the shaven head will take up the satrapy; to chase the sordid man who will then be against him. For fourteen years he will hold the tyranny.

NAPOLEON, 1793

Bonaparte (the shaven head) will retake Toulon the marine city in 1793 from the English, led by Sir Arthur Wellesley, who have made it a tributary. He will then overthrow the Directory (the sordid one) and put an end to the Republic. He will enjoy absolute power for fourteen years (9th November 1799–13th April 1814). This interpretation was made by le Pelletier who adds that 'the sordid one' may well mean the English!

Faux esposer viendra topographie,
Seront les cruches des monuments ouvertes:
Pulluler secte saincte philosophie,
Pour blanches, noirs, & pour antiques verts.

He will come to expose the false topography, the urns of the tombs will be opened. Sect and holy philosophy to thrive, black for white and the new for the old.

NATIONAL ASSEMBLY, 22nd DECEMBER 1789

On 22nd December 1789, the National Assembly changed the ancient regional districts of France into Departments. At St. Denis the tombs of the French kings will be violated and their ashes scattered. Anti-christian sects flourish and take the place of religion. People will accept that black is white and will accept new ideas for the old traditions.

15

Devant cité de l'Insubre¹ contree,	Before the city of the Insubrian
Sept and sera le siege devant mis:	lands, for seven years the siege
Le tres grand Roi y fera son entree,	will be laid; a very great king
Cité puis libre hors de ses ennemis.	enters it, the city is then free, away from its enemies.

Nostradamus here predicts a very long drawn out siege of Milan lasting seven years. The liberating king is probably a French one freeing Milan from its Spanish masters.

16

Entrée profonde par la grand Roine faicte	The deep entry made by the great Queen will make the place
Rendra le lieu puissant inaccessible:	powerful and inaccessible; the
L'armee des trois lions sera deffaite,	army of the three lions will be
Faisant dedans cas hideux & terrible.	defeated causing within a thing hideous and terrible.

QUEEN MARY AND THE CAPTURE OF CALAIS, 1558
The great Queen, Mary Tudor, held Calais 'engraved upon her heart' until it was recaptured by the Duc de Guise in 1558. England was at that time an ally of Spain through Mary's marriage and the three lions form part of the English Standard. This is a comparatively successful quatrain.

17

Le prince rare de pitié & clemence,	The prince who has little pity
Viendra changer par mort grand cognoissance:	or mercy will come through death to change (and become)
Par grand repos le regne travaillé,	very knowledgeable. The king-
Lors que le grand tost sera estrillé.	dom will be attended with great tranquillity, when the great one will soon be fleeced.

¹ *Insubre*—Latin, *Insubria* = the area around Milan.

Les assiegés couloureront leur paches,	The besieged will colour their
Sept jours apres feront cruelle issue	pacts, but seven days later they
Dans repoulsés feu, sang. Sept mis	will make a cruel exit: thrown
à l'hache	back inside, fire and blood,
Dame captive qu'avoit la paix	seven put to the axe the lady
tissue.	who had woven the peace is a
	captive.

An obscure quatrain which apparently describes a treacherous enemy who, while being besieged, pretends to sue for peace, but seven days later makes a disastrous attack. Line 4 is quite possible for that period. The peace of Cambrai, in 1529, was known as the Ladies' Charter because it was negotiated by the mother of Francis I and the aunt of Charles V.

Le fort Nicene ne sera combatu,	The fort at Nice will not engage
Vaincu sera par rutilant metal	in combat, it will be overcome
Son faict sera un long temps debatu,	by shining metal. This deed will
Aux citadins estrange espouvantal.	be debated for a long time,
	strange and fearful for the
	citizens.

Nice has been captured twice since Nostradamus wrote the Prophecies, in 1891 and 1705, both times by the French.

Ambassadeurs de la Toscane langue,	Ambassadors of the Tuscan
Avril & Mai Alpes & mer passer:	language will cross the Alps
Celui de veau[1] exposera l'harangue,	and the sea in April and May.
Vie Gauloise ne venant effacer.	The man of the calf will deliver
	an oration, not coming to wipe
	out the French way of life.

CAVOUR IN PARIS, 1856

The good relations which existed between Napoleon III and the Pope were spoiled when Cavour arrived in Paris in 1856 to plead the cause of Italian unity. The Congress at Paris took place in the months Nostradamus mentions, April and May. The reason for calling him man of the calf is obscure but fascinating, a typical

[1] *de veau*—Some commentators think this should be *de Vaud*, a Swiss Canton.

Nostradamus contortion of facts. Cavour was the envoy of Turin, and Torino means the city of the bull, it was called Augusta Taurinorum by the Romans, and Cavour is thus the offspring of the calf.

21

Par pestilente inimitié Volsicque,	By the pestilential enmity of
Dissimulee chassera le tyran:	Languedoc, the tyran dis-
Au pont de Sorgues se fera la	simulated will be driven out
traffique,	The bargain will be made on
De mettre à mort lui & son adherent.	the bridge at Sorgues to put to death both him and his follower.

Probably a bridge at Sorgues, the main town on the river of the same name. It belonged to the Vatican States until 1791. Langue doc was a large province to the west of the Rhône.

22

Les citoyens de Mesopotamie,[1]	The citizens of Mesopotamia
Yrés encontre amis de Tarraconne,[2]	angry with their friends from
Jeux, ritz, banquetz, toute gent	Tarraconne; games, rites, ban-
endormie	quests, every person asleep, the
Vicaire au Rosne, prins cité, ceux	vicar at Rhône, the city taken
d'Ausone.[3]	and those of Ausonia.

POPE PIUS VI, 1799

Mesopotamia is used several times by Nostradamus but it is not wholly clear which town he meant. He does not seem to refer to modern Iraq, and therefore it probably describes a European town. The Venaissin between the Rhône and the Durance and Avignon in particular seem to fit the prediction very well. The vicar in line 4 was the Pope Pius VI whom Nostradamus had captured and imprisoned at Valence in 1799. The second part of line 4 describes how a French army led by General Chaupionne recaptured Rome and then went on to Naples in 1799.

[1] *Mesopotamie*—Nostradamus means by this 'land between two rivers' It could be modern Iraq or in France, Avignon, between the Rhône and the Durance, or Paris between the Seine and Marne.

[2] *Tarraconne*—Either from Latin, *Tarroca*, Tarragona in Catalonia, or from Tarraconensis, the north-eastern part of Roman Iberia.

[3] *Ausone*—Southern Italy, most probably Naples.

Le Royal sceptre sera contrainct de prendre, *Ce que ses predecesseurs avoient engaigé:* *Puis que l'aneau on fera mal entendre,* *Lors qu'on viendra le palais saccager.*	The Royal sceptre will be forced to take that which his predecessors had pledged. Because they do not understand about the ring when they come to sack the palace.

Hugh Allen, an unreliable commentator on Nostradamus, wrote in 1943 that the scene of this pawnbroking of Royal Jewels would take place in Buckingham Palace! This is a very obscure quatrain.

L'enseveli sortira du tombeau, *Fera de chaines lier le fort du pont:* *Empoisonné avec oeufz de Barbeau,* *Grand de Lorraine par le Marquis du Pont.*[1]	He who was buried will come out of the tomb, he will make the strong one out of the bridge to be bound with chains. Poisoned with the roe of a barbel, the great one from Lorraine by the Marquis du Pont.

The barbel is a freshwater fish found throughout most of Europe. The Grand one of Lorraine is probably the Duke of that name, Charles III, who was taken to be reared in the French Court. The Marquis du Pont-à-Mousson was held by the heir to the Duchy of Bar. After Bar passed to the house of Lorraine the title was given to the younger sons of the Duke of Lorraine. The quatrain predicts that among these families the Duke is to be poisoned by the Marquis, that is, by one of the younger sons.

Par guerre longue tout l'exercite expuiser, *Que pour souldartz ne trouveront pecune:* *Lieu d'or d'argent, cuir on viendra cuser,*[2] *Gualois aerain, signe croissant de Lune.*	Through long war all the army exhausted, so that they do not find money for the soldiers; instead of gold or silver, they will come to coin leather, Gallic brass, and the crescent sign of the Moon.

[1] *Marquis du Pont*—The younger son of the house of Lorraine had the title of Marquis de Pont-à-Mousson.

[2] *cuser*—Latin, *cusare*. O.F. cudere = to coin money.

It is suggested that this quatrain refers to soldiers being paid with money made from leather after a severe war. Line 4 is very obscure

26

Fustes & galees autour de sept navires,	Foists and galleys around seven ships, a mortal war will be let
Sera livree une mortelle guerre:	loose. The leader from Madrid
Chef de Madric recevra coup de vivres,[1]	will receive a wound from arrows, two escaped and five
Deux eschapees & cinq menees à terre.	brought to land.

NOVEMBER 1555

In November 1555 some privateers from Dieppe attacked a Spanish fleet in the Channel. *Vivres* is then translated as *virer*, a nautical verb to attack. Apparently the privateers concentrated upon the Admiral's flagship and they succeeded in capturing it and four other ships who came to its aid and towed them to Dieppe.

27

Au cainct[2] *de Vast*[3] *la grand cavalerie,*	At the wall of Vasto the great cavalry are impeded by the
Proche à Ferrage empeschee au bagaige:	baggage near Ferrara. At Turin they will speedily commit such
Pompt à Turin feront tel volerie,	robbery that in the fort they
Que dans le fort raviront leur hostaige.	will ravish their hostage.

There are nine villages in France with the name of Vast plus a monastery near Arras and a harbour near Cherbourg. The reference may equally apply to Alphonso II, Marquis de Vasto (1502–44) who from 1537 onwards was Governor of Milan. He retired to Asti in 1554 and this may be what is meant by Ferrara as it was a duchy of the house of Este—and was seized by the Papal States in 1597.

[1] *Vivres*—Alternative *vires* = arrows, seems better in context, or *virer* = to attack. .

[2] *caint*—O.F., belt or waist. Possibly used here for encircling wall?

[3] *Vast*—Uncertain.

Le capitaine conduira grande proie,	The captain will lead a great
Sur la montaigne des ennemis plus	herd on the mountain closest
proche,	to the enemy. Surrounded by
Environné, par feu fera tel voie,	fire he makes such a way, all
Tous eschappez or¹ trente mis en	escape except for thirty put on
broche.	the spit.

Most commentators understand 'put on a spit' as meaning to be run through. I think it is Nostradamus' way of describing them being burnt alive.

Le grand Duc d'Albe se viendra	The great one of Alba will come
rebeller	to rebel, he will betray his great
A ses grans peres fera le tradiment:	forebears. The great man of
Le grand de Guise le viendra	Guise will come to vanquish
debeller,	him, led captive with a monu-
Captif mené & dressé monument.	ment erected.

This is at first sight a very clear quatrain, but it is not very accurate. The Duke of Alba was the main Spanish general, and the Duke de Guise the main French one. Unfortunately de Guise never triumphed over Alba, yet alone take him captive. It is doubtful whether Nostradamus saw Alba crossing over to the French side, but he did fight with the French from 1555–7 against the Vatican states.

Le sac s'approche, feu, grand sang	The sack approaches, fire and
espandu	great bloodshed. Po the great
Po, grand fleuves, aux bouviers²	rivers, the enterprise for the
l'entreprinse,	clowns; after a long wait from
De Gennes, Nice, apres long	Genoa and Nice, Fossano,
attendu,	Turin the capture at Savigli-
Foussan, Turin, à Savillon la	ano.
prinse.	

Nice, Fossano, Turin and Savigliano were all in Piedmont but all except Nice had been lost to the House of Savoy. Genoa was an independent state under Habsburg domination.

¹ *or*—Misprint, in all editions for *hors* = without, except for.
² *bouviers*—O.F. = either clowns or cowherdsmen.

De Languedoc, & Guienne plus de dix,	From Languedoc and Guienn more than ten thousand wi
Mille voudront les Alpes repasser:	want to cross the Alps agai
Grans Allobroges¹ marcher contre Brundis	The great Savoyards marc against Brindisi, Aquino an
Aquin & Bresse les viendront recasser.	Bresse will come to drive the back.

These place names are obscure because they are all so separate Languedoc and Guienne were in South-western France. Bres belonged to Savoy until 1601. Brindisi is in South Italy an together with Aquino, belonged to the kingdom of the Tw Sicilies. The action is totally unclear.

Du mont Royal naistra d'une casane,²	From the bank of Montereal will be born one who bores an
Qui cave, & compte viendra tyranniser	calculates becoming a tyran To raise a force in the marche
Dresser copie de la marche Millane,	of Milan, to drain Faenza an
Favene, Florence d'or & gens espuiser.	Florence of gold and men.

DE' MEDICI FAMILY

This may have been directed at one of the de' Medicis who cam from an area of Florence called Montereale. Milan belonged t the Habsburgs, Faenza was part of the Papal states and Florence as above, belonged to the de' Medicis, but the action is again obscure.

Par fraude regne, forces expolier,³	The kingdom stripped of i
La classe obsesse, passages à l'espie:	forces by fraud, the flee blockaded, passages for th
Deux fainctz amis se viendront rallier,	spy; two false friends will com to rally to awaken hatred for
Esveiller haine de long temps assoupie.	long time dormant.

¹ *Allobroges* = inhabitants of Savoy.
² *casan*—low Latin, *casana* = bank.
³ *expolier*—O.F. = plunder, strip, despoil.

This is one of Nostradamus' general prophecies which may have been fulfilled several times since it was written; mainly it is interpreted as the Fall of France in 1940, line 3 describing the Germans and the Russians, and the last line Anglo-French connections.

34

En grand regret sera la gent Gauloise	The French nation will be in great grief, vain and light-hearted, they will believe rash things. No bread, salt, wine nor water, venom nor ale, the greater one captured, hunger, cold and want.
Coeur vain, legier croirera temerité:	
Pain, sel, ne vin, eaue: venin ne cervoise	
Plus grand captif, faim, froit, necessité.	

FRANCE, 1940 *continued*

It is usually accepted that his quatrain carries on from the last, No. 33, and Nostradamus slipped up forgetting to change them about to muddle the reader as to their chronology. This is another general description of the Fall of France and its occupation under the Germans, which lasted until 1944.

35

La grand pesche viendra plaindre, plorer	The great fish will come to complain and weep for having chosen, deceived concerning his age: he will hardly want to remain with them, he will be deceived by those (speaking) his own tongue.
D'avoir esleu, trompés seront en l'aage:	
Guiere avec eux ne voudra demourer,	
Deçeu sera par ceux de son langaige.	

HENRI III

Henri III, the third son of Catherine de' Medici was elected King of Poland on the interpretation that Poland chose its kings in an unrestrained manner '*pesche*'. On the premature death of his brother Charles IX, he had to escape from Poland and resume his claim to the French throne. This upset the arrangements made by Poland and France to found dynasties. He was deceived (and also assassinated) by a fellow Frenchman, Jacques Clément.

Dieu, le ciel tout le divin verbe à l'unde,
Porté par rouges sept razes à Bisance:
Contre les oingz trois cens de Trebisconde,
Deux loix mettront, & l'horreur, puis credence.

God, the heavens, all the divine words in the waves, carried by seven red-shaven heads to Byzantium: against the anointed three hundred from Trebizond, will make two laws, first horror then trust.

The seven red heads are almost certainly Cardinals, but what were they doing on their way to Constantinople? Perhaps they were trying to convert the Sultan? It seems very unlikely and there is no recorded incident that I can find to substantiate this.

Dix envoyés, chef de nef mettre à mort,
D'un adverti, en classe guerre ouverte:
Confusion chef, l'un se picque & mord,
Lerin, stecades¹ nefz cap dedans la nerte.²

Ten sent to put the captain of the ship to death, are altered by one that there is open revolt in the fleet. Confusion, the leader and another stab and bite each other at Lerins and the Hyerès, ships, prow into the darkness.

This dramatic quatrain heralds the attempted assassination of a naval commander. The Lerin Islands are off Cannes and the Hyerès off Toulon.

L'aisné Royal sur coursier voltigeant,
Picquer viendra si rudement courir:
Gueulle, lipee, pied dans l'estrein pleignant
Trainé, tiré, horriblement mourir.

The elder royal one on a frisky horse will spur so fiercely that it will bolt. Mouth, mouthfull, foot complaining in the embrace; dragged, pulled, to die horribly.

DEATH OF CROWN PRINCE FERDINAND, 1842

The heir of Louis Philippe was thrown and dragged by a frisky horse, and died on 13th July 1842.

¹ *stecades*—Latin, *Stoechades* = the Islands of Hyerès.
² *nerte*—O.F. = Black, or Greek, *nerthe* = underneath.

Le conducteur de l'armeé Françoise,	The leader of the French army
Cuidant perdre le principal phalange:	will expect to lose the main phalanx. Upon the pavement of
Par sus pave de l'avaigne & d'ardoise,	oats and slate the foreign nation will be undermined
Soi parfondra par Gennes gent estrange.	through Genoa.

Dedans tonneaux hors oingz d'huile & gresse,	Within casks anointed outside with oil and grease twenty-one
Seront vingt un devant le port fermés,	will be shut before the harbour, at the second watch; through
Au second guet par mont feront prouesse:	death they will do great deeds; to win the gates and be killed
Gaigner les portes & du guet assommés.	by the watch.

It seems as though Nostradamus is describing a second Trojan horse which is trying to capture a seaport. They succeed in entering the town but are killed by the guards.

Les oz des piedz & des main enserrés,	The bones of the feet and the hands locked up, because of
Par bruit maison long temps inhabitee:	the noise the house is unin-habited for a long time. Digging
Seront par songes concavent deterrés,	in dreams they will be un-earthed, the house healthy and
Maison salubre & sans bruit habitee.	inhabited without noise.

Nostradamus seems to have believed in ghosts, because this is a description of a haunted house which is exorcized when the bones of the victim are removed. Perhaps an occupant of the house dreamt of the grave which led to the discovery of the skeleton?

Deux de poison saisiz nouveau venuz,
Dans la cuisine du grand Prince verser:
Par le souillard tous deux au faicts congneuz
Prins que cuidoit de mort l'aisné vexer.

Two newly arrived have seized the poison, to pour it in the kitchen of the great Prince. By the scullion both are caught in the act, taken he who thought to trouble the elder with death.

This is a detailed, specific quatrain in which two conspirators on a Prince's kitchen staff try to poison him. They are caught red-handed by the kitchen boy but it appears that only one is captured so possibly his accomplice got away.

CENTURY VIII

34
35
36
37**   Charles I of England
38
39
40
41*   Napoleon III
42*   Louis Philippe d'Orléans
43*   Defeat of Louis Napoleon, 1870
44
45
46**F? War linked with Paul VI and Kennedy Brothers
47
48?   1st February 2769?
49?   6th February 1971
50*   Capture of Tunis, 1573
51
52
53*   Napaoleon's failure to invade England
54
55
56*   Scotland and Charles II
57*   Napoleon I
58   James II and William of Orange, 1588
59*F? East and West in 20th Century?
60*?   Napoleon II?
61?
62
63
64*? Nazis and Britain
65*   Marshal Pétain, 1940–2
66
67
68*   Death of Cardinal Richelieu and Louis XIII, 1642–3
69
70
71**   1607
72*   Ravenna, 1512
73
74*F? The U.S.A.
75*   Portuguese king and son assassinated, 1908
76*   Cromwell

KEY: * Of interest. F? Possibly referring to the future.

PAU, NAY, LORON plus feu qu'à sang sera.
Laude nager, fuir grand au surrez.
Les agassas¹ entree refusera.
Pampon,² Durance les tiendra enferrez.

Pau, Nay, Loron will be more of fire than blood, to swim in praise, the great one to flee to the confluence (of rivers). He will refuse entry to the magpies Pampon and the Durance will keep them confined.

NAPOLEON I

Although the names in the first line are all small towns in Western France, Nostradamus does appear to be talking about a man rather than places. The capital letters also indicate a more fanciful reading by anagram, PAU, NAY, LORON becomes NAPAULON ROY—Napoleon the King. The spelling of Napoleon's name with an 'au' instead of an 'o' was commonplace, and Nostradamus' orthography is not at all reliable. The connection of the *agassas* or Pius would refer to Pius VI and VII who were both imprisoned by Napoleon. The confluence of rivers refers to Valence where the Rhône and Isère meet and where Pius VI was taken to die in 1798–9. Pius VII was taken to Savona and then on to Fontainebleau in 1872, therefore neither was imprisoned near the Durance of line 4. But Durance did lie near Avignon which belonged to the Papacy until 1791, where the Rhône and the Durance meet.

Condon & Aux & autour de Mirande
Je voi du ciel feu qui les environne.
Sol Mars conjoint au Lion puis marmande
Fouldre, grand gresle, mur tombe dans Garonne.

Condom and Auch and around Mirande, I see fire from the sky which encompasses them. Sun and Mars conjoined in Leo, then at Marmande, lightning, great hail, a wall falls into the Garonne.

All the towns mentioned are in the Departement of Gers in the south-west, except for Marmande which is about 50 miles north. The wall may be falling here or in some other Garonne town such as Bordeaux, Agen or Toulouse?

¹ *agassas*—Provençal, *agassa* = a magpie, known in French as pie, which is also the French spelling of Pius. A typical Nostradamus convolution.

² *Pampon*—Doubtful, possibly Gk., *Pamponeros* = all depraved?

Au fort chasteau de Viglanne[1] &
Resviers
Sera serré le puisnay de Nancy:
Dedans Turin seront ards[2] les
premiers,
Lors que de dueil Lyon sera transi.

Within the strong castle of Vigilance and Resviers the younger born of Nancy will be shut up. In Turin the first ones will be burned, when Lyons will be transported with grief.

THE DUKE DE MERCOEUR

The names in the first line of this quatrain are difficult to decipher, the best combinations are in Italy. There is a castle built by the Scaligers of Verona on the promontory at the south of Lake Garda. Another stands at Malescino. Also on the lake between San Vigilio and the Riviera is the monastery founded by St. Francis. Thus we have three possible sites on the Garda. Nancy is the capital of Lorraine, and the cadet a younger brother or branch of the family. It is most likely to refer to Nicholas, Duke of Mercoeur, the father-in-law of Henri III, who did not die until 1577. So what Nostradamus is trying to say can be summarized thus. The Duke of Mercoeur will be confined in a castle on Lake Garda. Turin, in line 3, belonged to the French when Nostradamus wrote. 'Ards' is a difficult word for which to find a definite meaning.

Dedans Monech[3] le coq sera receu,
Le Cardinal de France apparoistra
Par Logarion[4] Romain sera deceu
Foiblesse à l'aigle, & force au coq
naistra.

The cock will be received into Monaco, the Cardinal of France will appear; He will be deceived by the Roman legation; weakness to the eagle, strength will be born to the cock.

This prediction did not come true, in fact just the opposite if one accepts that Logarion is a misreading for legation. It is concerned with the struggle for power in the Mediterranean between the French and Spanish. Monaco had nominal independence under the Grimaldis but was bound by Treaty to help Spain. Nostra-

[1] *Viglanne*—Most likely San Vigilio and the Riviera, but could be Rubbiera and Vignola.
[2] *ards*—Possibly from *ardere* = to burn, but uncertain.
[3] *Monech*—Monaceis = Monaco.
[4] *Logarion*—Other texts have legation, which reads much better in the context.

damus predicts that this protection will move to Franco, which occurred in 1614. The French Cardinal who intrigued so much during Nostradamus' time is probably a reference to Charles, second Cardinal of Lorraine (1524–74). Reading Logarion as legate, there were two in France, the viceregal legate at Avignon and another as Papal Ambassador. Nostradamus describes a legate deceiving the French, but in spite of this he foresees the Habsburg power declining and that of France growing. In fact the exact opposite occurred. Monaco became a closer ally to the Spanish when a garrison took over from 1605–41, and the French were driven out of Italy in 1559.

5

Apparoistra temple luisant orné,	There will appear a shining
La lampe & cierge à Borne &	ornate temple, the lamp and
Bretueil.	candle at Borne and Breteuil.
Pour la lucerne le canton destorné,	For the canton of Lucerne
Quand on verra le grand coq au	turned aside, when one will see
cercueil.	the great cock in his shroud.

This seems to predict that the Canton of Lucerne will be overcome, and that at the same period a great French king would die. This has not occurred.

6

Charte fulgure à Lyon apparente	Lightning and brightness are
Luisant, print Malte subit sera	seen at Lyons shining, Malta
estainte,	is taken, suddenly it will be
Sardon,[1] *Mauris*[2] *traitera decep-*	extinguished. Sardon, Maurice
vante,	will act deceitfully, Geneva to
Geneve à Londes à coq trahison	London, feigning treason to-
fainte.	wards the cock.

FRANCE, SWITZERLAND, SAVOY AND ENGLAND
c. 1560

Malta was an independent state until the Revolution. The Turks attacked it in 1565. Maurice, according to legend, was a saint, a leader of a Theban legion who were annihilated because they refused to murder Christians. His cult is strong in Switzerland and Savoy. Sardon may stand for Sardinia which belonged to the House of Savoy after 1720. Nostradamus thus indicates that the

[1] *Sardon*—Sardinia is the most likely interpretation for this word.
[2] *Mauris*—Probably St. Maurice, patron Saint of much of French Alps and of Savoy.

308

Savoy held both regions. The connection between Geneva and London probably describes Elizabeth I's involvement with Calvin in the Conspiracy of Amboise (1566).

7

Verceil, Milan donra intelligence, *Dedans Tycin[1] sera faite la paye.[2]* *Courir par Siene eau, sang, feu par Florence.* *Unique choir d'hault en bas faisant maie.[3]*	Vercelli, Milan will give the news, the wound will be given at Pavia. To run in the Seine, water, blood and fire through Florence, the unique one falling from high to low calling for help.

Very obscure except for the fact that Vercelli and Pavia belonged to the Duchy of Milan and was finally taken over by the Habsburgs until the 19th Century.

8

Pres de Linterne[4] dans de tonnes fermez, *Chivaz[5] fera pour l'aigle la menee,* *L'esleu cassé lui ses gens enfermez,* *Dedans Turin rapt espouse emmenee.*	Near Focia enclosed in some tuns Chivasso will plot for the eagle. The elected one driven out, he and his people shut up, rape with Turin, the bride led away.

The village of Focia which occupies the old site of Linternum is unlikely to be the subject of this. Chivasso, a few miles north-east of Turin, was occupied by the French, and Nostradamus sees it plotting on behalf of the Emperor. Is the leader of the Chivasso plot exiled or sent to another town?

[1] *Ticin*—Latin, *Ticinum* = Pavia.
[2] *la paye*—Possible alternative is the plague.
[3] *maie* = (a) Kneading-trough. (b) *Ma aie*, help me!
[4] *Linterne*—Now Focia near Naples.
[5] *Chivaz* = Chivasso.

Pendant que l'aigle & le coq à Savone
Seront unis Mer Levant & Ongrie,
L'armee à Naples, Palerne, Marque d'Ancone
Rome, Venise par Barb'[1] *horrible crie.*

While the eagle is united with the cock at Savona, the Eastern Sea and Hungary. The army at Naples, Palermo, the marches of Ancona, Rome and Venice a great outcry by the Barbarian.

At Savona Nostradamus foresees an alliance between the Emperor and the French. Both the Levant and Hungary belonged to the Turks except for the small area the Habsburgs retained and paid for. Naples and Palermo were in the Habsburg kingdom of the Two Sicilies, and Ancona belonged to the Papal States. Does Nostradamus envisage a Moslem invasion of Italy which will suddenly unify the Christian faces?

10

Puanteur grande sortira de Lausanne,
Qu'on ne seura l'origine du fait,
Lon mettra hors toute le gente loingtaine
Feu veu au ciel, peuple estranger deffait.

A great stench will come from Lausanne, but they will not know its origin, they will put out all the people from distant places, fire seen in the sky, a foreign nation defeated.

MARXISTS OR CALVINISTS

The stench from Lausanne probably refers to the Calvinist centre that it became in the 16th Century, and in particular while Calvin's second-in-command, de Bèze, was teaching there. A more modern meaning applies it to the very frequent meetings of early Marxists there.

11

Peuple infini paroistra à Vicence
Sans force feu brusler la Basilique
Pres de Lunage deffait grand de Valence,
Lors que Venise par more prendra pique.

A multitude of people will appear at Vicenza without force, fire to burn the Basilica. Near Lunage the great one of Valenza defeated: at a time when Venice takes up the quarrel through custom.

[1] *Barb'*—short for either barbarian, or the enigmatic Aenobarb = the red bearded one. See I. 74, II. 49, V. 45 etc.

Les bien aisez subit seront desmis
Par les trois freres le monde mis en
   trouble,
Cité marine saisiront ennemis,
Faim, feu, sang, peste & de tous
   maux le double.

Those at ease
cast down, the v
trouble by three br
enemies will seize th
city, hunger, fire, blood, p
all evils doubled.

THE KENNEDY BROTHERS?

It appears that when three brothers appear in positions of power during a century, those at ease, i.e. America will suddenly suffer trouble. The marine city seized by their enemies, whom I doubtfully connect with the Asian Antichrist, could be Formosa or even Singapore or Hong Kong. It will be fascinating to see what the youngest Kennedy brother will do during the next few years. Nostradamus also mentions the three brothers in his Epistle which will appear in full in the following book.

De Flora issue de sa mort sera
   cause,
Un temps devant par jeune & vieille
   bueira,
Par les trois lys lui feront telle
   pause,
Par son fruit sauve comme chair
   crue mueire.

The cause of her death will be issued from Florence, one time before drunk by young and old; by the three lilies they will give her a great pause. Save through her offspring as raw meat is dampened.

Florence belonged to the de' Medicis and several daughters of that name, Catherine and Marie in particular, married into the Royal Family of France, as denoted by the fleur de lis. The last line probably means that poison was put into the meat—after all the Medicis were renowned for their mastery of poison.

...enir la grand cappe[1]
...roublee,
Pour l'esclaircir les rouges mar-
cheront,
De mort famille sera presque
accablee.
Les rouges rouges le rouge assome-
ront.

To support the great troubled Cappe; the reds will march in order to clarify it; a family will be almost overcome by death, the red, red ones will knock down the red one.

EXTREMISM IN THE FRENCH REVOLUTION

Cappe here probably is the shortened form of Capulet, the name of the French Royal family line. The French are described as not supporting the great Caputian family troubled by the Revolution. Republicans will march against them so that the family has to take enforced refuge in the Temple. The Royal Family will be almost completely destroyed except for the King's sister, Elizabeth, and possibly the eldest son, Louis XVII (see V. 1). Then the extremists, the red, red ones will guillotine the more moderate revolutionaries, the Girondins. Possibly the name of Robespierre (the red stone) is hinted at in the last line?

20

Le faux messaige par election fainte
Courir par urban rompu pache
arreste,
Voix acheptees, de sang chappelle
tainte,
Et à un autre l'empire contraicte.

The false message about the rigged election to run through the city stopping the broken pact; voices bought, chapel stained with blood, the empire contracted to another one.

This apparently describes the election of a Holy Roman Emperor who uses bribery 'voices bought' to attain his ends. The false election will be followed by a short war, which ends when the Pretender is murdered.

21

Au port d'Agde trois fustes
entreront
Portant d'infect non foi & pesti-
lence
Passant le pont mil milles embleront,
Et le pont rompre à tierce resistance.

Three foists will enter the port of Agde carrying the infection and pestilence, not the faith. Passing the bridge they will carry off a million, the bridge is broken by the resistance of a third.

[1] *cappe*—Here stands for Capulet instead of the more usual meaning of Pope.

20th CENTURY?

The enormity of the figure of these victims of the plague make the quatrain somewhat suspect. The figures are more suitable for the 20th Century, as for instance Biafra and Pakistan. Agde is a sea-port in the south-west of France, between Narbonne and Marseilles. Could it possibly be an indirect reference to the Second World War?

22

Gorsan, Narbonne, par le sel advertir	Coursan, Narbonne through the salt to warn Tuchan, the grace of Perpignan betrayed; the red town will not wish to consent to it, in a high flight, a copy flag and a life ended.
Tucham, la grace Parpignam trahie,	
La ville rouge n'y vouldra consentir.	
Par haulte vol drap gris vie faillie.	

COMMUNISM IN FRANCE?

A difficult quatrain. There are many Communist strongholds in present-day France around Perpignan, the red town. The rest is obscure.

23

Lettres trouvees de la roine les coffres,	Letters are found in the queen's chests, no signature and no name of the author. The ruse will conceal the offers; so that they do not know who the lover is.
Point de subscrit sans aucun nom d'hauteur	
Par la police[1] seront caché les offres.	
Qu'on ne scaura qui sera l'amateur.	

THE CASKET LETTERS

Unfortunately there is no proper noun to finally determine this quatrain but in that Nostradamus knew of Mary Queen of Scots and probably met her, while summoned to the Court in 1556, it may apply. The Casket Letters were documents relating to the murder of Darnley and events of 1567. The Earl of Morton produced them before commissions in London and York. The originals disappeared after 1584 and their authenticity has always been held in doubt.

[1] *police*—O.F. = (*a*) Ruse. (*b*) Government.

Le lieutenant à l'entree de l'huis,	The lieutenant at the door of
Assommera la grand de Perpignan,	the house, will knock down the
En se cuidant saulver à Monpertuis.	great man of Perpignan. Think-
Sera deceu bastard de Luisgnan.	ing to save himself at Mont-
	pertuis, the bastard of Lusignan
	will be deceived.

The family of Lusignan died out before Nostradamus' time but ruled Jerusalem and Cyprus until 1489, its titles passing to the house of Savoy. Nostradamus' patron, the Count de Tende, Governor of Provence, was the son of the Grand Bastard of Savoy, as he was known. If this is so then Montpertuis is almost certainly the Perthus Pass in the Pyrenees, and Nostradamus must have envisaged Tende defeating the Spanish around Rousillan (Perpignan) and then finding himself trapped in the Pyrenees with the Spanish blocking his return route to France.

25

Coeur de l'amant ouvert d'amour fertive	The heart of the lover, awakened by furtive love will
Dans le ruisseau fera ravir la Dame,	ravish the lady in the stream. She will pretend bashfully to
Le demi mal contrefera lassive,	be half injured, the father of
Le pere à deux privera corps de l'ame.	each will deprive the body of its soul.

A possible history of incest and rape among Royalty? The plot is clear but the references too general to be of any use.

26

De Caton es[1] trouves en Barcellonne,	The bones of Cato found in
Mis descouvers lieu retrouvers & ruine,	Barcelona, placed, discovered, the site found again and ruined.
Le grand qui tient ne tient vouldra Pamplonne.	The great one who holds, but does not hold, wants Pamplona,
Par l'abbaye de Montferrat bruine.	drizzle at the abbey of Montserrat.

None of Cato's famous family died at Barcelona, and only C Pacius Cato died in Spain, at Tarragona.

[1] *es*—Alternative reading, *os* = Bones. O.F., *ez* means planks o boards.

La voye auxelle l'une sur l'autre forniz[1]	The auxiliary way, one a upon the other, Le Mu,
Du muy desert hor mis brave & genest	deserted except for the brave one and his genet. The writing
L'escript d'empereur le fenix[2]	of the Phoenix Emperor, seen
Veu en celui ce qu'à nul autre n'est.	by him which is (shown) to no other.

This is set in Provence and the aqueduct is probably the one which ran from the River Saigne to Fréjus. A jennet is a small black horse. The commander with the Phoenix-like qualities is more of a problem.

Les simulacres d'or & argent enflez,	The copies of gold and silver
Qu'apres le rapt au lac furent gettez	inflated, which after the theft were thrown into the lake, at
Au desouvert estaincts tous & troublez.	the discovery that all is exhausted and dissipated by the debt.
Au marbre script prescript inter-getez.	All scrips and bonds will be wiped out.

INFLATION AND PAPER MONEY

This quatrain may well be describing the monetary inflation which hit Europe during the nineteen twenties and again in the sixties and seventies. It is one of the few quatrains I have not translated literally, as it is too complex, and have used that of Dr. Fontbrune (1939). It is an interesting idea for a man who lived long before paper money (the copies of gold and silver) were ever used.

Au quart pillier l'on sacre[3] *à Saturne.*	At the fourth pillar which they dedicate to Saturn split by
Par tremblant terre & deluge fendu	earthquake and by flood; under
Soubz l'edifice Saturnin trouvee urne,	Saturn's building an urn is found gold carried off by
D'or Capion ravi & puis rendu.	Caepio and then restored.

[1] *forniz* = (a) Arch. (b) Brothel. In this case Nostradamus is describing an aqueduct.
[2] *fenix* = (a) The Phoenix. (b) The Phoenician.
[3] *sacrere*—O.F. = to dedicate.

Saturn's building presumably means a temple dedicated to him, or the Church of Saint Saturnin (Sernin) in Toulouse. Under the fourth pillar an urn of gold will be found, stolen by Caepio who was a Roman consul who plundered Toulouse (106 BC). The treasure never reached Rome, for which Caepio was impeached and expelled from the Senate.

30

Dedans Tholoze non loing de Beluzer[1]
Faisant un puis long, palais d'espectacle,[2]
Tresor trouvé un chacun ira vexer,
Et en deux locz & pres del vasacle.[3]

In Toulouse, not far from Beluzer making a deep pit a palace of spectacle, the treasure found will come to vex everyone in two places and near the Basacle.

UNDISCOVERED TREASURE IN TOULOUSE
Beluzer is as yet unidentified by all Nostradamus' commentators. Quatrain 29 indicated that gold would be found when a pillar was struck by lightning, but here it seems more likely to be the result of men digging or a chance find, perhaps the two places referring to two different discoveries. This may be a quatrain yet to be fulfilled.

31

Premier grand fruit le prince de Perquiere
Mais puis viendra bien & cruel malin,
Dedans Venise perdra sa gloire fiere
Et mis à mal par plus joune Celin.

The first great fruit of the prince of Perchiera, then will come a cruel and wicked man. In Venice he will lose his proud glory, and is led into evil by the younger Selin.

MUSSOLINI AND VICTOR EMMANUEL III
When Mussolini led the Fascists in revolt the first prize that fell to him was the Prince of Pescheria, i.e. Victor Emmanuel himself, who, at Pescheria did one of the noblest acts of his reign. He had gone to the front after Caporetto, and took command in person rejecting all proposals of surrender and determined to fight it out.

[1] Beluzer—Unidentified name, or anagram?
[2] Nostradamus presumably means a theatre.
[3] vasacle = The mill section of Toulouse, also of the castle protecting the main bridge and gate to the city.

The Council of War was also held at Pescheria. The cruel one is Mussolini, who will lose his glory in Venice and be delivered to the hands of the younger Selin. Since Selin means crescent or moon, Nostradamus foresaw some connection with Islam, which did not occur.

32

Garde toi roi Gaulois de ton nepveu	French king, beware of your
Qui fera tant que ton unique fils	nephew who will do so much
Sera meutri à Venus faisant voeu,	that your only son will be
Accompaigné de nuit que trois & six.	murdered while making his
	vows to Venus; accompanied
	at night by three and six.

A clear prophecy which does not seem to have taken place.

33

Le grand naistra de Veronne & Vincence,	The great one who will be born of Verona and Vincenza who
Qui portera un surnon bien indigne.	carries a very unworthy sur-
Qui à Venise vouldra faire vengeance.	name; he who at Venice will wish to take vengeance, himself
Lui mesme prins homme du guet & signe.	taken by a man of the watch and sign.

MUSSOLINI

The great one born in the North of Italy, where both towns mentioned are situated, bearing an unworthy name, is Mussolini which literally means muslin maker. The vengeance he desires was against those powers who frustrated his dream of Mare Nostrum. The last line, more difficult, implies that he is taken in a snare by a man who watches and ambushes—presumably Hitler, who became Mussolini's inspiration.

Apres victoire du Lyon au Lyon	After the victory of the Lion
Sur la montaigne de JURA Secatombe[1]	over the Lion, there will be great slaughter on the mountain
Delues[2] *& brodes*[3] *septieme million*	of Jura; floods and dark-coloured people the seventh (of
Lyon, Ulme à Mausol mort & tombe.	a million), Lyons, Ulm at the mausoleum death and the tomb.

The Jura mountains run through Franche-Comté which belonged to the Habsburgs until 1674. If *brodes* can be understood as dark-haired people, rather than dark skinned, this may refer to the Spanish. However this is another quatrain where the vast amount of the figure suggests the present century.

Dedans l'entree de Garonne & Baise	At the entrance to Garonne and Baise and the forest not
Et la forest non loing de Damazan	far from Damazan, discoveries
Du marsaves[4] *gelees, puis gresle & bize*	of the frozen sea, then hail and north winds. Frost in the
Dordonnois gelle[5] *par erreur de mezan.*[6]	Dardonnais through the mistake of the month.

This seems to be a general summary of unseasonable weather which will occur in all the above mentioned places.

[1] *Secatombe*—An obvious misprint for hecatombe.

[2] *Delues*—Uncertain, possibly from Latin, *diluvies* = flood/destruction

[3] *brodes*—Yet again these strange people derived from the O.F., *brode* = black, brown and decadent.

[4] *marsaves*—Compound word made up from O.F., *mar* = sea and O.F., *save* = discovery.

[5] *gelle*—O.F., without extra syllable for scansion = frost.

[6] *mesan*—From Latin, *mensa* = a month by metathesis.

Sera commis conte oingdre aduché[1]
De Saulne & sainct Aulbin &
  Bell'oeuvre[2]
Paver de marbre de tours 'loing
  espluché
Non Bleteram resister & chef
  d'oeuvre.

It will be committed against
the anointed brought from
Lons le Saulnier, Saint Aubin
and Bell'oeuvre. To pave with
marble taken from distant
towers, not to resist Bletteram
and his masterpiece.

A difficult quatrain with an enigma, see footnote. Bletterans is in
Franche Comté which used to belong to the Habsburgs until 1647.

La forteresse aupres de la Tamise
Cherra par lors le Roi dedans serré,
Aupres du pont sera veu en chemise
Un devant mort, puis dans le fort
  barré.

The fortress near the Thames
will fall when the king is locked
up inside. He will be seen in his
shirt near the bridge, one facing
death then barred inside the
fortress.

CHARLES I

One of Nostradamus' more exciting quatrains, and reasonably
exact too. After his defeat and captivity Charles I was taken to
Windsor Castle overlooking the Thames, in December 1648. He
remained there until 9th January 1649. In a sense the castle did
fall because it was in the hands of the Parliamentarians. On 30th
January after a trial, Charles was beheaded dressed in a white
shirt. The nearest bridge would be London Bridge, for Westminster
Bridge was not built at this time. This quatrain is definitely connected with IX. 49.

[1] *aduché*—Provençal, *aducha* = brought.
[2] *Bell'oeuvre*—Most probably an enigmatic place-name or it may
translate literally 'beautiful work'.

Le Roi de Blois dans Avignon regner
Un autre fois le peuple emonopole[1]
Dedans le Rhosne par murs fera
   baigner
Jusques à cinq le dernier pres de
   Nolle.[2]

The King of Blois will reign in Avignon, once again the people covered in blood. In the Rhône he will make swim near the walls up to five, the last one near Nolle.

Qu'aura esté par prince Bizantin,
Sera tollu par prince de Tholoze.
La foi de Foix par le chef Tholentin,
Lui faillira ne refusant l'espouse.

He who will have been for the Byzantine prince will be taken away by the prince of Toulouse. The faith of Foix through the leader of Tolentino will fail him, not refusing the bride.

The identity of the characters here is completely unclear. A Byzantine prince is either a Sultan or a Moslem leader; the prince of Toulouse may be its Archbishop or any one of the hereditary Montmorency family. Tolentino is part of the Papal States so presumably its leader is the Pope. Foix belonged to the House of Navarre.

Le sang du Juste par Taurer la
   daurade,[3]
Pour se venger contre les Saturnins[4]
Au nouveau lac plongeront la
   marinade.[5]
Puis marcher contre les Albanins.[6]

The blood of the Just for Taur and La Duarade in order to avenge itself against the Saturnines. They will immerse the band in the new lake, then they will march against Alba.

If one accepts that the two churches stand for Toulouse, the quatrain seems to imply that the inhabitants are fighting both Calvin-

[1] *emonopole*—A difficult compound Nostradamus word. Probably the nearest is the Greek, *aimapnoos* meaning bloodthirsty, or *aimatopotes*, blood drinker.

[2] *Nolle*—Probably an enigmatic proper name; possible Nola in Italy, but it does not fit the context.

[3] *Taurer la daurade* = Two Churches in Toulouse. (*a*) St. Saturnin du Taur. (*b*) Sainte Marie de la Daurade.

[4] *Saturnins*—Either those of Saturn or of St. Saturnin.

[5] *marinade*—Provençal, *marinade* = (*a*) Band. (*b*) Servants, household.

[6] *Albanins*—Probably the troops of the Duke of Alba, the Habsburg general for Emperors Charles V and Philip II. Just possibly Albanian mercenaries.

ism, or the Huguenots, as well as a Spanish attack led by the Duke of Alba.

41

Esleu sera Renad ne sonnant mot;	A fox will be elected without
Faisant le faint public vivant pain	speaking one word, appearing
d'orge,[1]	saintly in public living on
Tyranniser apres tant à un cop,[2]	barley bread, afterwards he will
Mettant à pied des plus grans sus la	suddenly become a tyrant
gorge.	putting his foot on the throats
	of the greatest men.

NAPOLEON III

Napoleon III was indeed as cunning as a fox and when elected President was known as '*le Taciturne*'. The prediction of line 3 was fulfilled by the *coup d'état* he exerted to make way for the Second Empire, 2nd December 1851. He certainly used his newly acquired power to fulfil line 4.

42

Par avarice, par force & violence	Through avarice, through force
Viendra vexer les siens chiefz	and violence the chief of Or-
d'Orléans,	léans will come to vex his
Pres saint Memire[3] *assault &*	supporters. Near St. Memire,
resistance.	assault and resistance. Dead in
Mort dans sa tante diront qu'il dort	his tent they will say he is asleep
leans.	inside.

LOUIS PHILIPPE D'ORLÉANS

Louis Philippe will upset his supporters and will engage in combat around St. Merri (not *Memire*). That Nostradamus got the title of Orléans is astonishing because the founder of the House was the brother of Louis XIII, born long after Nostradamus' death. After his victory Orléans is unable to cope and sleeps like a dead man within his tent.

[1] *vivant pain d'orgue*—Has a secondary meaning—to feather one's nest, which is singularly appropriate.

[2] *cop*—Alternative spelling of coup, for the rhyme.

[3] *St. Memire*—An unidentified place name.

Par le decide¹ de deux choses bastars
Nepveu du sang occupera le regne
Dedans lectoyre seront les coups de
dars
Nepveu par peur plaire l'enseigne.

Through the fall of two bastard creatures the nephew of the blood will occupy the throne. Within Lectoure there will be blows of lances, the nephew through fear will fold up his standard.

THE DEFEAT OF LOUIS NAPOLEON, 1870

The only important nephew in French history occurred over 300 years after Nostradamus' death; Louis Napoleon, son of King Louis, of Holland who was the brother of Napoleon I. The two bastards that fall are presumably the government of Louis Philippe, for whom Nostradamus has little liking, and that of the Second Republic. Lectoyre is an anagram of Le Torcey, a suburb of Sedan, the scene of Louis Napoleon's defeat by the Germans and Prussians. He ordered a flag of surrender to be hung on Sedan's church and then on its citadel, after which the Emperor formally surrendered to the Germans at Douchery two miles away from Le Torcey, in 1870.

Le procreé naturel dogmion,²
De sept à neuf du Chemin destorner
A roi de longue & ami au mi-hom,
Doit à Navarre fort de PAU
prosterner.

The natural offspring of Ogmios will turn off the road from seven to nine. To the king long friend of the half man, Navarre must destroy the fort at Pau.

Ogmios turns up in several quatrains; he was the Celtic equivalent of Hercules or Mercury. Apart from this, the only clear fact seems to be the destruction of the fortress at Pau when Henri IV of Navarre was born.

¹ *decide*—From Latin, *decidere* = to fall.
² *Ogmion* = the Celtic Hercules.

*La main escharpe & la jambe
    bandes,
Longs puis nay de Calais portera.
Au mot du guet la mort sera tardee
Puis dans le temple à Pasques
    saignera.*

With his hand in a sling and his leg bandaged, the younger brother of Calais will reach far. At the word of the watch, the death will be delayed, then he will bleed at Easter in the Temple.

*Pol mensolee mourra trois lieus du
    Rosne[1]
Fuis les deux prochains tarasc
    destrois:
Car Mars fera le plus horrible
    trosne,
De coq & d'aigle de France, freres
    trois.*

Paul the celibate will die three leagues from Rome, the two nearest flee the oppressed monster. When Mars will take up his horrible throne, the Cock and the Eagle, France and the three brothers.

WAR LINKED WITH PAUL VI AND KENNEDY BROTHERS

The last Pope Paul before the present Paul VI died in 1621. The linking of the present Pope with the three Kennedy brothers helps us to date the quatrain in the near future. The present Pope will die either just outside Rome, or in France if the Rhône is intended. At this point the two allies (cf. V. 78 and VI. 50) are troubled, threatened by a great war. The Cock stands for France who appears to have an important role to play, and the Eagle stands for U.S.A. the home of the Kennedy brothers.

*Lac Trasmenien portera tesmoig-
    nage,
Des conjurez serez dedans Perouse,
Un despolle contrefera le sage,
Truant Tedesque de sterne &
    minuse.*

Lake Trasimene will bear witness of the conspirators locked up inside Perugia. A fool will imitate the wise one, killing the Teutons, destroying and cutting to pieces.

[1] possible misspelling for Rome or Rhône.

Saturne en Cancer, Jupiter avec Mars,
Dedans Feurier Chaldondon[1] *salva-terre.*
Sault Castalon[2] *affailli de trois pars,*
Pres de Verbiesque[3] *conflit mortelle guerre.*

Saturn in Cancer, Jupiter with Mars in February 'Chaldondon' salva tierra. Sierra Morena besieged on three sides near Verbiesque, war and mortal conflict.

According to Wöllner the astrologer, the closest we will come to this conjunction is 1st February 2769. I cannot offer a further opinion on this very difficult verse.

Saturn: au beuf joue en l'eau, Mars en fleiche,
Six de Feurier mortalité donra,
Ceux de Tardaigne[4] *à Briges si grand breche,*
Qu'à Ponteroso[5] *chef Barbarin mourra,*

Saturn in Taurus, Jupiter in Aquarius. Mars in Sagittarius, the sixth of February brings death. Those of Tardaigne so great a breach at Bruges, that the barbarian chief will die at Ponteroso.

According to Wöllner again, this conjunction occurred in 1736 and not again in the foreseeable future. However McCann (1942) says that it occurred on 6th February 1971 so Nostradamus seems to have been wrong on both counts, unless it refers to those Mafia chiefs who were put on an island off Sardinia in enforced exile in 1971?

La pestilence l'entour de Capadille,
Un autre faim pres de Sagont s'appreste:
Le chevalier bastard de bon senille,
Au grand de Thunes fera trancher la teste.

The plague around Capellades, another famine is near to Sagunto; the knightly bastard of the good old man will cause the great one of Tunis to lose his head.

[1] *Chaldondon*—Possibly from Latin, *Chaldens* = a soothsayer, otherwise incomprehensible.
[2] *Sault Castalon*—Probably Latin, *Saltus Castulonensis* = Sierra Morena.
[3] *Verbiesque*—An unsolved place name, probably near to Sierra Morena.
[4] *Tardaigne*—Almost definitely misreading for Sardaigne = Sardinia.
[5] *Ponteroso*—Unidentified, may mean the red bridge.

1573. CAPTURE OF TUNIS

This quatrain is a very successful hit for Nostradamus. In 1573 (after Nostradamus' death in 1566), Don John of Austria, the bastard son of Charles V the old man, recaptured Tunis for his half-brother, Philip of Spain. Although there is no record of a famine, Spain was suffering from sporadic outbursts of plague between 1570–4.

51

Le Bizantin faisant oblation,	The Byzantine makes an obla-
Apres avoir Cordube à soi reprinse:	tion after having taken back
Son chemin long repos pamplation,[1]	Cordoba. A long rest on his
Mer passant proi par la Colongna[2]	road, the vines cut down, at
prinse.	sea the passing prey captured
	by the Pillar.

In this, Nostradamus seems to predict that the leader of Constantinople, whatever nation it might be, will invade Spain near Cordoba, having first made an offering to the Gods. Cordoba had belonged to the Arabs until 1031, and then to the Moslems until 1236. Line 4 may suggest that this Turkish leader, or whatever, is likely to be caught when returning through the Pillars of Hercules, i.e. Gibraltar.

52

Le roi de Blois dans Avignon regner,	The king of Blois to reign in Avignon, from Amboise and
D'amboise & seme[3] *viendra le long de Lyndre*	'Seme' the length of the Indre: claws at Poitiers holy wings
Ongle à Poitiers sainctes aesles ruiner	ruined before Boni. . . .
Devant Boni.[4]	

Line 1 is identical to the first line of VIII. 38. The various rivers are in France. Either the final line was not completed or was cut by the Catholic censor because it was dangerous or heretical. It is a pity because, with it, one might have gleaned some meaning from this quatrain.

[1] *pamplation*—Dubious, probably from Latin, *pampinatio* = to cut vines.
[2] *Colongna*—From *Collonnes d'Hercule* = Gibraltar.
[3] *seme*—Possibly the Seine, otherwise not identified.
[4] *Boni*—Incomplete line.

Dedans Bolongne vouldra laver ses fautes,	Within Boulogne he will want to wash away his misdeeds, he
Il ne pourra au temple du soleil,	cannot at the temple of the
Il volera faisant choses si haultes	Sun. He will fly away, doing
En hierarchie n'en fut oncq un pareil.	very great things: In the hierarchy he had never an equal.

NAPOLEON'S FAILURE TO INVADE ENGLAND

Many commentators apply this to Napoleon by reading Bolongne as Boulogne, but there is just a possibility that it may mean Bologna in the Papal States. Westminster Abbey, which Napoleon could not enter by conquest, was traditionally built on the Temple of Apollo, which was destroyed by an earthquake in AD 154. Napoleon flew so high as to think of taking Russia as well as England. Certainly he had no equal during his lifetime.

Soubz la colleur du traicte mariage,	Under the colour of the marriage treaty, a magnanimous
Fait magnanime par grand Chyren selin,	act by the 'Chyren selin': St.
Quintin, Arras recouvrez au voyage	Quintin and Arras recovered on the journey; By the Spanish
D'espaignolz fait second banc macelin.	a second butcher's bench is made.

Entre deux fleuves se verra enserré,	He will find himself shut in
Tonneaux & caques unis à passer outre,	between two rivers, casks and barrels joined to cross beyond:
Huict poutz rompus chef à tant enferré,	eight bridges broken, their chief run through so many times,
Enfans parfaictz sont jugetez en coultre.[1]	perfect children's throats slit by the knife.

Specific details of an unknown battle.

[1] *coultre*—O.F. = knife.

La bande foible le terre occupera
Ceux de hault lieux feront horribles cris,
Le gros troppeau d'estre coin troublera
Toute pres D. nebro descouvers les escris.

The weak band will occupy the land, those of high places will make dreadful cries. The large herd of the outer corner troubled, near Edinburgh it falls discovered by the writings.

SCOTLAND AND CHARLES II

Dinebero is taken as meaning Edinburgh, through a phonetic pun, 'Edinbro''. This quatrain then describes very clearly the battle of Dunbar which took place 25 miles east of the city. Charles II landed in Scotland in 1650. The highlanders (line 1) were more numerous than the Cromwellians but their position was weak. (The phrase *estre en coin* is interesting because before the battle the Scots boasted they had Cromwell cornered 'in a pound'.) Therefore the weaker band, the Cromwellians, routed the Scots on 3rd September. Perhaps line 4 can be explained by the fact that Cromwell took possession of all the papers in the Scottish War Office?

57

De soldat simple parviendra en empire,
De robe courte parviendra à la longue
Vaillant aux armes en eglise on plus pire
Vexer les prestres comme l'eau fait l'esponge.

From simple soldier he will attain to Empire, from the short robe he will grow into the long. Brave in arms, much worse towards the Church, he vexes the priests as water fills a sponge.

NAPOLEON I

From a simple lieutenant Napoleon attained to the government of the French Empire. He exchanged his short consular robe for the long robe of Imperial Majesty. Although brave in battle he mishandles the Clergy, and troubles the priests by the abolition of the Clergy just as much as water fills a sponge. An explicit quatrain to describe Napoleon's progress.

Regne en querelle aux freres divisé, *Prendre les armes & le nom* *Britannique* *Tiltre Anglican sera guard advisé,* *Surprins de nuict mener à l'air* *Gallique.*	A kingdom divided by two quarrelling brothers to take the arms and the name of Britain. The Anglican title will be advised to watch out, surprised by night (the other is), led to the French air.

JAMES II AND WILLIAM OF ORANGE, 1688

Since Nostradamus' death there have been no brothers fighting for the English throne, the loser fleeing to France. The nearest this came to fulfilment was when James II and his son-in-law, the Anglican William of Orange, came to open disagreement in 1688. The Anglican Church may well have exerted influence on the Catholic James II, but nevertheless he fled to France 'to take the Gallic air'.

Par deux fois hault, par deux fois *mis à bas* *L'orient aussi l'occident faiblira* *Son adversaire apres plusieurs* *combats,* *Par mer chassé au besoin faillira.*	Twice put up and twice cast down, the East will also weaken the West. Its adversary after several battles chased by sea will fail at time of need.

EAST AND WEST, 20th CENTURY

This seems again to describe the geopolitical state of the 20th Century better than any other. From this quatrain it appears that Asia will make two violent attacks upon the Western Powers which will affect them somewhat. But finally the East will lose at sea.

Premier en Gaule, premier en *Romanie* *Par mer & terre aux Anglois &* *Paris* *Merveilleux faitz par celle grand* *mesnie* *Violent terax perdra le NOR-* *LARIS.*	First in Gaul, first in Roumania, over land and sea against the English and Paris. Marvellous deeds by that great troop, violent, the wild beast will lose Lorraine.

Napoleon II is the only French leader to lose the Lorraine, but
the rest of the quatrain does not fit him well. James Laver applies
it to Napoleon I, saying he can be described as first in France and
in Rome. This may be a split quatrain describing father and son,
or maybe Nostradamus was confused, and saw the two men as one.

61

Jamais par le descouvrement[1] du jour	Never by the revelation of day-
Ne parviendra au signe sceptrifere[2]	light will he attain the mark of
Que tous ses sieges ne soient en sejour,	the sceptre bearer. Until all his sieges are at rest, bringing to
Portant du coq don du TAG[3] amifere.	the Cock the gift of the armed legion.

The Cock bearing the gift of arms is the Cock symbolizing France,
which was an obscure symbol until the Revolutionaries adopted it.
The rest most commentators apply to Napoleon III; although I
am not happy with this interpretation I cannot find a better.

62

Lors qu'on verra expiler[4] le saint temple,	When one sees the holy temple plundered, the greatest of the
Plus grand du rosne leurs sacrez profaner:	Rhône profaning their sacred things; because of them a very
Par eux naistra pestilence si ample.	great pestilence will appear,
Roi fuit injuste ne fera condamner.	the king, unjust, will not condemn them.

A very general quatrain in which an unjust king commits sacrilege
which results in a plague.

63

Quand l'adultere blessé sans coup aura	When the adulterer wounded without a blow will have
Merdri la femme & le filz par despit,	murdered his wife and son out of spite; his wife knocked down,
Ferme assoumee l'enfant estranglera:	he will strangle the child; eight captives taken, choked beyond
Huit captifz prins, s'estouffer sans respit.	help.

[1] *descouvrement*—O.F. = discovery.
[2] *sceptrifere*—Latin = sceptre bearing, i.e. royal.
[3] *TAG*—Variant in editions, *tagma* = body of soldiers or legion.
[4] *expiler*—Latin, *expilare* = to rob, plunder.

Too general to identify.

64

Dedans les isles les enfans trans-portez, *Les deux de sept seront en desespoir,* *Ceux terrouer[1] en seront sup-portez,* *Nom pelle[2] prins des ligues fui l'espoir.*	The infants transported into the islands, two out of seven will be in despair. Those of the soil will be supported by it, the name 'shovel' taken, the hope of the leagues fails.

NAZIS AND BRITAIN

This quatrain is applied by most modern commentators to Britain, besieged by the Nazis in the Second World War. But even with this, *pelle* is not satisfactorily deciphered.

65

Le vieux frustré du principal espoir, *Il parviendra au chef de son empire:* *Vingt mois tiendra le regne à grand pouvoir,* *Tiran, cruel en delaissant un pire.*	The old man disappointed in his main hope, will attain to the leadership of his Empire. Twenty months he will hold rule with great force, a tyrant, cruel, giving way to one worse.

MARSHAL PÉTAIN, 1940–2

If one accepts that most general quatrains are assumed to occur in France, as I do, this may well refer to that country in 1940. In that year on 10th July, a rump session of the French Assembly invested Pétain with plenary powers until a new constitution could be formed. After increasing pressure from the Germans to collaborate he handed most of his powers over to Laval on April 1942.

[1] *terrouer*—O.F. = soil, land, ground.
[2] *pelle*—This has never been deciphered. Garencières got nearest with his suggestion of Montpellier.

Quand l'escriture D.M.[1] *trouvee,*	When the inscription D.M. is
En cave antique à lampe descouverte,	found in the ancient cave,
Loi, Roi, & Prince Ulpian[2]	revealed by a lamp. Law, the
esprouvee	King and Prince Ulpian tried,
Pavillon rogne & Duc sous la	the Queen and Duke in the
couvert.	pavilion under the cover.

Many commentators have suggested very ingenious solutions for
D.M., but as I say in the footnote, it is just the equivalent of There
Lies . . . in English. James Laver takes it to mean *du manuscrit*,
of the manuscript. It probably ties in with the puzzling quatrain
of IX. 84.

PAR. CAR. NERSAF, à ruine	Paris, Carcassone, France to
grand discord,	ruin in great disharmony,
Ne l'un ne l'autre aura election,	neither one nor the other will
Nersaf du peuple aura amour &	be elected. France will have
concorde.	the love and good will of the
Ferrare, Callonne grande protection.	people, Ferara, Colonna great
	protection.

Par. and *Car.* probably stand for Paris and Carcassonne, but
NERSAF is not a very good anagram for France, although by the
rules one is allowed to change one letter. Although Ferara was
joined with the Franco-Papal troops fighting Spain in 1557,
Colonna was always firmly pro-Spanish. The key to this quatrain
lies in the word *Nersaf*.

Vieux Cardinal par le jeune deceu,	The old Cardinal is deceived by
Hors de sa change se verra desarmé,	the young one, he will find him-
Arles ne monstres double soit	self disarmed, out of his
aperceu,	position: Do not show, Arles,
Et Liqueduct & le Prince em-	that the double is perceived,
bausmé.	both Liqueduct and the Prince
	embalmed.

[1] *D.M.*—Probably stands for Latin inscription, *Diis Manibus* which
was put on many Roman tombstones.

[2] *Ulpian*—Ulpius a Roman name, e.g. Trojan's was Marcus Ulpius
Trojanus.

Cardinal Richelieu is supplanted by the younger Cinq Mars and loses the favours of Louis XIII and has to resign. But at Arles he will receive a copy of a treaty with Spain, signed by Cinq Mars and the king's brother, in 1642. He tells the king of this treachery, and although very ill, travels to Paris on a barge. *Liqueduct* means literally 'led by the water', an excellent description of the Cardinal's voyage. But the Cardinal died at the end of 1642 and the king five months later, and as Nostradamus says, both bodies were embalmed.

69

Aupres du jeune le vieux ange baisser	Beside the young one the old angel falls, and will come to rise above him at the end; ten years equal to most the old one falls again, of three two and one, the eighth seraphin.
Et le viendra surmonter à la fin:	
Dix ans esgaux au plus vieux rabaisser,	
De trois deux l'un huitiesme seraphin.	

This quatrain seems to describe the rivalry of favourites; apart from this it is very obscure.

70

Il entrera vilain, mechant, infame	He will enter, wicked, unpleasant, infamous, tyrannizing over Mesopotamia. All friends made by the adulterous lady, the land dreadful and black of aspect.
Tyrannisant la Mesopotamie,	
Tous amis fait d'adulterine d'ame,	
Terre horrible, noir de phisonomie.	

Usually Mesopotamia has described Avignon, at the joining of the Rhône and the Durance. If this is so, the villain is the Cardinal Legate governing it in place of the Pope.

71

Croistra le nombre si grand des astronomes	The number of astrologers will grow so great, that they will be driven out, banned, and their books censored. In the year 1607 by sacred assemblies so that none will be safe from the holy ones.
Chassez, bannis & livres consurez,	
L'an mil six cents sept par sacre glomes	
Que nul aux sacres ne seront asseurez.	

This dating appears successful when reading other commentators who all apply it to the Council of Malines of 1607 which banished astrology. But I can find no record of this Council existing at all. It was probably invented by a prejudiced commentator of Nostradamus! Therefore this quatrain must be counted as a definite failure, despite the dating.

72

Champ Perusin d'enorme deffaite
Et le conflit tout au pres de Ravenne,
Passage sacre lors qu'on fera la feste,
Vainqueur vaincu cheval manger la venne.

Oh what a huge defeat on the Perugian battlefield and the conflict very close to Ravenna. A holy passage when they will celebrate the feast, the conquerer banished to eat horse meat.

RAVENNA, 1512

This is probably a retrospective quatrain which had already occurred when Nostradamus wrote the Prophecies. Both Perugia and Ravenna were Papal States and this quatrain describes accurately enough the victory of Gaston de Foix at Ravenna in 1512.

73

Soldat barbare le grand Roi frappera,
Injustement non esloigné de mort,
L'avare mere du fait cause fera
Conjurateur & regne en grand remort.

The king is struck by a barbarian soldier, unjustly, not far from death. The greedy will be the cause of the deed, conspirator and realm in great remorse.

If used correctly the word '*barbare*' refers to the pirates from Barbary (Algeria), but it is used widely for Moslems and others not of the Christian faith.

74

En terre neufue bien avant Roi entré
Pendant subges lui viendront faire acueil,
Sa perfidie aura tel recontré
Qu'aux citadins lieu de feste & receuil.

A king entered very far into the new land while the subjects will come to bid him welcome; his treachery will have such a result that to the citizens it is a reception instead of a festival.

The new land is an interesting phrase because it was one of the names for America in Nostradamus' day. If the U.S.A. is meant, the verse implies that a world leader comes to that country and is given an excellent welcome whereas the whole time the guest is planning treachery. I wonder if the Chinese will visit the U.S.A. in the near future?

75

Le pere & fils seront meurdris ensemble	The father and son will be murdered together, the leader
Le prefecteur dedans son pavillon	within his pavilion. The
La mere à Tours du filz ventre aura enfle	mother at Tours will have her belly swollen with a son, a
Criche verdure de failles papillon.	verdure chest with little pieces of paper.

ASSASSINATION IN PORTUGAL, 1908?

The first line of this quatrain is very clear, the murder of a father and son. It cannot apply to France as no French kings and Dauphins were assassinated together. In the case of Louis XVI and his son there was over two years between the king's and his son's presumed death. There was no pregnant widow at Tours involved with the family. The most important father and son assassination outside France was in 1908, when Carlos I and Louis Philippe of Portugal were murdered at Lisbon. But still no explanation of the widow at Tours or the puzzling last line.

76

Plus Macelin[1] que roi en Angleterre	More of a butcher than a king
Lieu obscure nay par force aura l'empire:	in England, born-of obscure rank will gain empire through
Lasche sans foi, sans loi saignera terre,	force. Coward without faith, without law he will bleed the
Son temps approche si presque je soupire.	land; His time approaches so close that I sigh.

OLIVER CROMWELL

Apparently Nostradamus had little sense of time because Oliver Cromwell did not appear until over 30 years after his death (1599–1658). He is described as more of a butcher than a king

[1] *Macelin*—Latin, *macellum* = a meat basket. Used elsewhere with the above meaning by Nostradamus.

because of the bloodshed of the Civil War. He was of the Protestant faith and Nostradamus regards him as a heretic. He was of comparatively humble origins and attained his position through military force. The reference to his being a coward is interesting as Cromwell was supposed to wear a corselet of some kind, because he was afraid of assassination.

77

L'antechrist trois bien tost an-niehilez,	The antichrist very soon annihilates the three, twenty-
Vingt & sept ans sang durera sa guerre.	seven years his war will last. The unbelievers are dead,
Les heretiques mortz, captifs, exilez.	captive, exiled; with blood,
Sang corps humain eau rougi gresler terre.	human bodies, water and red hail covering the earth.

ANTICHRIST AND THREE BROTHERS. LENGTH OF THE WAR

Three separate Antichrists appear in Nostradamus' Epistle. It is usually accepted that Napoleon was the first and Hitler the Second, so the Third is still to come. Line 1 can be read either as 'the third Antichrist will soon be annihilated' or 'the Antichrist will soon annihilate the three', implying by this the three Kennedy brothers, two of whom are already dead. It makes more sense in this context to assume that the Antichrist is a way of life, i.e. Russian Communism or Chinese Communism, since obviously one man did not kill both brothers. It seems as though Edward Kennedy must be a psychological assassinee since even Nostradamus foresaw his death four hundred years ago! The war is a long one of attrition; it may refer to the length of time needed before the cities would be safe from harmful radioactive fallout. After the atomic bombing of Nagasaki and Hiroshima large black raindrops fell, full of dust. This was recorded by survivors so perhaps Nostradamus is not so far out when he speaks of red rain.

78

Un Bragamus[1] avec la langue torte	A soldier of fortune with
Viendra des dieux le sanctuaire,	twisted tongue will come to the
Aux heretiques il ouvrira la porte	sanctuary of the gods. He will
En suscitant l'eglise militaire.	open the door to heretics and raise up the Church militant.

[1] *Bragamus*—O.F. = broadsword, or Provençal, *Briamanso* = a soldier of fortune.

This is a general quatrain that can be applied either to France during the Wars of Religion (1562–98) or to Germany during the Thirty Years War (1618–48).

79

Qui par fer pere perdra nay de Nonnaire,[1]	He who loses his father by the sword, born in a Nunnery, upon this Gorgon's blood will conceive anew; in a strange land he will do everything to be silent, he who will burn both himself and his child.
De Gorgon sur la sera sang perfetant[2]	
En terre estrange fera si tant de taire,	
Qui bruslera lui mesme & son enfant.	

The legendary Gorgon was a hateful monster, who turned everyone who looked at her into stone. Nostradamus is therefore describing an appalling woman who causes a man to kill himself and the child he has had by her. An interesting footnote is that Hugh Allen in his book on Nostradamus 1943, applies this quatrain to himself, on page xii!

80

Des innocens le sang de vefue & vierge.	The blood of innocents, widow and virgin, so many evils committed by means of the Great Red One, holy images placed over burning candles, terrified by fear, none will be seen to move.
Tant de maulx faitz par moyen se grand Roge	
Saintz simulacres tremper en ardent cierge	
De frayeur crainte ne verra nul que boge.	

THE RUSSIAN REVOLUTION

The great Red One of line 2 is a revolution, but it is difficult to decide if the French or Russian Revolution is meant. I am inclined to accept the latter as the Communist Party is described as Red, and Nostradamus describes the French Revolutionary tricolour elsewhere. The first line would then refer to the deaths of the Czar and Czarina and their 'virgin' children. Line 3 smacks faintly of the influence of the Church through the priest Rasputin. The last line would then imply that Anastasia did not escape assassination, and that those who claim to be her are pretenders.

[1] *Nonnaire*—Low Latin, *nonneria* = nunnery.
[2] *perfetant*—Latin, *superfetens* = to conceive while pregnant.

Le neuf empire en desolation	The new empire in desolation
Sera changé du pole aquilonaire.	will be changed from the
De la Sicile viendra l'esmotion	Northern Pole. From Sicily will
Troubler l'emprise à Philip tribu-	come such trouble that it will
taire.	bother the enterprise tributary
	to Philip.

The first two lines make this quatrain sound very modern by the sheer scope of their concept. A ravaged empire moves itself and its civilization southwards, this might well occur after an atomic war. But the last two lines bring us back to 16th-Century Europe where Nostradamus seems to see a Habsburg civil war between Philip and Ferdinand over the division of Charles V's empire. The uprising against Philip is predicted as starting in Sicily.

Ronge long, sec faisant du bon valet,	Thin tall and dry, playing the
A la parfin n'aura que son congie[1]	good valet in the end will have
Poignant poison & lettres au collet	nothing but his dismissal; sharp
Sera saisi eschappé en dangie.[1]	poison and letters in his collar,
	he will be seized escaping into
	danger.

A valet who tries to poison his master is caught and dismissed.

Le plus grand voile hors de port de	The largest sail set out of the
Zara,	port of Zara, near Byzantium
Pres de Bisance fera son entreprinse,	will carry out its enterprise.
D'ennemi parte & l'ami ne sera,	Loss of enemy and friend will
Le Tiers à deux fera grand pille &	not be, a third will turn on both
prinse.	with great pillage and capture.

FOURTH CRUSADE, 1202

Another retroactive prophecy describing the atrocities of the Fourth Crusade, 1202. Venice agreed to cross to Egypt with the Crusaders for a large sum of money and half the plunder. The Crusaders could not raise the money and so they captured Zara (then Hungarian, now in Yugoslavia). The Pope excommunicated the whole Crusade, whereupon they sacked Constantinople (Byzantium) and set up Romania, the Roman Empire of the East.

[1] *congie* and *dangie*—The latter word shortened to keep the rhyme.

Paterne orra de la Sicile crie,	Paterno will hear the cry from
Tous les aprests du Goulphre de Trieste,	Sicily, all the preparations in the Gulf of Trieste; it will be
Qui s'entendra jusque à la Trina-crie[1]	heard as far as Sicily flee oh flee, so many sails, the dreaded
Tant de voiles, fui, fuiz, l'horrible peste.	pestilence!

The Spanish empire of the two Sicilies owned Catonia and Paternum, whereas Trieste belonged to Venice of the Habsburg branch. So this is probably a continuation of VIII. 81.

Entre Bayonne & à Saint Jean de Lux	Between Bayonne and St. Jean de Luz will be placed the
Sera posé de Mars la promottoire[2]	promontory of Mars. To the
Aux Hanix[3] *d'Aquilon Nanar*[4] *hostera lux,*[5]	Hanix of the North, Nanar will remove the light, then suffocate
Puis suffocqué au lict sans adjutoire.[6]	in bed without assistance.

NAPOLEON III'S DEATH?

Nostradamus foresees a war zone (Mars) between Bayonne and St. Jean de Luz in South-west France. The difficulty of interpretation lies in Hanix and Nanar, see below. Another suggestion is that the promontory is Biarritz, where Napoleon III, like Mars the God of War, retired into the arms of loving women when the North wind ceases to blow. *Hanix* would then come from the Greek, *ansiscus*, without force. Napoleon died from an operation for the stone, but his weak physical condition, because of his debauchery, may have made him much weaker.

[1] *Trinacrie* = Trinicia, poetic name for Italy.
[2] *promottoire*—Variant spelling of *promontoire*.
[3] *Hanix*—Possibly from Gk., *anikatos* = unconquerable, or Latin, *Hamaxaeci* = the nomads of Northern Europe.
[4] *Nanar*—Possibly Latin, *nonaria* = prostitute?
[5] *lux*—Latin = light.
[6] *adjutoire*—O.F. = assistance, aid.

Par Arani Tholoser ville franque,
Bande infini par le mont Adrian,
Passe riviere, Hutin[1] par pont la
*   planque*
Bayonne entrera tous Bihoro[2] criant.

Through Emani, Tolosa and Villefranche, an infinite band through the mountains of Adrian. Passes the river, Cambat over the plank for a bridge, Bayonne will be entered all crying Bigoree.

NAVARRE

The three towns of line 1 and the mountain of Adrian in line 2 are all close together on the south-western tip of the Spanish Pyrenees. The only river to the north between them and Bayonne is the Bidassoa. As I have said before, Bigorre was the battle cry of the Huguenots of Navarre, and the original Navarre covered the area south of the Pyrenees and north into France. It became a separate state in 1515 until it was reunified with France by the accession of Henri IV of Navarre to the French throne after Nostradamus' death.

Mort conspiree viendra en plein
*   effect,*
Charge donnee & voiage de mort,
Esleu, crée, receu par siens deffait.
Sang d'innocence devant foi par
*   remort.*

A death conspired will come to its full effect, the charge given and the voyage of death. Elected, created, received (then) defeated by his followers, in remorse the blood of innocence in front of him.

LOUIS XVI

The conspiracy to rob Louis XVI of both his crown and life is successfully carried off. The change to the position of constitutional king and his flight to Varennes (voyage of death) will be the final cause of his death. He will be defeated by his own nation who earlier elected him. His innocent blood will be a source of remorse to the French.

[1] *Hutin*—O.F. = dispute, combat, hostility.
[2] *Bihoro*—Bigorre was the battle cry of the Huguenots of Navarre.

Dans la Sardaigne un noble Roi viendra	A noble king will come to Sardinia, who will only rule for three years in the kingdom. He will join with himself several colours; he himself, after taunts, care spoils slumber.
Que ne tiendra que trois ans le royaume,	
Plusieurs couleurs avec soi conjoindra,	
Lui mesmes apres soin someil marrit[1] scome.[2]	

KING OF SARDINIA, 1798–1802

King Charles Emmanuel IV, when the French Republic took most of his lands retired to Sardinia where he reigned for three years (1798–1802). He then abdicated in favour of his brother, Victor Emmanuel I. He then went to Rome humiliated and unhappy and joined the Jesuit Order with whom he stayed until his death in 1819. This is one of the few times in modern history that Sardinia had its own king and not a titular one.

89

Pour ne tumber entre mains de son oncle,	In order not to fall into the hands of his uncle who slaughtered his children in order to reign. Pleasing with the people, putting his foot on 'Peloncle', dead and dragged between armoured horses.
Qui ses enfans par regner trucidez.[3]	
Orant[4] au peuple mettant pied sur Peloncle[5]	
Mort & traisné entre chevaulx bardez.	

I have not been able to decipher *Peloncle* and therefore the quatrain remains unbroken.

[1] *marrit*—O.F. = to afflict, spoil.
[2] *scome*—Latin, *scomma* = scoff, taunt, jeer.
[3] *trucidez*—Latin, *trucidare* = to slaughter, massacre.
[4] *Orant*—Latin, *orans* = pleading, arguing.
[5] *Peloncle*—Doubtful, possibly Pellonia, the goddess who put enemies to flight?

Quand des croisez un trouvé de sens trouble
En lieu du sacre verra un boeuf cornu
Par vierge porc son lieu lors sera comble
Par roi plus ordre ne sera soustenu.

When those of the cross are found their senses troubled, in place of sacred things he will see a horned bull, through the virgin the pig's place will then be filled, order will no longer be maintained by the king.

The men of the cross are either Crusaders, or Nazis. The bull may mean in Taurus, and the Virgin, Virgo, but it doesn't get us much further.

Frymy[1] les champs des Rodans[2] entrees
Ou les croisez seront presque unis,
Les deux brassieres[3] en Pisces rencontrees
Et un grand nombre par deluge punis.

Entered among the fields of the Rhône (dwellers) where those of the cross are almost united, the two lands meeting in Pisces and a great number punished by the flood.

The conjunction of Pisces with Venus is the time clue for this quatrain, linked with flooding above the Rhône.

Loin hors du regne mis en hazard voyage
Grand host[4] duira[5] pour soi l'occupera,
Le roi tiendra les siens captif ostrage
A son retour tout pays pillera.

Far distant from his kingdom, sent on a dangerous journey, he will lead a great army and keep it for himself. The king will hold his people captive and hostage, he will plunder the whole country on his return.

A very clear and dramatic quatrain which does not seem to have been fulfilled.

[1] *Frymi*—Misprint in some editions for *Parmi* = among.
[2] *Rodans*—Latin, *Rhodanus* = the Rhône, or possibly its people.
[3] *brassieres*—lead strings, probably standing for Venus who was bound to Mars by an unbreakable thread forged by Vulcan.
[4] *host*—O.F., *ost* = army.
[5] *duira*—O.F., *duire* = to lead.

Sept mois sans plus obtiendra prelature
Par son deces grand scisme fera naistre:
Sept mois tiendra un autre la preture
Pres de Venise paix union renaistre.

For seven months, no longer, will he hold the office of prelate, through his death a great schism will arise; for seven months another acts as prelate near Venice, peace and union are reborn.

1590?

The only popes to live for less than seven months after election were Sixtus V, Urban VII, who died after two weeks, followed by Gregory XIV, who died after ten months, all in 1590. But unfortunately there is no record of a schism.

94

Devant le lac ou plus cher fut getté
De sept mois, & son host desconfit
Seront Hispans par Albanois gastez
Par delai perte en donnant le conflict.

In front of the lake where the dearest one was destroyed for seven months and his army routed; Spaniards will be devastating by means of Alba, through delay in giving battle, loss.

BAY OF CADIZ, 1596

Ward applies this quatrain to the English attack on Cadiz by Essex, Howard and Raleigh in June 1596. In line 1 the word *cher* becomes treasure or valuables, because the ships were heavy with booty having come in from a seven months' voyage. Cadiz bay is called a lake because the word Gaddir, from which Cadiz comes, means 'an enclosed space'. Forty galleons and thirteen warships were destroyed. What makes this quatrain so interesting is that Nostradamus must have foreseen the war between Spain and England, whereas when he wrote England's queen was the wife of Spain's king (Mary Tudor).

95

Le seducteur sera mis en la fosse
Et estaché jusques à quelque temps,
Le clerc uni le chef avec sa crosse[1]
Picante droite attraira[2] *les contens.*

The seducer will be placed in a ditch and will be tied up for some time. The scholar joins the chief with his cross. The sharp right will draw the contented ones.

[1] *crosse*—O.F. = possibly abbey; or cross.
[2] *attraire*—O.F. = to draw, attract.

La synagogue sterile sans nul fruit	The sterile synagogue without any fruit, will be received by the infidels, the daughter of the persecuted (man) of Babylon, miserable and sad, they will clip her wings.
Sera receu entre les infideles	
De Babylon la fille du porsuit	
Misere & triste lui trenchera les aisles.	

FLIGHT OF JEWS TO MOSLEMS, *c.* 1550–1566

This prophecy was already partly fulfilled in Nostradamus' lifetime. After the wave of persecution that they were suffering in Christian countries, the Sultan of Turkey, Suleiman the Magnificent, offered hospitality to Jews who came and settled in Constantinople, and Salonika in particular. One of them became very powerful and in 1566, the year of Nostradamus' death, Don Joseph Nassi was created Duke of Naxos and became the principal adviser to Selim II.

97

A fin du VAR changer le pompotans,	At the end of the Var the great powers change; near the bank three beautiful children are born. Ruin to the people when they are of age; in the country the kingdom is seen to grow and change more.
Pres du rivage les trois beaux enfants naistre.	
Ruine ay peuple par aage competans.	
Regne ay pays changer plus voir croistre.	

KENNEDYS?

In X. 100 'pempotan' stands for England. The problem is to decide whether it does so in this case, probably not. The river Var flows into the Mediterranean between Cannes and Nice and it was the approximate border of Savoy in Nostradamus' time. The three beautiful brothers who bring trouble to the nation may link up with the Kennedy theme. Certainly the U.S.A. was changing during their lifetimes and presumably was growing in influence to become a world power.

98

Des gens d'eglise sang fera espandu,	Of the church men the blood will be poured forth as abundant as water in (amount); for a long time it will not be restrained, woe, woe, for the clergy ruin and grief.
Comme de l'eau eu si grand abondance;	
Et d'un long temps ne sera restranche	
Ve, ve[1] au clerc ruine & doleance.	

[1] *Ve, ve*—Latin, *vae* = alas, woe.

Another quatrain about the Persecution of the Clergy *c.* 1792 in France.

99

Par la puissance des trois rois tempoulz,
En autre lieu sera mis le saint siege:
Où la substance & de l'esprit corporel,
Sera remis & receu pour vrai siege.

Through the powers of three temporal kings, the sacred seat will be put in another place, where the substance of the body and the spirit will be restored and received as the true seat.

The only time that the Pope's seat has been moved from the Vatican to date is when Pope Pius VI was moved to Valence and died there. Pius VII managed to return to Rome. Maybe one of the future Popes will move out of the Vatican. Lines 3 and 4 imply a revival of religious fervour.

100

Pour l'abondance de larme respandue
Du hault en bas par le bas au plus hault.
Trop grande foir par jeu vie perdue
De soif mourir par habondant deffault.[1]

By the great number of tears shed, from top to bottom and from the bottom to the very top, a life is lost through a game with too much faith, to die of thirst through a great deficiency.

A nonsensical quatrain to present-day readers.

[1] The whole of this line is difficult. It probably means drowned, or even to drink oneself to death.

CENTURY IX

1
2
3
4
5*   National Assembly, 1848
6
7
8
9   Nîmes, 1557
10
11*   England, 1649–56
12
13
14
15
16*** General Franco and de Rivera
17*   French Revolution
18** Louis XIII
19
20*** Louis XVI flight to Varennes
21
22
23*   Louis XVI and his son
24
25
26
27*   Louis XVII?
28
29*   Capture of Calais, 1558
30
31?
32
33

347

```
34***    Louis XVI and Saulce
35*      Ferdinand of Bulgaria, 20th Century
36*F?    Kennedy brothers
37
38
39
40*      Battle of St. Quentin, 1557
41
42***    Battle of Lepanto, 1571
43
44
45
46
47?      Francis II, 1559–60?
48*?
49**     Execution of Charles I, 1649
50*      Henri IV
51**     20th Century?
52*      Peace of Cateau Chambresis, 1559
53
54
55**     Influenza epidemic, 1918
56
57
58
59
60
61
62       Magic practices?
63
64
65***F?  The Space Race
66
67
68*      The sack of Lyons, 1793
69
70
71
72
73*?     18th February 1981
74
75
76
```

348

77***   Fates of Marie Antoinette and Mme. du Barry
78
79
80
81
82
83*F?   An earthquake on 10th April?
84**   Tomb of St. Peter?
85
86*   3rd July 1851
87
88*   1557. Calais
89*   Louis Philippe, 1830–48
90**   Hitler
91
92**F? New York?
93**   Louis XIV
94
95
96
97
98
99*   Napoleon's retreat from Moscow
100**? Pearl Harbour, 1941

KEY: * Of interest. F? Possibly referring to the future.

Dans la maison du traducteur de Bourc[1]

Seront les lettres trouvees dur la table

Bourgne, roux, blanc chanu tiendra de cours,

Qui changera au nouveau connestable.

In the house of the translator from Bourg letters will be found on the table. One-eyed, red- and white-haired will hold the course, which will change for the new constable.

This is a fascinating quatrain. One of the best known 16th-Century French scholars was a man called Etienne de la Boétie. If '*Bourc*' stands for Boétie then the prophecy makes some sort of sense, in that the latter had a famous quarrel with the then Constable of France, Anne de Montmorency over the publication of a book, 'La Servitude Voluntaire'. Nostradamus seems to predict that Boétie would have even more trouble with the Constable's successor, Henri de Montmorency. This did not occur as Boétie died four years before Anne de Montmorency, in 1563. See also IX. 81.

Du hault du mont Aventin voix ouïe,

Vuidez, vuidez de tous les deux costez,

Du sang des rouges sera l'ire assomie,[2]

D'Arimin Prate, Columna[3] *debotez.*[4]

A voice is heard from the top of Aventine Hill. Go, go, all on both sides! The anger will be appeased by the blood of the red ones. From Rimini and Prato, Colonna expelled.

Another quatrain centred around the feuds of the Vatican states with the great Italian families, the Colonnas and the Orsinis etc. In Nostradamus' time they were allied to the Spanish and thus got deeply involved with the Vatican's anti-Spanish policies of Pope Paul IV.

[1] *Bourc* = Bourg, north of Bordeaux; the inhabitants were called Bourcais.

[2] *assomie*—O.F. = to appease.

[3] *Columna*—Original spelling of the Colonnas of Rome.

[4] *desbotez*—O.F., *debouter* = expell, drive out.

La magna vaqua[1] *à Ravenne grand trouble,*	The Magnavacca near Ravenna in great trouble, led
Conduictz par quinze enserrez à Fornase	by fifteen shut up at Fornese; at Rome two monsters with
A Rome naistre deux monstres à teste double	double heads are born, blood, fire, floods, the greatest in the
Sang, feu, deluges, les plus grands à l'espase.	air.[2]

This is similar to the last quatrain with the added enigma of *magna vaqua*, literally 'the great cow'. It seems to be involved with the Papal states and the Vatican, together with hanging and two-headed monsters, two of which were shown to Nostradamus in his capacity of prophet in the early 1560s near Salon, when he declared them to predict a disunited France to come.

L'an ensuivant descouvertz par deluge,	The following year revealed by a flood, two leaders elected, the
Deux chefs esluez le premier ne tiendra	first will not hold on; for one of them refuge in fleeing shadows,
De fuir ombre à l'un d'eux le refuge,	the victim plundered who maintained the first.
Saccager case[3] *qui premier maintiendra.*	

Another quatrain describing a discovery, or treasure, combined with vague threats.

Tiers doit du pied au premier semblera.	The third toe will look like the first one of a new king, of low
A un nouveau monarque de bas hault	height, he who will occupy as a tyrant Pisa and Lucca, to
Qui Pise & Lucques Tyran occupera	correct the fault of his predecessor.
Du precedant corriger le deffaut.	

[1] *magna vacca*—Either the valley and port named Magnavalca between Ravenna and Ferrara, or an unsolved name?

[2] i.e., hanged.

[3] *case*—Provençal *casa* = victim of hunt or the hunt.

The third estate, established for a second time in 1848, will seem no more than a toe of the first, i.e. very insignificant. Louis-Napoleon found it easier to deal with than did Napoleon I. In 1831 Louis Napoleon was involved with Italian revolutionaries and helped to try to seize Civila Castellana which is in Tuscany as are Pisa and Lucca. The fault of Napoleon's predecessor was Napoleon II's failure to obtain real power.

6

Par la Guienne infinité d'Anglais.
Occuperont par nom d'Anglaquitaine
Du Languedoc Ispalme[1] Bour-
delois.
Qu'ils nommeront apres Barboxi-
taine.[2]

A great number of English in Guienne will occupy it, calling it Anglaquitain. In Languedoc, Ispalme, Bordelais which they will name after Barboxitaine.

The English occupied Guienne, the Languedoc and Bordelais steadily between the 12th and 15th Centuries, but not since Nostradamus' lifetime. Bordelais was one of the centres of English dominance in southern France. Perhaps Ispalme is a misprint for Lapalme near Narbonne? Barboxitaine seems to mean 'the Beard's' south-western France, the Beard being the man variously referred to as Bronze Beard or Aenobarbe (see V. 59). Not a successful quatrain on the whole.

7

Qui ouvrira le monument trouvé
Et ne viendra le serrer promptement.
Mal lui viendra & ne pourra
prouvé,
Si mieux doit estre roi Breton ou
Normand.

The man who opens the tomb when it is found, and who does not come and shut it immediately; evil will come to him, no one will be able to prove it. It might have been better were he a Breton or a Norman King.

Another quatrain about the discovery of a tomb, and it may be linked with I. 27. The last line is suitably enigmatic: I. 27 is regarded by some as being a threat against the opening of Nostradamus' tomb which happened all the same in 1813.

[1] *Ispalme*—Unidentified place name.
[2] *Barboxitaine*—Probably derived from Barbe-Occitanie, Barbe referring to the enigmatic Bronzebeard and Occitanie, the medieval name for the Mediterranean coast.

Puisnay Roi fait son pere mettre à mort,	The younger son will put his father, the king to death, after the quarrel, to a death very dishonest. Writings found, suspicion will bring remorse, when the chased wolf lies on the bedcover.
Apres conflit de mort tres inhoneste:	
Escrit trouvé soubson donra remort,	
Quand loup chassé pose sus la conchette.	

Although the statement of a younger son taking over his father's throne, in a way that involves murder, sounds quite reasonable, it is hard to find any possible fulfilment since Nostradamus' lifetime, and also of the strange details of the last two lines.

9

Quand lampe ardente de feu inextinguible,	When the lamp burning with eternal fire, will be found in the temple of the Vestals. A child found (in the) fire water passing through the sieve, Nîmes to perish in water, the markets will fall in Toulouse.
Sera trouvé au temple des Vestales,	
Enfant trouvé feu, eau passant par trible:[1]	
Perir eau Nimes, Tholose cheoir les halles.	

1557

Nostradamus may have cheated on this verse because in 1557 the most enormous cloudburst occurred over Nîmes (popularly held to be the site of a Temple of Diana, tended by the Vestal Virgins). The water was over six feet deep in some places and many of the beautiful monuments were uncovered. But nothing remarkable occurred in Toulouse around that time.

10

Moine moinesse d'enfant mort exposé,	The child of a monk and a nun will be exposed to die, to die by a she bear, and carried off by a boar; the army will be camped near Foix and Parmiers, Carcassonne will raise the pillage against Toulouse.
Mourrir par ourse & ravi par verrier.[2]	
Par Foix & Pamyes le camp sera posé.	
Contre Tholose Carcas, dresser forrier.	

[1] trible—Mod. French, crible = a sieve.
[2] verrier—Probably made up by Nostradamus from Latin, verez = a boar.

A quatrain set in South-west France, the first part describing the tragic circumstances and death of a baby, the second part great military events.

11

Le juste à tort à mort l'on viendra mettre	They will come to put the just man wrongfully to death, publicly in the midst he is extinguished. So great a plague will be born in this place that the judges will be forced to flee.
Publiquement & du millieu estaint:	
Si grande peste en ce lieu viendra naistre,	
Que les jugeans¹ fouir seront contraint.	

ENGLAND, 1649–56

This quatrain is usually applied to England. It states that after someone is unjustly executed, a great plague occurs in that place causing the people who caused the death to flee. It is understood to describe Charles I who was beheaded in 1649, his death to be followed by the great plague of London 1655–6.

12

Le tant d'argent de Diane & Mercure	The great amount of silver of Diana & Mercury, the images will be found in the lake. The sculptor looking for new clay, both he and his followers will be soaked in gold.
Les simulacres au lac seront trouvez,	
Le figulier cherchant argille neufve	
Lui & les siens d'or seront abbrevez.	

Another treasure quatrain relating in particular to that in Toulouse of VIII. 28–30.

13

Les exilez autour de la Soulonge	The exiles around Sologne, led by night to march into Auxas, two from Moderna for the cruel one of Bolognia; put, discovered, by the fire of the Buzançais.
Condus de nuit pour marcher à Leuxois,	
Deux de Modene truculent² de Boulogne,	
Mis descouvers par feu de Burancois.	

¹ *jugeans* = judges, again invented by Nostradamus.
² *truculent*—From Latin, *truculentus* = ferocious, hard, cruel.

354

*Mis en planure chaulderone d'in-
    fecteurs,*[1]
*Vin, miel & l'huile, & bastis sur
    forneaulx*
*Seront plongez sans mal dit mal
    facteurs*
*Sept. fum extaint au canon des
    borneaux.*

The dyers' cauldrons put in a
flat place, wine, honey and oil
and built over furnaces. They
will be drowned, without saying
or doing an evil thing, seven of
Borneaux, the snake extinguished from the cannon.

A typical, unintelligible Nostradamus quatrain at its worst.

15

Pres de Parpan les rouges detenus
*Ceux du milieu parpondrez menez
    loing:*
*Trois mis en pieces, & cinq mal
    soustenus,*
*Pour le Seigneur & Prelat de
    Bourgoing.*

The red ones detained near
Perpignan, those in the middle,
ruined, led far away. Three cut
into pieces and five badly
supported for the Lord and
Prelate of Burgundy.

Perpignan belonged to Spain until 1659, and red was the colour
of the Spanish. Nostradamus seems to foresee a Franco-Spanish
struggle around the Pyrenees. The Governor of Burgundy, in
Nostradamus' time the Duke of Aumale died in 1573, the country
had four (not five) bishops under him.

16

De castel[2] *Franco sortira l'assem-
    blee*
*L'ambassadeur non plaisant fera
    scisme:*
Ceux de Ribiere seront en la meslee
*Et au grand goulphre desnier ont
    l'entree.*

From Castille Franco will bring
out the assembly, the ambassadors will not agree and cause a
schism. The people of Riviera
will be in the crowd, and the
great man will be denied entry
to the Gulf.

FRANCO AND DE RIVERA

This is an extraordinary verse with the names of two personages in
it. The Dictator Primo de Rivera and also Francisco Franco, who
helped depose him, and was exiled to Morocco, returning trium-
phantly when his party came to power. The last line is held to
describe Franco's exile when he was not allowed to cross the Medi-

---

[1] *infector*—Latin, dyer.
[2] *castel* = Castille.

355

terranean (*goulphre*) to his native Spain. Castel should be read a Castille. See III. 8.

Le tiers premier pis que ne fait Neron,	The third one firstly does worse than Nero, go, flow, brave
Vuidez vaillant que sang humain respandre:	human blood. The furnace will be rebuilt, a golden century;
R'edifier sera le forneron,	(then) death, a new king and
Siecle d'or, mort, nouveau roi grand esclandre.	great scandal.

THE FRENCH REVOLUTION

The third first is the National Convention of the Tiers État in Revolutionary France. Nostradamus describes it as being far crueller than Nero's reign with blood flowing freely from the guillotines. The machine will be put at the Place de la Révolution opposite the Tuileries, where formerly tile kilns were built. The golden century of the Kings Louis XIV–XVI is over! The great scandal is possibly a reference to the killing of the Royal Family. See also III. 59.

Le lis Dauffois portera dans Nancy Jusques en Flandres electeur de l'empire,	The lily of the Dauphin will be taken as far as Nancy, the elector of the empire as far as
Neufve obturee au grand Mont-morency,	Flanders. A new prison for the great Montmorency, to the
Hors lieux provez delivre à clere peyne.	usual place delivered up to Clerepeyne.

LOUIS XIII

Louis XIII was the first bearer of the lilies of France and the title of Dauphin since Nostradamus' death. He entered Nancy in September 1633. The city of Treves had been recovered the year before by the Maréchal d'Estrées who re-established the authority of the Elector. However in 1633 the Elector was carried off by the Spanish and taken as a prisoner to Brussels (*Flandres*). At the same time 1632, a revolt was led in southern France by the great Montmorency. His family pleaded for his release in vain, but did obtain the doubtful privilege of execution by a private, rather than public, executioner. He was beheaded in the court of the prison Hôtel de Ville, quite recently built, i.e. 'not in the usual place'. '*Delivre à clere peyne*' has two meanings. It means delivered to clear punishment, but also *clere peyne* is declared by some commentators to be the name of the executioner. A typical Nostradamus pun. I have not been able to verify the name. It first appears in a commentary by Jaubert, 1656.

19

Dans le millieu de la forest Meyenne,	In the middle of the Mayenne forest, the Sun in Leo, the
Sol au lyon la fouldre tombera.	lightning will fall. The great
Le grand bastard issu du Grand du Maine,	bastard born of the great man of Maine, on that day a point
Ce jour fougeres pointe en sang entrera.	will enter the blood of Fougères.

Mayenne in North-western France has a large forest west of the city. Fougères is about twenty miles further west, the seat of a great family bearing the name which died out in the 13th Century. It was used in the 15th Century by Diane de Poitiers, Henri II's mistress, and also by Henri III when he was still Duke of Anjou. No other great families are connected with the house, and the Fougères line was long dead, unfortunately for Nostradamus.

20

De nuict viendra par la forest de Reines,	By night will come through the forest of Reins two partners, by
Deux pars vaultort Herne[1] la pierre blanche,	a roundabout way, the Queen, the white stone. The monk-
Le maine noir[2] en gris dedans Varennes	King dressed in grey at Var- ennes the Elected Capet causes
Esleu cap. cause tempeste feu sang tranche.	tempest, fire and bloody slicing.

LOUIS XVI's FLIGHT TO VARENNES, 1791

The royal couple, Louis XVI and his wife, Marie Antoinette, will go by night through the forest of Reins, having fled from the Tuileries through a secret door in the Queen's apartment. They lost their way and chose an extremely bad route (*vaultort*), The *pierre blanche* probably refers to the affair of the diamond necklace which demolished Marie Antoinette's fragile popularity with the French people. It may also refer to the fact that her lady in waiting said that the Queen's hair turned white overnight, and that she normally wore white dresses. The King was wearing a

[1] *Herne*—Anagram for *Reine*.
[2] *noir*—Usual anagram for king.

simple grey suit (perhaps the word monk refers to his earlier impotence), when they entered Varennes. He was a Capet, an elected king, the first France had ever had, and as Nostradamus declares, was the cause of a revolution and the shedding of blood. *Tranche* is the verb meaning to slice, and the sound is particularly apposite in this context of the guillotine.

21

Au temple hault de Blois sacre Solonne,	At night, the high temple of Blois at Sacré Solonne a priest
Nuict pont de Loire, prelat, roi pernicant[1]	on the Loire bridge, a king dying; a messenger, victory for
Curseur[2] *victoire aux marestz de la lone*[3]	the marshes on the water. Destruction for a priestly gift
Don prelature de blancs à bormeant.[4]	from the whites.

Sacré Solonne is the church of Saint Solenne, the Cathedral at Blois. Nostradamus repeats in several quatrains his conviction that France would gain a king from Blois.

22

Roi & sa court au lieu de langue halbe,[5]	The king and his court in the place of the clever tongue, in
Dedans temple vis à vis du palais.	the temple, facing the palace.
Dans le jardin Duc de Mantor & d'Albe.	In the garden the Duke of Mantua and Alba, Alba and
Albe & Mantor poignard langue & palais.	Mantua dagger, tongue and the palace.

The key to this quatrain lies in the identities of Mantor and Alba. In 1536 the places of Alba and Mantua had been joined together by Charles V. The ruler from 1550-87 was Gonzaga who did suffer an assassination attempt at Casale, but not at Blois. Also the famous Château de Blois does not face the Cathedral.

[1] *pernicant*—From either Latin, *pernecare* = to kill, or *pernix* = swift.
[2] *curseur*—O.F. = runner, messenger.
[3] *lone*—Provençal, *lona* = a pool, still water.
[4] *abormeant*—Latin, *aboriri* = to miscarry. Provençal, *abouriment* = destruction.
[5] *halbe*—O.F., *habler* = to talk a lot.

Puisnay jouant au fresch dessouz la	The younger son playing out-
tonne,	doors under the arbour, the
Le hault du toict du milieu sur sa	top of the roof on the middle of
teste,	his head. The father king in the
Le pere roi au temple fait Solonne,	Temple is solemn, sacrificing,
Sacrifiant sacrera fum de feste.	he will consecrate the smoke of
	the feast.

LOUIS XVI AND HIS SON

The younger child is the second son of Louis XVI and his wife
who was allowed out to play in the Temple gardens while Louis
was imprisoned in a tower away from the rest of his family. Line 3
actually repeats this fact, and we continue on to the King's gloomy
future when he will be sacrificed to the Festival of Revolution.

24

Sur le palais au rochier[1] des	At the palace from the balcony
fenestres	of the windows, the two little
Seront ravis les deux petits royaux,	royal ones will be carried off.
Passer aurelle[2] Luthece[3] Denis	To pass Orléans, Paris and the
cloistres	cloisters of Saint Denis, a nun,
Nonain, mallods[4] avaller verts	the flies devouring the green
noiaulx.	pits.

St. Denis was about ten miles from Paris in Nostradamus' age. All
that is clear in this verse is the fact that two young royal children
are kidnapped.

[1] *rochier*—Derived from roche, and in the context of windows probably
means a balcony.

[2] *aurelle*—Latin Aurelianum, Orléans.

[3] *Luthece*—Latin, Lutetia, Paris.

[4] *mallods?*—O.F., malots = flies? malois = wicked? or Latin, malum =
an apple?

Passant les ponts venir pres des rosiers,[1]
Tard arrivé plustot qu'il cuidera,[2]
Viendront les noves[3] *espaingnolz à Beziers,*
Qui icelle chasse emprinse[4] *cassera.*

Crossing the bridges to come near the Roisiers, sooner than he thought, he arrived late. The new Spaniards will come to Béziers, so that this chase will break the enterprise.

Nostradamus' new Spaniards are the interesting point in this quatrain. Béziers was on the Spanish invasion route about fifty miles north-east of the pre-1659 border. The river is probably the one which became the Canal du Midi.

Nice sortie sur nom[5] *des letres aspres,*
La grande cappe[6] *sera present son sien,*
Proche de Vultry aux murs de vertes capres
Apres plombin[7] *le vent à bon essien.*

Departed by the bitter letters the surname of Nice, the great Cappe will present something, not his own; Near Voltai at the wall of the green columns, after Piombino the wind in good earnest.

De bois la garde vent chez rond pont sera,
Hault le receu frappera le Daulphin,
Le vieux teccon[8] *bois unis passera,*
Passent plus oultre du duc le droit confin.

The forester, the wind will be close around the bridge, received highly, he will strike the Dauphin. The old craftsman will pass through the woods in a company, going far beyond the right borders of the Duke.

LOUIS XVII

This quatrain may be another confirming the escape of the Dauphin who was reported dead in June 1795. It implies that he is taken out of France, but the method is very obscure. The possible

[1] *rosiers*—Either the place or rosebushes.
[2] *cuiderer*—O.F. = to think.
[3] *noves*—O.F. = new.
[4] *emprinse*—O.F. = enterprise.
[5] *sur nom*—Either surname or 'under the name of'.
[6] *cappe*—Referring to Pope as a Cope, modern French, Cape.
[7] *plombin*—Either of Piombino, or leaden, from lead.
[8] *teccon*—O.F. = a game played with a ball. Possibly from Gk., *tekton*, a craftsman?

reference to a ball game would be in context with amusing a ten-year-old child. See V. 1.

28

Voille Simacle[1] port Massiliolique,[2]	The Allied fleet from the port of
Dans Venice port marcher aux	Marseilles, in Venice harbour
Panons:	to march against Hungary. To
Partir du goulfre & Sinus[3]	leave from the gulf and the bay
Illirique,	of Illyria, devastation in Sicily,
Vast[4] à Socile, Ligures coups de	for the Ligurians, cannon shot.
canons.	

This quatrain covers a lot of ground, geographically. We have Panonia, Hungary, Marseilles, and the gulf of Illyria which is the Adriatic sea, but despite so many place names I cannot decipher it.

29

Lors que celui qu'à nul ne donne	When the man will give way to
lieu,	none, will wish to abandon a
Abandonner vouldra lieu prins non	place taken, yet not taken;
prins:	Ship afire through the swamps,
Feu nef par saignes, butiment[5] à	bitumen at Charlieu, St. Quin-
Charlieu,	tin and Calais will be recap-
Seront Quintin Balez[6] reprins.	tured.

CAPTURE OF CALAIS, 1558

The last line of this quatrain is interesting. The fall of Calais to the French was unexpected when the Duke de Guise recaptured it on 6th January 1558. St. Quentin was given back to the French in the general settlement of 1559.

[1] *Simacle*—Gk., *symmachos* = allied with, auxiliary.
[2] *Massiliolique*—Latin, *Masilioticus* = of Marseilles.
[3] *Sinus*—Latin = a bay.
[4] *Vast*—Latin, *vastum* = destruction, devastation.
[5] *butiment*—O.F. = bitumen—a mineral pitch, asphalt.
[6] *Balez*—Probably anagram for Calais.

*Au port de P.U.O.L.A. & de saint
  Nicolas,
Perir Normande au goulfre phana-
  tique,[1]
Cap.[2] de Bizance raues crier helas,
Secours de Gaddez[3] & du grand
  Philipique.*

At the port of Pola and Saint
Nicolo, a Normand will punish
in the Gulf of Quarnero: Cape
to cry alas in the streets of
Byzantium, help from Cadiz
and the great Philip.

All the places mentioned, except Cadiz, are in Yugoslavia. If
Philip is intended to be Philip II, Nostradamus was predicting a
Franco-Turkish attack on the Habsburgs in the south, with the
Spaniards helping against the French.

*Le tremblement de terre à Montara,
Cassich[4] saint George[5] à demi per-
  fondrez,
Paix assoupie, la guerre esveillera,
Dans temple à Pasques abismes
  enfondrez.*

The trembling of the earth at
Mortara the tin island of St.
George half sunk; drowsy with
peace, war will arise, at Easter
in the temple abysses opened.

The St. George islands here seem unlikely to be Great Britain
because it is unusual to suffer earthquakes so far outside the earthquake zone, and secondly an earthquake in Mortara would incur a
disturbance of over 1,000 miles from Britain. This one is left for
the reader.

[1] *phanatique?*—Latin, *Sinus Flanaticus* = the Gulf of Quaerno?
[2] *Cap*—Probably apocope of Capet, the French Royal line.
[3] *Gaddez*—Latin, *Gades* = Cadiz.
[4] *Cassich*—probably from Greek Cassiterides, the tin islands, a name
given to Cornwall and the Scilly Isles.
[5] *saint George*—Probably England, as he was adopted as patron saint
in the 14th Century.

De fin porphire profond collon trouvee
Dessoubz la laze¹ escriptz capitolin:²
Os poil retors Romain force prouvee,
Classe³ agiter ay port de Methelin.

A deep column of fine porphyry is found, inscriptions of the Capitol under the base; bones, twisted hair, the Roman strength tried, the fleet is stirred at the harbour of Mitylene.

Hercules Roi de Romme & d'Annemarc⁴
De Gaule trois Guion⁵ surnommé
Trembler l'Italie & l'unde de sainct Marc⁶
Premier sur tous monarque renommé.

Hercules, king of Rome and of 'Annemarc' three times the leader of France to be surnamed (de Gaule). Italy will tremble and the waters round St. Mark, the first to be renowned over all (the) kings.

Perhaps a reference to General de Gaulle? For Annemarc see also IV. 27.

Le part solus mari sera mitré,
Retour conflict passera sur le thuille:
Par cinq cens un trahir sera tiltré,
Narbon & Saulce par conteuax avons d'huile.

The partner, solitary but married, will be mitred, the return, fighting will cross over the Tuileries. By five hundred one traitor will be ennobled, Narbonne & Saulce, we will have oil for knives.

LOUIS XVI AND SAULCE

This is one of the most extraordinary of the quatrains. When Louis XVI and Marie Antoinette were stopped at Varennes (IX. 20) they passed the night at the house of a man named Saulce (line 4). The Sauces (modern spelling) have been chandlers and *marchands-épiciers* there since the 16th Century. The fact that the king alone is mitred refers to Louis' return to the Tuileries on 20th June 1792 when the mob invaded the palace, and the king

¹ *laz*—Greek = foot or base.
² *capitolin*—Belonging to the Capital of Rome—i.e. latin.
³ *Classe*—Latin, *classis* = fleet.
⁴ *Annemark?* Hungary and Bohemia, Moravia.
⁵ *Guion*. O.F. guide, chief, leader.
⁶ *Saint Marc*. Venice, of whom he is the patron.

was forced to wear the revolutionary cap of liberty, which looks very like a mitre. It is thought that *couteaux* in line 4 should be read as *quartants*, which means oil sold in retail, which was exactly what Saulce did. In Thiers' History of France, he states that the mob when they returned (*retour*) to the Tuileries (*thuile*), for a second time, numbered exactly five hundred. A very convincing quatrain.

35

Et Ferdinand blonde sera descorte,[1]	And the fair-haired Ferdinand
Quitter la fleur suivre le Macedon.[2]	will be detached to abandon the
Au grand besoin faillira sa routte,	flower and to follow the
Et marchera contre le Myrmidon.[3]	Macedonian. In great need
	his course will fail him and he
	will march against the Myrmi-
	dons.

FERDINAND OF BULGARIA, 20th CENTURY

This may well describe King Ferdinand of Bulgaria with the Macedonians, Germans and Greeks during the Second World War.

36

Un grand Roi prins entre les mains	A great king captured by the
d'un Joine,	hands of a young man, not far
Non loing de Pasque confusion coup	from Easter, confusion, a state
coultre:[4]	of the knife. Everlasting cap-
Perpet.[5] *captifs temps que fouldre*	tives, times when the lightning
en la husne,	is on the top, when three
Lorsque trois freres se blesseront &	brothers will be wounded and
meutre.	murdered.

KENNEDYS?

If this refers to the Kennedys, the theme of three bothers from America, which runs through the Prophecies, this verse indicates that the brothers are murdered and that this may happen around Easter. Since J. F. Kennedy died on 22nd November 1963 and Robert Kennedy on 6th June 1968, perhaps another assassination

[1] *descorte*—O.F. = detached, in disagreement.

[2] *Macedon*—Nostradamus probably means the Spanish.

[3] *Myrmidons*—Achilles' tribe, renowned for their obedience to all commands.

[4] *coultre*—Latin, *culter* = a knife.

[5] *Perpet*—Probably apopope of Latin, *Perpetualis* = everlasting.

364

may occur around April, with perhaps a storm thrown in, 'the lightning on the top'. Equally the lightning may refer to a gun on the top of a tall building, as happened at Dallas in 1963.

37

Pont & malins en Decembre versez,
En si haut lieu montera la Garonne:
Murs, edifices, Tholose renversez,
Qu'on ne scaura son lieu avant
  matronne.[1]

Bridges and milk overturned in December, the Garonne will rise to a very high place. Walls, buildings, Toulouse overthrown, so that none will know his place before Matronne.

38

L'entree de Blaye par Rochelle &
  l'Anglois,
Passeraontre le grand Aemathein[2]
Non loing d'Agen attendr le
  Gaulois,
Secours Narbonne deceu par entre-
  tien.

The entry at Blaye for la Rochelle and the English, the great Macedonia will pass beyond; not far from Agen the Gaul will wait,[3] help from Narbonne misled by a conversation.

39

En Arbissel à Veront[4] & Carcari,
De nuict conduitz pour Savonne
  attrapper,
Le vifz Gascon Turbi, & la
  Scerry
Derrier mur vieux & neuf palais
  gripper.

In Albisobla to Veront & Carcara, led by night to seize Savona, the swift Gascon, La Turbie and l'Escarene, to seize the old and new palace behind the wall.

[1] matronne—May well be disguised place name.
[2] Aemathein—Latin, Emathia = poetic name for Macedonia and Thessaly.
[3] will wait—Alternatively, he will wait for the Frenchman . . .
[4] Veront—Not Verona as other places close to Albisola; unsolved place name?

Pres de Quintin dans la forest
bourlis[1]
Dans l'abbaye seront Flamens
ranches,[2]
Les deux puisnays de coups mi
estourdis
Suitte oppressee & garde tous
aches.

Near St. Quentin, deceived in
the forest, in the Abbey the
Flemish will be cut up. The two
youngest half-stunned by blows,
their followers crushed, and the
guard all cut to pieces.

BATTLE OF ST. QUENTIN, 1557

Before the battle of St. Quentin in 1557 the Spaniards seized the
Abbey of Vermandois: this was followed by the battle on 10th
August 1557.

41

Le grand Chyren[3] soi saisir
Avignon,
De Romme letres en miel plein
d'amertume.
Letre ambassade partir de Chanig-
non,[4]
Carpentras pris par duc noir rouge
plume.

The great 'Chyren' will seize
Avignon, from Rome will come
honeyed letters full of bitter-
ness. The letter and embassy to
leave from Chanignon, Carpentras taken by the Black
Duke with the red feather.

Henri II is here seen to capture Avignon, which belonged to the
Papacy, but unfortunately it did not come into French hands
until 1791, although it was twice occupied in 1663-4 and 1768-74.
The letters are doubtless from an irate Vatican. Chanignon is still
undeciphered. Carpentras is near Avignon and was part of the
Pope's lands.

[1] bourlis?—Possibly a proper name or derivative of boucle = deceived?
[2] ranches—Error for tranches in all editions.
[3] Chyren—Anagram for Henryc?
[4] Chanignon—Unsolved place or proper name.

De Barcellonne, de Gennes & *Venise,*	From Barcelona, from Genoa and Venice, from Sicily a
De la Secille peste Monet¹ unis	pestilence allied with Monaco;
Contre Barbare classe² prendront la *vise*	they will take aim against the barbarian fleet, the barbarian
Barbare, pulse bien loing jusqu'à *Thunis.*	driven as far back as Tunis.

BATTLE OF LEPANTO, 7th OCTOBER 1571

This prophecy was well fulfilled in 1571 when the allied fleets of the Papacy, Venice and Spain crushed the Turks at Lepanto. By 1573 Don John of Austria the leader of the expedition went on to recapture Tunis. Much of the Turkish fleet was composed of ships from their ally the Algerian Barbari, or pirates.

43

Proche à descendre l'armee Cruci- *gere³*	Ready to land, the army of the Cross will be watched for by the
Sera guettez par les Ismaëlites⁴	Ismaelites; struck from all sides
De tous cottez batus par nef *Raviere⁵*	by the ship Raviere, quickly attacked by ten chosen galleys.
Prompt assaillis de dix galeres *eslites.*	

This is probably a continuation of the last quatrain.

44

Migres migre de Genesve trestous,	Leave, leave Geneva everyone,
Saturne d'or en fer se changers,	Saturn will change from gold
Le contre RAYPOZ⁶ exterminera *tous,*	into iron. Those against RAYPOZ will all be exterminated.
Avant l'a ruent de ciel signes fera.	Before the rush the sky will show signs.

---

¹ *Monet*—Unusual spelling for Monech, Monaco from Latin, *Herculi Monoeciis.*

² *classe*—Latin = fleet.

³ *Crucigere*—Bearing a cross, a Crusader.

⁴ *Ismaëlites*—Biblical name for the Arabs.

⁵ *Raviere*—O.F., *raviere* = impetuosity. Nostradamus must be hinting at an unsolved name here.

⁶ *RAYPOZ*—An anagram, but not solved except for one suggestion. Zopyre who betrayed Babylon to Darius.

Geneva was famous in Nostradamus' time as being the Protestant equivalent of the Vatican because Calvin made it his centre. Nostradamus is either warning the victims of a Calvinist purge, or warning them that they will be attacked by Philip II. Raypoz is another unsolved personal name.

45

Ne sera soul jamais de demander,
Grand Mendosus¹ obtiendra son Empire
Loing de la cour fera contremander,
Pimond, Picard, Paris, Tyrron² le pire.

There will never be a single person to ask, great Mendosus will attain his Empire. Far from the court he will have countermanded Piedmont, Picardy, Paris, Tuscany the worst.

Mendosus is an anagram for the family of Vendôme, earlier spelt Vendosme, in which case the quatrain should describe either Henri IV, or his father Anthony de Navarre, Duke de Vendosme. Unfortunately despite this excellent lead the rest of the quatrain is very obscure. Piedmont was Italian and belonged to Savoy, Picardy is a Normandy province of France.

46

Vuidez, fuyez de Tholose les rouges
Du sacrifice faire expiation,
Le chef du mal dessouz l'ombre des courges
Mort estranger carne omination.³

Be gone, flee from Toulouse the red ones, make expiation for the sacrifice. The main cause of evil in the shadow of the gourds, dead, to strangle the prognostication of flesh.

47

Les soulz signez d'indigne delivrance,
Et de la multe auront contre advis,
Change monarque mis en perille pence,⁴
Serrez en caige se verront vis à vis.

The undersigned to an infamous delivery, and receiving contrary advice from the crowds; a monarch changes, thoughts are put in danger, shut in a cage they will see each other face to face.

¹ Mendosus—Erroneous, or an anagram for Vendosme, the Bourbon branch who won the French throne in 1594.
² Tyrron—Probably from Latin, Tyrrheni = the Etruscans.
³ carne ominatio—Prognostic of flesh.
⁴ pence—This may either be from penser, to think, or if Nostradamus knew some English, pence.

Possibly this quatrain can be applied to Francis II, 1559–60?

48

La grand cité d'occean maritime,	The great city of the maritime
Environnee de maretz en cristal:	ocean, surrounded by a swamp
Dans le solstice hyemal[1] & la prime[2]	of crystal; in the winter solstice and the spring will be tried by a
Sera tempté de vent espouvantal.	dreadful wind.

This is described by Allen (1943) as the destruction of Central Park, and by Boswell (1941) as the destruction of Tokyo, but by Russian chemical bombs. The latter was almost correct in his own prediction i.e. Nagasaki and Hiroshima 1945.

49

Gand & Bruceles marcheront contre Envers	Ghent and Brussels march against Antwerp; the Parlia-
Senat du Londres mettront à mort leur Roi	ment of London will put their king to death; the salt and wine
Le sel & vin lui seront à l'envers,	will oppose him; because of
Pour eux avoir le regne en dessarroi.	them he will have the kingdom in trouble.

EXECUTION OF CHARLES I, 1649

This quatrain implies that lines 1 and 2 are simultaneous. Charles I was executed in 1649 new style, or 1648, old style, when New Year's day was held on 25th March. Philip IV made great attempts to reconquer the Netherlands but by 1648 they were anxious to get the Dutch out of the war, and ceded to them several key towns. By doing this, they closed the Scheldt which ruined Antwerp. Note that the quatrain is also numbered 49, the date of King Charles' death, a very fortunate coincidence. See VIII. 37.

50

Mandosus tost viendra à son hault regne	Mendosus will soon come to his great reign putting behind
Mettant arriere un peu de Nolaris:	somewhat the Nolaris; the pale
Le rouge blaisme, le masle à l'interregne	red one, the man in the in- terregnum, the frightened
Le jeune crainte & frayeur Barbaris.	young man and the fear of the Barbaric ones.

[1] *hymal*—Latin, *hiemalis* of winter.
[2] *prime*—O.F., springtime.

Mendosus as we saw in IX. 45 and X. 18, is an anagram of Vendosme, and Nolaris one of the Lorraine, the home of the Guise family. The quatrain says that Vendosme, Henri IV, will soon come to the throne and relegate the house of Guise to the wings. The '*rouge blesme*' is probably the old Cardinal of Bourbon, pallid from age and red in his Cardinal's robes. He was proclaimed King Charles X in 1589 but died the next year. The '*masle*' is the Duke de Mayenne who was Lieutenant-General during the interregnum. The young man is the Duke de Guise, and Barbaris is Philip II of Spain who claimed the throne of France through his daughter Isabella.

51

Contre les rouges sectes se banderont,	Against the red ones sects will unite, fire, water, iron, the rope will weaken through peace. Those who plot are at the point of dying except one who above all will ruin the world.
Feu, eau, fer, corde par paix se minera,[1]	
Au point mourir, ceux qui machineront,	
Fors un que monde surtout ruinera.	

20th CENTURY

This quatrain must have a 20th-Century interpretation. The Reds here fit in a modern politico-social setting better than anywhere else. The conditions described existed between the two World Wars. In line 1 are Fascism, Nazism, Communism etc., and in line 2 the rope obviously refers to the Corde Sanitaire. Line 3 describes the wretched western statesmen, most of whom were appeasers like Chamberlain and Pétain. The exception is Hitler in line 4 who certainly attempted to fulfil this prediction.

52

La paix s'approche d'un costé, & la guerre	Peace approaches from one side; and war never was the pursuit of it so great. Men and women moan, innocent blood on the land, and this will be throughout the whole of France.
Oncques ne feut la poursuitte si grande,	
Plaindre homme, femme, sang innocent par terre	
Et ce fera de France à toute bande.	

PEACE OF CATEAU CAMBRESIS, 1559

On 13th April 1559, the King of France declared that he would stop fighting the Spanish and turn his attention to liquidating the

[1] *se miner*—O.F. = to ruin, destroy, spoil.

heretics in France. The peace is between France and Spain, the war the civil war between Catholics and Huguenots, declaring a time of bloodshed for all of France.

53

Le Neron jeune dans les trois cheminées	In three chimneys the young Nero will make the living pages thrown out to burn. He is happy who will be far from such happenings; three of his family will ambush him to death.
Fera de paiges vifs pour ardoir[1] getter,[2]	
Hereux qui loing sera de telz menees,	
Trois de son sang le feront mort guetter.	

There is one record of a young man being thrown into a fireplace by his prince in the historical novels of Rafael Sabatini; otherwise I can offer no clue.

54

Arrivera au port de Corsibonne,[3]	There will arrive at Porto Corsini, near Ravenna, one who will plunder the lady. The legate from Lisbon in the deep sea; hidden under a rock they will carry off seventy souls.
Pres de Ravenne qui pillera la dame,	
En mer profonde legat de la Ullisbonne	
Souz roc cachez raviront septante ames.	

The Dame here may well be the Catholic Church that is plundered at Porto Corsini, eight miles north of Ravenna.

55

L'horrible guerre qu'en l'occident s'apreste	The dreadful war which is prepared in the West, the following year the pestilence will come, so very horrible that young, nor old, nor animal (will survive) blood, fire, Mercury, Mars, Jupiter in France.
L'an ensuivant viendra la pestilence,	
Si fort horribles que jeune, vieux, ne beste,	
Sang, feu, Mercure, Mars, Jupiter en France.	

[1] *ardoir*—O.F. = to burn.
[2] *getter*—O.F. spelling of *jeter* = to throw.
[3] *Corsibonne* = Porto Corsino, the port of Ravenna.

This quatrain is usually applied to the First World War which was followed by the dreadful influenza epidemic of 1917–18, governed by the conjunction of Mercury, Mars and Jupiter.

56

Camp pres de Noudam passera Goussan ville,	The army near Noudan will pass Goussainville, and will
Et à Maiotes[1] laissera son ensigne,	leave its mark at Maiotes; in an
Convertira en instant plus de mille,	instant more than a thousand
Cherchant les deux remettre en chaine & legne.[2]	will be converted, looking for the two to put back chain and firewood(?).

Houdan and Goussainville are both to the west of Paris. But Maiotes is still unsolved and I cannot find a clear meaning for *legne.*

57

Au lieu de DRUX[3] un Roi reposira,	In the place of DRUX a king
Et cherchera loi changeant d'Anatheme,	will rest, and will look for a law to change Anathema. While the
Pendant le ciel si tres fort tonnera,	sky thunders so loudly the king
Porter neufve Roi tuera soimesme.	will kill himself at the new gate.

58

Au costé gauche à l'endroit de Vitry	To the left side of the place of
Seront guettez les trois rouges de France;	Vitry the three red ones of France will be watched. All
Tous assomez rouge, noir non murdri	those killed red, the black not murdered, in safety reassured
Par les Bretons remis en asseurence.	by the Bretons.

[1] *Maiotes*—Either a place name, Mantes? or from the Greek, *memaotes* = keen soldiers.
[2] *legne*—Possibly Provençal, *legna* = firewood, Loomis?
[3] *DRUX*—Possibly anagram for Dreux?

A la Ferté prendra la Vidame
Nicol tenu rouge qu'avoit produit la
vie.
La grand Loisne naistra que fera
clame.[1]
Donnant Bourgongne à Bretons par
envie.

At the Ferté Vidame he will take, Nicol the red who had produced life; to the great Louise who acts secretly one will be born, who gives Burgundy to the Bretons through envy.

Conflict Barbar en la Cornere noire.
Sang espandu trembler la d'Almatie,
Grand Ismaël[2] *mettra son pro-*
montoire,
Ranes[3] *trembler secours Lusitanie.*

In a black head-dress the Barbarian fights, blood shed, Dalmatia trembles. The great Ismaël will make his promontory, Frogs tremble under aid from Portugal.

La pille faite à la coste marine,
La cita nova & parents amenez
Plusieurs de Malte par le fait de
Messine,
Estroit serrez seront mal guardon-
nez.

The plunder taken on the sea coast, in the new city and relations brought forward; Several of Malta through the deeds of Messina, will be closely shut up, poorly rewarded.

Au grand de Cheramon agora
Seront croisez par ranc tous
attachez,
Le pertinax[4] *Oppie,*[5] *& Man-*
dragora,[6]
Rougon[7] *d'Octobre le tiers seront*
laschez.

To the great one of Cheramon agora will all the crosses by rank be attached, the long lasting Opium and Mandrake, the Rougon will be released on October the third.

MAGIC PRACTICES?

A very odd verse. Ceramon-agora was actually the name of a town in Asia Minor which is believed to be present-day Usak.

[1] *clame*—Latin, *clam* = secretly.
[2] *Ismaël* = An ancestor of the Arab nation, therefore Arabs.
[3] *ranes*—Latin, *rama* = a frog.
[4] *pertinax*—Latin = long lasting.
[5] *Oppie*—Greek = opium.
[6] *Mandragoras*—Gk. = mandrake.
[7] *Rougon*—Unsolved place name.

Both the herbs of opium and mandrake had mysterious virtues and were used in occult practices.

63

Plainctes & pleurs cris & grands urlemens	Complaints and tears, cries and great howls, near Narbonne and Bayonne and in Foix; oh what dreadful calamities and changes, before Mars has revolved a few times.
Pres de Narbon à Bayonne & en Foix	
O quel horrible calamitz changemens,	
Avant que Mars revolu quelques fois.	

Each revolution of Mars lasts 687 days, which may be relevant if the quatrain is to be taken literally. The rest is obscure.

64

L'Aemathion[1] passer montz Pyrenees,	The Aemathian will cross the Pyrenees in March, Narbonne will not make any resistance. He will carry on a very great intrigue by land and sea, Cap. having no land in which to stay safely.
En Mars Narbon ne fera resistance,	
Par mer & terre fera si grand menee	
Cap.[2] n'ayant terre seure pour demeurance.	

65

Dedans le coing de luna[3] viendra rendre,	He will come to take himself to the corner of Luna, where he will be taken and placed on foreign land. The unripe fruit will be the subject of great scandal, great blame, to the other great praise.
Ou sera prins & mis en terre estrange,	
Les fruitz immeurs seront à la grand esclandre	
Grand vitupere à l'un grande louange.	

SPACE RACE?

If Luna is to be taken literally as the moon, this quatrain makes surprising sense. The first two lines describe the astronaut deliberately going to the moon, 'taken' in his capsule and landing. The 'unripe fruit' may intend to imply that the rockets are not yet

[1] *Aemathian*—Either Macedonian or Thessaly as before IX. 38.
[2] *Cap.*—Nostradamus' usual shortening of the Capetian name of the French royal line.
[3] *luna*—Possibly Lunigiana, or even the Moon?

374

ready for such intensive flight. The scandals and blame are the deaths and dangers suffered by all astronauts whether American or Russian. Note that Nostradamus is aware that one country or side gets great praise and benefit from the space race, but that the other receives only blame from its citizens. The USA has halted its space programme while that of the USSR is continuing apace.

66

Paix, union sera & changement,	There will be peace, union and
Estatz, offices bas hault, & hault bien bas.	change, estates and offices (that were) low, (are) high,
Dresser voyage le fruict premier torment,	those high, very low. To prepare for a journey torments the
Guerre cesser, civil proces debatz.	first child; war to cease, legal processes, debates.

This could apply to any post-war period.

67

Du hault des montz à l'entour de Lizer	From the top of the mountains around Isère, a hundred
Port à la roche Valen cent assemblez	assembled at the gate to the Valencian rock; from Château-
De chasteau neuf pierre late en donzere	neuf, Pierrelatte, in Douzère; against the Crest, Romans
Contre le crest Romans foi assemblez.	assembled in faith.

Crest is probably a shortening of Chrestiens, Christians, which makes this obscure verse imply some sort of religious strife.

68

Du mont Aymar[1] sera noble obscurcie,	The noble of Mount Aymar will become obscure, the evil
Le mal viendra au joinct de sonne & rosne.[2]	will come at the junction of the Saone and the Rhône, soldiers
Dans bois caichez soldatz jour de Lucie,[3]	hidden in the woods on Lucy's day, there never was so horrible
Qui ne fut onc un si horrible throsne.	a throne.

[1] *Mont Aymar*—Possibly Montelimart? or by the mountain of slaughter.
[2] Junction of the rivers is at Lyons.
[3] *Lucie*—St. Lucy's day, 13th December.

375

Two facts are obvious in this quatrain, Lyons and December the 13th. This is probably describing the sack of Lyons in 1793 which was performed by the Revolutionary soldiers and was a great scandal at the time. Mount Aymar is still unclear.

69

Sur le mont de Bailly & la Bresle[1]
Seront caichez de Grenoble les fiers,
Oultre Lyon, Vien. eulx si grande gresle,
Langoult[2] en terre n'en restera un tiers.

On the mountain of Sain Bel and l'Arbresle[1] will be hidden the proud people of Grenoble Beyond Lyons, at Vienne there will be such great hail, locust on the land, not a third of it will remain.

70

Harnois trenchant dans les flambeaux cachez
Dedans Lyon le jour du Sacremont,[3]
Ceux de Vienne seront trestous hachez
Par les cantons Latins[4] Mascon ne ment.

Sharp armour hidden in the torches at Lyons, on the day of the sacrament; all those of Vienne will be cut to pieces by the Latin cantons, Mâcon does not lie.

71

Au lieux sacrez animaux veu à trixe,[5]
Avec celui qui n'osera le jour:
A Carcassonne pour disgrace propice,
Sera posé pour plus ample sejour.

Animals with hair seen at the holy places with one who does not dare (to face) the day; Carcassonne is suitable for the disgrace, and will be left for a longer stay.

[1] The most likely two combinations.

[2] langoult—O.F., langouste = a locust, not a lobster as in modern French.

[3] jour du Sacrament—Understood as Corpus Christi, the first Thursday after Trinity Sunday.

[4] Latins—Possibly the Grisoné where most of the Italian-speaking Swiss live.

[5] trixe—Greek, thrix = hair or wool, possibly sheep in this context?

Encor seront les saincts temples pollus,	Again the holy temples will be polluted and plundered by the
Et expillez par Senat Tholossain,	Senate of Toulouse; Saturn
Saturne deux trois cicles revollus,	having completed two or three
Dans Avril, Mai, gens de nouveau levain.[1]	cycles in April and May there will be people of a new leaven.

The cycle of Saturn is 29·5 years, so two or three cycles can be added presumably to the date of the sack of Toulouse. Nostradamus appears to think that the Calvinists will take over and despoil the churches. It is possible that line 3 means two × three cycles of Saturn, i.e. six, which would be 177 years, a figure Nostradamus mentions also in the Preface.

Dans Foix entrez Roi ceiulee[2] *Turbao,*	The king enters Foix wearing a blue turban, he will reign for
Et regnera moins revolu Saturne,	less than a revolution of Saturn;
Roi Turban blanc Bisance coeur ban,	the king with the white turban, his heart banished to Byzan-
Sol, Mars, Mercure pres de la hurne.[3]	tium, Sun, Mars and Mercury near Aquarius.

18th FEBRUARY 1981

This verse apparently describes a Moslem or Eastern invasion, because of the turbans. Foix is understood to belong to a blue-turbaned man, king for less than 29·5 years. Then the white figure appears, in some way connected with Constantinople (Byzantium). According to McCann (1942) this quatrain is dated by the planets as 18th February 1981.

[1] *levain*—i.e. Protestants disputing the Eucharist.
[2] *ceiulee*—Latin, *caeruleus* = blue.
[3] *hurne*—Variant spelling of *l'urne*, Aquarius.

377

Dans la cité de Fersod[1] homicide,
Fait & fait multe beuf arant ne
macter,[2]
Retour encores aux honneurs d'Arte-
mide,
Et à Vulcan corps morts sepultures.[3]

In the homicidal city of Fertsod, again and again many
oxen plough, not sacrificed;
again a return to the honours of
Artemis, and to Vulcan the
corpses of the dead to bury.

De l'Ambraxie & du pays de
Thrace
Peuple par mer mal & secours
Gaulois,
Perpetuelle en Provence la trace,
Avec vestiges de leur coustume &
loix.

From Arta & the country of
Thrace, people ill by sea, help
from the Gauls; in Provence
their perpetual trace and rem-
nants of their customs and laws.

This seems to describe the Greeks returning to ask aid from
Southern France, and particularly Provence, of which their early
colonial settlers were particularly fond.

Avec le noir[4] Rapax & sanguin-
aire,
Issu du peaultre[5] de l'inhumain
Neron
Emmi[6] deux fleuves main gauche
militaire,
Sera murtri par Joine cheulveron.[7]

With the rapacious and bloody
king, sprung from the pallet of
inhuman Nero; between two
rivers, the military on the left
hand, he will be murdered by a
bald young man.

[1] *Fertsod?—La Ferté—*Sodom?
[2] *macter,* Latin, *mactare* = to slaughter.
[3] *sepultrer—*O.F. to bury.
[4] Anagram for *roi,* king, or the black one?
[5] *peaultre* = pallet, brothel, rudder, (Laver).
[6] *emmi—*O.F., = between.
[7] *chaulveron—*Diminutive of *chauve* = bald.

Le regne prins le Roi conujera,[1]
La dame prinse à mort jurez à sort,
La vie à Roine fils on desniera,
Et la pellix[2] *au sort de la consort.*

The kingdom taken, the King will plot, the lady taken to death by those sworn by lot; they will refuse life to the Queen's son, and the mistress suffers the same fate as the wife.

FATE OF MARIE ANTOINETTE AND MME. DU BARRY

After the Royal Family's imprisonment, Louis XVI was executed in January 1793. He was condemned by the Convention who elected these powers to itself. However, the Queen, who was not executed until the following October, had a newly created revolutionary tribunal to judge her which was served by a jury selected by lot. This was an institution unknown to France in Nostradamus' day. The third line tells the fate of Louis XVII whether he died or lived abroad is irrelevant, his kingdom was denied to him. Finally the most interesting line of all. While the Queen was imprisoned in the Conciergerie, the old mistress of Louis XV, Mme. du Barry, was taken for a while to the prison of Sainte Pelagie. An impressive quatrain.

La dame Greque de beauté laydique,[3]
Hereuse faicte de procs innumerable,
Hors translater au regne Hispanique,
Captive prinse mourir mort miserable.

The Greek lady of the beauty of Lais is made happy by innumerable suitors; transferred out to the Spanish kingdom she is captive taken to die a wretched death.

It has been suggested that the incomparable lady is in fact democracy, which was founded in Greece, and which starts to die out in Europe beginning with Spain in 1936.

[1] *conjuera*—Alternative, will make advances?
[2] *pellex*—Latin = mistress or concubine.
[3] *laydique*—Lais was the most beautiful woman in Corinth. Possibly means ugly from *laid*?

Le chef de la classe[1] par fraude
   stratageme,
Fera timides sortir de leurs galleres,
Sortis meutris chef renieur de
   cresme,
Puis par l'embusche lui rendront les
   saleres.

The leader of the fleet through deceitful trickery will make the scared ones come out of their galleys. Come out, murdered, the leader to renounce the holy oil. Then through an ambush they give him his deserts.

80

Le Duc voudra les siens exterminers
Envoyera les plus forts lieux
   estranges,
Par tyrannie Pize & Luc ruinera,
Puis les Barbares sans vin feront
   vendanges.

The Duke will wish to kill his followers, he will send the strongest to the strangest places; through tyranny he ruins both Pisa and Lucca, then the Barbarians will harvest grapes without wine.

81

Le Roi rusé entendra ses embusches
De trois quartiers ennemis affaillir,
Un nombre estranges larmes de
   coqueluches[2]
Viendra Lemprin[3] du traducteur
   faillir.

The crafty king will understand his ambushes, from three sides the enemies threaten; a large amount of strange tears from the hooded (ones), the splendour of the translator will fail.

Perhaps the translator in this quatrain is the same as in IX. 1, in trouble with the church and the state?

82

Par le deluge & pestilence forte
La cité grande de long temps
   assiegee,
La sentinelle & garde de main
   morte,
Subite prinse, mais de nul oultragee.

By the flood and the great plague the great city is assailed for a long time. The sentry guard killed by hand, sudde captured, but none wronged.

Another vague, general quatrain; a great city which is suffering from the plague and flooding, is seized by a surprise attack at night.

[1] classe—Latin = fleet.
[2] coqueluches = hooded men, i.e. monks.
[3] Lemprin?—Greek, lampros = splendour.

Sol vingt de Taurus si fort terre trembler.	The sun in twenty degrees of Taurus, there will be a great
Le grand theatre rempli ruinera,	earthquake; the great theatre
L'air ciel & terre obscuroir & troubler	full up will be ruined. Darkness and trouble in the air, on sky
Lors l'infidelle Dieu & sainctz voguera.	and land, when the infidel calls upon God and the Saints.

AN EARTHQUAKE ON 10th APRIL

The day but not the year of this great earthquake is given; such an apocalyptic verse makes one think of the Los Angeles fault. 'Sol vingt de Taurus' means twenty days after the sun moves into Taurus which is April 10th

Roi exposé parfaira l'hecatombe,	The king discovered will complete the slaughter once he has
Apres avoir trouvé son origine,	found his origin: a torrent to
Torrent ouvrir de marbre & plomb la tombe	open the tomb of marble and lead, of a great Roman with the
D'un grand Romain d'enseigne Medusine.[1]	Medusine device.

TOMB OF ST. PETER?

Yet another verse about the discovery of a tomb. The key lies in the word Medusine. If it is an anagram of Deus in me, this would mean it was the real tomb of St. Peter, as that was his emblem, and that the one which was declared to be found some years ago is of another early Pope.

Passer Guienne, Languedoc & le Rosne,	To pass Guienne, Languedoc and the Rhône from Agen,
D'Agen tenans de Marmande & la Roole,	holding Marmande and La Réole; to open the wall through
D'ouvrir par foi par roi[2] *Phocen*[3] *tiendra son trosne*	the king, Marseilles will hold its throne a battle near St.
Conflit aupres saint Pol de Mauseole.[4]	Paul-de-Mausole.

---

[1] *Medusine*—Device of Medusa? Device of Pegasus? Device of 'Deus in me'?

[2] *par roi*—Possibly *parroi* = wall?

[3] *Phocen* = Marseilles.

[4] *St. Paul de Mausole*—A convent, then an asylum (where Van Gogh stayed) just outside St. Rémy.

Du bourg Lareyne ne parviendront droit à Chartres	From Bourge-la-Reine they will not come straight to Chartres,
Et feront pres du pont Anthoni panse,[1]	they will pause near the Pont d'Anthony: seven as crafty as
Sept pour la paix cantelleux comme martres.	martens for peace they will enter with weapons into a
Feront entree d'armee à Paris clause.	closed Paris.

3rd JULY 1815

The seven allied nations who joined against Napoleon were Austria, England, Prussia, Portugal, Sweden, Spain and Russia, they entered Paris on 3rd July 1815. The city was stripped of its troops when the French army was evacuated to Chartres taking up positions on the way to the Loire, passing Bourge-la-Reine and the Pont d'Anthony under which it is reputed to have camped.

Par la forest du Touphon[2] essartee,	In the cleared forest of Tou-
Par hermitage sera posé le temple,	phon the temple will be placed
Le duc d'Estampes par sa ruse inventee,	near the hermitage. The Duke of Étampes through the ruse he
Du mont Lehori prelat donra exemple.	invented will give an example to the priest of Montlhery.

The clue to this verse probably lies in the title in line 3. Three of the kings of France's greatest mistresses held the title, first Anne de Pisseleu, then Diane de Poitiers, and later Henri IV's Gabrielle d'Estrées. I cannot get any further with this.

[1] panse. should be *pause* to rhyme with line 4.
[2] *Touphon*—Doubtful. There is a place called Forfou but it has no forest. Possibly from the Gk., *tophion* = a plaster quarry, or French, *touffe* = a clump.

Calais, Arras secours à Theroanne,	Calais & Arras help to·Théro-
Paix & semblant simulera les-	uanne, the spy will simulate
coutte,[1]	peace and semblance; the
Soulde[2] *d'Alabrox*[3] *descendre par*	soldiers of Savoy go down by
Roane	Roanne; those people who
Destornay peuple qui deffera le	would stop the rout turned
routte.[4]	away.

1557

This quatrain must be dated 1557 since Calais fell to the French in 1558. Both Arras and Théronanne belonged to Spain. When Calais fell, Philip II, husband of the English Queen, lost all rights to Calais. On 5th February 1556 the Treaty of Vaucelles was declared between France and Spain. Therefore this quatrain was probably written between the Truce and the Spanish attack of 1557. Savoy (Allobrox) was almost completely French occupied at this period, so it is possible that a garrison of soldiers was sent up after St. Quentin. The borders of Savoy were only thirty-five miles from Rouanne.

89

Sept ans sera Philip fortune pro-	Fortune will favour Philip for
spere,	seven years, he will cut down
Rabaissera des Arabes l'effaict,	again the exertions of the
Puis son midi[5] *perplex rebours*	Arabs. Then, in the middle a
affaire	perplexing, contrary affair,
Jeune ognion[6] *abismera son fort.*	young Ogmios will destroy his
	stronghold.

LOUIS PHILIPPE, 1830–48

The first seven years of Louis Philip's reign, 1830–8 were extremely fortunate. He managed to subdue the Arabs and consolidate the French occupation of Algeria. In the middle of his reign, 1838–40, he will be troubled by the Eastern question and the result will be shameful for him. Finally the French proclaiming the new republic, 24th February 1848, will dethrone him and keep him under guard.

[1] *l'escoute*—O.F. = a spy.
[2] *soulde*—O.F. = pay or mercenaries.
[3] *Allobrox* = classical inhabitants of Savoy.
[4] *routte*—Either O.F., *route* = rout; or *route*—road?
[5] *son midi*—Either in middle age, or to the South?
[6] *ogmios*—The Celtic Hercules.

Un capitaine de la grand Ger-
manie
Se viendra rendre par simulé
secours
Un roi des rois aide de Pannonie,[1]
Que sa revolte fera de sang grand
cours.

A captain of the greater Germany will come to deliver false
help; king of kings; to support
Hungary; His war will cause a
great shedding of blood.

HITLER

The Greater Germany sounds uncannily like the Grossendeutsch-
land of Hitler's Third Reich. The second line is brilliant. Hitler
invaded Poland under the pretence of giving help, as Nostradamus
says elsewhere. Hitler for a time was a king of kings, lord of all he
surveyed. He also captured Hungary and the war he started killed
about 14 million people among the soldiers of both sides, and
according to some estimates as many again among the civilian
population, and quite probably more.

L'horrible peste Perynte[2] *& Nico-*
polle,[3]
Le Chersonnez[4] *tiendra & Marcel-*
oyne,[5]
La Thessalie vastera l'Amphi-
polle,[6]
Mal incogneu & le refus d'Anthoine.

The dreadful plague at Perinthus and Nicopolis will take the
Peninsula and Macedonia; it
will lay waste Thessaly and
Amphipolis, an unknown evil,
and refused by Anthony.

The Anthony here may be Anthony of Navarre, father of Henri IV,
but the setting of the quatrain in Greece makes this unlikely.

[1] *Panonia*—Classical Hungary.
[2] *Perinthus*—Modern Eski Eregli
[3] *Nicopolis*—Modern Preveza.
[4] *Chersonnez*—Either the Gallipoli peninsular (Chersonese) or the
Poloponnesus.
[5] *Marceloyne*—Probably error for Macedoine.
[6] *Amphipolis*—Near modern Salonika.

Le roi vouldra dans cité neuf entrer	The king will want to enter the
Par ennemis expugner[1] lon viendra	new city, they come to subdue
Captif libere faulx dire & per-	it through its enemies; a captive
petrer	falsely freed to speak and act;
Roi dehors estre, loin d'ennemis	the king to be outside, he will
tiendra.	stay far from the enemy.

NEW YORK?

This may refer to New York, as in I. 87, VI. 97 and X. 89, and continue the three quatrains describing the city being attacked during the next war. This is a logical possibility which must be futuristic as it has not occurred to date. The king far from the enemy is probably the President in some secret underground shelter from which he will continue to direct the war.

Les ennemis du fort bien eslongnez,	The enemies are very far from
Par chariots conduict le bastion,	the strong man, the bastion is
Par sur les murs de Bourges	brought by wagons. Above the
esgrongnez,	crumbled walls of Bourges
Quand Hercules battra l'Haema-	when Hercules strikes the
thion.[2]	Macedonian.

LOUIS XIV

This quatrain tells that when Aemathion, who can here stand for Louis XIV, has pushed back his enemies and consequently enlarged the borders of France, bastions of earth were constructed in the fortification system of Vauban. At this time Bourges falls into decay when its Grosse Tour (great tower) fell into ruin during Louis' reign. The final line refers to a labour of Hercules, which was in this case the lengthy Languedoc canal. Started in 1666 and finished in 1681 at a cost of 34,000,000 francs it was the wonder of the times. It also freed the French from dependency on the Western area of the Mediterranean and became their equivalent of the Pillars of Hercules, i.e. Gibraltar.

[1] *expugnare*—Latin = to subdue, capture, storm, violate etc.
[2] *Haemathion*—As Aemathion, Macedonian or from Thessaly.

Foibles galleres seront unies ensemble,
Ennemis faux le plus fort en rampart:
Faible assaillies Vratislaue tremble,
Lubecq & Mysne tiendront barbare part.

Weak galleys will be joined together, the false enemy is strongest on the ramparts. Bratislava trembles, the weak attacked, Lubeck & Meissen will take the Barbarian's side.

Le nouveau faict[1] conduira l'exercite,[2]
Proche apamé[3] jusques au pres de rivage,
Tendant secour de Milannoile[4] eslite,
Duc yeux privé à Milan fer de cage.

The new fact will lead the army, almost cut off as far as to the river bank, holding for help from the Milanese élite; the Duke loses his eyes in an iron cage in Milan.

Milan belonged to the Habsburgs until 1859. A lot of commentators equate the last line with Mussolini but the quatrain is really too general.

Dans cité entrer excercit[5] desniee,
Duc entrera par persuasion,
Aux foibles portes clam[6] armee amenee,
Mettront feu, mort de sang effusion.

The army denied entry to the city, the Duke will enter through persuasion; secretly the army led to the weak gates, they put it to fire, death and flowing of blood.

De mer copies[7] en trois parts divisees,
A la seconde les vivres failliront,
Desesperez cherchant champs Helisees,
Premier en breche entrez victoire auront.

The forces at sea divided into three parts, the second one will run out of supplies; in despair looking for the Elysian Fields, the first entering the breach will have victory.

[1] Or the newly made one?
[2] *exercitus*—Latin = army.
[3] *apamé*—Greek, *apamao* = to cut off.
[4] Almost certainly means Milanese.
[5] *exercite*—Latin, *exercitus* = army.
[6] *clam*—Latin = secretly.
[7] *copies*—Latin, *copia* = troops, army.

Here are two battles; we start with a naval one and end up on land. Apart from the fact that the Elysian Fields were the Greek heaven, I cannot decipher this muddled quatrain.

98

Les affligez par faute d'un seul taint, *Contremenant*[1] *à partie opposite,* *Au Lygonnois mandera que contraint* *Seront de rendre le grand chef de Molite.*[2]	Those afflicted through the fault of a single infected one, the transgressor will be in the opposite party. He will send to the Lyonnais and compel that they should be given up to the great leader of Molite.

99

Vent Aquilon fera partir le siege, *Par murs gerer cendres, chauls, & pousiere,* *Par pluie apres qui leur fera bien piege,*[3] *Dernier secours encontre leur frontiere.*	The north wind will cause the seige to be raised, to throw over the walls cinders, lime and dust; afterwards through rain which does them much harm, the last help is met at their frontier.

RETREAT FROM MOSCOW?

If Aquilon is a synonym for North, most commentators take this as describing Napoleon's retreat from Moscow. He finds help only at the frontiers of his empire having lost so many men on the expedition (the rain and snow which does them such harm).

100

Navalle pugne[4] *nuit sera superee,*[5] *Le feu naves*[6] *à l'Occident ruine:* *Rubriche neufue la grand nef coloree* *Ire à vaincu, & victoire en bruine.*	A naval battle will be overcome at night. Fire in the ruined ships of the West, a new coding the great ship coloured anger to the vanquished and victory in a mist.

[1] *Contremenant*—Error for *contrevenant*.
[2] *Molite?*—either from Melita, Malta, or Greek, *molos* = war?
[3] *piege*—Provençal, *piegi* = worse, harmful.
[4] *pugne*—Latin, *pugna* = battle.
[5] *superee*—Latin, *superatus* = overcome.
[6] *naves*—Latin = ships.

Pearl Harbour was attacked in the very early morning by the Japanese planes. The great tankers were set alight to the ruin of America, the West. I think 'the new coding' of line 3 is the formula for this new type of attack which finally brings anger to a defeated Japan and hazy glimpses of victory to a stunned America. The 'colour' of the ship probably refers to camouflage.

CENTURY X

1   France. Vichy Régime
2
3
4*   Battle of Worcester, 1651
5
6*   9th September 1557
7
8*   15th June 1856
9
10*   Napoleon
11
12*   1591?
13
14
15
16*   Louis XVIII
17*   Madame Royale, 1787–99
18*   Henri of Navarre
19*   Elizabeth of England?
20   Post-Fascist Italy?
21
22**   Abdication of Edward VIII, 1936
23   Louis XVIII
24*   The Hundred Days, 1815
25
26**   Death of Robert Kennedy. Britain and Common Market

27
28
29
30
31
32

33
34**   Napoleon and the King of Naples
35
36   British Isles?
37
38**   Henri of Navarre
39***   Mary Queen of Scots and Francis II
40**.   Abdication of Edward VIII, 1936
41
42*   Pax Britannica
43*   Louis XVI
44*   Henri III
45*   Henri of Navarre
46
47
48*   Spanish Civil War followed by World War II
49***F?   New York's water supply poisoned?
50
51*   France and Germany, 1871
52
53
54
55**   Francis II and Mary Queen of Scots
56
57
58*   Louis XIV
59*   1560
60
61
62
63
64*   Italy 19th Century
65
66**   Polaris in Scotland from U.S.A.
67
68
69
70
71*?   The U.S.A.?
72*F?   The Third Antichrist and War
73
74**   War in 20th Century, probably at end of 1970s
75**   *continued*

KEY: * Of interest. F? Possibly referring to the future.

A l'ennemy l'ennemy foi promise
Ne se tiendre les captifs retenus:
Prins preme¹ mort & le rest en chemise,
Damné le reste pour estre soustenus.

To the enemy, the enemy faith promised will not be kept, the captives retained; one is taken near to death and the rest in their shirts, the rest damned for being supporters.

FRANCE—VICHY RÉGIME

This is usually read as a general quatrain about the Vichy régime, when the Germans failed to make collaboration a two-way proposition to the French people.

Voille gallere voil de nef cachera,
La grande classe² viendra sortir la moindre.
Dix naves³ proches le tourneront poulser,
Grande vaincue unis à foi joindre.

The ships sail will hide the sailing galley, the great fleet will cause the lesser one to go out. Nearby ten ships will turn to drive it back, the great one conquered united to join in faith.

There seems possibly to be a connection between this quatrain and IX. 100. It describes a naval battle with ships either camouflaged or hidden by a smoke screen. The great one who is conquered may then refer to the U.S.A. who joins the Allies after Pearl Harbour. Alternatively it may apply to one of the many actions in the Mediterranean 1940–1943.

En apres cinq troupeau ne mettra hors un
Fuytif pour Penelon⁴ l'aschera,
Faulx murmurer secours venir par lors,
Le chief le siege lois habandonnera.

After the fifth will not put out a flock, a fugitive will be turned loose for Penelon. Falsely to murmur, then to come in aid, then the chief will abandon the siege.

The key word in this quatrain is Penelon which is not definitely deciphered, see below.

¹ *preme*—O.F. = next, close, near.
² *classe*—Latin, *classis* = fleet.
³ *naves*—Latin, *navis* = ship.
⁴ *Penelon?*—Possibly an anagram for Polone, Poland?

Sus la minuict conducteur de l'armee	At midnight the leader of the army will run away, suddenly
Se saulvera, subit evanoui,	disappeared. Seven years later,
Sept ans apres la fame non blasmee	his reputation unblemished, to
A son retour ne dira oncq oui.	his return 'yes' will not once be said (i.e. many times).

BATTLE OF WORCESTER, 1651

After his defeat at the Battle of Worcester, Charles II fled to France via Scotland, in disguise. His usurper Cromwell actually reigned for seven years, and Charles was restored in 1560. It is a general quatrain but can be applied to these events quite accurately.

Albi & Castres feront nouvelle lique,	Albi & Castres will make a new alliance, nine Arians Lisbon
Neuf Arriens[1] Lisbons & Portugues,	and the Portuguese; Carcassonne, Toulouse will join their
Carcas, Tholosse consumeront leur brigue	intrigue when a new chief is the monster from the Lauragues.
Quand chef neuf monstre de Lauragues.	

The new Arians are the interesting subject here. Unfortunately it is most likely that Nostradamus was reverting to the Crusade (1208–13) of the Albigensians.

Sardou[2] Nemans si hault desborderont,	The Gardon will flood Nîmes so high that they will think
Qu'on cuidera[3] Ducalion renaistre,	Ducalion has been reborn.
Dans le collosse la plus part fuiront,	In the colossus the greater part will flee, Vesta's fire appears
Vesta sepulchre feu estaint apparoistre.	extinguished in the tomb.

[1] *Arriens* = (a) The 13th Century heretics. (b) People now dwelling in Afghanistan.
[2] *Sardon*—Error for Gardon.
[3] *cuider*—O.F. = To think, believe.

According to Jaubert a storm broke out at Nîmes in 1557 which lasted from 5 a.m. to 9 p.m., and this combined with a flood from the Gardon. Apparently many antiquities were revealed when the flood waters withdrew. Menard's History of Lyons confirms the flood as 1 p.m. to 9 p.m. but does not mention the Gardon.

7

Le grand combat qu'on appreste à Nancy,	The great fight that they prepare at Nancy, Aemathien will say I subjugate all; the British Isles through wine and salt are in trouble, Hem. mi Philip two, Metz will not hold for long.
L'aemathieu dira tout je soubmetz,	
L'isle Britanne par vin, sel, en solci,	
Hem. mi deux Phi. long temps ne tiendra Metz.	

The reference to wine and salt connect this quatrain in some manner to England, see IX. 49. But I am not happy with any of the ingenious comments to date. It seems more probable that '*deux Phi.*' refers to Philip II attacking French-occupied Lorraine. Metz was finally ceded in 1648 but was in French control from 1552, in which case Nostradamus is only stating a known fact. Nancy was handed back to its Duke in 1661 having been occupied for twenty-seven years.

8

Index & poulse parfondra[1] le front	With index finger and thumb he will wet the forehead, the Count of Seneglia to his own son, through several, Venus in short order, three are wounded to death in seven days.
De Senegalia le Conte à son filz propre	
Les Myrnarmee[2] par plusieurs de prin front	
Trois dans sept jours blesses mors.	

15th JUNE 1856

On this date the Prince Imperial, son of Napoleon III, was baptized. His godfather was Pope Pius IX who was the son of Count Mastoi Ferretti of Senigallia. Venus is interpreted as the Empress Eugenie but line 4 is still unexplained.

[1] *perfundere*—Latin = to sprinkle, moisten.
[2] *Mimnermia*—A surname of Venus.

De Castillion figuires jour de brune,	In the Castle of Figueras on a
De fame infame naistra souverain prince.	misty day a sovereign prince will be born of an unworthy
Surnon de chausses perhume lui posthume,	woman. The surname of Chausses on the ground will
Onc Roi ne faut si pire en sa province.	make him posthumous, never was a king so bad in his province.

See X. 11 also for this verse. Loomis suggests this verse describes one of Nostradamus' Antichrists.

10

Tasche de murdre enormes adulteres,	Stained with murder and enor-
Grand ennemi de tout le genre humain	mous adulteries, great enemy of all mankind, he will be worse
Que sera pire qu'ayeulx, oncles ne peres	than his ancestors, uncles and fathers, in steel, fire and water,
En fer, feu, eau, sanguin & inhumain.	bloody and inhuman.

NAPOLEON

The epithet of line 2 was applied to Napoleon Bonaparte by the Venetian ambassador, Morenigo.

11

Debbouz louchere du dangereux passage	In the dangerous passage underneath Junquera, the post-
Fera passer le posthume sa bande,	humous one will cross his men. To cross the Pyrenean moun-
Les monts Pyrens passer hors son bagaige	tains without his baggage the duke will hasten to Perpignan
De Perpignam courira duc à tende.	from Tende.

This obscure verse seems to be related to X. 9, particularly the reference to the posthumous child.

Esleu en Pape, d'esleu sera mocqué,	Elected as Pope, he will be
Subit soudain esmeu prompt &	mocked when elected, suddenly
timide,	and unexpectedly moved,
Par trop bon doulz à mourir pro-	prompt and timid: Caused to
vocqué,	die through too much goodness
Crainte estainte la nuit de sa mort	and kindness he will fear for the
guide.	guide killed on the night of his
	death.

1591?

This is normally applied to the Cardinal Santa Severina who was elected Pope Gregory XIV, but died two months later in 1591, the election being declared illegal. However his successor Innocent IX also died in under two months.

13

Soulz la pasture d'animaux rumi-	Beneath the food of ruminating
nant[1]	animals, led by them into the
Par eux conduicts au ventre herbi-	centre of the food place;
polique[2]	soldiers hidden, their weapons
Soldatz caichez les armes bruit	being noise, tried not far from
menant,	the city of Antibes.
Non loing temptez de cité Anti-	
polique.	

14

Urnel Vaucile[3] *sans conseil de soi*	'Urnel Vaucile' without a plan
mesmes.	of his own, bold, timid for fear
Hardit timide par crainte prins	of being taken and captured;
vaincu,	accompanied by several pale
Accompaigné de plusieurs putains	whores converted in the Car-
blesmes	thusian convent at Barcelona.
A Barcellonne aux chartreux con-	
vaincu.	

The interpretation here depends on the *Urnel Vaucile* line, which has no connections to date with the monastery at de Urgel, near Llanos to the town of the same name. The Carthusian monastery mentioned is that of Mont Allegro.

[1] i.e. under a load of hay.
[2] Into the market place?
[3] *Urnel Vaucile?*—Llanos de Urgel? Plain of Urgel?

Pere duc vieux d'ans & de soif chargé,	The father duke old in years and troubled with thirst, on the last day his son denying him the jug: into the well plunged alive he will become dead: the Senate to the son a death long and light.
Au jour extreme filz desniant les guiere[1]	
Dedans le puis vif mort viendra plongé,	
Senat au fil[2] la mort longue & legiere.	

A son is hanged for giving his thirsty father an excess of water, by putting him down the well! Impossible to place this quatrain.

Heureux au regne de France, heureux de vie	Happy in the kingdom of France, happy in life, ignorant of blood, death, anger and rage. By a flattering name he will be envied, a king robbed, too much faith in the kitchen.
Ignorant sang mort fureur & rapine,	
Par nom flateurs seras mis en envie,	
Roi desrobé trop de foi en cuisine.[3]	

LOUIS XVIII

When he is happily re-established on the French throne, Louis XVIII will not die a violent death but lives happily. He was given the name of Louis le Desiré (line 3). His guilt will lie in the fact that he does not sufficiently occupy himself with the public good, and that he is a renowned glutton.

La roine Ergaste[4] voiant sa fille blesme,	The barren queen, seeing her pale daughter because of unhappiness locked up in her stomach. Lamentable cries will then come from Angoulême and the marriage to the cousin greatly impeded.
Par un regret dans l'estomac encloz,	
Cris lamentables seront lors d'Angoulesme,	
Et au gemain mariage fort clos.	

MADAME ROYALE, 1787–99

The *Roine Ergaste* is a queen confined to the manual labour found in any penitentiary. When imprisoned in the Temple Marie

---

[1] *l'aiguiere*—Mod. French = jug.
[2] *fil*—Probably should read *filz* = son.
[3] i.e. in his servants.
[4] *Ergaste*—Ergastulus = penitentiary?

Antoinette was compelled to sew her own clothes. The adjective can also mean captive, which indeed the Queen was. She sees her daughter, Madame Royale, pale with the family misfortunes. Madame Royale was betrothed to the Duke of Angoulême in 1787, and married him in 1799. It is suggested that her childless marriage '*l'estomac enclos*' was due to her sufferings with her family in the Temple.

18

Le ranc Lorrain fera place à Vendosme,
Le hault mis bas & le bas mis en hault,
Le filz d'Hamon[1] sera esleu dans Rome,
Et les deux grands seront mis en deffault.

The house of Lorraine will make way for Vendôme, the high put low and the low exalted. The son of Hamon will be elected in Rome, and the two great ones will be put at a loss.

HENRI DE NAVARRE

This is a very successful prophecy for Nostradamus. Henri IV, Duke of Vendôme will eclipse the house of Lorraine, and Henri IV, earlier known as '*le petit Béarnais*' will be elevated to the high rank of king of France. This son of Hamon, i.e. heretic, will be accepted as King in Rome. The two great ones who lose out on this are the two Pretenders, the Duke de Guise and the Duke de Mayenne.

19

Jour que sera par roine saluee
Le jour apres le salut, la priere,
Le compte fait raison & valbuee,[2]
Par avant humbles oncques ne feut si fiere.

The day she will be saluted as queen, the prayer the day after the blessing. The account is right and valid, once humble, there was never a woman so proud.

Suggested as applying to Elizabeth I of England when she succeeded to her sister, the childless Mary Tudor.

[1] *Hamon*—Mamon in some editions.
[2] *valbuee*—Unsolved word. *Valable* is suggested as an alternative?

Tous les amis qu'auront tenu parti,	All of the friends who have belonged to the party, put to death and looked for the uncouth letters. The public possessions, the great one annihilated by six, never were the Roman people so wronged.
Pour rude en lettres mis mort & saccagé,	
Biens publiez pat sixe grand neanti,[1]	
Onc Romain peuple ne feut tant outragé.	

POST-FASCIST ITALY

This quatrain applies accurately to post-Fascist Italy, and in Nostradamus' day it made little sense. The drastic remedy makes it appear more modern.

21

Par le despit du Roi soustenant moindre,	Through the king's spite in supporting the lesser one, he will be murdered presenting the jewels to him. The father wishing to impress his son with nobility did what the Magi once used to do in Persia.
Sera meurdri lui presentant les bagues,	
Le pere au filz voulant noblesse poindre	
Fait comme à Perse jadis feirent les Mague:	

22

Pour ne vouloir consentir à divorce,	For not wanting to consent to the divorce, which then afterwards will be recognized as unworthy, the King of the islands will be forced to flee, and one put in his place who has no sign of kingship.
Qui puis apres sera cogneu indigne,	
Le Roi des Isles sera chassé par force	
Mis à son lieu que de roi n'aura signe.	

ABDICATION OF EDWARD VIII, 1936.
10th DECEMBER

Edward VIII's abdication was not popular among the British people, who had little love for Mrs. Simpson. Edward was therefore forced to leave Britain because of her social standing, '*cogneu indigne*'. Finally George VI, who was not in line for the kingship is forced to accede to the throne. See also X. 40.

[1] *neantir*—to annihilate.

Au peuple ingrat faictes les remonstrances,	Remonstrances are made to the ungrateful people, then the army will seize Antibes. In the arch of Monaco the complaints will occur, and at Fréjus the shore will be taken by one from the other.
Par lors l'armee se saisira d'Antibe,	
Dans l'arc Monech feront les doleances	
Et à Frejus l'un l'autre prendra ribe.[1]	

LOUIS XVIII

When Louis XVIII issued a proclamation urging fidelity to the new régime the only place that remained loyal to Napoleon was Antibes. Both Louis and Napoleon used Fréjus; the former to embark for England, the latter when embarking for Elba.

24

Le captif prince aux Italles vaincu	The captive prince conquered in Italy will cross from Genoa to Marseilles by sea; by a great effort the foreigners will be overcome except for a gun shot, a barrel of bees' honey.
Passera Gennes par mer jusqu'à Marseille,	
Par grand effort des forens[2] survaincu	
Sauf coup de feu barril liqueur d'abeille.	

THE HUNDRED DAYS, 1815

This quatrain must be linked with IV. 26 in which Napoleon's emblem of bees also appears. Napoleon, a closely guarded prisoner on Elba, escapes by sea in March and lands at Cannes, near Marseilles. He is overcome again at Waterloo, where he seeks death in vain, and the bees of his emblem spill all their sweetness.

25

Par Nebro ouvrir de Brisanne[3] passage,	Through the Ebro will be opened a passage to Brissane far away the Tago will make a demonstration. The outrage will be committed in Pelligoux, of the great lady sitting in the orchestra.
Bien eslongez el tago fara muestra,	
Dans Pelligauxe[4] sera commis l'outrage	
De la grand dame assise sur l'orchestra.	

[1] *ribe*—Provençal, *riba* = bank, shore.
[2] *forens*—O.F. = foreigner, stranger.
[3] *Brisanne*—Unsolved place name.
[4] *Pelligaux*—Unsolved place name.

Le successeur vengera son beau frere,
Occupera regne souz umbre de vengeance,
Occis ostacle son sang mort vitupere,
Long temps Bretaigne tiendra avec la France.

The successor will avenge his handsome brother and occupy the realm under the shadow of vengeance, he, killed, the obstacle of the blameworthy dead, his blood; for a long time Britain will hold with France.

DEATH OF SECOND KENNEDY BROTHER.
BRITAIN AND COMMON MARKET

The quatrain seems to indicate that Robert Kennedy will die following the death of his handsome brother, J. F. Kennedy. It is interesting to note that Nostradamus foresees two brothers killed within a short period of time. Robert Kennedy's stand in the name of his dead brother does him no good. One wonders what it will bring to Edward Kennedy. The last line seems to imply that once de Gaulle is dead, Britain's relationship with the Common Market is a particularly successful one. See I 26, VIII. 46, 77.

Par le cinquieme & un grand Hercules
Viendront le temple ouvrir de main bellique,
Un Clement, Iule & Ascans recules,
Lespe, clef, aigle n'eurent onc si grand picque.

Through the fifth and a great Hercules they will come to open the temple with the hand of war; one Clement, Julius and Ascans put back, the sword, the key, the eagle never once felt so great a dislike.

Second & tiers qui font prime musicque
Sera par Roi en honneur sublimee,
Par grasse & maigre presque demi etique
Rapport de Venus faulx rendra deprimee.

Second and third make first class music they will be sublimely honoured by the king: Through fat and thin, even half emaciated, to be made debased by the false report of Venus.

De Pol MANSOL dans caverne caprine[1]
Caché & prins extrait hors par la barbe,
Captif mené comme beste mastine
Par Begourdans amenee pres de Tarbe.

In the great cave of Saint Paul de Mausole, hidden and seized, pulled out by the beard, the captive led like a mastiff animal, by the people of Bigorre brought near to Tarbes.

St. Paul de Mausole is just outside Nostradamus' birthplace of St. Rémy. The quatrain seems to describe the capture of a goat, or goatboy, who is taken to Bigorre in Navarre.

30

Nepueu & sang du sainct nouveau venu,
Par le surnom soustient arcs & couvert
Seront chassez mis à mort chassez nu,
En rouge & noir convertiront leur vert.

Nephew and of the blood of the newly created saint, through his surname he will sustain the arches and the roof. They will be driven out naked and chased to their deaths, their green will be converted to red and black.

31

Le saint Empire viendra en Germanie
Ismaelites[2] *trouveront lieux ouverts.*
Anes vouldront aussi la Carmanie,[3]
Les soustenens de terre tous converts.

The Holy Empire will come to Germany, the Arabs will find open places; the asses will also want Carmania, the supporters completely covered with earth.

32

Le grand empire chacun an devoir estre
Un sur les autres le viendra obtenir,
Mais peu de temps sera son regne & estre,
Deux ans aux naves se pourra soustenir.

The empire each year should become great. One will come to hold (power) over all the others. But his kingdom and life will last a short time. In two years he will be able to maintain himself in his ships.

[1] *caprinus*—Latin adjective = pertaining to goats.
[2] *Ismaelites*—Not Jews but Arabs, who claim descent from Ishmaël, son of Abraham.
[3] *Carmanie*—Either the Persian province at the entrance to the Persian Gulf, or an unsolved anagram.

La faction cruelle à robbe longue,
Viendra cacher souz les pointus poignars
Saisir Florence le duc & lieu diphlongue[1]
Sa descouverte par immeurs & flaugnards.[2]

The cruel party with long robes will hide sharp daggers underneath. The Duke to seize Florence and the place of two words. Its discovery through young ones and flatterers.

Gaulois qu'empire par guerre occupera
Par son beau frere mineur sera trahi,
Par cheval rude voltigiant trainera,
Du fait le frere long temps sera haï.

The Gaul who gains his empire through war will be betrayed by his younger brother-in-law. He will be dragged by an untrained nervous horse, for the act the brother will be hated for a long time.

NAPOLEON AND THE KING OF NAPLES

The King of Naples, Joachim Murat, married Napoleon's younger sister Caroline. He first betrayed Napoleon in 1814, but sided with him in 1815. He was also a renowned cavalry leader. Apparently, according to Robb (1942) this quatrain converted the eminent Professor Jacques Barzun of Colombia University, and Professor Siceloff, who stated that the chances of this quatrain being fulfilled were 'about zero'.

Puisnay royal flagrand d'ardent libide,
Pour se jouir de cousine germaine,
Habit de femme au temple d'Arthemide:
Allant murdri par incognu du Marne.

The younger son of a king flagrant with burning lust to enjoy his first cousin. Women's attire in the temple of Diana going to be murdered by the unknown man from Marne.

The last line suggests that a Duke of Mayenne or Maine will be involved in a royal scandal, but unfortunately though a probable situation, it does not seem to tie in with anything specific.

[1] *diphlongue*—Erratum for *diphtongue* = double word.
[2] *flaugnards*—Provençal = flatterer or wheedler.

36

*Apres le Roi du saucq guerres
parlant,
L'isle Harmotique[1] le tiendra à
mespris,
Quelques ans bous rongeant un &
pillant
Par tyrannie à l'isle changeant pris.[2]*

After the king (of the stump?)
speaks of wars, the United
Island will despise him. For
several years the good one
gnaws and pillages, through
tyranny on the island its values
change.

The United Islands may well be the British Isles, bringing the
date to after 1603. Line 3 probably describes the privateers of the
late 16th Century and early 17th Century, such as Drake, Hawkins
and Raleigh. But it is difficult to interpret the adjective *'de soucq'*
as applying to James I.

37

*L'assemblee grande pres du lac de
Borget,
Se ralieront pres de Montmelian,
Marchans plus oultre pensif z feront
proget
Chambry, Moraine combat sainct
Julian.*

The great crowd near to the
lake of Le Bourget, they will
rally near to Montmelian,
going further ahead the
thoughtful ones draw up a plan,
Chambery, St. Julian de Maur-
ienne, fight.

38

*Amour alegre non loing pose le siege,
Au sainct barbar seront les garni-
sons,
Ursins[1] Hadrie pour Galois feront
plaige,
Pour peur rendus de l'armee du
Grisons.[3]*

'Light of love' will not hold the
siege for long, for the converted barbarian will be all the
garrisons; the Ursins and Adria
give security for the French, for
fear of the army being handed
over to the Grisons.

HENRI OF NAVARRE

Henri's usual nickname among his contemporaries was 'Vert
Galant', which is very close to Nostradamus' *'armour allegre'*.
During the Siege of Paris, 1590, Henri could not hold the siege
for longer than four complete months, because of the advance of
the Duke of Parma from Flanders. Nostradamus describes the
city garrison as devoted to things converted and barbarous, by

[1] *Harmotique*—Dubious probably from Greek, *armoskitos* = joined
together, fitting together?
[2] *pris*—Mod. French, *prix*.
[3] *Grisons* = The people of South-east Switzerland.

which he means that they were the clerical revolutionaries. Henri also changed his religion to get the French throne. The last two lines are unclear.

39

Premier fils veufve malheureux marriage,	The first son, a widow, an unfortunate marriage without any children: two islands thrown into discord. Before eighteen years of age, a minor: of the other even lower will be the betrothal.
Sans nuls enfans deux isles en discorde,	
Avant dixhuict incompetant eage,	
De l'autre pres plus bas sera l'accord.	

MARY QUEEN OF SCOTS AND FRANCIS II

This is one of Nostradamus' notoriously successful quatrains, and appears to have been understood by the French Court of the time. Francis II, the eldest son of the widowed Catherine de' Medici, marries Mary Stuart, an unfortunate marriage which was childless. Because of Mary's return to Scotland she caused discord between England and her own country. Francis was still not quite eighteen years old when he died (seventeen years, ten months, fifteen days). His younger brother Charles IX was betrothed to Elizabeth of Austria when only eleven years old. This quatrain is quite astonishingly accurate.

40

Le jeune nay au regne Britannique,	The young born to the realm of Britain, which his dying father had commended to him. Once he is dead, London will dispute with him, and the kingdom will be demanded back from the son.
Qu'aura le pere mourant recommandé,	
Icelui mort LONOLE[1] donra topique,	
Et à son fils le regne demandé.	

ABDICATION OF EDWARD VIII, 1936

This refers back to X. 22. Edward VIII is the true heir to the British throne which was left to him by his dying father. But he will cause scandal (*topique*) in London by his behaviour with Mrs. Simpson, and public hostility towards her earlier divorce caused the King to abdicate, the kingdom taken back from him by the people and given to his brother.

[1] *Lonole*—Probably erratum for *Londres* = London.

En la frontiere de Caussade &
    Charlus,
Non guieres loing du fonds de la
    vallee,
De ville franche musicque à son de
    luths,
Environnez combouls[1] & grand
    mytee.[2]

On the boundary of Caussade and Caylus, not very far from the depths of the valley, music from Villefranche to the sound of lutes, surrounded by cymbals and a great (deal) of stringed (instruments).

All the places mentioned are small villages within fifty miles of Agen where Nostradamus once lived. Perhaps here he is just describing a festival he witnessed?

Le regne humain d'Anglique geni-
    ture,
Fera son regne paix union tenir,
Captive guerre demi de sa closture,
Long temps la paix leur fera
    maintenir.

The human reign of English offspring will cause the kingdom to remain united in peace. Half captured in his enclosure in the war, for a long time peace will be maintained by them.

PAX BRITANNICA

This is a general but very apt quatrain, which describes Britain and the Pax Britannica of the 19th Century, or possibly the long peace England enjoyed under Walpole and the early Georges. The first is more acceptable because of England's vast influence in the 19th Century.

Le trop bon temps trop de bonté
    royale:
Fais & deffois prompt subit
    negligence,
Legier croira faux despouse loyalle,
Lui mis à mort par sa benevolence.

Too much of good times and too much royal bounty, made and quickly undone by sudden negligence. He will lightly believe false his loyal wife whom in his benevolence he puts to death.

LOUIS XVI

Louis XVI was put to death because he did not bother to apply himself properly to affairs of state. The weakness and irresolution of character that he displayed, and the great ease with which he

---

[1] *combouls*—Greek, *kumbalon* = cymbal.

[2] *mytee*—Dubious, possibly from *mitos* = a stringed instrument?

elieved reports that his wife, Marie Antoinette was involved, other
han as a dupe, in the affair of the Diamond Necklace; all these,
lus his kindness, left him defenceless before the Revolutionaries.

44

Par lors qu'un Roi sera contre les siens,
Natif de Blois subjugera Ligures.
Mammel,[1] Cordube & les Dalmatiens,
Des sept puis l'ombre à Roi estrennes[2] & lemurs.[3]

Where a king is (chosen) against his people a native of Blois will subdue the League. Mammel, Cordoba and the Dalmatians; of the seven then a shadow to the King, new money and dead ghosts.

HENRI III

See VIII. 38 and 52 which also discuss a king from Blois. It
probably refers to Henri III of France who will subjugate the
League (line 2). He was descended from the Court of Blois and
Nostradamus elsewhere calls him 'le grand du Blois'. The seven in
the final line is yet another reference to the seven children of
Catherine de' Medici.

45

L'ombre du Regne de Navarre non vrai,
Fera la vie de fort illegitime:
La veu promis incertain de Cambrai
Roi Orleans donra mur legitime.

The shadow of the kingdom of Navarre is not true, it will make the life of a strong man illegal. The uncertain vow promised at Cambrai,[4] the king at Orléans will give a lawful boundary (wall).

HENRI IV OF NAVARRE

Henri of Navarre has still only a shadow of a kingdom since he
has not yet gained true possession of France. He did lead an
irregular life with many mistresses, including the wife of Balagny,
the governor of Cambrai, to whom Henri gave in return the
hereditary possession of the town (line 3). Orléans may represent
here either the family or the town.

[1] *Mammel*—Unsolved place name; perhaps Mamel, in the Baltic?
[2] *estrennes* = Handsel, earnest money, or New Year money.
[3] *lemur*—Latin, *lemures* = spirits of the dead.
[4] Cambrai—A reference to the Peace of Cambrai 1529 when the
French gave up their claims to Flanders.

Vie sort mort de L'OR vilaine indigne,
Sera de Saxe non nouveau electeur:
De Brunsuic mandra d'amour signe,
Faux le rendant aux peuple seducteur.

Because of the gold, the life, fate and death of an unworthy sordid man: he will not be the new Elector of Saxony. From Brunswick he will send for a sign of love, the false seducer giving it to the people.

This quatrain appears to be set in Germany, and to state that Saxony will not have a new Elector. Maurice did not enter the fight against Charles V until 1552 while the Duchy of Brunswick played no significant role in the 16th Century, so maybe this quatrain is reasonably accurate.

De Bourze ville à la dame Guirlande,
L'on mettra¹ sus par la trahison faicte,
Le grand prelat de leon par Formande,²
Faux pellerins & ravisseurs defaicte.

In the town of Burgos, at the Garland lady they will give the verdict on the treason committed; the great prelate of Leon through Formande, undone by false pilgrims and thieves.

Du plus profond de l'Espaigne enseigne,
Sortant du bout & des fins de l'Europe,
Troubles passant aupres du pont de Laigne,
Sera deffaicte par bands sa grand troppe.

Banners from the furthest corners of Spain, coming out from the ends and borders of Europe. Trouble passing near the bridge of Laigne, its great army will be routed by bands (of men).

SPANISH CIVIL WAR FOLLOWED BY WORLD WAR II
The first lines describe well enough the Spanish Civil War and the involvement of the Germans and Italians. Nostradamus sees this trouble growing, i.e. the Second World War, until it is stretched all over Europe. Laingnes a town forty odd miles north-west of Dijon was occupied by the Germans. It is interesting to note that

¹ *mettra*—Literally, impose a verdict.
² *Formand?*—Formentera, the Balearic island?

Nostradamus sees the occupying army as being routed by its enemies the Allied Forces, as it was in 1944 and 1945.

49

Jardin du monde au pres du cité neufve,	Garden of the world near the New City, in the road of the
Dans le chemin des montaignes cavees,	hollow mountains. It will be seized and plunged in the tank,
Sera saisi & plongé dans la Cuve,	forced to drink water poisoned
Beuvant par force eaux soulfre envenimees.	with sulphur.

NEW YORK POISONED THROUGH ITS WATER SUPPLY?

This is a fascinating quatrain with the idea of a water supply of a whole city being poisoned, more suited to James Bond than Nostradamus. The *cité neuf* is New York. The *jardin du Monde* is probably a way of describing it as a world centre. The next line is interesting. Could a road of hollow mountains be the nearest Nostradamus could get towards describing a skyscraper? I am not quite sure what the tank is, perhaps Nostradamus is trying to indicate the controls or reservoir of the water supply poisoned with sulphuric acid? See IV. 97, IX. 92.

50

La Meuse au jour terre de Luxembourg.	By day, the Meuse in the land of Luxembourg, will find
Descouvrira Saturn & trois en lurne,	Saturn and three in Aquarius; mountain and plain, town, city
Montaigne & plein, ville, cité & Bourg,	and borough; flood in Lorraine betrayed by the great urn.
Lorrain deluge trahison par grand hurne.	

51

Des lieux plus bas du pays de Lorraine,	Some of the lowest places in the county of Lorraine will be
Seront des basses Allemaignes unis,	united with the lower Germanies. Through the people
Par ceux du siege Picards, Normans, du Maisne,	of the seats of Picardy, Normandy and Maine, they will be
Et aux cantons ce seront reunis.	reunited to the cantons.

FRANCE AND GERMANY, 1871

Lorraine and the regions to the South (*plus bas*) such as Alsace, were united to Lower Germany with the consent of those defeated in the Siege of Paris in 1871, the people of France, Picards, Normans and from Maine. All those areas suffered German occupation. Lorraine did not return to France until 1919.

52

Au lieu[1] *où LAYE & Scelde se marient,*	At the place where the Laye and the Scheldt join the
Seront les nopces de longtemps maniees,	marriage will be arranged a long time ago. At the place in
Au lieu d'Anvers où la crappe[2] *charient*[3]	Antwerp where the chaff is carried a young undefiled wife,
Jeune vieillesse consorte intaminee.	and old age.

An obscure marriage between a very young girl and an old suitor which takes place at Ghent.

53

Les trois pellices de loing s'entre-batron,	Three prostitutes will quarrel for a long time; the greatest
La plus grand moindre demeurera à l'escoute:	will remain to hear the least. The great Selin will no longer
Le grand Selin n'en fera plus patron,	be her patron, she will call him fire, shield, a white rout.
Le nommera feu pelte blanche routte.	

If Selim does refer to Henri II here this would describe his many royal mistresses, presumably rivals to Diane de Poitiers, such as Gabrielle d'Estrées. I imagine 'white rout' is intended to mean a lily-livered coward!

54

Nee en ce monde par concubine fertive,	Born into this world of a furtive concubine, at two raised high
A deux hault mise par les tristes nouvelles,	by the bad news. She will be taken captive among enemies
Entre ennemis sera prinse captive,	and brought to Malines and Brussels.
Et amené à Malings & Bruxelles.	

[1] *lieu*—Ghent.
[2] *crappe*—O.F. = chaff.
[3] *charier*—O.F. = to carry, to cast about.

Les malheureuses nopces celebreront,
En grand joye mais la fin mal-
heureuse:
Mary & mere nore desdaigneront.
Le Phybe mort & nore plus
piteuse.

The unfortunate marriage will be celebrated with great joy, but the end is unhappy. The mother will despise the daughter-in-law Mary, the Apollo dead and the daughter-in-law more pitiful.

FRANCIS II AND MARY QUEEN OF SCOTS, 1558–60

The word Mary is spelt with a *y* in the original, and this makes it quite likely to refer to Mary Queen of Scots and her unhappy wedding, see X. 39. Catherine de' Medici disliked Mary intensely and the latter called the Queen Mother 'a merchant's daughter'. The strange word Phybe may well mean Francis II, Mary's husband, if one takes the first syllable (*Phy*) (*phi*) for F. and the *be* for beta, second letter of the alphabet, thus F II, Francis II. They married in 1558 and Francis died in 1560.

Prelat royal son baissant trop tiré,
Grand fleux de sang sortira de sa
bouche,
Le reign Anglique par regne
respiré,
Long temps mort vif en Tunis
comme souche.

The royal priest bowing too low, a great flow of blood will come out of his mouth. The Anglican reign, a realm breathing, for a long time dead as a stump, living in Tunis.

Le soublevé ne cognoistra son
sceptre,
Les enfants jeunes des plus grands
honnira:
Oncques ne fut un plus ord[1] cruel
estre,
Pour leurs espouses à mort noir[2]
bannira.

The uplifted one will not know his sceptre, he will disgrace the young children of the greatest ones. There was never so filthy and cruel a being, for their wives, the king will banish them to death.

[1] *ord*—O.F. = filth.
[2] *noir*—Usual Nostradamus anagram for king.

Au temps du dueil que le felin
    monarque,
Guerroiera le jeune Aemathien:
Gaule bansler perecliter la barque[1]
Tenter Phossens[2] au Ponant entre-
    tien.

At a time of mourning the
feline monarch will make war
with the young Aemathien.
France to shake, the bark will
be in danger, Marseilles to be
tried, a talk in the West.

LOUIS XIV

Aemathien, the child of the dawn, that is the sun, must refer here
to Louis XIV who adopted the sun as his device and was also
called the Sun King. When there is a time of mourning for Louis
XIII, the wily monarch, Philip IV of Spain, will go to war against
Aemathien. France is shaken by the civil war of the Fronde, and
the bark of the Papacy is threatened by the development of
Jansenism. Phossen is Marseilles, which Louis XIV entered by
breaching the walls in 1660. A year earlier he went to the West of
France (Ponant means Occident) and on the island of Bidussoa
concluded the peace of the Pyrenees and his marriage with the
Infanta Maria Theresa. The island is still called l'Isle de la
Conférence.

Dedans Lyons vingt cinq d'une
    alaine,
Cinq citoyens Germains, Bressane,
    Latins,
Par dessous noble conduiront longue
    traine,
Et descouverts par abbois les
    matins.

In Lyons, twenty-five of the
same breath, five citizens, Germans, Bressans, Latins, under
a noble they will lead a long
train and are discovered by the
barking of the mastiffs.

1560

In September 1560 five citizens from Lyons and twenty others,
including some German Protestants, entered into a conspiracy to
hand over the city to the Huguenots. It was suspected at the time
that the main people behind the plot were the Prince de Condé
and the Vidame de Chartres. It was discovered in time by the
guards.

[1] la barque = the Papacy, bark of St. Peter.
[2] Phossens = Phoceans, founders of Marseilles.

Je pleure Nisse, Mannego, Pize, Gennes, *Savone, Sienne, Capue, Modene, Malte:* *Le dessus sang & glaive par estrennes,* *Feu, tremblera terre, eau, malheureuse nolte.*[1]	I weep for Nice, Monaco, Pisa, Genoa, Savona, Siena, Capua, Modena and Malta. The blood and sword above for a gift, fire, the earth will tremble, water, an unhappy reluctance.

Betta,[2] *Vienne, Emorre,*[3] *Sacarbance,*[4] *Voudront livrer au Barbares Pannone:* *Par picque & feu, enorme violance,* *Les conjurez descouvers par matrone.*	Betta, Vienna, Emort, Sopron, they will want to deliver Hungary to the Barbarians; great violence through pike and fire, the conspirators discovered by a matron.

This quatrain appears to be linked with the following ones, X. 62 and 63, but they are all very obscure.

Pres de Sorbin pour affaillir Ongrie, *L'herault de Bude les viendra advertir:* *Chef Bizantin, Sallon de Sclavonie,* *A loi d'Arabes les viendra convertir.*	Near Sorbia in order to assail Hungary, the herald of Brudes will come to warn them. The Byzantine chief, Salona of Slavonia, he will come to convert them to Arab law.

[1] *nolte*—Probably from Latin, *noluntas* = unwillingness.
[2] *Betta?*—Possibly Baetis, the Guadalquivir River?
[3] *Emmore*—Uncertain place name.
[4] *Sacarabance*—Latin, *Scarbantia* = modern Sapron.

Cydron,[1] Raguse,[2] la cité au
    sainct Hieron.[3]
Reverdira le medicant succours,
Mort fils de Roi par mort de deux
    heron,[4]
L'Arabe Ongrie feront un mesme
    cours.

Cydonia, Ragusa, the city holy
to Hieron, the healing help will
make it green again, the king's
son dead because of the death of
two heroes, Arabia and Hungary
will take the same steps.

64

Pleure Milan, pleure Luques,
    Florance,
Que ton grand Duc sur le char
    montera,
Changer le siege pres de Venise
    s'advance,
Lors que Colomne[5] à Rome chang-
    era:

Weep Milan, weep Lucca and
Florence, when your great
Duke climbs into the chariot.
To change the seat it advances
close to Venice when at Rome
the Colonnas will change.

ITALY 19th CENTURY

When the Grand Duke left Italy, Austria abandoned the province
of Venetia to Napoleon III, who gave it in turn to Victor Emmanuel. Florence became the latter's new capital until the seat of
all Italian government was moved to Rome, when the temporal
powers of the Papacy declined.

65

O vaste Romone ta ruine s'approche,
Non de tes murs de ton sang &
    substance;
L'aspre par lettres fera si horrible
    coche,
Fer poinctu mis à tous jusques au
    manche.

O great Rome your ruin draws
near, not of your walls but of
your blood and substance; the
harsh one in letters will make
so horrid a notch, pointed steel
wounding all up to the sleeve.

[1] Cydonia—Now modern Canea.
[2] Ragusa—Now Dubrovnik.
[3] Hieron?—Dubious personal name?
[4] heron—Mostly regarded as a false rhyme for heroes.
[5] Colonne—A great Roman family, the Colonnas.

Le chef de Londres par regne
l'Americh,
L'isle de l'Escosse tempiera par
gellee:
Roi Reb auront un si faux ante-
christ
Que les mettra trestous dans la
meslee.

The London premier through American power will burden the island of Scotland with a cold thing. Reb the King will have so dreadful an antichrist who will bring them all into the troubles.

POLARIS IN SCOTLAND AND U.S.A.

A most interesting quatrain. The Premier of London at the time specified was Harold Macmillan who had a good relationship with America. It was during his office that Scotland was burdened with the cold thing (the Polaris submarines). Roi Reb sounds strange but links this even firmly with another antichrist to come who will lead all of them, i.e. Britain and U.S.A. into trouble.

67

Le tremblement si fort au mois de
Mai,
Saturne, Caper, Jupiter, Mercure
au beuf:
Venus aussi Cancer, Mars en
Nonnay,[1]
Tombera gresse lors plus grosse
qu'un euf.

A very great trembling in the month of May, Saturn in Capricorn. Jupiter and Mercury in Taurus. Venus also in Cancer, Mars in Virgo, then hail will fall greater than an egg.

The accumulation of planets in the zodiac here referred to is apparently very rare, but all it predicts here is an earthquake in May and a great fall of hail. The dates are April 1929 or May 3755.

[1] Nonnay = Virgo, as nonnay comes from Nonne, or Nonnain a nun, and virgin.

L'armee de mer devant la cité tiendra *Puis partir sans faire langue alee,* *Citoyens grande proie en terre prendra,* *Retourner classe,*[1] *reprendre grand emblee.*[2]	The army of the sea will stand before the city then depart without making a long passage. A great prey of citizens will be taken on land, the fleet returns to seize (by) great robbery.

Le fait luisant de neuf vieux esleué *Seront si grand par midi aquilon,* *De sa seur propre grande alles*[3] *levé.* *Guyant meurdri au buisson d'ambellon.*[4]	The shining deed of the new old one exalted, will be so great in the south and north. Raised by his own sister great crowds arise, fleeing is murdered in the bushes at Ambellon.

L'oeil par object ferra telle excroissance, *Tant & ardente que tumbera la neige,* *Champ arrousé viendra en descroissance,* *Que le primat succumbera à Rege.*	Because of an object the eye will swell so much, burning so greatly that the snow will fall. The watered fields will start to shrink when the Primate dies at Reggio.

La terre & l'air gelleront si grand eau, *Lors qu'on viendra pour jeudi venerer,* *Ce qui sera jamais ne feut si beau,* *Des quatre pars le viendront honnorer.*	The earth and air will freeze so much water when they come to venerate on Thursdays. He who will come will never be as fair as the few partners who come to honour him.

U.S.A.?

This is interesting in that the Christian Sabbath is Sunday, for Jews it is Saturday, and for Muslims, Friday. Could Thursday possibly refer to the United States unique tradition of Thanksgiving, which is held on a Thursday?

[1] *classe*—Latin, *classis* = a fleet.
[2] *emblee*—O.F. = robbery or thieving.
[3] *alles*—O.F. = trip, speed, crowd.
[4] *ambellon?*—Dubious, possibly village of Ambel?

L'an mil neuf cens nonante neuf sept mois,	In the year 1999, and seven months, from the sky will come the great King of Terror. He will bring back to life the great king of the Mongols. Before and after War reigns happily.
Du ciel viendra un grand Roi deffraieur.	
Resusciter le grand Roi d'Angolmois.[1]	
Avant que Mars regner par bonheur.	

3rd ANTICHRIST WAR

In this gloomy prediction Nostradamus seems to foresee the end of the world at the Millennium, the year 2000. He was greatly influenced in this by medieval thinking which held all millenniums in great dread. From the verse it appears that first we must suffer the Asian antichrist 'the King of Mongols' before the advent of this new and terrifying figure. Note that Nostradamus expects war both before and after his coming. See IV. 50, X. 74, 75.

Le temps present avecques le passé	The present time together with the past will be judged by the great man of Jupiter. Too late will the world be tired of him and disloyal through the oath-taking clergy.
Sera jugé par grand Jovialiste,	
Le monde tard lui sera lassé,	
Et desloyal par le clergé juriste.	

By *Jovialiste* Nostradamus means a follower of Jupiter, and, by extension, a pagan. The quatrain has been applied to both Rabelais and Voltaire, but was probably intended as a dig at Calvin, Nostradamus' arch enemy.

An revolu du grand nombre septiesme	The year of the great seventh number accomplished, it will appear at the time of the games of slaughter, not far from the age of the great millennium, when the dead will come out of their graves.
Apparoistra au temps Jeux d'Hecatombe,	
Non esloigné du grand eage milliesme	
Que les entres sortiront de leur tombe.	

[1] *Angolmois*—Not Angoumois in Western France but the anagram of the O.F., *Mongolois*.

At the time of the seventh number (could this mean at the end of the 1970s?), war will break out again on an immense scale. The date will not be far from the millennium, which it isn't, see X. 72. The last line is purely horrific unless Nostradamus had some vision of the last judgment.

75

Tant attendu ne reviendra jamais	Long awaited he will never
Dedans l'Europe, en Asie appar-	return in Europe, he will
oistra	appear in Asia; One of the
Un de la ligue islu du grand	league issued from great
Hermes,	Hermes, he will grow above all
Et sur tous rois des orientz croistra.	other powers in the Orient.

WAR IN THIS CENTURY (*continued*)

This may refer to the last quatrain, The King of Horror will appear in Asia, not Europe and will wax powerful over the Eastern countries? See X. 72.

76

Le grand senat discernera la pompe	The great Senate will see the
A l'un qu'apres sera vaincu chassé,	parade for one who afterwards
Ses adherans seront à son de	will be driven out, vanquished.
trompe,	His adherents will be there at
Biens publiez ennemis deschassez.	the sound of a trumpet, their
	possessions for sale, the enemies
	driven out.

No setting is given to the reader for these general events.

77

Trente adherens de l'ordre des	Thirty members of the order of
quiretres[1]	Quirites, banished, their
Bannis leurs biens donnez ses	belongings given to their bold
adversaires,	adversaries. All their good
Tous leurs bienfais seront pour	actions will be taken as wrong,
desmerites	the fleet scattered, delivered up
Classe[2] espargie[3] delivrez aux	to the Corsairs.
consaires.	

[1] *quiretres* = (*a*) Roman citizens in their civil capacity. (*b*) Low Latin, renowned warriors.

[2] *classe*—Latin, *classis* = a fleet.

[3] *espargie*—O.F., *espargier* = tò sprinkle, dispense.

This is usually accepted as referring to post-Fascist Italy, and the corsairs are then understood to be the Russians, who received a large part of the Italian navy.

78

Subite joie en subite tristesse	Sudden joy into sudden sadness
Sera à Romme aux graces embras-sees.	will beat Rome for the graces embraced; Mourning, cries,
Deuil, cris, pleurs, larm. sang excellent liesse	tears, weeping, blood, excellent rejoicing, contrary bands sur-
Contraires bandes surprinses & troussees.	prised and trussed up.

79

Les vieux chemins seront tous embelis,	The old roads will all be improved, they will go to (a
L'on passera à Memphis somentrée,[1]	place) similar (to) Memphis. The great Mercury of Hercules'
Le grand Mercure d'Hercules fleur de lis	fleur de lis, will cause land, sea
Faisant trembler terre, mer & contree.	and country to tremble.

80

Au regne grand du grand regne regnant	In the kingdom of the great one reigning with a great rule by
Par force d'armes les grands portes d'airain	force of arms he will cause to be opened the great gates of
Fera ouvrir le roi & duc joignant,	brass; the king and duke allied the port demolished, the ship
Port demoli nef à fons jour serain.	(sunk) to the bottom and a serene day.

81

Mis tresor temple citadins Hesperi-ques	Treasure is placed in a temple by Western citizens withdrawn
Dans icelui retiré en secret lieu,	therein to a secret place, the
Le temple ouvrir les liens fameli-ques.	temple to open by hungry bonds, recaptured, ravished, a
Reprens ravis proie horrible au milieu.	terrible prey in the midst.

[1] *somentré*—From Greek, *symmetros* = like, resembling.

AMERICAN OR SPANISH WEALTH?

During the 16th Century gold poured into Spain from her possessions in the New World. Could Nostradamus be taken literally in this case, that a great amount of treasure is hidden in some Spanish Cathedral? However, problems arise with line 3. How can a bond be hungry? It has been suggested that this is an imaginative description of economic crisis in the United States (Hesperiques' other meaning) to be followed by a riot at Fort Knox, the greatest gold hoard in the world.

82

Cris, pleurs, larmes viendront avec coteaux
Semblant fouir donront dernier assault.
Lentour parques planter profons plateaux,
Vifs repoulsez & meurdris de prinsault.[1]

With the knives will come cries, tears and weeping, seeming to flee they will make a final assault around the parks they will set up high platforms, the living pushed back and murdered instantly.

83

De batailler ne sera donné signe,
Du parc seront contraint de sortir hors,
De Gand lentour sera cogneu l'ensigne,
Qui fera mettre de tous les siens à mors.

The signal will not be given to fight, they will be obliged to go out of the park; the banner around Ghent will be recognized, he who will put all his followers to death.

84

La naturelle à si hault hault non bas
Le tard retour fera marris contens,
Le Recloing[2] ne sera sans debatz
En empliant & pendant tous son temps.

The illegitimate girl so high, high not low, the late return will make the grieved ones contented. The Reconciled one will not be without disputes by employing and wasting all his time.

ELIZABETH I

Some people regard line 1 as describing Elizabeth Tudor whom Pope Paul IV declared to be a bastard through the illegality of her

[1] *de prinsault*—O.F. = firstly, at once, immediately, etc.
[2] *Recloing*—Dubious? Possibly derived from Latin, *recolligo* = to regain, be reconciled?

420

mother's marriage. She was considered to be one also by most English Catholics.

85

Le vieil tribung au point de la trehemide.	The old tribune on the point of trembling will be pressed not
Sera pressee captif ne deslivrer,	to give up the captive. The old,
Le veuil non veuil ne mal parlant timide	not old speaking timidly of the evil to free his friends in a law-
Par legitime à ses amis livrer.	ful manner.

FRANCE, 1940–3

This quatrain has been mentioned as a general description of France between 1940–3 when Marshal Pétain was negotiating with the Germans about prisoners of war who were being used as slave labour.

86

Comme un griphon viendra le roi d'Europe	The king of Europe will come like a griffon, accompanied by
Accompaigné de ceux d'Aquilon,	those of the North; he will lead
De rouges & blancz conduira grand trappe	a great troop of red and white, they will go against the king of
Et iront contre le roi de Babilon.[1]	Babylon.

ALLIED FORCES, 1815

The King of Europe was the Allied Forces which marched against Napoleon, the king of Egypt, before he was made first Consul. The great army of red and white uniforms are the tunics of the English and the Austrians. The English may well be described as from the North, as also Russia.

87

Grand roi viendra prendre port pres de Nisse	A great king will come to anchor near Nice, the death of
Le grand empire de la mort si enfera	the great empire is thus accom- plished. He will place his
Aux Antipolles posera son genisse,	heifer in Antibes, plunder at
Par mer la Pille tout esvanoira.	sea, all will vanish.

[1] *Babylon*—In medieval texts the King of Egypt is often called the King of Babylon.

Piedz & cheval à la seconde veille
Feront entree vastient tour par la mer,
Dedans la poil¹ entrera de Marseille,
Pleurs, cris, & sang onc nul temps si amer.

Foot and horse at the second watch, they will make an entry laying waste all at sea. He will enter the port of Marseilles, tears, cries and blood, never a time so bitter.

De brique en marbre seront les murs reduits
Sept & cinquante annees pacifiques,
Joie aux humains renoué Laqueduict,
Santé, grandz fruict joye & temps melifique.²

The walls will change from brick to marble, seventy-five peaceful years. Joy to people, the aqueduct reopened, health abundant fruit, joy and mellifluous times.

LOUIS XIV

This general quatrain seems to describe the prosperity of France under her great King Louis XIV.

Cent fois mourra le tyran inhumain.
Mis à son lieu scavant & debonnaire,
Tout le senat sera dessoubz sa main,
Faché sera par malin themeraire.

A hundred times the inhuman tyrant will die and a wise and carefree man put in his place. He will have the whole senate in his hands, he will be troubled by a wretched scoundrel.

NAPOLEON IN ST. HELENA

Napoleon is dying a hundred deaths through his enforced captivity; in his place is elected Louis XVIII, often called 'le debonnaire'. Both houses of Parliament, the Senate, will profess devotion to their new king down to the last man. The trouble referred to in the final line was the assassination of the Duke de Berry in line for the throne through his father, Charles X.

¹ *poil*—Usually regarded as erratum for *port*.
² *melific*—From Latin, *mellificus* = honey making. Nostradamus probably meant to write *mellifluus*.

Clergé Romain l'an mil six cens &
   neuf,
Au chef de l'an feras election
D'un gris & noir de la Compagne
   issu,
Qui onc ne feut si maling.

In the year 1609, the Roman Clergy at the head of the year will have an election; one of grey and black come forth from Campania, never was there one as wicked as he.

Pope Paul V reigned from 1605 to 1621 as Pope. But in the year 1609 he fell ill, and according to contemporary reports, there was a great deal of intriguing going on in the Courts of France and Rome should the Pope die an opportune death.

Devant le pere l'enfant sera tué:
Le pere apres entre cordes de jonc,
Genevois peuple sera esvertué
Gisant le chief au milieu comme un
   tronc.

In front of the father the child will be killed, the father afterwards between ropes of rushes. The people of Geneva will be exerted, the chief lying in their midst like a trunk.

La barque neufve recevra les
   voyages,
Là & aupres transferont l'empire,
Beaucaire, Arles retiendront les
   hostages
Pres deux colomnes trouvees de
   paphite.

The new Bark will go on voyages, there and nearer they will transfer the empire. Beaucaire & Arles will retain the hostages near where two columns of porphyry are found.

PIUS VI, 1799

This quatrain implies that the Papacy will be moved as in I. 32, and V. 45 etc. Both Beaucaire and Arles are near the Rhône river which borders Valence where Pope Pius VI died in captivity in 1799.

De Nismes, d'Arles, & Vienne	Scorn from Nîmes, Arles and
contemner,	Vienne, not to obey at all the
N'obei tant à l'edict Hespericque:[1]	Western edict; in order that
Aux labouriez[2] *pour le grand*	the great may condemn the
condamner,	tormented, six escape in
Six eschappez en habit seraphicque.[3]	Franciscan garb.

Dans les Espaignes viendra Roi	Into Spain will come a very
trespuissant,	powerful king, he will subju-
Par Mer & terre subjugant or midi,	gate the south by land and sea.
Ce mal fera rabaissant le croissant,	This evil will cause a lowering
Baisser les aesles à ceux du vend-	of the crescent again, a lowering
redi.[4]	of the wings of the people of
	Friday.

PHILIP II OF SPAIN

The nearest this appears to come to fulfilment is Philip II of Spain
who persecuted the Moors, made several futile expeditions
to North Africa and was involved in the Battle of Lepanto
1571.

Religion du nom des mers vaincra,	The religion called after the
Contre le secte fils Adaluncatif,[5]	seas will overcome, against the
Secte obstinee deploree craindra,	sect of the son Adaluncatif; the
Des deux blessez par Aleph &	stubborn lamentable sect will
Aleph.	fear the two men wounded by
	A & A.[6]

This quatrain should be easy to solve but is not. The anagram for
Adaluncatif is still unbroken. The A's in line 4 are not much help
since a great number of Arab names begin with A.

[1] *Hesperique*—Western? American? Spanish?
[2] *labourier*—O.F. = to be tormented.
[3] *seraphique*—The true name of the Franciscan order is the Order of
Seraphim.
[4] The Mahometans celebrate their Sabbath on a Friday.
[5] *Adaluncatif*—Unsolved name, possibly containing Calif among the
anagram?
[6] A & A—Aleph, letter A in Hebrew. Alif in Arabic.

Triremes pleines tout aage captif,
Temps bon à mal, le doux pour
amertume;
Proie à Barbares trop tost seront
hastifs,
Cupid de veoir plaindre au vent la
plume.

Triremes full of captives of all
ages good times for bad, sweet
ones for the bitter; hasty they
will be too quickly prey for
the Barbarians anxious to see the
plume (of smoke) wail in the
wind.

La splendeur claire à pucelle
joyeuse,
Ne luira plus long temps sera sans
sel:
Avec marchans,[1] ruffiens loup
odieuse,
Tous pesle mesle monstre univer-
selle.

For the joyful maiden the
bright splendour will shine no
more, for a long time she will
lack salt. With merchants,
bullies, odious wolves all confusion the universal monster.

FRENCH THIRD REPUBLIC

The Third Republic in France was typified as Marianne, and so
might refer in a general way to France between 1940–4, lacking
wisdom 'salt' in her behaviour. The confusion and beasts refer to
the Nazi invasion.

La fin le loup, le lyon, beuf, &
l'asne,
Timide dama[2] seront avec mastins,
Plus ne cherra à eux la douce
manne,
Plus vigilance & custode aux
mastins.

The end of the wolf, the lion,
ox and the ass, the timid deer
will be with the mastiffs. No
longer will the sweet manna
fall upon them; more vigilance
and guarding for the mastiffs.

[1] *marchands*—May mean mercenaries here?
[2] *dama*—Latin = a deer:

Le grand empire sera par Angleterre,
Le pempotam¹ des ans plus de
trois cens:
Grandes copies² passer par mer &
terre,
Les Lusitains³ n'en seront pas
contens.

A great empire will be for England, the all powerful for more than 300 years. Great forces cross by land and sea. The Portuguese will not be content.

GREAT BRITAIN

In this interesting quatrain Nostradamus foresees a great future for Britain lasting for three hundred years. Most people take it from the reign of Elizabeth to that of Victoria, fifty years longer than prophesied. It is unclear what the Portuguese have to do with this, and line 3 is also tricky, does it refer to English forces, or to the forces that will end Britain's greatness? A good ambiguous twist with which to end in the typical Nostradamus tradition.

¹ *pempotam*—From the Greek, *pan* = all, and the Latin, *potens* = powerful.

² *copies*—Latin, *copia* = troops.

³ *Lusitains*—Classical name for Portuguese.

INDEX

428

433

434

EXPLORE THE FRONTIER OF PSYCHIC KNOWLEDGE

__**THE AIRMEN WHO WOULD NOT DIE**   04273-1 – $2.50
John G. Fuller

__**CHARIOTS OF THE GODS?**   04381-9 – $2.50
Erich Von Däniken

__**THE HUMAN AURA**   05321-0 – $2.75
Nicholas Regush

__**MY SEARCH FOR THE GHOST OF**   04011-9 – $1.95
FLIGHT 401
Elizabeth Fuller

__**PHONE CALLS FROM THE DEAD**   04559-5 – $2.25
D. Scott Rogo and Raymond Bayless

__**PSYCHIC ARCHAEOLOGY**   05000-9 – $2.50
Jeffrey Goodman

__**WE ARE THE EARTHQUAKE**   04991-4 – $2.75
GENERATION
Jeffrey Goodman

__**THE STAR PEOPLE**   05513-2 – $2.75
Brad and Francie Steiger

Available at your local bookstore or return this form to:

Berkley Book Mailing Service
P.O. Box 690
Rockville Centre. NY 11570

Please send me the above titles. I am enclosing $_____
(Please add 50¢ per copy to cover postage and handling). Send check or money order—no cash or C.O.D.'s. Allow six weeks for delivery.

NAME_____

ADDRESS_____

CITY_____STATE/ZIP_____

62AP

MS READ-a-thon—
a simple way to start youngsters reading

Boys and girls between 6 and 14 can join the MS READ-a-thon and help find a cure for Multiple Sclerosis by reading books. And they get two rewards — the enjoyment of reading, and the great feeling that comes from helping others.

Parents and educators: For complete information call your local MS chapter. Or mail the coupon below.

Kids can help, too!

Temples sacrez prime facon Romaine	Temples consecrated in the early Roman fashion, they will
Rejecteront les goffres[1] fondements	reject the broken foundations;
Prenant leurs loix premieres & humaines,	taking their early human laws, expelling almost all the cults of
Chassant, non tout des saincts les cultements.	the saints.

A RELIGIOUS REVIVAL

A general quatrain predicting a return to the simpler religious precepts and practices, and a rejection of the elaborate cult of saints in the Roman Catholic Church. It may have been intended for the Huguenots of Nostradamus' own time.

9

Neuf ans le regne le maigre en paix tiendra,	For nine years the thin man will keep a peaceful rule, then
Puis il cherra[2] en soif si sanguinaire:	he will fall into so bloody a thirst that a great nation will
Pour lui grand peuple sans foi & loi mourra,	die for him without faith or law; killed by a much better
Tué par un beaucoup plus debonnaire.	natured man.

Three specific elements combine in this quatrain, which do not seem to have occurred as yet. A very thin ruler will, after a nine year peace, plunge his nation into a disastrous war. His death, in turn, will be caused by someone with right or good on his side. It has been suggested that this could be the Nazi party coming to power in the elections of 1930, and that Roosevelt is the good-natured opponent, but this gives a wrong time factor.

10

Avant long temps le tout sera rangé,	Before long everything will be organized; we await a very evil
Nous esperons un siecle bien senestre	century. The state of the masked and the solitary ones
L'estat des masques & des seuls bien changé,	greatly changed, few will find that they wish to retain their
Peu trouverant qu'à son rang vueille estre.	rank.

[1] *Goffre*—Romance = deep, broken.
[2] *cherra*—O.F., *choir* = to fall.

A general description of the French Revolution in which the state of two particular social orders was dangerous to maintain and became greatly changed. The first were the Court (*masques*), and the second the Clergy, who were abolished in 1790. Both classes suffered financial loss and many faced death because of their social rank or function throughout the early years of the Revolution.

11

Le prochain fils de l'aisnier parviendra,
Tant esleue jusque au regne des fors:[1]
Son apre gloire un chacun la craindra,
Mais ses enfans du regne gettez[2] *dehors.*

The following son the elder will succeed, very greatly raised to a kingdom of privilege. His bitter renown will be feared by all, but his children will be thrown out of the kingdom.

NAPOLEON?

The first line is extremely difficult because of the multitude of possible meanings of *prochain* and *aisnier*. *Prochain* may mean next, nearest, younger or favourite, and *aisnier* either elder or a falcon (*l'ainier*) giving a metaphor of a bird of prey similar to Napoleon, the eagle. If it does refer to Napoleon, he was the second son and he was elected to a kingdom and privilege, from being the son of a Corsican middle-classs family he became Emperor. He was feared in Europe and his children were deprived of kingship by Louis XVIII. However, Napoleon's nephew, Louis Napoleon, re-established himself in 1852 and ruled until the Third Republic of 1871.

12

Yeux clos, ouverts d'antique fantasie,
L'habit des seuls seront mis à neant:
Le grand monarque chastiera leur frenaisie,
Ravir des temples le tresor par devant.

Their eyes closed, open to the old fantasy, the habit of priests will be abolished. The great monarch will punish their frenzy, stealing the treasure in front of the temples.

[1] *fors*—O.F., Privileges.
[2] *gettez*—Alternative spelling of jettez = to throw.